The Heartland of U.S. Empire

In the series *Asian American History and Culture*,
edited by Cathy Schlund-Vials and Rick Bonus.
Founding editor, Sucheng Chan; editors emeriti,
David Palumbo-Liu, Michael Omi, K. Scott Wong,
Linda Trinh Võ, and Shelley Sang-Hee Lee.

ALSO IN THIS SERIES:

Rebecca Jo Kinney, *Mapping AsiaTown Cleveland: Race and Redevelopment in the Rust Belt*

Linh Thùy Nguyễn, *Displacing Kinship: The Intimacies of Intergenerational Trauma in Vietnamese American Cultural Production*

Tritia Toyota, *Intimate Strangers: Shin Issei Women and Japanese American Community, 1980–2020*

Ruth Maxey, ed., *The Collected Short Stories of Bharati Mukherjee*

Y-Dang Troeung, *Refugee Lifeworlds: The Afterlife of the Cold War in Cambodia*

George Uba, *Water Thicker Than Blood: A Memoir of a Post-Internment Childhood*

Long T. Bui, *Model Machines: A History of the Asian as Automaton*

erin Khuê Ninh, *Passing for Perfect: College Impostors and Other Model Minorities*

Martin F. Manalansan IV, Alice Y. Hom, and Kale Bantigue Fajardo, eds., *Q & A: Voices from Queer Asian North America*

Heidi Kim, *Illegal Immigrants/Model Minorities: The Cold War of Chinese American Narrative*

Chia Youyee Vang with Pao Yang, Retired Captain, U.S. Secret War in Laos, *Prisoner of Wars: A Hmong Fighter Pilot's Story of Escaping Death and Confronting Life*

Kavita Daiya, *Graphic Migrations: Precarity and Gender in India and the Diaspora*

A list of additional titles in this series appears at the back of this book.

Thomas Xavier Sarmiento

The Heartland of U.S. Empire

Race, Region, and the Queer Filipinx Midwest

TEMPLE UNIVERSITY PRESS
Philadelphia • Rome • Tokyo

TEMPLE UNIVERSITY PRESS
Philadelphia, Pennsylvania 19122
tupress.temple.edu

Copyright © 2026 by Thomas Xavier Sarmiento
All rights reserved
Published 2026

Library of Congress Cataloging-in-Publication Data

Names: Sarmiento, Thomas Xavier, author.
Title: The heartland of U.S. empire : race, region, and the queer Filipinx Midwest / Thomas Xavier Sarmiento.
Other titles: Asian American history and culture.
Description: Philadelphia : Temple University Press, 2026. | Series: Asian american history and culture | Includes bibliographical references and index. | Summary: "This book approaches discursive and affective formations of the Midwest from the vantage of queer, diasporic, and decolonial Filipinxness to foreground the imperial foundations of America's heartland and thus U.S. national and cultural identities and to reconfigure the texture of the U.S. Filipinx diaspora"— Provided by publisher.
Identifiers: LCCN 2025053112 (print) | LCCN 2025053113 (ebook) | ISBN 9781439927663 (cloth) | ISBN 9781439927670 (paperback) | ISBN 9781439927687 (pdf)
Subjects: LCSH: Filipino American sexual minorities—Middle West—Social conditions. | Filipino Americans—Middle West—Ethnic identity. | Filipino Americans—Cultural assimilation—Middle West. | Sexual minorities—Middle West—Social conditions. | Filipinos—Middle West—Social conditions. | Filipino diaspora. | Imperialism—Social aspects—Middle West.
Classification: LCC HQ73.4.F55 S37 2026 (print) | LCC HQ73.4.F55 (ebook)
LC record available at https://lccn.loc.gov/2025053112
LC ebook record available at https://lccn.loc.gov/2025053113

The manufacturer's authorized representative in the EU for product safety is Temple University Rome, Via di San Sebastianello, 16, 00187 Rome RM, Italy (https://rome.temple.edu/).
tempress@temple.edu

∞ The paper used in this publication meets the requirements of the American National Standard for Information Sciences—Permanence of Paper for Printed Library Materials, ANSI Z39.48-1992

Printed in the United States of America

9 8 7 6 5 4 3 2 1

*For Richard
and Bella and Bayani*

Contents

Acknowledgments — ix

Introduction: Imagining a Queer Filipinx Midwest — 1

Part I: The Philippines Queering the Midwest

1. Elegies for St. Louis: The Midwest as Filipinx America's Primal Scene — 31
2. Tracing the Queer Filipinx Midwest: The Heartland's Archives of U.S. Empire in the Philippines — 63

Interlude

3. Sensing the Queer Filipinx Midwest: Geographic Nostalgia and Melancholia in Bienvenido Santos's Exile Literature — 95

Part II: The Midwest Queering Filipinx Diaspora

4. Filipinas in the Wild West — 125

5. "See[ing] the World Not as It Is, but as It *Should* Be": Queer Filipinx Midwesterners and Postracial-Postimperial Televisuality   151

Conclusion: "Looking Back at Looking Forward": Toward a Queer Cartography of the U.S. Filipinx Diaspora   193

Notes   201
Bibliography   239
Index   257

Acknowledgments

The Heartland of U.S. Empire has been over a decade in the making, spanning U.S. regions and time zones. I am happy to see it out in the world. It began as a dissertation with the mentorship of Kale Bantigue Fajardo, Kevin P. Murphy, Jigna Desai, Roderick Ferguson, Josephine Lee, and Lisa Sun-Hee Park at the University of Minnesota. I have appreciated their continued advice and support postgraduation. Lisa and Kale planted the seed to study Asian Americans in the Midwest early in my graduate career, which has blossomed into a positive research and teaching trajectory I had not anticipated.

I have been lucky to read, think, write, and dialogue with Donna Doan Anderson, Constancio Arnaldo, Paul Michael Leonardo Atienza, Christine Balance, Nerissa Balce, José-Héctor Cadena, Ryan Cartwright, Bianet Castellanos, Lily Chen, Genevieve Clutario, Denise Cruz, Shilpa Davé, Adrian De Leon, Josen Diaz, Robert Diaz, Yuri Doolan, Linda España-Maram, JC Fermin, Tanya González, Vernadette Gonzalez, Terese Guinsatao Monberg, Scott Herring, Juliana Hu Pegues, Angela Hubler, Mingwei Hwang, Douglas Ishii, Michele Janette (mentor extraordinaire), Mary Joyce Juan (kasama), Sara Kearns, Ava Kim, Joo Ok Kim, Rebecca Jo Kinney, Abby Knoblauch, Shelley Lee, Sara Luly, Allan Lumba, Joyce Mariano, Phillip Marzluf, Kimberly McKee, Paul Nadal, Andy Oler, Valerie Padilla Carroll, Karla Padrón, Gabriell Padua, Chris Perreira, Kong Pha, Joe Ponce, Elliott Powell, Marcy Quiason, Thea Quiray Tagle, Alden Sajor Marte-Wood, Joy Sales, Sarita See, Harrod

Suarez, Jasmine Kar Tang, Lisa Tatonetti, MT Vallarta, Tessa Winkelmann, and Nicolyn Woodcock.

To Sony Coráñez Bolton, Matthew Chin, Kareem Khubchandani, Ian Shin, and James Zarsadiaz: It is truly a privilege to be a member of the boy luck club. I cherish the community that we have built over the years and across cities. Thank you for being writing partners, sounding boards, and confidants.

My colleagues in the Department of English at Kansas State University have provided generative feedback during colloquia over the years. I also have had the honor of presenting parts of the book at Missouri State University and Wellesley College and for Humanities Kansas.

A University Small Research Grant; a College of Arts and Sciences Research, Scholarship, and Creative Activities Faculty Enhancement Award; a sabbatical leave, all from Kansas State University; and an External Faculty Fellowship from the Suzy Newhouse Center for the Humanities at Wellesley College supported research and writing time. Karin Westman has consistently supported my efforts at Kansas State. Eve Zimmerman, Lauren Cote, Antonio Arraiza Rivera, Weihong Bao, Genevieve Clutario, Susan Ellison, Rebeca Hey-Colón, Annette Lienau, Nikhil Rao, and Yoon Sun Yang made my time at the Newhouse so memorable and productive. Rachel Moore and Mariana Urera provided helpful research assistance.

Min Song introduced me to the world of academic publishing, and Martin F. Manalansan IV and Rick Bonus shepherded this book at a critical juncture. Shaun Vigil at Temple University Press has been such a pleasure to work with. I am glad to be a part of the Asian American History and Culture series edited by Cathy Schlund-Vials, Shelley Sang-Hee Lee, and Rick Bonus. Many thanks to the two anonymous reviewers who provided such insightful comments to enrich the book. Ria Unson graciously shared her artwork for the book cover.

My friendships with Angela Brooks, Michael Contreras, Jan Estrellado, Agustín Orozco, and Kirk Riggin have sustained me across decades. My parents, Bayani and Bella, have been waiting excitedly for this book to come out—maraming salamat po for all your love and support; I am proud to be your son. Love also goes out to my siblings, Anne Lisa, Jasmin, Jennifer, and Michael, who always welcome me home, and to my Espinosa, Vandermoore, and Cinco niblings, who make being a guncle so much fun. And to the Dowdell family, thank you for welcoming me into the fold.

Finally, Richard Dowdell and our cats have made the Midwest home. Richard has been an astute listener and reader all these years, giving me clarity whenever I have been stuck. He always ensures that I am fed delicious meals, properly packed for research travel, and well rested. This book really could not have been written without him. He is still my teenage dream.

The Heartland of U.S. Empire

Introduction

Imagining a Queer Filipinx Midwest

I am queer, the son of Filipinx immigrants,[1] and a transplant to the U.S. Midwest.[2] I currently live and work in a small college town in the Flint Hills region of northeast Kansas, the ancestral land of the Kanza (now the Kaw Nation) and home of the first operational public land-grant institution in the United States. In 2016, my parents visited my new home state during the Fourth of July. Having lived most of their lives in California, they were excited to see a part of the country unfamiliar to them. My father is a U.S. Air Force veteran who served during the Vietnam era, and in his later years, he has become more interested in military culture. Knowing this but also to visit a local tourist site I had yet to see, I planned a trip to nearby Fort Riley, a U.S. Army installation founded in 1853 to "provide protection for the movement of people and trade over the Oregon-California and Santa Fe Trails" and the current home of the First Infantry Division (also known as the Big Red One).[3] While visitors are welcome, the base requires them to proceed through a series of security checkpoints, which can be unsettling for queer, Brown immigrant bodies such as ours—though my father's navy-blue patriotic shirt, emblazoned with "USA PROUD" and featuring the American flag and armed soldiers in defensive positions, and green camouflage shorts may have eased our passage.

Successfully driving on base, we visited the U.S. Cavalry and First Infantry Division Museums and the Custer House. The U.S. Cavalry Museum features the material culture of the U.S. Cavalry from the Revolutionary War through its inactivation in 1950, the First Infantry Division Museum chronicles the history of this army division from World War I to the present day, and the Custer House allows visitors to tour Brevet Major General George A. Custer's living quarters during his tenure as leader of the Seventh Cavalry Regiment and prior to his so-called "last stand" at the Battle of the Little Bighorn / the Battle of the Greasy Grass against the Lakhóta (Lakota), Northern Cheyenne, and Arapaho.[4] As my parents and I walked the museum grounds and observed unironic displays of U.S. invasion, empire, and settler colonialism, I silently reflected on the irony of three former colonial subjects, Filipinxs in the heartland, learning about how the colonizer regarded those they colonized, including us/our people.

An inset case titled "New Missions" in the U.S. Cavalry Museum references the Philippines. The display affirms the supposed successful end of continental U.S. frontier expansion and the seemingly logical movement of U.S. empire outward (figure I.1).

The display's primary label reads:

> The Wounded Knee engagement, 1890, marked an end to the Indian Wars. Over the next quarter century, the cavalry's role would be transformed from frontier guardian to protector of America's interests beyond our borders. Beginning with the Spanish–American War, 1898, followed by the Philippine Insurrection, 1899–1902, and Boxer Rebellion, 1900, and concluding with the Mexican border troubles of 1911–1916, mounted units were called upon to protect American lives and property.

Below this problematic text, with its anachronistic reference to massacres as "wars" and trivialization of continued struggles for independence as an "insurrection," is a map with pins of the aforementioned locations, stereoscope images of cavalrymen in Florida, Cuba, and the Philippines, photos of soldiers in the Philippines and China, and a photo of the Buffalo Soldiers (the all-Black Ninth and Tenth Cavalry Regiments) in Cuba. Lingering over the different elements of the case, I literally felt both seen and erased, anathema in this Midwestern rendering of the nation. The display perpetuates the misnomer of the Philippine–American War as an "insurrection," presuming the United States as rightful governor of the Philippines and disavowing Filipinx struggles for independence from Spain prior to U.S. intervention. It also links U.S. discourses of Manifest Destiny, Native genocide, Black incorporation, and tropical imperialism, revealing the interracial intimacies of U.S. empire.

An adjacent inset case titled "Philippine Insurrection" describes cavalry efforts, which consisted of "daily and nightly patrols by small detachments commanded by junior officers," during the Philippine–American War. Whereas the display label presents American soldiers as simply doing their

Figure I.1 Display case of "New Missions" beyond the continental United States in the U.S. Cavalry Museum. (*Photo by Thomas Xavier Sarmiento, July 2016.*)

job, it expectedly portrays Filipinx fighters as savage, "armed with bolos and rifles" and engaging in "fighting [that] was bitter and often times [*sic*] brutal." The case includes two photos of U.S. cavalrymen, a rifle, a pistol, a medal, a cigar box, and a bamboo waist belt; the latter two objects are labeled as "souvenirs" brought back to the United States by the Thirteenth Cavalry (figure I.2). While the particular terms under which such souvenirs were acquired are left unaddressed, violence surely figures centrally.

Figure I.2 Display case of the "Philippine Insurrection" in the U.S. Cavalry Museum. (*Photo by Thomas Xavier Sarmiento, July 2016.*)

In a display that willfully centers a predominantly White American perspective, Filipinxs are nevertheless present as specters floating in the silences. As a Filipinx person, I oriented to the negated object of these displays, lamenting my parents' and my presence as inheritors of colonial subjectivity and the contradiction of being aligned with the racial Other of these displays yet expected to affiliate with their racist patriotism because of our nationality. We silently took in these visuals, perhaps unable to articulate the ambivalence and pain of being cast as enemies of the state. Despite often being the only party in various areas of the museum, we somehow stood out. It felt as if the contents of the displays were not meant for us (they likely were not)—a bittersweet affirmation of Sara Ahmed's claim that "bodies stand out when they are out of place."[5]

The U.S. Cavalry Museum makes palpable not only the United States' imperial projects in the Philippines but also two key points at the heart of this book: the role of the Midwest region in the project of U.S. transpacific empire building and the paradox of Philippine and Filipinx absent presence in the region and the nation. Although the Philippines and Filipinxs are not the primary subjects and objects of these exhibits within the museum, their presence is undeniable. As a Filipinx person living in Kansas, while walking through these exhibits with my immigrant parents, whose parents and grandparents (my grandparents and great-grandparents) lived through Spanish, U.S., and Japanese occupations in the Philippines, I paradoxically felt seen in this museum, nestled in the rural Midwest. While the museum interpellates me as a colonial subject and forces me to adopt the imperial gaze, it also provides a grammar to connect the Philippines and the Midwest—bridging my existence—in its avowal of the archipelago and leaves marginal space for me to disidentify with the normative narrative of nation. I do not imagine the museum draws a considerable number of visitors, given its regional and active military location. So, while the museum avows the United States' imperial past, such an acknowledgment, as Sarita See argues, ironically becomes a means for erasure.[6] The requirement that people must visit the site poses a barrier to knowledge acquisition. Tucked away in the middle of the country, on a military base in northeast Kansas, the museum is not readily accessible. And yet, the museum and Fort Riley more broadly aptly materialize how the Midwest is the heartland of U.S. empire.[7]

From its very founding, Fort Riley, originally named Camp Center for its perceived location in the center of the North American continent that land surveyors presumed would be owned by the United States, is a technology of U.S. empire building.[8] In providing a space for troops to assemble as they defended the incursion of White settlers and squatters from Native peoples whose lands the U.S. government stole and later training troops for combat in the series of U.S. wars on the continent and abroad, this military installation roots U.S. empire in America's heartland. The U.S. Cavalry Museum and the Custer House not only preserve the U.S. Army's history but also bear the history of U.S. empire, with the former documenting the military's tactics and travels and the latter honoring a military leader associated with the so-called Indian Wars. Curiously, whereas the U.S. Cavalry and First Infantry

Division Museums acknowledge the military's presence in the Philippines throughout its time as a U.S. colony, the Fort Riley history web page omits the Spanish- and Philippine-American wars, concealing the traces of U.S. empire in the Philippines. Such an omission is significant, given the Philippines was the United States' only colony in Asia (officially from 1898 to 1946). However, as Philippine and Filipinx American studies scholars and scholars of U.S. empire have demonstrated, this epistemic omission is not necessarily surprising given discourses of American exceptionalism distinguishing U.S. imperialism from that of Europe.[9] American exceptionalist discourse understands U.S. imperial expansion as benevolent in its drive to promote liberal democratic values in contrast to the European empires of yore from which the United States wrested itself. In documenting the presence of the Philippines and Filipinxs in a modest local museum situated within a sizable army base in the middle of the country, I point to seemingly unexpected sites in the nation's quintessential region that purportedly represents its idealized identity and values to resignify America's heartland as the heartland of U.S. empire.[10] I also transform discourses of Filipinx diaspora that cordon off Filipinxs from the Midwest. These rhetorical moves drive *The Heartland of U.S. Empire: Race, Region, and the Queer Filipinx Midwest*.

If Fort Riley represents the military arm of U.S. empire, then the Oz Museum might represent its cultural arm. The museum is located in Wamego, a town of close to 4,500 residents that was named after a Potawatomi chief and has developed a tourist economy out of L. Frank Baum's *Oz* series and its adaptations. Anchored by the Oz Museum, which opened in 2003, Lincoln Avenue, Wamego's main thoroughfare, also features Oz Winery and used to include Toto's Tacoz. Since Baum's children's novel did not specify where in Kansas Dorothy, Toto, Aunt Em, and Uncle Henry live, many places in the state often associate themselves with Oz. Whether or not you are a fan of the *Oz* stories, the museum is a fun local attraction—and thus another place I took my parents to during their first visit to Kansas. The lobby is dressed as Aunt Em and Uncle Henry's farm, and as you enter through the home's front door, you are whisked away into Munchkinland. Alongside mannequin displays of select scenes from the 1939 film are various memorabilia of the book series, the MGM film, various stage productions, including *The Wiz* and *Wicked*, and contemporary film adaptations, including *The Muppets' Wizard of Oz* and *Oz the Great and Powerful*. It truly feels like you have left the Flint Hills prairie and stepped into a fantasy world. The museum's immersive environment is not unlike Disneyland, with its kitschy and eclectic feel. For me, its un-museum-ness models queer archival practices, finding value where others may see detritus.

Though present in the Fort Riley museums, the Philippines is less apparent in the Oz Museum. *The Wonderful Wizard of Oz*'s production context and its allegorical referents mainly drive the connection between Oz and U.S. empire in the Philippines. In *Model-Minority Imperialism*, Victor Bascara reads Baum's novel in its 1900 sociohistorical context to suggest its anti-imperialist undertones. For him, the novel can be read as "a text of anti-imperialism for its sympathy for the oppressed, even though that sympathy resulted in the displacement of one colonizer in favor of another."[11] He cites economist Hugh Rockoff's reading of the novel, which forwards "the Winkies, the yellow people enslaved by the Wicked Witch of the West," as symbolic of the United States' newly acquired Filipinx wards.[12] When Dorothy first arrives in Oz, she affirms to the Witch of the North that Kansas is "a civilized country"[13]; and when she inadvertently defeats the Wicked Witch of the West with a bucket of water, "Dorothy's first act was to call all the Winkies together and tell them that they were no longer slaves."[14] As an allegory of the United States' benevolence toward Filipinxs (the Winkies) and vanquishment of tyrannical Mother Spain (the Wicked Witch of the West), Dorothy's quest in the novel is not unlike the United States' imperial pursuits in the Philippines.

Recognizing the text and its quintessential Midwesternness as an archive of U.S. empire queers (in the sense of spoiling, ruining, and troubling) the mythology of the nation's middle as a nowhere place removed from settler colonialism and overseas imperial expansion. Hence, even though Wamego's Oz Museum may not explicitly bear the traces of U.S. empire in the Philippines, that genealogy nevertheless is part of its narrative. As a self-identified "friend of Dorothy," I did not anticipate living in between two places that would resonate with my ethnic and sexual identities and inspire a queer diasporic Filipinx reimagining of the Midwest. Sensing those "textural" moments of surprise—what Andy Oler understands as "those things that might usually be overlooked or plowed under" and that invite us "to take what exists and to make meaning from [them], both out of [their] actual, material existence and out of our experience of [them]"—this book approaches discursive and affective formations of the Midwest from the vantage of queer, diasporic, and decolonial Filipinxness to foreground the imperial foundations of America's heartland and thus U.S. national and cultural identities and to reconfigure the texture of the U.S. Filipinx diaspora.[15]

I begin this book with my personal experience of the Midwest region to illustrate how a noncoastal point of origin for Asian America yields different insights about migration, nation, empire, and identity.[16] As Gayatri Gopinath argues, "a turn to the region is, quite often, a turn to the personal and autobiographical. Engagements with the region, scholarly or otherwise, are often inextricably linked to the project of narrating the self, even as these engagements attempt to deconstruct an essentialist logic of identity, place, and belonging."[17] The scale of region can be thought of as local and thus more intimate than the scale of nation and its corollary, diaspora. In its subnational sense, region operates as a kind of minoritarian position, as it often is subordinate to other identitarian positions such as national, racial-ethnic, and diasporic affiliation. However, as this book reveals, a regional sensibility gives texture to national and diasporic experiences; the regional, the local, is often the means through which people understand themselves in space and time. And because of its often-subordinate status to nation and diaspora, the regional can figure as a queer formation that resultantly has the capacity to engender alternative socialities.

In a cultural moment when U.S. national politics are extremely divisive, fueled by the election of the country's first Black president, Barack Obama (whose maternal side hails from Kansas), in 2008 and exacerbated by Donald Trump's succession in 2016 and reelection in 2024, the Midwest region remains central in key debates about the nation's social, economic, and moral investments precisely because it often is synonymous with the so-called real America. That "real America" is code for White, middle class, heterosexual, and Christian. And although the Midwest obviously is composed of more diverse sociocultural identities, discursive representations of the region as rural and politically conservative persist in both U.S. national and minority cultures. To counter this powerful narrative, this book recovers and recontextualizes a range of cultural representations in museum exhibits, literature, film, archival repositories, theater, and television that document Filipinxs in the Midwest since the early twentieth century. By doing so, it transforms the region into a critical site of transpacific U.S. empire building as well as a queer diasporic geography of Filipinx America. Each chapter is organized around what I call queer Filipinx Midwest tropes that engage with literary, visual, archival, and performative texts produced by and/or about Filipinxs located in the middle of the country. I employ a queer, decolonial Filipinx methodology that traces how narratives of America's heartland position Filipinxs in the region as nonnormative due to their racial, gender, sexual, and national statuses. By locating Filipinx presence in the geographic heart of the United States, I unsettle the boundaries between nation and empire, domestic and foreign, and normative and queer. Such a discursive move aims to trouble who can belong where and when, from both dominant and subaltern perspectives.

Heartland of U.S. Empire engages and connects the growing body of scholarship on queer nonmetronormativities, Asian American studies "east of California," and critical studies of the Midwest.[18] By tracing diasporic Filipinx routes not only from the Philippines to the United States but importantly from and to regions *within* the United States as well as Filipinx roots in America's heartland, I bring into productive tension the transnational and translocal. I also create a space for different cultural narratives of the nation's geographic interior to emerge—one that prominently features U.S. empire, Asian migrations, and nonnormative genders and sexualities in the discursive formation of the region. Such epistemic interventions are a response to the dominant cultural imaginaries of the region that result in normative sociocultural identities coming to define its geographic identity. The notion of Black people, Indigenous people, people of color (BIPOC), queer and trans* (QT) people, migrants, refugees, adoptees, Muslims, Buddhists, other religious minorities, and people who subscribe to progressive or radical political ideologies as Midwestern, for example, runs counter to ruling discourses of the region and suggests such nondominant polities are out of place or are regional exceptions. I argue that groups outside the stereotypical Midwestern mold are discursively queer to the region; in fact, their very presence queers the hegemonic narrative of the region, thereby calling into question who and what can be considered Midwestern in the first place. I also argue that queerness is not only a sociocultural phenomenon but a spatial and locational one as well.

As a transplant to the Midwest from Southern California, I am acutely aware of how my ethno-racial-sexual embodiment and my secondary geographic location seem incongruent with each other to regional insiders and outsiders, including myself. However, rather than normalize such a seeming contradiction that renders certain bodies out of place, I interrogate the sources of this thought that has material, and sometimes deadly, consequences. Focusing on the specific case of Filipinxs in the Midwest, I illumine not only the queerness of the region—how the region both queers bodies that read as out of place and is home to queer bodies—but also its imperial foundations. Challenging normative ideas about queerness, Filipinxness, and the Midwest, I theorize the Midwest as not merely the heartland of the U.S. nation but more accurately as the heartland of U.S. empire. Such a conceptualization underscores imperialism as endemic to the United States' national identity, decenters the coasts as the exclusive locus for queer and Asian American theorizing, and reveals the constellation of colonial and diasporic formations unique to the United States' geographic interior.

As Christine Balance rightly points out, "Ideas of American nationhood are themselves imperialist imports."[19] And if the Midwest figures "less a distinct region than the nation's heartland, the essence of Americanism," as William Barillas observes, then locating queer diasporic Filipinx cultural representations here lays bare the region-as-nation's imperialist underpinnings.[20] Given the Philippines' status as the United States' first and only Asian colony and that Filipinx Americans make up the third largest U.S. Asian ethnic group (with an estimated total population of 4.4 million in 2021) and are among the fastest growing U.S. immigrant populations, examining diasporic Filipinx history and culture in the context of the Midwest enriches the extant scholarship on Filipinxs in the U.S. diaspora and challenges popular misconceptions regarding the region and its connection to national and transnational concerns.[21]

A Queer Filipinx Midwest

The Midwest is not the first place you might think of for a study of U.S. empire in the Philippines and diasporic Filipinx culture. Its relational unexpectedness positions it as structurally queer to Philippine and diasporic Filipinx geographies, ontologies, and epistemologies. And yet, as See provocatively asserts, "America's heartland is riven by its transoceanic empire, and the most interior states can be mapped . . . by the Philippines."[22] Focusing on Filipinxs in the Midwest at once challenges America's heartland as the province of Whiteness, as removed from transpacific U.S. territorial expansion, and unsettles the Philippines as always origin for diasporic Filipinxs.

The Midwest played a crucial role in facilitating the cultures of U.S. imperialism in the Philippines at the turn of the twentieth century, though such specificity often is underacknowledged, from Michiganian scientists and politicians influencing knowledge about and governance of the Philippines; to Hoosier, Nebraskan, North Dakotan, and South Dakotan servicemen deployed to fight in the Spanish– and Philippine–American wars (one of whom fired the first shot that reputedly started the latter[23]); to pensionadxs (government- as well as nongovernment-sponsored students) studying at land-grant universities such as Iowa State, Kansas State, Illinois, and Minnesota starting in 1903; to the 1904 St. Louis World's Fair's display of over a thousand native Filipinxs. Because Midwesterners were "over there," in the Philippines, at the turn of the twentieth century, Filipinxs have been "over here," in the Midwest, since the early twentieth century.[24] University of Michigan zoologist Joseph Beal Steere brought Filipino teen guide Mateo Francisco to Michigan in 1875 (Francisco returned to the Philippines in 1887).[25] Filipino Santiago Artiaga enrolled at the University of Michigan in September 1900, earning a BS in civil engineering in 1904 and returning to the Philippines.[26] The 1910 U.S. Census listed two Filipinos living in Minnesota.[27] And Filipinx immigrants gathered at the Muehlebach Hotel in downtown Kansas City, Missouri, on December 30, 1917, to commemorate Philippine national hero José Rizal.[28] As this brief history indicates, Filipinxs are not new immigrants to the region.

Although space and place have been key optics in Filipinx American studies, much of that scholarship has focused on the tropics and the role of water in connecting archipelagic geographies.[29] Informed by such pathbreaking scholarship yet forging an alternative pathway, this book retreats to the interior United States, to its "amber waves of grain" and riverine tributaries, to address the heterogeneity within the U.S. Filipinx diaspora. Such a move departs from the transnational turn in Asian American and American studies that emerged in the 1990s and 2000s—within which Filipinx American studies scholars were at the forefront[30]—not to discount the importance of thinking transnationally but rather to reconceptualize discursive meanings of home and diaspora beyond the nation.[31] As the following chapters reveal, home is not always an ocean away, nor is diaspora always on the scale of the national.

The concept of a queer Filipinx Midwest engenders a different sense of queerness, race, nation, diaspora, empire, and region. To place *queer*, *Filipinx*, and *Midwest* adjacent to one another is to hold in tension the contradictions of queer and Filipinx discursive absence and material presence in the Midwest. A queer Filipinx Midwest invites you to reimagine America's heartland beyond Whiteness, nationalism, patriotism, and rurality; it also pivots away from hegemonic imaginaries of the U.S. Filipinx diaspora as rooted in (sub)urban coastal centers—especially California—invested in hetero-repro-normative social and community formations and oriented toward the Philippines.[32] As a discursive formation born out of cultural production, it foregrounds the queer and Filipinx roots and routes of the Midwest, thereby transforming dominant cultural perceptions of both the American region and the U.S. Filipinx diaspora. The queer Filipinx Midwest that emerges once we recognize the Midwest as the heartland of U.S. empire essentially is a project of queer-of-color critique—what José Muñoz so beautifully describes as "a structuring and educated mode of desiring that allows us to see and feel beyond the quagmire of the present" and "the rejection of a here and now and an insistence on potentiality or concrete possibility for another world."[33] The queer Filipinx Midwest that comes to life in these pages is inspired by such a utopian vision and is a love letter to queers of color in the heartland whose existence often is rendered unintelligible.

In remapping the Midwest as the heartland of U.S. empire, this book forwards region as a generative, albeit undervalued, analytic for reading race, sexuality, and migration. Whereas ethnic studies tends to focus on the national and the transnational, given nation and empire's roles in producing ethno-racial social formations, and area studies, an outgrowth of the Cold War, engages both nation and region, the latter often constituting a bloc of adjacent nations, *region* in the subnational sense appears provincial.[34] The Midwest largely has remained peripheral in published Asian American studies scholarship, and even when it appears as a notable part of Asian American experience, it has not been positioned as the fulcrum on which critical analysis pivots.[35] This book addresses this considerable lacuna by both figuring the space of the Midwest as central to the narrative of Asian American experience and framing the place of the Midwest as crucial for understanding why people of Asian descent are perpetually foreign in the dominant U.S. national imaginary.³⁶ A queer Midwest–centric approach to Asian America loosens the grip of demographic density for determining sociocultural significance and underscores geography's role in contextualizing the experiences of Asians in the United States,³⁷ reminding us that racialization and other forms of alienation are thoroughly spatialized.³⁸

Subnational region is a productive lens through which to explore the nuances of the U.S. Filipinx diaspora. My previous work on queer Filipinx and peminist (Filipina/x American feminist) cultural production has emphasized the heterogeneity of the Filipinx diaspora as a response to the heteronormative tendencies ethno-racial cultural nationalisms often produce.³⁹ However, normativity also is geographic. A regional approach to U.S. Filipinx diaspora reveals the predominance of the West Coast, especially California, as a cultural referent in much of Filipinx American critique—a form of metronormativity.⁴⁰ For example, Benito Vergara presents Daly City, California, as the capital of Filipinx America; Linda España-Maram, Dawn Mabalon, and Dorothy Fujita-Rony historicize the labor of mostly Filipino men during the early twentieth century in Los Angeles, Stockton (California), and Seattle, respectively; Theodore Gonzalvez and Dylan Rodríguez feature Pilipino cultural nights, evenings of Philippine cultural dances often interwoven with dramatic-comedy skits themed to diasporic Filipinx identity and community, as staples on California college campuses; Carlos Bulosan's novel *America Is in the Heart*, canonical in Asian American literature, fictionalizes Filipino labor and organizing up and down the West Coast; and Jessica Hagedorn's novel *The Gangster of Love* begins in San Francisco.⁴¹ In recognizing the geographic norms of diaspora, I turn to the Midwest to mine its queer potentialities given its peripheral status within Filipinx American discourses. This dialectic between normative and queer calls to mind Ahmed's observation that "queer is, after all, a spatial term, which then gets translated into a sexual term, a term for a twisted sexuality that does not follow a 'straight line,' a sexuality that is bent and crooked."⁴² Hence, the notion of being out of place underscores how the image of Filipinxs in the Midwest materializes a queer (nonsexual) orientation.⁴³

Gopinath's turn to region in analyzing queer diasporic aesthetic practices is instructive for understanding the epistemological stakes of this book. Region poses opportunities to "bypass the nation" and "to grasp the texture of regionally inflected gender and sexual formations"; it yields "a new mapping of space and sexuality" that "rejects dominant cartographies that either privilege the nation-state or cast into shadow all those spaces, and gender and sexual formations, deemed without value within the map of global capital."⁴⁴ And although region might function as an intermediary "third term" between nation and diaspora,⁴⁵ queerness frustrates such "conventional indices of spatial scale" as being discrete, illuminating moments when they "collide, collapse, and coalesce."⁴⁶ A regional optic also transforms our sense of time, departing from a linear progress narrative steeped in colonial notions of development, modernity, and heteronormativity toward a narrative that embraces simultaneity and alterity.⁴⁷ Similar to Gopinath's use of region as method, I focus on region to see, feel, and understand queerness, race, nation, diaspora, and empire differently, to engender new ways of knowing how it feels to be Filipinx in America.

My approach to region, then, is necessarily affective. In being here in the Midwest, inhabiting particular noncoastal spaces and places, I have come to experience the "keen awareness of the smallness and specificity that necessarily and ironically accompanies" the "wild heterogeneity" of Filipinx America and the Philippines, as See puts it, "an order of particularity often illegible to outsiders or perceived as too narrow and hence valueless."⁴⁸ See's observation unsettles the perceived wholeness of Filipinx ethno-racial formation while calling out the systems of knowledge within and beyond academe that occlude the material reality and ontological significance of recognizing Filipinx experience as socially, culturally, and geographically inflected. Similarly, Gopinath highlights the work of queer scholarship as a practice of "document[ing], analyz[ing], archiv[ing], and valu[ing] the small, the inconsequential, and the ephemeral."⁴⁹ She notes that the aesthetic practices of queer diaspora "allow us to apprehend bodies, desires, and affiliations [that are] rendered lost or unthinkable within normative history" but rather are "ingrained in small acts and everyday gestures that play out not on the stage of the nation but in the space of the region."⁵⁰

Heartland of U.S. Empire enacts a queer diasporic Filipinx Midwestern aesthetic practice that blends See and Gopinath's sense of minoritarian cultural critique. Empirical data might dismiss the study of Asians in general and Filipinxs specifically in the Midwest as statistically insignificant because of their marginal demographic representation (Asians represent 4.3 percent and Filipinxs represent 0.6 percent of the total twelve-state Midwest region; Asian Midwesterners represent 12.3 percent of the total Asian American population; and Filipinx Midwesterners represent 8.9 percent of the total Filipinx American population as of the 2020 U.S. Census) and affirm California as representative, given that the majority of Asians and Filipinxs reside there (29.4 percent of Asian Americans and 39.3 percent of Filipinx Americans as of the 2020 U.S. Census).⁵¹ However, numbers only tell a partial story, and these numbers in particular only tell a contemporary story. Much like Scott Herring, who problematizes census data to distinguish geographic imaginaries (in his case, the rural/urban divide), I focus more on the cultural aspects of geography, those which are "in excess of empirical geographic specificities or the faulty logic of population density" and more "context-specific, phantasmic, performative, subjective, and ... [oftentimes] standardizing."⁵²

Although numbers certainly matter, I am less concerned with strict demographic representation and more with discursive imagination.[53] At the same time, culture and affect are limited. Although region might be a way to queer nation, diaspora, and empire, it also can reinforce hetero-nationalisms premised on nostalgia for a fictive innocence.[54] Still, the imaginary is a powerful construct that does not necessarily heed reality (i.e., empirical evidence) to narrate its sometimes-problematic past and plausible future presents.[55]

Geographer Yi-Fu Tuan presents region as "primarily a construct of thought, the most active mode of human experiencing."[56] He notes that "region . . . is far too large to be known directly. It has to be constructed by symbolic means."[57] For him, region is a type of place whose scale is too vast for most people to experience directly. Rather than being simply a finite place with fixed boundaries, region comes into being as a place *and* space largely through discursive, affective, and imaginative means. The queer Filipinx Midwest this book forwards thus takes form by engaging with products of human creation and acts of creative thinking—poetry, film, short stories, essays, memoirs, novels, drama, television, and museum exhibits—to imagine Otherwise.[58] The cultural texts I engage throughout the book convey Midwestern and Filipinx experiences of one another. They form an assemblage that creates the queer Filipinx Midwest, what Herring understands as a "coalition" and Karen Tongson sees as a "constellation" of objects and occurrences.[59]

My turn to region ultimately is a provocation to imagine more capacious modes of knowing and being that exist in the shadow of normativities—social, cultural, and geographic. Herring's rural orientation and Tongson's suburban orientation provide models for queer anti-metronormative critiques, which are attentive to the differentials of race, class, gender, and sexuality tempered by space and place, that this book aligns with.[60] Herring forwards a critical queer anti-urbanism as a method to negate the "compulsion to urbanism," which entails the urban as the pinnacle of queer modernity and denigrates the nonurban/rural, and to "critically negotiate the relentless urbanisms that often characterize any U.S.-based 'gay imaginary.'"[61] As the title of his book suggests, the concept of *another country* is a project that involves both reimagining *country* and ushering in another space and place beyond the metronorm. Such a project very much resonates with my reimagining the heartland as not a "vast banana [and coconut] wasteland"[62] nor a space of metroimperial exception.[63] Tongson's queer-of-color suburban imaginaries likewise are a creative project that invites us to recognize "spatial Others," the queer denizens who inhabit suburbia contrary to national discourses of "white flight" and queer metronormativity.[64] Such a project "reorient[s] our spatial perspective to account for *local* [original emphasis] migrations that intersect with queer of color regionalisms in the United States."[65] This attention to the microscale that both scholars prioritize echoes See and Gopinath's orientation toward the small and seemingly insignificant, and like theirs, my work is not simply about excavation and accumulation but also crucially about conceptualization, of thinkability.

Region in this book is the means through which another Filipinx America emerges. As Tongson's regional focus on suburban Southern California is less "a local addendum to national narratives" and more a recognition of the region "as a conceptual and topographical nexus for an American empire bound up with histories of sexuality, race, and desire,"[66] so too is my regional pivot to the Midwest. Moreover, in the same way that Herring's anti-urbanism is not meant to replace queer urbanity for rurality but rather to underscore the metronormative bias of queer studies, I forward the queer Filipinx Midwest as an intervention into the unconscious urban coastal normativities that buttress Asian diaspora studies.[67] But unlike Tongson and Herring's geographic foci, which coincide with population densities that cut across regions, my singular regional focus cuts across population densities. That is, despite the Midwest's synonymity with Middle America, which might connote suburbia or rurality, the Midwest morphs into these demographic scales as needed, including the urban. What is more, unlike suburbia or the rural, the Midwest region has a particular history and contemporary meaning irreducible to the more generic preceding terms. Nevertheless, my inward geographic turn resonates with Tongson's archival "sprawl" and Herring's "paper cut politics"—minor annoyances that may do little damage on their own but can effect social, cultural, and political transformations as "an aggregate"—as the examples I present appear eclectic yet connected by transits of empire and build upon one another to progressively undercut the normative beliefs espoused by Asian and non–Asian Americans that Asians are practically nonexistent in this part of the country.[68] Proffering the queer Filipinx Midwest is a performative gesture that brings into being a critical Asian American geography that can help us to understand both Asian America and the Midwest differently.

Houses and Homes

Heartland of U.S. Empire can be abbreviated with the acronym *HoUSE*, or *house*. Such a configuration is apt, as this book aims to place empire as foundational to the U.S. nation's heartland, its symbolic home. Empire figures as the house, the structure that shapes the heartland's ontology. However, much like built homes, the foundations, supporting beams, and other structural supports are often hidden and thus acknowledged as an afterthought, if at all. Only when the support structure fails or when renovations are in order do we get to see the frames that prop up the façade. As scholars of U.S. empire have argued, American exceptionalism enables the nation to forget that it is an empire.⁶⁹ However, when American exceptionalism fails, it reveals the discursive and material efforts that have gone into masking its largely invisible operation. Such a failure for me is the presence of queerness and Filipinxs in the Midwest; Filipinxs' very being in a place presumed to be incompatible with and thus inconceivable to their existence belies the region's mythology of White Americana.

Since the Midwest is Indigenous land, its imagined Whiteness rests on an inherently cracked foundation based on land theft. The Northwest Ordinance (1787) expanded the footprint of the United States along the Great Lakes, sanctioning White settlement on the Indigenous lands of the Peoria, Kaskaskia, Piankashaw, Wea, myaamiaki (Miami), Mascoutin, Odawa (Ottawa), Sauk (Sac), Mesquaki (Meskwaki; Fox), Kickapoo, Bodewéwadmik (Potawatomi), Ojibwe, Chickasaw, Lënape (Delaware), saawanwa (Shawnee), Wyandot, Dakhóta (Dakota), Seneca, Ho-Chunk, and Menominee that would become Illinois, Indiana, Michigan, Minnesota, Ohio, and Wisconsin.⁷⁰ The Louisiana Purchase (1803) further expanded the nation's territory westward into lands the United States first imagined as "Indian Country," a space for the refugee populations of Indigenous peoples being forced out of the East, including the Cherokee, Chickasaw, Choctaw, Muskogee (Creek), and Seminole, and that eventually would become Iowa, Kansas, Minnesota, Missouri, Nebraska, North Dakota, and South Dakota. The influx of settlers to the region and ongoing U.S. antagonism toward Native peoples resulted in the usurpation of Baxoje (Ioway), Sauk (Sac), Mesquaki (Meskwaki; Fox), Kaw, Osage, Pawnee, Jiwere (Otoe), Nutachi (Missouria), Peoria, Kaskaskia, Piankashaw, Wea, Quapaw, saawanwa (Shawnee), Lënape (Delaware), Kickapoo, Omaha, Dakhóta (Dakota), Ponca, Lakhóta (Lakota), Arapaho, Cheyenne, Ho-Chunk, Nakoda, and Ojibwe homelands.⁷¹

Geographer James Shortridge's oft-cited study of the region indicates White settlement during the nineteenth century played a central role in creating the dominant image of the region as a pastoral idyll,⁷² papering over the violence of Native removal and genocide and of Black enslavement sanctioned by fugitive slave laws that were foundational to the region's becoming.⁷³ By the early twentieth century, with established small towns and a robust agricultural economy, the region transformed into America's heartland, the quintessential representation of the nation's core values, which rest on White supremacy.⁷⁴ However, as Owen Cantrell points out, this period, which has served as a template for White America's nostalgia for simpler times, also marks the decline of small-town life.⁷⁵ Nevertheless, the heartland myth endures. As Victoria Johnson reveals, the origins of broadcast television are rooted in Midwesternness and the heartland values and perceived averageness it inspires—"the 'all-American' cultural values of populism ... a commitment to family, [and] a belief in free enterprise and progress within tradition."[76] For Kristin Hoganson, the heartland ethos of American culture is connected to the Cold War and the desire for national security in the face of racialized domestic threats alongside political economic foreign threats,[77] which have resurged in the early twenty-first century.[78]

Heartland of U.S. Empire is a home renovation project that queers the joists, frames, and trusses that prop up America's heartland mythology by highlighting its normative aesthetics and its role in engendering queer subjects who must appear as out of place for the myth to hold. In so doing, the book also rearticulates the Midwest as a rightful home and homeland for BIPOC, LGBTQ+ (lesbian, gay, bisexual, transgender, queer, and related identities), and others perceived as anomalous and discrepant in and to the region.[79] It contributes to scholarship that intervenes in the heartland's assumed Whiteness and straightness, such as *American Studies*' double special issue "Unsettling Global Midwests" (Perreira et al. and Sarmiento et al.), Britt Halvorson and Joshua Reno's *Imagining the Heartland*, Monica Trieu's *Fighting Invisibility*, Sook Wilkinson and Victor Jew's edited collection *Asian Americans in Michigan*, Brent Campney's *Hostile Heartland*, Linda Allegro and Andrew Grant Wood's edited collection *Latin American Migrations to the U.S. Heartland*, and the Twin Cities GLBT (gay, lesbian, bisexual, transgender) Oral History Project's *Queer Twin Cities*.[80]

To be sure, home is fraught. Even as we recognize the presence of BIPOC and LGBTQ+ peoples in the region, our sense of belonging is not without ambivalence. The murders of Vincent Chin, Brandon Teena, Nireah Johnson, Brandie Coleman, Jason Gage, Cha Vang, Srinivas Kuchibhotla, Rekia Boyd, Dontre Hamilton, Michael Brown, Laquan McDonald, Philando Castille, and George Floyd, among so many others, underscore the precarity of being BIPOC and/or LGBTQ+ and thus out of place in America's heartland and the United States as a whole. As Chandan Reddy explains, *home* for queer and trans* people of color raises the historic practices of housing disenfranchisement for people of color as well as the homo- and transphobia of some home lives for queer and trans* people; it also signifies the paradox of national non/belonging.[81] If the nation is home and the heartland is the idealized form of the nation, then *Heartland of U.S. Empire* queers and Filipinizes articulations of American inclusion.[82] Reddy notes that "[drag ball] 'houses' [featured in Jennie Livingston's documentary *Paris Is Burning*] never replace the 'home.' ... [They] are the site from which to remember the constitutive violence of the home, and the location from which to perform the pleasures and demands of alternative living, while at the same time functioning as an 'interlocutionary device' between homes and queer subjects."[83]

In a similar vein, this book is not an attempt to replace commonsense understandings of the Midwest region or the U.S. nation per se; rather, it enacts a queer diasporic disidentificatory practice of knowing and being that interrogates why queered racialized bodies are perceived as out of place in the middle of the country and invites you to savor the queer diasporic Filipinx Midwestern cultural practices that exist in spite of the constant threat of erasure.[84] However, unlike the drag houses that function as "counter-cultures and alternative social formations that provide both support and community for the urban queers of colors interviewed in Livingston's documentary," the house I forward is less a literal and symbolic support structure for queer diasporic Filipinx Midwesterners than it is a call to see the Midwest as the heartland of U.S. empire, to recognize the region and thus nation's ontology as necessarily imperial in form.[85]

While this book foregrounds region to rework nationalist discourses, the Midwest is not a generic region per se. Certainly, my study of Filipinxs in the Midwest resonates, for example, with Leslie Bow's and Khyati Y. Joshi and Jigna Desai's works on Asian Americans in the South. And while such critical regional approaches to Asian America and Asian diaspora are related in their intervention in ethno-racial nationalisms, the Midwest's particularity as a region that transcends its regional specificity reveals its paradoxical exceptional status as an analytic. Unlike other regions in the United States, the Midwest often is a synecdoche for the nation and, for historian Andrew Cayton, figures as an "anti-region."[86] Barillas clarifies that the Midwest as national heartland "concedes the region's strengths to the nation while ascribing its weaknesses only to the Midwest."[87] That is, *heartland* as a regional signification reflects pride in the nation, whereas *Midwest* as regional demarcation activates public derision of the nonurban.

Notwithstanding this distinction between the Midwest as both synecdoche for the nation and geographic particularity associated with provincialism, a critical regional approach to the Midwest recognizes that regions are connected to both the local and the global.[88] As Cheryl Temple Herr asserts, "Critical regionalism ... allows for understanding places seeking some form of relation beyond that woven by capital. In fact, the key to a critical regionalist methodology for cultural studies is the relationality of regionalism."[89] In the age of globalization, studying the subnational regional may seem unsexy in contrast to the global. However, the transnational is a constellation of localities in global drag. Contrary to popular perceptions, the Midwest is not landlocked (a charge of insularity; as if movement across regions is impossible via land). The Great Lakes border the northeast central states, the Mississippi River basin flows in eleven of the twelve states that make up the region, and transportation via land, air, and sea places the area in the national and transnational circuits of people and goods.[90]

To study region is to study relations.[91] Gopinath argues that an analysis of queer diasporic regional aesthetics "enables and demands that connections be made between fields of thought, geographic areas, and temporalities that would otherwise not be grasped readily through standard disciplinary approaches."[92] She notes that "framing queerness through the region, and the region through queerness, provides us with an alternative mapping of sexual geographies that links disparate transnational locations and allows new models of sexual subjectivity to come into focus."[93] Hoganson's historiography of the heartland recasts the Midwest as a dynamic place of movement and connection, from Kickapoo free and forced migrations, to northern European diasporas remaining connected to Europe, to cattle ranching that traversed the Canadian and Mexican borderlands, to hog farming crossing the Pacific and Atlantic Oceans, to seed and plant imports, to telecommunication advances.[94] Likewise, the *GLQ* special issue "Queering the Middle" conceptualizes the U.S. heartland as "a point of both return and departure, simultaneously a catalyst for movement and a marker of stasis."[95] Such cartographies challenge the perception that the subnational regional is less robust than epistemic formulations of nation, diaspora, and the transnational; instead, they reveal the "promiscuous intimacies," as Gopinath puts it, "of our past histories as they continue to structure our everyday present, and determine our futures."[96]

Accordingly, I frame the Midwest as an affirmative space of connection, reworking the trite notion of "flyover country" by appropriating the hub-and-spoke model of air transportation and applying it to the circuits of U.S. empire. Normative understandings of the Midwest as "static and inward-looking, the quintessential home referenced by 'homeland security,' the steadfast stronghold of the nation in an age of mobility and connectedness, the crucible of resistance to the global, the America of America First," occlude its contributions to national empire building.[97] However, as See argues, the structure of U.S. empire as "progressivist imperialism" transforms Philippine referents in the heartland as "anomalous."[98] Her research on the University of Michigan Museum of Natural History and the Frank Murphy Memorial Museum (honoring the last American governor-general of the Philippines), both of which are notable for their accumulation of Philippine objects prior to and during the American colonial period, reveals how U.S. empire in the Philippines is simultaneously a direct result of Midwestern entanglement abroad and removed from Michiganian museological accumulation.[99] As opposed to framing this book primarily as a story about U.S. empire that happens to emanate from the Midwest or about the Midwest that happens to engage U.S. empire, I hold both narratives in tension to disrupt the normative discourses that often shape them.

To imagine Filipinxs in the Midwest is to rearticulate diaspora and nation. If Filipinxs seem queer to the region, appearing as out of place and thus discrepant and anomalous—tropes that signify Asian American regional racial formations—then their belonging (or not) has everything to do with the history of U.S. empire in the Philippines and constructions of nation and diaspora in the Philippines and the United States. For example, whereas Allan Isaac introduces Filipinxs as "noncitizen nonaliens" during the colonial period, revealing the ambiguous juridical status of Filipinx nationality,[100] See suggests that Filipinxs more fittingly are "foreign in a domestic space" to indicate the curious presence and absence of the Philippines and Filipinxs in the United States.[101] Isaac and See illumine the liminal position of Filipinxs in U.S. culture, further underscoring the importance of the middle zone as a productive vantage point. And although Kale Fajardo's sea-based diaspora in *Filipino Crosscurrents* may seem to reinforce the dominance of the transpacific in Filipinx diaspora studies, his emphasis on the in-between resonates with the metaphor of the middle a Midwest regional orientation affords.[102]

The queer Filipinx Midwest is a diasporic formation that interrogates the bounds of both the U.S. and Filipinx American nations. If the heart of Filipinx America is geographically coastal, then an a-coastal vantage point enables a critique of that ethno-racial national formation. This epistemological and ontological inquiry veers away from the Philippines as always the home to which Filipinxs refer. Such ideas build on Harrod Suarez's conceptualization of diaspora as "less . . . the historical condition of dispersal than . . . the conceptual question of movement through politicized spaces and histories. . . . Its political purchase resides in how it mobilizes a different orientation in the world, one that may disrupt the empirical orientations situating subjects within the structures of globalization."[103] This alternative orientation queers the normative dialectical chronotopes of nation and diaspora by positing that nation emerges from diaspora, which is precisely the work of the queer Filipinx Midwest.[104]

In queering the orientation of diaspora through region, I advance the discourse of queer diasporas. In *The Feeling of Kinship*, David Eng presents queer diasporas as a critical methodology that focuses on "queerness, affiliation, and social contingency" and "declines the normative impulse to recuperate lost origins, to recapture the mother or motherland, and to valorize dominant notions of social belonging" premised on sanguineous kinship.[105] The refusal "to recapture the . . . motherland" is crucial in my conceptualization of the Midwest as a queer diaspora of Filipinx America as I decenter the Philippines as origin of Filipinx diaspora and diasporic Filipinxs' object of desire. Whereas Eng employs queer diasporas "as a rejoinder to the political and psychic dilemmas of queer liberalism," I use queer diasporas as a framework to rethink the space of the U.S. metropole by mapping diaspora to microgeographies of the nation—namely, region—to reimagine notions of home and non/belonging.[106] In so doing, I unsettle the normative logics of diaspora studies by refusing to position the receiving nation as diaspora writ large. As Gopinath rightly points out, our understanding of diaspora must "account for the movements and dispersals that happen within, rather than simply across, dominant nation-state boundaries"; doing so "refram[es] the nation-state itself as 'diaspora space.'"¹⁰⁷ As the history and reality of the Midwest attests, Native dispossession and relocation, settler colonialism, and post/colonial migration pervade the region's existence. Fajardo's crosscurrents framework slightly diverges from Eng and Gopinath's focus on diaspora over nation by considering the flows between nation/homeland and nation/diaspora.¹⁰⁸ Moreover, Desai and Martin Joseph Ponce both forward *beyond* to emphasize diasporic hybridity that emerges in excess of nation.¹⁰⁹ I rework these subtleties by recognizing diaspora within diaspora.¹¹⁰

The queer Filipinx Midwest rescales diaspora from nation to region, from transnational to translocal. The queerness of the Midwestern Filipinx diaspora denotes not only LGBTQ+ identities and communities but also how Midwestern Filipinxs do not necessarily desire the Philippines as the normative object of diasporic longing. In my case, as a U.S.-born Filipinx who grew up in Southern California among many Filipinxs, I see the Philippines as more my parents' and grandparents' home than mine. During college, I became involved in Filipinx American activism and ambivalently pondered the group's orientation toward the Philippines, which sometimes eclipsed U.S.-based Filipinx concerns. While I do not want to reinforce a false dichotomy between the Philippines and the United States for Filipinx Americans and see migrant generational distinctions as tied to nationality and biological kinship, both of which can perpetuate heteronormativity, I do want to question what it means for the Philippines to be home for Filipinxs regardless of birthplace. As a Midwest transplant, I view my home as California—a homeland, where my family is, where I grew up, came out, and formed queer kinship; but even though I sometimes feel out of place in the middle of the country, it also has become a home, the home I make with my partner and our cats in a town where we have made connections.¹¹¹ My sense of home is thus multiple, ambivalent, and not oriented to nation.

From Nowhere to Now Here

Isaac remarks that Filipinx presence in the United States can be described as being "everywhere and nowhere," using Andrew Cunanan's "enigmatic unrecognizability" (in the wake of his murdering fashion designer Gianni Versace in 1997) to illumine the paradox of Filipinxs being one of the country's dominant Asian ethnic groups and yet often unintelligible in the national imaginary because of imperial amnesia.¹¹² *Heartland of U.S. Empire* reworks this apt metaphor by highlighting Filipinxs being everywhere *in* nowhere, the so-called hinterlands of the U.S. diaspora that overlap with the country's geographic and discursive middle. As Martin Manalansan, Chantal Nadeau, Richard Rodríguez, and Siobhan Somerville state in their introduction to

"Queering the Middle," "The middle creates less a magisterial panoramic perspective than a queer vantage."[113] Similarly, Denise Cruz attends to the middle engendered by transpacific thought through the trope of *midway*, writing, "While a midway refers to the middle, the halfway point that bisects a geographical distance, in North America in the 1890s and 1900s *midway* [original emphasis] became associated specifically with the exhibits that were becoming increasingly popular as large public entertainments.... [A] midway also signifies the in-betweens of space, time, or process and encapsulates the geopolitical shifts that are crucial to transpacific femininities."[114] Cruz's insights help to recast the 1904 St. Louis World's Fair, which she mentions and which I address in chapter 1, as a middle event as opposed to simply a national-imperial one. And instead of denigrating the Midwest as the so-called middle of nowhere, I follow the editors of "Queering the Middle" and see it as "the middles of somewhere and elsewhere," a geography of possibility and plausibility.[115] However, in queering and Filipinizing the Midwest and regionalizing the U.S. Filipinx diaspora, I reorder *nowhere* as a space and place of *now here*. *Now here* is a rhetorical move that responds to Asian American and American studies as well as popular discourses that position QTBIPOC as out of place in the Midwest. Recognizing the Midwest as the heartland of U.S. empire enables us to acknowledge these marginalized subjectivities as now here in the region.

Now here is a queer diasporic regional practice of seeing, feeling, and knowing that buttresses this book; it is not a claim of novelty, for, as previously discussed, Filipinxs have been in the region for quite some time. It is a provocation to remember and reckon with the history and afterlife of U.S. empire in the Philippines in the seemingly unexpected spaces and places of the nation. As See astutely observes, "the remembering of Filipinos in America reveals the capitalist colonial nightmare of the American Dream."[116] To recognize Filipinxs and other nonnormative subjects as now here in the Midwest is to perform the work of recovery, reorientation, and reimagination; it not only introduces new archives that lay bare the violence of U.S. imperialism but more importantly challenges us to see the world differently and create spaces and places that are more habitable.

Ponce's queer diasporic reading—"a practice of connectivity, of seeking out relationalities that form beyond the strictures of normative social boundaries"—is instructive for my analysis of queer diasporic Midwestern Filipinx cultural formations that emerge when adopting a *now here* instead of *nowhere* mentality of the middle/Midwest.[117] The texts I read relate to one another in the feelings of strangeness, dislocation, and longing they engender in both their narrative worlds and their audiences. The queer affects I uncover are more reflective of my disidentificatory interpretations than they are intrinsic to the texts themselves, which resonates with Tongson's turn to queer theory to read the relocated (whom for her are "the queers, immigrants, and people of color who know that inhabiting the suburbs promises privilege but experience it otherwise"): "The relocated (sometimes by choice, at other times by circumstance) are not as often found in literature as they are read in and through queer theory: in the incidental moments of queer imagining we happen upon through the yearnings and formative moments of discovery that may theoretically lead to elsewhere, but which bring us inevitably back to those shared, secret nowheres."[118] Thus, in threading together Filipino weathering in Bienvenido "Ben" Santos's literature of exile (chapter 3) and Filipina wildness in M. Evelina Galang's peministt stories (chapter 4) as instances of queer regional intimacies, I offer an alternative way of looking at text, a queer-regional gaze. Such a performance explodes the norms of region, nation, empire, and diaspora.

Imagining Asian America from the Midwest enables us to see a different story about the United States. Instead of exclusion, we encounter stories of refuge and incorporation as well as isolation and singularity (of being the "only one").[119] Although this book focuses on Filipinxs, it finds resonance with other Asian ethnic groups whose presence in the region stems from transpacific U.S. imperialism—from Chinese immigrants fleeing racist violence along the West Coast during the late nineteenth century,[120] to Japanese and Korean war brides migrating to military towns, including Fort Riley, following World War II and the Korean War,[121] to Korean children being adopted by mostly White families following the Korean War,[122] to Vietnamese and Hmong refugees resettling in big cities and small towns following the Vietnam War,[123] to professional-class Indian immigrants being recruited by universities, hospitals, and industries after the Immigration Act of 1965.[124]

BIPOC are everywhere in the Midwest. In the PBS docuseries *Asian Americans* (2020), when legislator Mee Moua states, "This is our country," she challenges us to acknowledge that Asians are American and that they belong here, not simply in the national abstract but in particular regional places like the Twin Cities, Minnesota.[125] The notion of *now here* ushered by a queer Filipinx Midwest cartography that rejects the region as discursively belonging to White cis-heterosexuality and being empty of QTBIPOC and recognizes it instead as the heartland of U.S. empire gestures toward what See refers to as a "queer horizon": a "wandering," "oblique" perspectival approach to abstracted U.S. landscapes that betrays a history of racial-sexual imperial violence and genocide and enables us to see such horrors beneath the mask of beauty.[126]

Itinerary

Heartland of U.S. Empire enacts Gopinath's mode of queer curation that places seemingly unlike subjects and objects in relation to one another to render legible queerness: modes of everyday life that resist the normative logics of empire, nation, diaspora, and region as well as ethno-racial and queer social formations.[127] However, whereas she engages the scale of the region insofar as it unearths aesthetic practices that transcend normative spatial and temporal borders, I interrogate region itself to illustrate how a change in scale engenders a change in queer diasporic racialized ontology and epistemology. My foregrounding of and focus on a singular subnational region offers a sustained engagement with the so-called local as it radiates simultaneously inward and outward—that is, the Midwest is both singular and polyvalent. Hence, rather than read the Midwest comparatively, I remain with the Midwest to emphasize the rich diversity of the singular.

Akin to Tongson's cloverleaf freeway interchange metaphor that stitches queer-of-color suburban imaginaries, an eclectic assemblage of texts that place Filipinxs in the Midwest from the turn of the twentieth century to the present intersect with one another to map the queer Filipinx Midwest.[128] They reveal a series of critical nodes in the translocal and transnational circuits of U.S. imperialism. These texts express culture's capacity to document and inspire. Responding to See's assertion that "American imperialism is animated by a powerful sense of entitlement that is profoundly bound up with the aesthetic," I turn to literary and cultural texts by and about Filipinxs in the Midwest to access an archive that exceeds colonial knowledge.[129] Such an epistemological move aims to unsettle the coherence of the U.S. imperial nation-state, as opposed to bolstering it or calling for queer Filipinx inclusion within it.

Part I, "The Philippines Queering the Midwest," illustrates how Midwesterners in the Philippines since the late nineteenth century and Filipinxs in the Midwest since the turn of the twentieth century queer discourses of the Midwest through such cross-racial embodied presences across regions, nations, and empire. Composed of chapters 1 and 2, this section traces how the Filipinx body on display at the turn of the twentieth century and subsequently documented in Midwestern archival repositories reveal the Midwest's entrenched ties to U.S. empire in the Philippines. Both chapters focus on how Filipinx presence in the Midwest unsettles the discourse of the region as being removed from transpacific U.S. territorial expansion and queers the image of the Midwest as always White, straight, Christian, middle class, and disconnected from global circuits of empire and transnational trade.

Chapter 1, "Elegies for St. Louis: The Midwest as Filipinx America's Primal Scene," centers on the 1904 Louisiana Purchase Exposition, commonly referred to as the 1904 St. Louis World's Fair, and its infamous Philippine Exhibit, which showcased over a thousand people representing various ethno-religious groups from the archipelago. St. Louis is a Filipinx primal scene of U.S. imperialist subjection. I put Aimee Suzara's *Souvenir* (2014), a collection of poems based on her archival research on the 1904 St. Louis World's Fair, in conversation with Marlon Fuentes's *Bontoc Eulogy* (1995), a mockumentary that links the filmmaker to a fictitious ancestor, Markod, who supposedly was displayed at the fair, and Jesse Lee Kercheval's "The Dogeater" (1987), a short story that imagines the fair's aftermath. Reading these elegiac narratives about the fair and its Philippine Exhibit with a queer Filipinx Midwestern sensibility, I emphasize the fair's regional geography and illustrate the Midwest as foundational to U.S. empire in the Philippines and to U.S. Filipinx diaspora.

Chapter 2, "Tracing the Queer Filipinx Midwest: The Heartland's Archives of U.S. Empire in the Philippines," draws attention to the siting of archival materials that trace the colonial ties between the United States and the Philippines in the Midwest. That scholars regularly travel to see the University of Michigan's impressive Philippine collection and the Missouri History Museum's archive of the 1904 St. Louis World's Fair, for example, often without focusing on their physical location in the Midwest, contributes to the discursive erasure of Filipinx connections to the region. This chapter revisits the University of Michigan archive with a queer diasporic Filipinx Midwestern eye to foreground its regionality.[130] The chapter also considers minor Midwestern archival traces at the University of Minnesota, Kansas State University (K-State), and the University of Kansas (KU). I argue that this disparate—yet considerable in the aggregate—assemblage of Midwest archives concerning the Philippines belies the Midwest's irrelevance to Philippine and diasporic Filipinx history.

Chapter 3, "Sensing the Queer Filipinx Midwest: Geographic Nostalgia and Melancholia in Bienvenido Santos's Exile Literature," is an interlude that bridges parts I and II by discussing how analyzing Filipino/American writer Santos as a Midwest author simultaneously queers the meaning of the Midwest and the U.S. Filipinx diaspora. While Santos is hailed in both Philippine and Asian American letters, few scholars have read him as Midwestern. However, as a pensionado at the University of Illinois, a Rockefeller Fellow and Exchange Fulbright Professor in the famed Iowa Writers' Workshop, and a Distinguished Writer in Residence / creative writing professor at Wichita State University for nearly a decade, Santos and his literature certainly have been shaped by and shape Midwestern culture. (As an English professor at Kansas State University whose maternal side hails from the Bicol region in the Philippines, I feel a fictional kinship with Santos's personal ties to Bicol and later professional life in the Wheat State.) This intermediary chapter functions as an apt introduction to part II, as it reveals how translocal Filipinx cultural production remaps conventional understandings of homeland, diaspora, nation, and sociality.

Santos's oeuvre, which is intimately tied to his lived experience, draws attention to alternative Filipinx migration routes that bypass California and the West Coast more broadly. Spanning the early 1940s to the early 1990s, his writings provide a multisensory, polysemous depiction of middle-class Filipinxs who migrated to the metropole first as students and later as young professionals as opposed to manual laborers—a common narrative in Asian American history.[131] His stories also illumine the exilic structure of feeling that emerged in response to the Philippines' entrance into World War II as a colony of the United States and to the U.S.-backed authoritarian regime of Ferdinand Marcos during the 1970s and 1980s. Importantly, their particular settings "east of California" reveal the provisional conditions of possibility the Midwest affords to Filipinxs in exile from both the imagined Philippine homeland and the locus of diasporic Filipinx American community along the urban West and East Coasts—namely, queer homosocial intimacies.

Part II, "The Midwest Queering Filipinx Diaspora," features an array of contemporary Filipinx Midwest cultural productions and circulations that queer the boundaries of the U.S. Filipinx diaspora by rethinking questions of home, homeland, nation, and belonging through queer embodiment, sociality, and translocality. Starting with the presumption that Filipinxs are consonant with the Midwest and thus are included in the subject of part II's title ("The Midwest"), chapters 4 and 5, which make up this section, together function as invitations to resee both region and diaspora through the prism of queer Filipinx Midwestern culture. The narrative and performative works featured in this section rework the ontological and epistemological, or onto-epistemological, dimensions of Filipinx postcolonial-diasporic subjectivity, writing, singing, and speaking back to the Midwestern colonial gaze presented in part I and against the coastal urban hegemony of Filipinx America.

Chapter 4, "Filipinas in the Wild West," reads Galang's collection of short stories *Her Wild American Self* (1996) alongside A. Rey Pamatmat's stage play *Edith Can Shoot Things and Hit Them* (2011), both of which feature representations of strong, unruly Filipinas from the American heartland, to explore the racialized gendered limits and possibilities of regionality. These queer-peminist narratives of domesticity present Filipinxs in the Midwest as being in (and not out of) place, reworking the referents *home* and *homeland*. I use *wild* as a metaphor to analyze Galang's and Pamatmat's portrayal of young women's gender transgression vis-à-vis Midwestern aesthetics. In establishing the connections among place, racialized gender and sexuality, and feminist and queer sensibilities, I reveal how the U.S. heartland activates alternative ways of living and being for minoritized subjects that are geographically informed.

Chapter 5, "'See[ing] the World Not as It Is, but as It *Should* Be': Queer Filipinx Midwesterners and Postracial-Postimperial Televisuality," looks at Fox's teen musical dramedy *Glee* (2009–2015) and NBC's workplace sitcom *Superstore* (2015–2021), both of which feature queer Filipinx characters residing in Midwest suburbs, to revel in the rise of queer Filipinx Midwestern mainstream visibility while also interrogating what such occurrences mean in a supposedly postracial and postimperial moment. Reading both series through a diasporic queer postcolonial Filipinx lens, I argue that the seemingly marginal appearance and presence of charismatic queer Filipinx characters in the contemporary U.S. heartland frustrates the nation's imperial amnesia and magnifies its anxieties concerning race and empire as it assiduously attempts to move past them. Such queer Filipinx Midwestern bodies figure as allegorical specters of the nation's racial-colonial past, harbingers of the nation's inability to move beyond its past in the present, and beacons that propel queer Filipinx Midwesterners to live in the future present.

The conclusion, "'Looking Back at Looking Forward': Toward a Queer Cartography of U.S. Filipinx Diaspora," returns to St. Louis via the Missouri History Museum's 2004 exhibit on the 1904 World's Fair (a new, more decolonial exhibit opened in 2024) and relates it to the Eisenhower Presidential Museum's display of the Philippines on the eve of independence in Abilene, Kansas, to reflect on the paradoxical remarkability and unremarkability of queer(ed) Filipinxs in America's heartland. By locating Filipinxs in the geographic center of the U.S. nation and placing them at the heart of the narrative, the museological, literary, filmic, archival, performative, and televisual materializations of the queer Filipinx Midwest that this book features map alternative images of diasporic Filipinx identity and experience and U.S. regional and national identities, histories, and realities. Such a cartographic move ultimately rewrites the cultures of U.S. empire as domestically situated and intrinsic to the nation's symbolic heart, the Midwest, thereby positioning Filipinx Midwesterners not as anomalous subjects but rather as vectors who point us toward new(er) and nuanced ways of interpreting region, nation, empire, diaspora, home, desire, and belonging.

I

The Philippines Queering the Midwest

1

Elegies for St. Louis

The Midwest as Filipinx America's Primal Scene

The 2020 PBS docuseries *Asian Americans* surprisingly begins with the story of Antero Cabrera, an Igorot (an Indigenous peoples of the Cordillera Mountain Range of northern Luzon, Philippines, made up of several ethnolinguistic groups) preteen who migrated to the United States as one of the 1,100-plus Filipinxs displayed at the 1904 St. Louis World's Fair.[1] Unsurprisingly, Cabrera's story is not framed in regionally specific terms but rather as part of a national story about Asian America. Similarly, the history of Filipinx America tends to focus on nation-to-nation movement, even as it acknowledges particular locales. For example, the eighteenth-century "Manilamen" settlement of St. Maló, Louisiana, and the early twentieth-century importation of Filipinxs to St. Louis to showcase U.S. imperial investments in Asia understandably are part of the mosaic of the U.S. Filipinx diaspora as opposed to local stories.[2] Perhaps the ethno-racial emphasis of *Filipinx* ushers a national frame, as *Filipino* itself only came into being as a unified demonym following the Philippine Revolution.[3] Nevertheless, the nation is a composite of local and regional sites that make up the whole. For me, the issue lies with certain local geographies predominating as representative of the national as well as other local geographies becoming subsumed under the abstract national.

A few points about the PBS docuseries strike me. After the opening title sequence, a montage of group photographs of various early Asian American immigrants appears on screen with the following voice-over narration: "They come from all corners of Asia. . . . They all dream of new possibilities in

America."[4] A cut to a photograph of a lone dark-skinned boy wearing a loincloth appears as the narrator continues, "Every dreamer has a story. One is twelve-year-old orphan, Antero Cabrera, who sets off from the Philippines in 1904 to see the land of riches he's always heard about."[5] The juxtaposition of group photos captured from some distance and formal family portraits with Cabrera's up-close, high-angle, full-body profile photo not only cues the episode's first segment but also draws attention to his subjectivity and sets the series' tone that Asian Americans are not faceless hordes but singular plurals, a part of the whole. Cabrera's story serves as a catalyst to link the story of Asian America to U.S. empire in the Philippines at the turn of the twentieth century. Viewers learn how Cabrera came to be in St. Louis because of his education by White American missionaries in the Philippines following the Philippine–American War, which presumably granted him fluency in English, as he "work[ed] as an interpreter and houseboy for anthropologist Albert Jenks."[6] Jenks, a University of Minnesota professor, was the fair's Philippine "Reservation" Anthropology Division head.[7]

In contrast to historical analyses of the fair, which tend to focus on the administrators and predominantly White fairgoers,[8] and Filipinx/American studies critiques of the fair, which tend to focus on the violence of human zoos, the docuseries presents an object of the fair as a subject with agency.[9] Certainly, the display of Filipinxs and other Indigenous peoples and peoples of color at world's fairs during the late nineteenth and early twentieth centuries is abhorrent. However, *Asian Americans* presents a different tone, as it employs talking heads, such as Filipina British writer Candy Gourlay, who acknowledges both the wonder and problems of the fair, and Cabrera's granddaughter Mia Abeya, who emphasizes the performative nature of the displays and the remittances Cabrera was able to send as a cultural performer. Although Cabrera's narrative balances the line between immigrant American dream and colonial subject, the series' leading with St. Louis, and by extension the Midwest, and U.S. empire in the Philippines charts a novel point of origin for Asian America consistent with Stephen Sumida's provocation in "East of California."

What surprises me about *Asian Americans* is its opening with Filipinxs in the Midwest. Historically, Filipinxs have been eclipsed in the story of Asian America, as Filipinx American studies scholars have argued.[10] To lead with a Filipinx story disrupts hegemonic perceptions of Asian America(ns). Moreover, starting with the St. Louis World's Fair plants Asian Americans right in the middle of the country. Though subtle, the series supports my argument that the Midwest is central to Asian American history and culture. You cannot tell the story of Asian America without the Midwest.

Formally known as the Louisiana Purchase Exposition, which commemorated the hundredth anniversary of the largest territorial acquisition by the

United States, the 1904 St. Louis World's Fair was an opportunity to showcase the United States' newly acquired Philippine colonial subjects—thereby connecting past and present expansion. However, the fair actually connects transatlantic and transpacific empires, as the Louisiana Purchase of 1803 was indicative of not only the United States' territorial expansion and settler colonialism west of the Mississippi River but also the decline of the French empire as a result of the Haitian Revolution.[11] Similar to other expositions of the late nineteenth and early twentieth centuries, the fair prominently featured human zoos, with over a thousand living stock ethno-regional Filipinx types in the Philippine "Reservation" alone, which spanned forty-seven acres (about 4 percent of the fairgrounds' 1,240 acres) on the southwestern edge,[12] making it "the largest exhibit at the Fair."[13] Such displays were designed to showcase a linear racial progress narrative from savagery to civilization, with the latter being secured through U.S. imperial tutelage. Among the ethno-regional Filipinx types put on display, the Igorot particularly garnered the most attention for their seminudity and consumption of dog meat, inciting both disgust and attraction. Subsequently, *Filipinx* and *dogeater* became entwined.[14]

For Filipinxs in the Philippines and in the diaspora, the 1904 St. Louis World's Fair is the primal scene of U.S. imperial subjection of the Filipinx body on continental American soil.[15] As such, it is an event and place to which Filipinxs return. And yet, in dominant diasporic Filipinx discourses, the Midwest is a place incommensurate with contemporary diasporic Filipinx life. While much scholarship in Filipinx American studies returns to the 1904 St. Louis World's Fair, it unwittingly neglects to center the regional geography in which that event takes place.[16] As such, my focus on the space and place of the fair and its afterlives figures as an epistemically queer take on the fair. If normative Filipinx American discourses of the fair emphasize the objectification of Filipinx bodies for the White imperial American gaze, then a queer Filipinx Midwest discourse of the fair looks askew to face the peripheral and the background.

This chapter foregrounds the U.S. interior as a critical geography of U.S. empire to highlight the regional foundations that undergird the U.S. Filipinx diaspora. Engaging three cultural objects that meditate on the fair and its afterlife—Suzara's debut collection of poems *Souvenir* (2014), Fuentes's experimental/mock documentary film *Bontoc Eulogy* (1995), and Kercheval's short story "The Dogeater" (1987)—I trace the geographies of diasporic Filipinx melancholia rooted in subnational region to queer hegemonic notions of the Midwest and the U.S. Filipinx diaspora. I read all three texts as elegiac to highlight the terrain of culture as the working-through of post/colonial grief.[17] My reference to elegy in this chapter exceeds its narrow poetic form and focus on a deceased person and instead connotes a melancholic tone for that which has passed.[18] Thus, even as Fuentes's film eulogizes a deceased fictive family member who was displayed at the fair and Kercheval's story sympathizes with a living elderly man who also was displayed at the fair and who himself laments the death of his wife, these texts alongside Suzara's poems work through the traumas of the fair's exploitation of colonized Filipinx bodies.[19]

Karen Weisman's gloss of elegy points to the form's performative nature. As an artistic expression to mourn loss, elegy "throws into relief the inefficacy of language,"[20] which resonates with See's theorization of Filipinx post/colonial melancholia as the inability to articulate loss through language and conveying it instead through affective embodiment.[21] Weisman observes elegy as a "mode of engaging with the disappointments *of* [original emphasis] time and place . . . a way of realizing what has been done to culture."[22] As a conscious contemplative form, time and place become suspended, and the material conditions that engender loss are laid bare.[23] Its concern with memorialization is not simply metaphoric but can engage with "the physical spaces of preservation."[24] Accordingly, Suzara and Fuentes's engagement with the physical archive and commemoration of the fair enact elegiac form. Ultimately, elegy enables a catharsis through creativity, in the creation of poetry and art (including prose and film).[25] Appropriate to my Midwest regional approach to diaspora and empire, which invokes metaphors of the middle, Weisman writes, "Between the extremes of life and death, joy and sorrow, the receding past and the swiftly moving present, falls the elegy as we know it today."[26] Exhibiting themes of ambivalence, liminality, and irresolution, the elegiac creative works I engage in this chapter illustrate the melancholic productivity of the middle, of both/and, of a refusal of extreme certitude.

Elegy's association with melancholia fittingly evokes the sense of arrestedness, of being stuck, that denotes the diasporic post/colonial Filipinx condition. In Freudian psychoanalysis, *melancholia* refers to improper mourning, as the subject is unable to "get over" a lost object.[27] I read this inability to "get over" as a liminal zone wherein the subject is unable to move forward or backward. Such a metaphoric middle ground resonates with the racialized diasporic subject who is neither of the home country left behind nor of the host country and its attendant racism as well as with the post/colonial subject for whom coloniality is not over but ongoing, even if formally disavowed.[28] What is more, locating the elegiac diasporic post/colonial Filipinx subject in the Midwest, in the middle of the continental United States, in the symbolic heart of the nation, evokes a further metaphor of the middle that reveals the ambivalence of the U.S. racial-imperial nation-state. As I outline in the introduction, the Midwest region is not an addendum to diasporic U.S. Filipinx discourse but instead an ontoepisteme that reimagines the center of axis as it turns us away from the norm and toward the minor but not insignificant. However, whereas Sigmund Freud casts melancholia as pathological, indicative of its structural queerness, I sympathetically read melancholia as symptomatic of power's refusal to relinquish itself and as a compass that points to alternative ontoepistemologies. Post/colonial melancholia is "insurgent" because it lays bare what empire has disavowed and "challenge[s] the idea that the past is closed, even as those who refuse to forget may be called crazy and unfit."[29]

I refuse to let go of St. Louis, which opens me up to different facets of this history that could have been discounted if I simply moved on. In returning to the primal scene of Filipinx America from the vantage of the middle, I counter the notion that U.S. imperialism is premised on the distancing of the normative American subject from the colonized racial (Filipinx) abject. Rather, empire is about intimacy.[30] As Juliana Chang rightly asserts, "the apparent alienness is produced by incorporation and intimacy as well as exclusion and alienation."[31] Chang's turn to narratives of domesticity in Asian American literature aims to reveal that Asian American subalternity constitutes American normative subjectivity. Reconceptualizing the Asian subaltern as interior to the U.S. nation shatters what *America* connotes. Likewise, recognizing Filipinxs in St. Louis as an index of Filipinx belonging to the U.S. nation shatters the illusion of Filipinx alienation. That Filipinxs are historically tied to the U.S. geographic interior proves they are central to the U.S. national imaginary.

The United States' disavowal of its status as an imperial power serves to smooth over the contradiction of Filipinxs being forcibly incorporated into, yet racially excluded from, the American national body politic at the turn of the twentieth century following President William McKinley's infamous decision to annex the Philippines in 1898.[32] However, the United States' post/colonial ambivalence speaks not simply to Filipinx racial difference but also to their alleged deviance from White heteronormativity. As Victor Mendoza asserts, the threat of the Filipinx in U.S. metroimperial consciousness at the turn of the twentieth century indicates not simply Filipinxs' "racial difference but also ... their gendered-sexual menace."[33] At the fair, Filipinx nudity ambivalently scandalized and titillated White American fairgoers, illustrating the entanglement of coloniality, racialization, gendering, and sexualization.[34] Framing the United States as "metroimperial" draws attention to the inadequacy of "nation" as its signifier; it also establishes connection between the continental United States and its overseas territories. Moreover, conceptualizing metroimperialism as constituted by social and sexual intimacies reveals the violent erotics of U.S. colonial governance as well as the U.S. public's discursive and material entanglements with Filipinxs on both sides of the Pacific Ocean. Rereading the fair as a key example of metroimperial intimacy located not simply in the Philippines, as much of Mendoza's work does, and rightly so, but critically in the continental United States' geographic interior works to anchor empire in the heart of the U.S. nation.

My focus on the intimacies of the fair reframes U.S. empire as an attractive rather than repelling force vis-à-vis its colonial wards. Moving beyond the fair's imperialist logics of objectification, order, and distance, I open a middle-ground space to attend to the range of intimacies and attractions between displayed Filipinxs and their audiences, composed of fairgoers, nonattending consumers of fair narratives during the early twentieth century, and contemporary viewers and readers of the fair's history. Located in the geographic middle of the nation-empire, the fair figures as an "interzone" of possibility.[35] Following Lisa Lowe's expansion of intimacy beyond "spatial proximity or adjacent connection,"[36] most often attributed to "conjugal and familial relations in the bourgeois home,"[37] to include also "the volatile contacts of colonized peoples,"[38] I collapse the discursive distance between the so-called modern from the primitive, the human and the inhuman.[39] Such an ontoepistemic shift reframes the fair and its popular shadow, the Philippine Exposition, from being primarily understood as cheap amusements that bolster U.S. colonial power to becoming sites of attraction that play out unstable colonial phantasies and desires.[40] It also emphasizes the spatio-political relation between the Philippines and the United States buttressed by imperialism.[41]

Re-membering St. Louis

Suzara's book of poetry, *Souvenir*, returns us to the open wound of the 1904 St. Louis World's Fair's Philippine Exhibit, indicating the ongoing significance of the fair to diasporic Filipinx subjectivity well into the twenty-first century.[42] The book is divided into four sections, entitled "Exhibit A" through "Exhibit D," which reconfigures its contents as evidence for readers to judge the acts of U.S. empire as opposed to serving the ends of museological display. The first "exhibit" traces Suzara's encounter with the Missouri History Museum's *The 1904 World's Fair: Looking Back at Looking Forward* exhibit, which opened in 2004 to commemorate the hundredth anniversary of the fair (and which I discuss in the book's conclusion).[43] The poems in this section imagine what the Filipinxs on display might have thought and said if they had been considered as more than mere objects of entertainment for mostly White fairgoers, thereby reversing the subjects and objects of the gaze.[44]

Whereas Exhibits A and B focus on the universalized Filipinx subjects as colonial objects of anthropology and science, Exhibits C and D focus on the particularized diasporic Filipinx subject embodied by the poet and her immigrant parents living in the Pacific Northwest during the 1980s. Seemingly disconnected, the book's sections reveal the "palimpsests" of multiple colonialisms and the primal scene of Filipinx subjection in the Midwestern United States as constitutive of diasporic Filipinx ontology more broadly.[45] Its narrative structure deviates from an Enlightenment linear telos and embraces relationality and repetition. The front matter that defines *souvenir* as a "token of remembrance; a memento" fittingly gestures to this sense of repetition as Suzara invites readers to remember and return to the fair. The French verb *venir*, meaning "to come," appears in *souvenir*, further revealing how the text functions as an invitation to engage the intimacies of the fair and its afterlife.[46]

Pertinent to my focus on the psychic dimensions of a regional-cum-universal wound in Filipinx America, Suzara opens with the following epigraph by French psychoanalyst Jacques Lacan: "I can feel myself under the gaze of someone whose eyes I do not see, not even discern. All that is necessary is for something to signify to me that there may be others there."[47] While the *I* in the passage refers to Lacan, the first-person pronoun interpellates the author (Suzara) and reader, reconfiguring who can be the subject. The passage signals the affective and geographic pull of psychic-social relations. From a diasporic post/colonial perspective such as Suzara's, the *I* is both subject, the focus of the sentences, and subjected, as they fall "under the gaze of" a spectral figure/force, metaphorizing the Real in Lacan's terms or the unconscious in Freud's terms. That the epigraph ends with "there may be others there" indicates a relational desire between the *I* and the mysterious "someone whose eyes I do not see." When read as the diasporic Filipinx American attuned to the remnants of the St. Louis World's Fair figured by "the gaze," the *I* becomes satisfied by "the gaze" directing them to "others there." The "others there" signify the wealth of knowledge of archival remains left by the displayed Filipinxs. Moreover, the notion that more than one "someone" likely exists suggests that Filipinxs in the Midwest are not anomalous but rather constitute a field. To mourn St. Louis for Filipinx America involves not only a temporal return but importantly a spatial one.

Although Suzara's biography places her outside of the Midwest—she first lived in Leonia, New Jersey (57), and then relocated to Kennewick, Washington (74)—her upbringing in the Pacific Northwest and her use of the frontier motif to describe her coming of age finds resonance with the Old Northwest and Manifest Destiny discourses that created the Midwest and that the 1904 World's Fair was celebrating in honor of the Louisiana Purchase centennial. Such a relationality is productive in generating alternative genealogies of diaspora premised on subnational region. Moreover, Suzara's intranational migrations reflect the actual dynamism of diaspora and intervene in the discourses of nation-diaspora, which often position these geographies as relationally static. That Suzara may not be of the Midwest does (and should) not preclude her from participating in its discursive construction.

The first section of the book, "Exhibit A: The Philippine Reservation," presents Suzara's intimate reflections of the fair as experienced during her archival research at the Missouri History Museum over a century after it took place. Like many Filipinxs, including myself, Suzara embarks on a pilgrimage to

St. Louis.[48] As a historical Filipinx/American site, St. Louis beckons us. The first poem, "Objects & Artifacts," opens with Suzara encountering the main gallery of *The 1904 World's Fair: Looking Back at Looking Forward* exhibit: "I see my ruddy face reflected / in the glass. And which is the ghost: this colonial woman, / . . . or me, gazing back?" (13). Suzara's use of first-person narration creates a sense of intimacy and foregrounds the subaltern as subject, even as the stanza ends with a question mark. The juxtaposition of Suzara's melanated complexion with the Victorian mannequin outfitted in "white taffeta" sets Suzara apart from "this colonial woman"; yet, Suzara's reflection in the glass, appearing between her and the figurative woman, creates a racial-gender relational intimacy. This first stanza sets the book's tone as a question: Through whose gaze might we reimagine the fair and its afterlife? Rather than didactically shifting the gaze from the colonizer to the colonized, Suzara employs point of view in her poems to present a ghostly perspective—those who are remaindered.[49]

The second poem, "Catalog of Objects," shifts to second-person narration, creating a sense of distance between the *I* of the opening poem but also placing the reader in the poet's shoes. Whereas the first and fourth stanzas list objects and portraits on display at the museum exhibit, the second, third, and fifth stanzas present a series of simple sentences that form a rhythm: "*You walk into the Missouri History museum. . . . // You dream that night . . . // . . . // You see the daguerreotypes of Filipinos, Native Americans, Eskimos, Arabs, and Japanese . . . You see your face reflected in the glass*" (15; original italics). Unlike the reflection that differentiates the *I*/author/narrator in "Objects & Artifacts," the reflection in "Catalog of Objects" aligns the *you*/author/narrator/reader with the portraits of Indigenous peoples and people of color hanging on the museum walls. Although the poem may appear to evoke scientific objectivity as it enumerates the objects on display, its use of *you* unsettles such a myth and invites readers to inhabit the physical and symbolic space of the Missouri History Museum. Moreover, restaging the first poem through the lens of *you* signifies the multiplicity and partiality of knowledge production as readers reencounter the exhibit and gravitate toward new artifacts.

In "Museum Note #2: What you bring," the *you* functions as a mode of address to a particular person, juxtaposing a presumable Filipino (gendered male) subject and the author/narrator.[50] The theme of weather opens the poem in true Midwestern fashion. While the first line/stanza (left justified) suggests a concern for colder weather in comparison to the tropics with the parenthetical aside "(no mention of weather)" that follows the packing of "one loin cloth," the second stanza (full justified, set on a right column that overlaps with the left column) presents a set of (self-)directives: "Don't bring those shoes that rub the inside of your right foot . . . Don't bring all those long-sleeves for Oakland evenings" (29). The author/narrator's point of view places her outside the Midwest region, as she appears to worry whether the displayed Filipinxs can weather the four seasons of the U.S. interior and to be less familiar with the heat (and humidity) of Midwestern summers.[51] In chapter 3, I discuss cold weather as the dominant imaginary of the Midwest, largely by non-Midwesterners, even though the Midwest also experiences triple-digit temperatures. Here, Suzara unwittingly debunks perceptions of Midwest climate. She also regionalizes diaspora by distinguishing St. Louis weather from that of Oakland. Although the author/narrator initially may be out of place in the Midwest, the culmination of her pilgrimage to St. Louis grants her intimate knowledge of the Filipinx Midwest, transforming the region from outpost to waypoint in the circuits of diasporic Filipinx ontoepistemologies.

The poems in "Exhibit A" are not just elegies to people connected to the event of the St. Louis World's Fair; they also are poems about place, the mourning of a place, and how to make sense of a situated event by inhabiting an imagined shared space despite distance in time. Two poems explicitly mention place: "World's Fair Box," which under its title denotes "*At the Missouri History Museum Library*" (24; original italics); and "Oral History," which denotes "*In the Listening Room at the Missouri History Museum Research Library*" (27; original italics). While other poems indicate where the author/narrator is located within their stanzas, this specific callout draws attention to the particular knowledge the writer gains from visiting and engaging with the Missouri History Museum archive.

Those who visit an archive are encountering not just materials but also the space and place that house and are connected to such materials (an argument I develop further in chapter 2). When Suzara describes her own experiences in the *I* or transposes them onto to a distanced *you*, she uses imagery and approximates sound through font style to give readers a sense of the archival space and the place that both house the fair's archive and served as the fairgrounds. In "World's Fair Box," Suzara describes the sanctity of the Missouri History Museum Library: "My eyes trace immense dark wood panels . . . / . . . The ceiling rises, arched into stained glass. I note the instinct / to clasp my hands in prayer" (24). Perhaps not distinct from other archival reading rooms, this particular library nevertheless commands reverence. Suzara uses the first two stanzas to build anticipation in accessing archival materials concerning Filipinxs displayed at the fair, including "manila folders labeled: / *Igorotte.* / *Negrito.* / *Visayan*" (24; original italics). I recall similar senses during my visit to the library in summer 2012; somehow, I felt this place was important as someone of Philippine descent, and I could not wait to start poring over materials not biologically connected to me and yet poignantly part of my heritage as a diasporic Filipinx Midwesterner. When the narrator "lift[s] the cardboard lid [of a box of photos]" and "the scent of forgotten dust flies to [her] nostrils," I am transported to the same place and recall the wonder and lament of encountering the ephemera of the displayed Filipinxs.

In "Oral History," Suzara presents four perspectives. The narrator is represented by the book's standard typeface. William Link, who attended the fair as a young person and participated in the Missouri History Museum's 1979 oral history project, is represented with a typewriter typeface. Archival material text is represented in bold typeface. And a displayed Filipinx person, quoted in Jose Fermin's book *1904 World's Fair: The Filipino Experience*, is represented by larger-sized italics. Although not all text is audio recorded, it evokes aurality. Coincidentally, I recall reading the transcript of Link's oral history interview and the passages Suzara quotes. Through the literal place of St. Louis, I am connected to another diasporic Filipinx person in search of place in the post/colonial metropole, and we are both connected to the Filipinxs who traversed the region before us. This communion through sonic-textual media invokes Balance's concept of disobedient listening. Disobedient listening "listen[s] against and beyond the dominant discourses that continuously constrain and narrow our understanding of the sonic and musical in Filipino America."[52] Such dominant discourses privilege the visuality of race and preoccupy themselves with static notions of domination and resistance.[53] In contrast, disobedient listening embraces relationality and improvisation. Disobediently listening to the St. Louis archive, excerpted in Suzara's "Oral History," enables us to hear the subaltern voices that *are* present and *can* speak.[54]

"Exhibit A" directly works to repair the primal scene of Filipinx subjection under U.S. empire as it restages the fair and its afterlife from the perspective of the displayed Filipinx. As the back matter of the book indicates, "Suzara's poetry flips the script to question the ethics of the imperial gaze."[55] Through first-person plural narration and dialogic address, Suzara transforms the object of racial melancholia into a subject as well, creating an intersubjective reparation.[56] The St. Louis Fair and the Igorot "dogeater" figure as the lost object for the (diasporic) Filipinx melancholic subject, though the meaning of that loss remains just out of reach. Recovering St. Louis and the "dogeater" as part of diasporic Filipinx heritage also involves avowing the imperial foundations of the U.S. nation-state. However, as Eng and Shinhee Han observe, the subject of racial melancholia does not simply experience a conflict within but rather is exposed to social forces and intersubjective dynamics. Since racialized subjects historically also are objects of the White imperial gaze, their ambivalent working-through of racial-imperial trauma is at once psychic and social.[57] In considering the social dimensions of (racial) melancholia, we begin to see that the attempt to recover what has been lost is informed by our subjective relation with others.

Accordingly, "Possession," "Philippine Souvenir Card #1," "Philippine Souvenir Card #2," "Norms," and "Good Boy" present the imagined voices of the displayed Filipinxs as speaking back to White American imperial fair organizers and fairgoers *and*, through space-time, responding to the desires of the melancholic diasporic Filipinx subject who longs for communion with their imagined forebears. While Filipinxs are captured in the fair's archive, their perspective is more exception than rule, given that the fair's archive focuses on White American colonial subjects (rather than its racial-colonial objects), a conundrum Genevieve Clutario addresses and circumvents by "weaving together 'fragments' and rereading documents to excavate the experiences and viewpoints of" the minoritized.[58] Similarly, Suzara builds on historical truth, stating the names of the colonized displayed ("In the Laboratory of the St. Louis World's Fair," "World's Fair Box," "Antero," and "Dear Ota Benga"), and speculates what they might have thought and said through poetic form.[59]

For example, "Philippine Souvenir Card #1" and "Philippine Souvenir Card #2," which refer to playing-card decks featuring official photographs sold as souvenirs to promote and remember the fair,[60] contextualize the static portraits of the displayed into dynamic characters who are real (figure 1.1).[61] "Card #1" functions as a response from the "sightless boy" who "stares back" at the author/narrator in "Objects & Artifacts": "Upon a kalabaw, I sit / tilling the perpetual rice / paddy of your imagination" (23). The "sightless boy" as literal object (playing card) and metaphoric object of U.S. empire becomes subject through Suzara's syntax (*I*) and interpellates the author, visitors of the exhibit, and organizers of the fair (*your*) as objects of his gaze, demonstrating the relationality of racial melancholia. The juxtaposition of the present continuous verb *tilling* with the adjective *perpetual* removes the object-subject from static colonial stereotype to living post/colonial being.[62] Moreover, the multiplicity of *your* renders museum visitors, including those who also are post/colonial kin such as Suzara or me, to coexist as intersubject and subjugator. Toward the end of the poem, the narrator challenges his scene of subjection when he quips, "You think you've succeeded in capturing me," which works to unsettle the foreclosure of his objecthood (23).

Likewise, the narrator of "Card #2" ends by critiquing anthropological epistemes: "We are Tagalog but / you . . . / . . . label us / simply 'A Native Group'" (30). The first-person plural renders racial melancholia a collective mourning and critique. I interpret the *you* as referring to both the Philippine Exhibit's anthropological organizer, Jenks, and exhibit audiences past and present. This dialogic address subverts the perceived passivity of the dis-

Figure 1.1 Display of Philippine souvenir playing cards in *The 1904 World's Fair: Looking Back at Looking Forward* exhibit at the Missouri History Museum, St. Louis. (*Photo by Thomas Xavier Sarmiento, August 2012.*)

played, indicating their knowingness of the performative nature of their display, even if misrecognized. The tone remains elegiac but does not foreclose agency. "Possession" also lays bare the performativity of Igorot dogeating—*the* abject act definitive of Filipinx subjectivity at the fair and that which haunts the contemporary diasporic Filipinx subject—declaring, "We roast dogs for your fancy: / the sacred turned to gluttony" (20).[63] These poems that fantasize displayed Filipinx agency attempt to repair the scene of imperial subjection at the fair and engender cathartic release.

In this first section of Suzara's collection, I also am drawn to minor moments that further illumine the palimpsests of St. Louis and reveal the geographic specificities of knowledge. For example, two entries not listed in the table of contents appear: "In the card file at the Missouri History Museum Research Library," followed by five file folder headings (26); and "MHM LRC Stacks," followed by four library catalog numbers (28).[64] Appearing without narrative context, both texts might not garner readers' attention. However, for those who have engaged with the materiality of an archive and more specifically with the Missouri History Museum's fair holdings, these seemingly insignificant letters and numbers serve as proof that we (Filipinxs) were (t)here (in St. Louis, both in the past and present). In fact, Suzara's poems derive from her direct experience with place and transport readers to the particular geographies of St. Louis vis-à-vis U.S. empire. Both "poems" provide a glimpse of the massive archive that exists in St. Louis and, through inference, hint at the primary and secondary sources that inform Suzara's work.

As mentioned earlier, the second half of *Souvenir* departs from St. Louis and turns inward, tracing Suzara's genealogy from the East Coast (Leonia, New Jersey, a suburb of New York City) to the West Coast (Kennewick, Washington, a rural city in the eastern part of the state with a history of racial segregation).[65] Instead of being representative of a generic diasporic Filipinx American narrative, these poems also read as regional like the first half of the book. A region-region analysis of Suzara's poems short-circuits expected narratives of nation and diaspora that figure subjects and objects as monolithic and universal. While Suzara's personal recollections reflect the specificities of her life that are distinct from the (sub)urban coasts, they also are a part of the constellation of diasporic Filipinx America.

Although Kennewick, Washington, is geographically outside of the Midwest, its geography, history, and economy find commonality with the U.S. interior. Like the Midwest, Eastern Washington is drier than its coastal counterpart, suitable for agriculture, and more rural than urban. The Lewis and Clark Expedition (1804–1806), which surveyed the United States' newly acquired territories west of the Mississippi River from the Louisiana Purchase (1803), traveled through Kennewick.[66] The metropolitan statistical area that Kennewick anchors has been and continues to be predominantly White.[67] The Columbia Center is "the only shopping center within a 100-mile radius," making it a regional retail destination not unlike the Mall of America in Minnesota (though Bloomington, a suburb of Minneapolis, where the mall is located, is not the only shopping center in that region).[68] In Suzara's poems about Kennewick, the motif of the frontier in "Fun on the Frontier" (a narrative poem that recounts the author/narrator's ambivalence about enjoying a county fair with a White friend) and "My Dad, the Filipino Cowboy" ("A Split Couplet" [63] about the author/narrator's father) links the West of the second half of the book with the Midwest of the first half.

"Exhibit C: Science" opens with an epigraph on Manifest Destiny, which stitches together St. Louis, the Gateway to the West, to Suzara's journey to Kennewick in 1980. Like the poems in Exhibits A and B, which relate the Filipinx diaspora to Indigenous and Black peoples ("Catalog of Objects," "Norms," "Bushman Shares a Cage With Bronx Apes," "Dear Ota Benga," and "Suture"), the poem "Science" aligns Filipinxness with Indigeneity. It cites "the Umatilla, Yakima, Nez Perce[,] and Colville" tribes of the Columbia River region who opposed White scientific dealings with the Kennewick Man, a prehistoric skeleton found on the banks of the Columbia River in 1996 (56). In addition, it uses irony to critique European scientific racism, thereby relating U.S. transpacific imperialism with continental settler colonialism.[69] The poem "It was cherry pie" also reworks the notion of "America," subtly invoking U.S. empire in the Philippines through region, as the author/narrator lists her family's multiple roots, from "Daet" to "Mangaldan" and "Manila," to "Niagara Falls," "Maryland," and "New Jersey" (60). Daet is the capital of the Camarines Norte province in the Bicol region, Mangaldan is a city in the Pangasinan province in the Ilocos region, and both regions are on the island of Luzon. Suzara's transregional citation makes the U.S. Filipinx diaspora tangible as opposed to simply metaphoric. The local Philippine and American cities are all part of Suzara's family's histories. They do not have to choose between claiming Filipinx or American ethno-nationalities; rather, both identities coexist in the locale of Kennewick, "in cherry & apple country" (60). Moreover, the nostalgic, pastoral tone of the poem evokes a sense of Americana—"at a time when people still did things like that: / greeted new neighbors with a pie" (60). And the author/narrator intimates a sense of belonging when she ends the poem with an invitation to play by a White kid (61). In "Guns & Satin Sheets," the author/narrator juxtaposes her father's present life in Kennewick—"go[ing] to the firing range / with his buddies Sem and Serg"—with his upbringing in Daet, reflecting, "How far away from . . . / the dirt roads where slim men stroll in tsinellas [slippers]," again using locality of place to contemplate identity, community, and belonging (64–65).

By way of closure, I want to briefly reflect on "Exhibit D: Objects & Artifacts," the final section of Suzara's collection. The title coincides with the first poem of the book. This cyclical structure invokes the (racial) melancholic subject who repeatedly returns to their primal wounding. The epigraph that introduces this final section also returns readers to Lacan and the gaze: "What determines me . . . is the gaze that is outside" (73). Interpreting Lacan's words in relation to Suzara the author and presumed narrator of the poems, I read the *me* as Suzara's subjectivity and "the gaze that is outside" as readers, such as myself, who analyze the meaning of her poetics to understand the diasporic Filipinx condition embodied by her.

While St. Louis fails to appear in the second half of the book, it nevertheless informs the diasporic melancholic Filipinx condition of alienation and ambivalence that haunts Suzara's poems based on her family's life in rural east Washington. Read as a whole, *Souvenir* illustrates both the social *and* psychic effects of U.S. empire in the Philippines. I read the poems in Exhibits C and D less as intrasubjective and more as intersubjective, following Eng and Han's assessment of Asian American racialization, with the author/narrator relating her family's estrangement in diaspora as a form of objectification consonant with the displayed Filipinxs at the fair. The souvenir as a concept stitches together Suzara's childhood memories of growing up in the ruins of U.S. Cold War military imperialism via a second-grade field trip to the Hanford Reservation ("Downwind: A Timeline": "Our souvenirs: brown irradiated marbles in little paper pouches" [74]) with the material cultural remains of U.S. transpacific territorial empire proudly displayed at the Missouri History Museum's World's Fair commemorative exhibit ("Objects & Artifacts": "If I were there: / 1904, a souvenir: / Which [playing-card] suit would I become?" [13]).[70] Suzara's poetic lament exposes the toxic nature of U.S. imperialism routed through region and proffers an alter-narrative of the minor, the objectified, the peripheral, thereby reimagining the meaning of St. Louis vis-à-vis Filipinx diaspora.

A Eulogy for St. Louis

Going backward in time, I move from Suzara's early twenty-first century poetic re-membering of St. Louis to Fuentes's late twentieth-century audiovisual meditation on St. Louis in his auto-ethnographic film *Bontoc Eulogy*, performing a racial melancholic search for the origins of diasporic Filipinx culture's attempt to work through the primal wound of Filipinx American subjection. Although many scholars have analyzed Fuentes's mock documentary, the extant scholarship neglects to center regional geographies in their analyses.[71] The filmmaker also overlooks geography as a theme of his film, instead describing it as "a film that deals with issues of race, difference, voyeurism, science as ideology, spectacle, memory, time—as the particularities of one's existence in the *here* [emphasis added] and now."[72] Fuentes concedes that the "respective visibility or materiality [of the numerous interrelated thematic strands of the film] really depends on *where* the viewer is *situated* [emphases added]."[73] I highlight the geographic unconscious that appears in Fuentes's interpretation of his film to (re)orient audiences to its geographic dimensions, given my situatedness in the Midwest and preoccupation with how place shapes ontoepistemology. In addition to St. Louis figuring as a metaphor for Filipinx subjection under U.S. empire, I argue that it is a material site through which diasporic Filipinxs ambivalently come into consciousness about the extent of U.S. empire in the Philippines. Rather than close read several scenes to support my argument (and rehash what other scholars have already observed and heard), I focus more on the film as a cultural object that often mediates diasporic Filipinxs' access to the fair. Revisiting *Bontoc Eulogy*, the urtext of diasporic Filipinx critiques of the fair, with an orientation to geography foregrounds St. Louis as a specific place in the constellation of the U.S. Filipinx diaspora, unsettling the notion of the Midwest as a nowhere for Filipinxs and revealing it to be a somewhere that we already unwittingly lay claim to.[74]

In Fuentes's discussion of the creative process of producing *Bontoc Eulogy*, the literal space and place of the fair recedes, simply serving as the background setting through which Fuentes can work through the melancholia of racial-colonial objectification. Like Suzara, Fuentes, as a diasporic Filipinx subject, shifts the gaze of the fair and its afterlife, endowing the abject object (the displayed Filipinx) with subjective agency by narrating the history, memory, and experience of the fair through Markod, a fictional descendent displayed there, and himself. The audiovisual form enables audiences to hear and see the displayed Filipinx as a subject whose desires do not align with the U.S. imperial regime. Unlike Suzara, Fuentes does not visit the actual site of the fair: "I never visited St. Louis. Like the 'homeland' [the Philippines], it is a state of mind, more valuable to me as an imaginary."[75] Whereas Suzara travels to the museum and archive that bring to life the fair and occupy the geographic origin of Filipinx American subjection, Fuentes travels to Washington, DC, accessing the fair and Philippine–American archives at the Smithsonian, Library of Congress, and National Archives.[76] His secondary route to St. Louis as metonym via the U.S. nation's capital not only attests to the significance of this regional event to the nation-empire but also illustrates the interaction among region, nation, transnation, and diaspora in making sense of identity. What is more, his reluctance to visit St. Louis reveals this Midwestern city's significance in the formation of diasporic Filipinx identity. The Midwest takes up space in his psyche and figures as an unconscious affect. As Filipinxs based in California (Suzara in the Bay Area and Fuentes in Los Angeles), Suzara and Fuentes exemplify the Midwest's connection to diasporic Filipinxs across regions within the U.S. diaspora. While California may be the demographic and cultural center of Filipinx America, the Midwest, and St. Louis more specifically, is core to the psychic life of Filipinx America.

As I read Fuentes's rumination on the filmmaking process, I mine for moments of the geographic/regional unconscious that materialize in his discursive framing of the fair as a temporal event. He explains his personal motive for making the film as a desire to "locate myself within historical narratives that define the Filipino in America."[77] Although *locate* may function metaphorically for him, it nevertheless denotes geographic place. Where Filipinxs belong in the United States connotes place and belonging in the physical and symbolic borders of the nation. In addition, an event is a specific happening in time *and* place. Only focusing on the temporal (historical) nature of the fair yields a partial narrative (though a complete narrative is an impossibility and not the goal of my analysis). Fictional cultural anthropologist Dr. Mia Blumentritt's conversation with Fuentes about the filmmaking process delves into the concepts of "in situ" and "in context" ethnography articulated by Barbara Kirshenblatt-Gimblett, addressing the film's place-based object—the Philippine Village,[78] an "exposition within an exposition" that metaphorizes the submerged and ambivalently dis/avowed colonial relationship between the Philippines and the United States.[79] *In situ*, defined as "in the natural or original position or place," points to authenticity.⁸⁰ However, as Fuentes intimates, Kirshenblatt-Gimblett's "display dichotomy can actually be used to frame the film as a personal reconstruction project."⁸¹ While the archival footage that appears in the film may be in situ, Fuentes's reconstruction of the Philippine Village unravels what is "in the natural or original position or place."⁸²

Again, the film's meditation on the abject object-subject of the fair, the displayed Filipinx, may suggest character is the film's primary focus; however, to be displayed requires a setting, a place. When discussing the farce of his ethnographic film, Fuentes points out his intentional "misdirection" in presenting an image of a Negrito but stating via text the person is Visayan, which Filipinx audiences are likely to recognize as the *méconnaissance* of U.S. imperial anthropology.⁸³ He describes such ethnic distinctions as geographic, illustrating how U.S. imperial anthropology, despite its attempts to delineate the progressive stages of civilization by distinguishing different ethno-regional groups—Igorot, Tagalog, Visayan, Negrito, Moro, and so on—results in flattening such regional differences under the national rubric "Philippine Reservation."⁸⁴ Similarly, my attention to geographic plurality aims to disrupt the unconscious homogenization of the U.S. Filipinx diaspora. While Fuentes privileges temporality, given its association with history and memory, my excavation of space and place that situates the film's content reveals the film is just as much about Filipinxs *in* the Midwest as it is about the history of Filipinxs displayed at the St. Louis Fair.

Filipinx in this context is not without complication, given the figure associated with Filipinx America's primal scene is the Igorot, an Indigenous body that conjures primitivity for White American colonial fantasies as well as authenticity for some diasporic Filipinxs who long for a precolonial past. Although U.S. colonial taxonomies positioned the Igorot as uncivilized in relation to Luzon's Christian lowlanders and the Visayans, the fair's geography lumped all peoples of the Philippines onto a "Reservation," thus blurring the lines of Philippine Indigeneity. What is more, north of the Philippine Reservation, separated by human-made Arrowhead Lake, Native Americans were also put on display to signify the United States' past. Such proximity not only links the United States' continental and transpacific conquests but also forges trans-Indigenous relationalities.⁸⁵ This is not to say all Filipinxs are Indigenous or that Indigenous peoples of the Philippines are equivalent to Native Americans; rather, the conditions of U.S. empire enable relationalities and intimacies among the differentially colonized that can disrupt the imperial tendency to divide and conquer.

Whereas analyses of *Bontoc Eulogy* have focused on the prologue, with the filmmaker/narrator repetitively listening to a gramophone that produces a different sound each time, I focus on the narrative middle, which takes viewers to the United States' geographic middle and serves as the impetus of Fuentes's production.[86] I read the film's title and premise as the mourning of the displayed Filipinxs at the fair, especially the Bontoc Igorot, who garnered the most attention from fairgoers. Thus, while the narrative entry point emerges from the narrator's search for the fate of his Bontoc grandfather, Markod, who left the Philippines and traveled to St. Louis but never returned as he intended, conforming to tropes of diasporic melancholia, the particularity of St. Louis as a place and event is the axis on which the story turns. However, the film's devotion to placing the narrator and Markod's story in the Philippines (about one-third of the film is set there) emphasizes the transnational and -regional connections of the Midwest. The narrator's desire to learn more about his Indigenous grandfather's history takes him to the heartland of U.S. empire.

As object-subject, Markod serves Fuentes's desires to recover a lost past. Accordingly, even though Fuentes figures as native informant, the film largely reinforces the ethnographic gaze.[87] However, two sequences shift from Fuentes's recovery narrative to Markod's experiential narrative at the fair. The first engenders a more expectant tone, whereas the second conforms to the expected elegiac tone of a dream deferred for minoritarian subjects. In the first, Fuentes translates Markod's observations of the fair, transforming him from displayed object to touristic subject. He begins the sequence, "When night fell, all the buildings were lit, the grounds transformed into a brightly pulsing landscape of light and darkness, the likes of which he [Markod] had never seen before." Black-and-white still shots of Festival Hall, the Cascades, and the Colonnade of States; the Palace of Varied Industries; and a bridge along the Great Basin illuminated against a black sky appear in measured succession, interlaced with black-and-white, high-angle, long-distance footage of a dark-skinned, muscular Filipino man wearing a conical hat and shorts and pounding a white textile sheet on a pile of white sheets, enveloped by his bright daylight surroundings. The juxtaposition in lighting establishes a stark difference between the grandeur of the central fairgrounds and the laboring Filipinx body. A recording of Markod speaking in his native tongue, similar to the recording that plays in the prologue, begins to play as additional interlaced shots featuring the illuminated Palace of Liberal Arts, Mines and Metallurgy, and Fine Arts appear.[88] The voice-over translates, "There were many small suns, so many that they could not be counted, and they made the whole place light on the darkest nights." Briefly, viewers experience the fair through Markod's perspective. This fabricated archival trace, albeit plausible, unsettles the fair as a site and event of pure subjection akin to Suzara's poems giving voice to the unrecorded.

The sequence continues with the narrator recounting, "He marveled at the giant bird cage, which contained hundreds of birds he had never seen. He was taken for a ride on the giant Ferris wheel." Photos of White American fairgoers walking and riding in cars appear on screen. The absence of Filipinx bodies alters the gaze of the film in these shots, as the point of view aligns with what the White fairgoer would have seen in the central fairgrounds but also places the White body as object of the gaze. The next part of the sequence continues with this theme. Footage appears of a light-skinned woman, whom Markod "was quite taken by," balancing a wood chair with her mouth while swaying her hips in the Mysterious Asia section of the Pike. The Orientalism of this scene again momentarily places Markod in the position of the gazer but complicates the power dynamics of the fair, as both he and the dancing woman ultimately are to be looked at rather than to be looking.[89] The film lingers as viewers watch her full performance, with Orientalist music fading in and synched to her movements before another voice-over narrates that "Markod's wonder never ceased." Footage of White men feeding white rats to a dog appears as the narrator shares Markod noting the need to fatten their dogs back home through similar practices. The scene cuts to a White woman, scantily clad in a white one-piece undergarment with a cinched waist, demonstrating her flexibility. Again, the camera lingers as viewers marvel and also imagine Markod marveling at her skills. The narrator remarks, "Markod wondered if her skills would have been very useful in the jungle," which reframes the gaze from hierarchically sexist to horizontally intersubjective. The next scene, which imagines Markod "enjoy[ing] watching the elephants plummet down the chute," lingers on the footage of elephants walking out of the chute pool, echoing Markod's wonderous gaze at the novelties the fair offered in contrast to his village in the Luzon mountains. Certainly, Markod's conditions of possibility are circumscribed by his status as a performer at the fair, but this sequence brings into relief the displayed Filipinx as also a desiring subject whose location in St. Louis granted them access to the pleasures of U.S. imperialism.[90]

In contrast, a second sequence presents Markod's less wonderous perspective of the fair, building toward the film's denouement. Viewers finally arrive at the origin of Markod's gramophone recordings. The narrator states, "Over the course of several months, Markod told the story of his people and his experiences at the fair." This ties together the earlier decontextualized voice recordings. Now, Markod's body appears on screen. Played by actor Enrico Obusan,[91] Markod wears a bahag (loincloth) and cap as he squats; talks into the gramophone; sits; and stands, squats, and plays a wind instrument on a rotating disk in an enclosed space decorated with hanging white sheets, so as to appear in a tent at the fair. While Markod is subjected to the viewers' gaze, the diegesis also places him as the subject with whom viewers might identify, as he provides a firsthand account of the conditions of the fair from the displayed position.

The sequence cuts to archival footage of U.S. military men marching on a dirt road (the first group holding band instruments and the second group holding rifles) during daylight, and Markod's recorded voice materializes: "There are people everywhere, and there is no silence until late at night when all the visitors are gone, and we are finally left alone." The scene cuts to a daytime overhead pan of the palaces during construction as Markod's speech continues: "No place to plant or hunt. No mountains or rivers. Their houses are tall as trees. And so many tiny suns light up the night. Yet of the many things that I have seen, there are very few that we would want with us in our mountains." The scene ends with a somber nondiegetic wind instrument melody. The tone of this sequence supports Markod's reflection on death/mortality (sparked by the deaths of a Negrito infant and two Bontoc men at the fair) and his longing for home and his wife and child in the Philippines. Its mise-en-scène places Markod in St. Louis, but in this sequence, Markod is estranged. As his body rotates on a disk, he is presented as a specimen to behold. Disillusioned, Markod no longer marvels at the illumination of imperial technology and finds the cacophony of the fair disruptive. The cultural and physical geography of the fair make palpable the stark contrast between the flatlands of the Midwest and the highlands of Luzon. Although this sequence conforms to normative scripts of diasporic Filipinx melancholia, that is but one of many ambivalent emotions Markod expresses in the film. In analyzing this sequence in relation to the one before it, I direct attention to the fair as a site that engenders both excitement and lament for Filipinxs past and present.

In her analysis of Fuentes's film, Balance proffers disobedient listening as a critical mode that engenders "new" meaning to seemingly self-evident cultural objects.[92] Disobedient listening enables us "to move through and beyond preoccupations with authenticity."[93] It also "defies the smooth yet violent framings of colonialism and imperialism's visual regime," challenging the primacy of the visual endemic to racialization and thus reorienting us toward the sonic to amplify processes of racialization.[94] By paying attention to sound and performance in *Bontoc Eulogy*, Balance guides us away from debates of authenticity and veracity and instead productively prompts us to consider the agential potential of memory and elegiac desire manifest in the film narrator's search for a usable past in Markod's phonographic recordings.[95] Building on Balance, I attend to the film's ambient "noise," so to speak—the environment, spatial frameworks, and place making—that Fuentes constructs to texturize Markod's narrative. The visualization of Filipinxs as primitive bodies on display through cinematographic focus and framing is enhanced by the diegetic (tribal drumming, Markod's native tongue) and nondiegetic (Fuentes's voice-over narration and English translation) sounds *and* the setting in which such bodies perform. Filipinx difference and being out of place materialize not simply through the visual but in concert with the sonic *and* spatial. While scenes of Igorot dancing and chanting occur in the Cordillera Mountains and the St. Louis fairgrounds, the film's editing unsettles geographic certitude, as voice-over and mise-en-scène are not always synched, disrupting the fiction of the real often attached to racial-colonial representations.[96] That both places could stand for the other reveals the slippage of the fair planners' fetish with ethnographic authenticity. My attention to the literal background enacts a kind of "disobedient listening," as I open myself up to other senses eclipsed by the visual.

Consonant with Fuentes's preoccupation with history and memory, Balance, Jan Christian Bernabe, and Fatimah Tobing Rony all engage issues of temporality in evaluating the film's ontoepistemic impact. For Balance, the prologue's repetitive acts of listening point to a relationship between time and narrative order. However, Fuentes's organizational flow is less prescriptive than it is imaginative, as he creates new content to fill in the gaps in the audiovisual archive rather than obsessing over what is irretrievably lost.[97] "Hear[ing] something new each time," the filmmaker/narrator demonstrates how the repetitiveness of post/colonial and diasporic racial melancholia can be productive as it refuses normative time and opens itself to queer temporalities.[98] Similarly, Bernabe considers Fuentes's "archive imperative"— "a critical, creative, and fundamentally political artistic praxis that, at core, troubles the certainties of knowledge production of American empire"—in terms of its queer temporality and its composite form that counters the linear telos of U.S. civilizing discourses.[99] Balance and Bernabe's attention to form unsettles cinematic veracity and amplifies subaltern agency and artistry.[100] Rony also marvels at Fuentes's artistry and explains how the end credit's revelation that the film is fiction forces audiences to "question how we know and learn how to tell time on and through the material form of film."[101] For Rony, time figures as an orientation device to place Filipinx subjectivity. Balance, Bernabe, and Rony do consider space and place, but given the film's themes of history and memory, temporality takes precedence in their analyses. And yet, the questions of diasporic history and memory are necessarily tied to geography, as Cristina Martinez-Juan observes in her analysis of the film, to the places inhabited, left behind, and of desired return, whether the Philippines, the United States, or somewhere in between.[102]

Although the narrator may reflect on the temporal distance between his Bontoc Igorot grandfather and himself, the spatial intimacy of the fairground attempts to marry the past and present.[103] Viewers see the narrator sitting on a white bench contemplating his grandfather's experience at and whereabouts after the fair. This bench is part of an expansive row of seating facing a band shell. As he is swallowed in the sea of white, the narrator's dark skin stands out, which parallels the juxtaposition of the fair's white-plastered,

Figure 1.2 Narrator/filmmaker Marlon Fuentes looking back at the camera/audience toward the end of *Bontoc Eulogy*. (*Marlon Fuentes and Bridget Yearian,* Bontoc Eulogy, *1995.*)

neoclassical architecture with the brown skin of native Filipinxs. At one point, the narrator looks directly at the camera, again disarming the power of the imperial gaze recurrent in the film (figure 1.2).

Although the present-day shots actually take place in San Diego's Balboa Park, the former site of the 1915 Panama–California Exposition, they are meant to evoke the St. Louis fairgrounds through their architectural grandeur.[104] Like Suzara's actual travel to St. Louis, Fuentes's staged mise-en-scène reveals memory is spatial as much as it is temporal. Returning to the site of the fair is an attempt to experience the past and to connect with real and imagined kin. Bernabe interprets a Philippine saying the narrator speaks in Filipino/Tagalog early in the film—"*Ang hindi lumilingon sa pinanggalingan, hindi makararating sa patutunguhan*"—as "Those who do not look back to their point of origin (or homeland) will not have the potential to reach their destinations."[105] The narrator speaks these words in relation to his loss of home and identity as a diasporic subject whose children are born in the United States and thus detached from their Philippine heritage. Archival footage of everyday life in U.S. colonial Manila moves across the screen as the narrator speaks and the melancholy sound of wind and percussive instruments play.

Accordingly, the narrator's melancholia is not simply temporal (looking back to the past) but crucially geographic in form (home, homeland, destination). While Manila and the Philippines may be the narrator's origin, his turn to St. Louis through his search for Markod reveals multiple origins.[106] Reflective of this book's larger argument, the Midwest is a point of origin for Filipinx America, and the Philippines is not the exclusive or even primary home for diasporic Filipinxs. Bernabe pluralizes *destination* (*patutunguhan*), even though the narrator does not in his translation, which also makes space for multiple homes and homelands. This multiplicity queers ethno-national notions of home and belonging, refusing the fetish of the origin.[107] The film itself queers the notion of origin, replacing the Forest Park architecture with that of Balboa Park to bring together fictive kin, which itself is a queering of bio-racial family formations. By inventing his direct kinship ties to the primal Filipinx/American past, Fuentes disrupts racial filiation and models queer diasporic aesthetic practice, making room for queerness in Filipinx America.[108]

While elegy and eulogy both concern mourning, eulogy works to honor the deceased. Fuentes's film is elegiac in its desire to know Markod, the narrator's lost descendant and symbol of diasporic Filipinx loss, but its framing as a eulogy reveals its productive ends in resolving racial melancholia.[109] As a creative object, the film proliferates alter-narratives to the colonial order of things. In his genealogical quest, the narrator-cum-filmmaker dredges up a barely hidden past that remains present, enjoining viewers to reckon with the ongoing legacies of U.S. empire in the Philippines manifest on both sides of the Pacific Ocean.

The film's narrative focus on Markod makes local the intimacies of transoceanic empire; however, as Bernabe illumines, Markod figures as a "queer composite Filipino body . . . capable of disrupting generic, colonial certitudes about race and racial classification that are the bedrock of American imperial archives."[110] As a singularity who stands in for heterogenous subalterns, Markod embodies the notion of "being singular plural" that Muñoz attributes to queer utopian performativity gleaned from Jean-Luc Nancy.[111] Markod and the narrator are mirrored protagonists. While the film can be read as a tribute to Markod (i.e., a eulogy), the narrator's subjective presence interrupts the objective gaze of conventional ethnography and documentary film (though indicative of elegy). The narrator's overt presence establishes a dialogic relationship between Markod and himself, even if neither directly speaks to the other. This dynamic is what blurs the film's form as pure eulogy or elegy, as the narrator stitches together the fragments of Markod's composite archival traces to produce a seemingly cohesive narrative that transforms displayed Filipinxs from spectacle into complex beings. And yet, the mystery of Markod's fate at the end of the film leaves viewers to generate their own conclusions. As I discuss in chapter 5, the disappearance of the Filipinx body can figure as a site of possibility as it resists full capture by hegemonic regimes of knowledge.[112]

Reckoning with the Figure of the Dogeater

If Fuentes attempts to piece together the afterlife of the fair, sparked by the uncertainty of Markod's whereabouts, Kercheval provides an extended reflection on what might have become of displayed Filipinxs in the story "The Dogeater." Going further back in time (and to a different place of production—from California to Iowa), I move from Fuentes's mid-1990s film to Kercheval's late 1980s fiction, which predates Hagedorn's acclaimed novel *Dogeaters* (1990), a work that most readers likely will associate with the literary referent for "dogeater."[113] Consonant with Suzara and Fuentes, Kercheval positions the subaltern Filipinx body as the narrative center and disidentifies with the fair's anthropological taxonomies premised on generic type, instead presenting a rounded representation of individual Filipinx humanity.[114] However, whereas Suzara and Fuentes deemphasize the dominant association of Filipinxs (particularly the Igorot) with dogeating, Kercheval does not shy away from it in an attempt to defang its discursive power.[115] As a White American author, Kercheval may not possess a melancholic relationship to St. Louis in the way that Suzara, Fuentes, and other Filipinxs on both sides of the ocean do, but her engagement with the fair and its afterlife illustrates the broader collective American wound of U.S. empire in the Philippines that emanates from the Midwest. Like Suzara and Fuentes, Kercheval draws from the U.S. imperial archive to give life to a fantasy of Filipinx humanity. "The Dogeater" was inspired by her chance encounter with a 1904 World's Fair guidebook, found among other forgotten library books, during one of her writing breaks while in college at Florida State University in the early 1980s.[116] And although she did not travel to the site of the fair, she has spent considerable time in the Midwest, as a master of fine arts student in the Iowa Writers' Workshop and as a professor at the University of Wisconsin–Madison.

Published in 1987 as the last story of *The Dogeater*, Kercheval's debut collection of stories, "The Dogeater," the only story to feature a person of Philippine descent, imagines the later life of one of the Igorot people displayed at the fair.[117] The story is set in New Orleans in 1981. This shift from the Midwest to the South challenges the notion that a subnational regional emphasis is insular. This cross-regional intimacy also highlights the palimpsests of U.S. empire and Filipinx diaspora that traverse space and time as well as the riverine link between the two port cities that weave French, Spanish, British, and American empires and map alternative borderlands.[118] The story's contemporary setting near an alternate origin site of the U.S. Filipinx diaspora (the eighteenth-century St. Maló "Manilamen" settlement) makes palpable the ongoing mourning of the displayed Filipinxs at the fair.

Whereas the sensational 1904 reportage, which remains frozen in the archive, presents the Igorot dogeater as a flat character and thus a stereotypical, dehumanized composite, Kercheval's story re-presents this figure as a rounded character with emotional substance and breathes life into a seemingly static past. As such, "The Dogeater" acts as a fissure that betrays the assumption that division, separation, and alienation always define racial-imperial formations both materially and discursively. I read the story as an opportunity to work through diasporic U.S. Filipinx melancholia as primarily perceiving the fair as violent and inhumane—which is undeniable. But like *Bontoc Eulogy*, "The Dogeater" reveals moments of cross-racial intimacies and pleasure.

The story's first five pages (about one-third of the total page count) develop protagonist John (pronounced "Yon") Santioc's characterization apart from his racial-ethnic identity. Only when he retrieves a book that his recently deceased wife, Louisa, "had [read] many times" to him—*The Book of the Fair: St. Louis 1904*—does he become a subject of American (racial) history.[119] Juxtaposing excerpts from *The Book* and John's memories, Kercheval reveals that John was the only child among the Igorot displayed at the fair, that he was picked up by a truant officer and sent to the Home for Wayward Children when he ventured into the city with one of the fair guards, and that he eventually left on a train bound for New Orleans, where he met his wife while working in City Cemetery No. 1.[120] As John reflects on his life, readers discover that he regrets not having fulfilled the Igorot custom of dog sacrifice when his grandmother had fallen ill at the fair, when his estranged daughter, Celeste, was born years later, and when his wife fell ill; if he had, according to the limited omniscient narrator who conveys John's private thoughts, he would not be alone now in his empty shotgun cottage in New Orleans. However, Celeste's visit at the story's end suggests hope. Although she seems initially embarrassed by the publicity of her father's alleged dogeating, in the end, she nonverbally reveals her respect for the Igorot practice of dog sacrifice to garner good fortune when John realizes that "she had come to show him the dog she was fattening for Anna Lynn's [her daughter's] wedding" (91).

Minimizing John's particular racial-ethnic identity, the story appears to motivate narrative conflict through a more universal concern: the death of a loved one. Louisa and John's possible interracial marriage (as Louisa's racial-ethnic identity is never confirmed) is unremarkable in its New Orleans context, as Louisiana only prohibited miscegenation between White and Black people (unlike California, where Filipino men were prohibited from marrying White women).[121] And yet, their seemingly typical marriage and the understandable pain John experiences upon Louisa's passing actually serve as an entry point to further examine the particulars of his life. Arguably, John's racial-colonial identity initially appears repressed, mirroring dominant U.S. culture's imperial disavowal, and John's diegetic and Kercheval's meta-narrative working-through of racial melancholia lay bare the traumas of U.S. empire in the heartland.

John opens *The Book* to a familiar entry, "*Filipinos at the Fair*," which reads:

> Because the Igorrotes [a common spelling of Igorot during the period of the fair] eat dogflesh, they aroused the Women's Humane Society to protest, but the Igorrotes insisted that the dogs were a necessary part of their daily and ritual lives, and their regular banquets of dog proved such popular occasions with the visitors that the Fair authorities were disinclined to register protest. (83)

On the next page, John sighs over a picture of "a small group of naked men standing attentively around a smoking pit fire. Beyond them, a large crowd of men and women in proper finery [look] on just as attentively" (83). Whereas this excerpt from *The Book* reproduces the spectacle of Igorot dogeating under the guise of ethnological documentation, John's own recollection of his lived experiences portrayed through such an authoritative text complicates any facile interpretation of experience, memory, and history. John's somatic response (sighing) to the photograph illustrates the ambivalence of diasporic Filipinx racial melancholia triggered by the objectification of the Filipinx body.[122] It at once recalls the abstract violence of being put on display to bolster the United States' colonial occupation of the Philippines and John's regional/local nostalgia of being with his family on the fairgrounds. As a two-dimensional snapshot of his experience at the fair, for John, "the black-and-white photographs . . . seemed such inadequate captors of time and place," thus revealing the limits of representation to fully capture an experience, a feeling, one's (in)humanity (83). Likewise, Kercheval's fiction remains a representation and cannot fully rectify the dehumanizing experience of the Philippine Reservation. Nevertheless, "The Dogeater" offers a more complex rendering of the Igorot experience at the fair, one that goes beyond spectacle.

Chang's concept of the racial inhuman provides an alternative approach to make sense of racialized traumatic literary representations. The racial inhuman is "the other for the normative, white, American citizen-subject" that orients us to recognize liberal humanism as an investment in White supremacy and heteropatriarchy.[123] Rather than giving into the seduction of (re)claiming the humanity of racialized subalterns who have historically been defined as sub- or superhuman, the racial inhuman enjoins us to revel in its dissident humanity. For Chang, the racial inhuman undoes the commonsense notion of the human, as "the inhuman is the alien that permeates the human, and the human that finds itself alien."[124] The inhuman already is part of the human; alterity constitutes the norm. Chang also connects the racial inhuman to *jouissance*, the Lacanian psychoanalytic affect she defines as "an annihilating sensation of terror, trauma, and ecstasy."[125] *Jouissance* is an excessive pleasure that threatens to overwhelm a subject with unbearable pain.[126] According to Chang, the racial inhuman produces *jouissance* in both majoritarian and minoritarian subjects who distance themselves from the racial inhuman and yet are captivated by their deviation from normative scripts.[127]

John is an example of Chang's racial inhuman. As "the dogeater," he is both revolting and riveting. Whereas Celeste is disturbed by the press's racist misrepresentation of her father (John is alleged to have stolen his neighbor's dog and eaten it), John remains unfazed and fixated on mourning both Louisa's death and his experience at the fair. Instead of reading the story as a rehumanization of the dehumanized Igorot/Filipinx subject of the fair, which, according to Chang, "chillingly resonates with the civilizing aims of colonization," as it leaves intact the notion of the human with Euro-American Enlightenment discourses, I view it as presenting an alternate humanity that exceeds the terms of White supremacy akin to Suzara and Fuentes's creative moves.[128] Reading the story as crystallizing John's inhumanity does not pathologize his Igorot/Filipinx excess; instead, doing so enables readers to recognize John as a subject, as opposed to an object of the fair, and reveals "the racial symptoms, fantasies, and unconscious of the U.S. nation-state."[129] John's inhumanity lays bare the racist-imperialist violence of the fair, which endures well after history turns into memory.

Though the newspaper headline *"Man Eats Dog"* that opens the story relies on a racist stereotype to hook readers in, this connection is quickly overwritten within the narrative (78). A different reporter, Delores LeBlanc, who writes a follow-up story, interprets John supposedly eating dog meat not as an ethnic marker but as a class marker. She assumes he ate his neighbor Mrs. Humphrey's dog because he is an elderly person on a fixed income and therefore presumably so poor that he must resort to unconventional food. She consequently suggests that any criminality accrues not to his individual Filipino body but rather to the collective U.S. body. In Delores's worldview, John stands out not because he is Filipino and thus automatically a dogeater, as the dominant cultural representations of Filipinxs during the 1904 World's Fair would have it, but because he is a casualty of a social welfare system that fails to adequately care for such vulnerable populations. In this way, the story transforms John from a particular racial-colonial protagonist into a universal human subject with whom readers, especially those who are not Filipinx, might identify.[130]

Once the plot transforms John from an abstract universal into a racially particular character, however, the story reveals the necessity of his Igorot identity for comprehending his material reality. For example, whereas enunciating *Igorrote* "would have had no meaning for [Delores] . . . the way it had no meaning" to the truant officer who apprehended him outside the fairgrounds, the story gives texture and meaning to his regionalized racial-colonial identity (84). Without the context of the fair, and by extension the United States' colonization of the Philippines, the signifier *Igorrote* indeed has no meaning; however, the plot relies on this added information to explain the relationship between the story's title, its main character, its conflict, and its resolution. In short, the plot requires John to be a particular subject for his story to be universal. Liberal humanism as abstract universality fails to cohere on the racial-colonial inhuman.

When, as a child, John goes into the city of St. Louis with Mike, one of the guards who had befriended him and snuck him out of the fairgrounds, "dressed right" in American drag, "wearing trousers and a buttoned shirt," John is excited he can pass unnoticed as a denizen of St. Louis (84). In shedding his bahag and covering up his naked body, John transforms again from a particularity into a universal. But in so doing, he becomes uninteresting to Midwesterners walking about the streets of 1904 St. Louis. Out of the context of the fair and disguised in foreign dress, from the perspective of the racial inhuman, John is no longer interpellated as a performing Igorot. Instead, he becomes simply a truant in the eyes of the law. When John is misidentified as a juvenile delinquent by a truant officer after Mike momentarily steps into a shop, his reason for being in St. Louis disappears—or rather, his particular existence undergoes repression by the force of universality, which becomes apparent when the officer places him in the Home for Wayward Children. There, John is mistaken for Italian, and his memories of the fair are rejected as "only hallucinations from when he had been so sick" with pneumonia after experiencing his first snow (85). Emblematic of dominant U.S. culture's desire to repress the nation's imperial past with the Philippines, this scene of *méconnaissance* reveals the problems with failing to acknowledge the particularity of John's Igorot identity and the presence of Filipinxs more generally in the Midwest. When John is separated from his Igorot/Filipinx subjectivity, the conditions of U.S. imperialism that brought him to the U.S. mainland interior are replaced by a proximate Whitened and abstract discourse of proper citizenship. Such a transformation also is indicative of assimilative colonization, wherein Indigenous peoples are legible as only in the past and become modern via Westernization.[131]

The reference to "his first snow" in St. Louis, however, regionalizes John's diasporic experience, negating the impulse to read him through a geographically universal lens. In fact, much of the story takes place in John's shotgun cottage, the architectural style of houses typically associated with New Orleans's working-class and non-White residents.[132] This intimate space metaphorizes the domestication of Filipinx Otherness, as John simultaneously appears abstracted in a home space that could be anywhere, although its very form is specific to the regional South. Moreover, given the long-standing presence of Filipinxs in Louisiana, John is less out of place than he seems.[133] John's migration from St. Louis to New Orleans via train illustrates the literal and symbolic transregional connections between these multi-imperial gateway cities that bypass the West and East Coasts. In paying attention to place, I am arguing that the intimacies of U.S. empire occur in unique locations, not simply amorphous geographies such as nation.

Instead of reconciling Filipinx colonial subjection, my reading of the figure of the Filipinx as dogeater rendered in Kercheval's obscure short story invites a reckoning with the regionalized "irreconcilabilities" of queered racial-colonial ambivalence on the part of colonizer and colonized.[134] *To reconcile* functions like a noun, as it promotes stasis, whereas *to reckon* aligns with its verb form, promoting the agitation of the seemingly settled. At the story's end, John elicits another somatic response—he smiles, but his smile is not in isolation, as his daughter Celeste responds with a smile (91). In contrast to John's sigh in reaction to the photographic objectification of Igorot dogeating for White public consumption, his smile in response to Celeste's performative gesture of reparation—the presentation of the Doberman she is fattening for her daughter's wedding—illustrates an intersubjective exchange unintelligible to dominant discourses. This narrative resolution of *jouissance* adds depth to John's racial-colonial melancholia, as his past does not completely foreclose his future. Rather than refute John as an Igorot/Filipinx dogeater, the story affirms it. The story reanimates the stereotype of the Filipinx as dogeater, though it places the marginalized object of the colonial gaze as the central narrative subject, capable of independent thought and bodily expression.

Moving on from St. Louis

The 1904 St. Louis World's Fair is an event in Philippine and Filipinx American histories, and St. Louis and the Midwest more broadly are foundational geographies to Filipinx psyches and socialities. Returning to St. Louis with a queer diasporic Filipinx Midwestern sensibility, I vivify the primal scene of Filipinx America to hold space for the regional, which often is eclipsed by the national and the transnational. The three creative texts I engage with in this chapter illustrate how the space and place of the fair matter just as much as the fair's symbolic status in relation to diasporic post/colonial Filipinx melancholia, laden as the latter is with tropes of temporality. Suzara's, Fuentes's, and Kercheval's elegiac creative responses to the fair reveal the power of culture in working through post/colonial racial melancholia. In their respective refusals to "get over" the fair, they dredge up the past—returning readers and viewers to the physical sites and scenes of subjection—so that the present and future will remember and re-member the fair's legacy as both concerning imperialism and intimacy.

As Diana Fuss observes in her meditation on the elegy, "Melancholia (endless and irresolvable mourning) has become the new consolation."[135] While elegies derive from melancholia, melancholia achieves relief from elegies. This feedback loop may seem counterproductive, but it enables the source of grief to remain tangible. The elegies for St. Louis that Suzara, Fuentes, and Kercheval present not only avow U.S. empire in the Philippines but also render the Midwest, America's heartland, as central to that narrative, thereby resignifying what actually might stand in for the nation's core values. Fuss explains how elegies are modes of address and a matter of ethics.[136] Elegies mourn the dead while enjoining the living to consider the significance of the dead. In the case of the 1904 World's Fair, Suzara's, Fuentes's, and Kercheval's elegies "repa[ir], resuscitat[e], and recla[im]" the inhumanity of displayed Filipinxs and proffer alter-narratives of people and places that recast them from dead to live subjects whose meanings cannot be known in advance.[137]

Before moving on from St. Louis, I would like to consider two last poems from Suzara that are not necessarily intertextual but nevertheless speak to each other as they illustrate the perspective of the middle. "Antero" is the last poem in "Exhibit A," while "Scissor-cut" is the last poem in "Exhibit C." "Antero" returns us to the beginning of this chapter with another perspective on Cabrera.[138] Like Kercheval's story, the poem begins with sensational headlines about the Igorot from the White gaze: "*The Call of The Wild! / Dog-Eating / Head Hunting*" (36; original italics). However, unlike Kercheval's story, the rest of the poem is told from Antero's point of view: "Now I help Jenks collect objects and people" (36). The last stanza queers Midwestern tropes of the frontier and grit, as Antero states, "We've grown a second skin; the mask / required to survive in this savage place" (36). Whereas the dominant discourse of the Midwest at the turn of the twentieth century figures Indigenous peoples of North America and the Philippines as "savage," Antero flips the script, challenging normative perceptions of Self and Other as he lays bare White America's lack of humanity for racialized humans deemed inhuman. Moreover, "the humid summers at Forest Park" are less familiar to the highlander Igorot than the cooler clime of Seattle, the next exposition they traveled to, ironically mirroring the climatological disorientation White Americans experienced in the lowland tropics that I discuss in chapter 2 (36). Again, place serves as a reference point in diasporic imaginaries.

"Scissor-cut" likewise anchors the narrative through place with the opening line "At the big house on 53rd avenue" (68). Suzara recounts another scene of nostalgic domesticity in Kennewick—"hanging out" with a childhood friend, Joy, who accidentally cuts her finger on "so-sharp, pointed surgical scissors" (Suzara's father is a surgeon) (68). This event triggers Suzara to reflect on her family's nonnormative diasporic position. She italicizes *normal* four times in the poem, which reminds her that despite a picturesque suburban upbringing, as a diasporic Filipinx family outside the capital(s) of Filipinx America, they are out of place.[139] The first three instances refer to the scissors Joy cuts herself with: "For these were not the *normal* kind [of scissors]," "we didn't have *normal* scissors / . . . / . . . / like *normal* families did" (68; original emphases). That object, however, is a cipher for diasporic queerness, as Suzara describes the "many things we [her family] did / that weren't *normal*," from Filipinx foodways ("sili," "Jufran," "bangus," "rice," "soy sauce"), to language ("*arrai!* . . . / . . . / never *ouch!*"), to transnational family formations (talking to her grandparents "on a long-distance call" across the ocean) (69; original italics). Suzara cuts this elegiac interlude by returning to the diegetic present as she nurses Joy's wound. The narrative middle of the poem metaphorizes the significance of the middle as a space, place, position, and relation. Delving beyond the surface, the poem bears witness to Suzara's psychic pain, her split subjectivity rent from colonial raciality.

Both poems illumine the middle as generative. Whereas the protagonist of "Antero" occupies an intermediary position as linguistic translator, the protagonist of "Scissor-cut" inhabits the space between Filipinx and American. Although both protagonists figure as liminal, they are not disembodied; rather their embodiment is multiple and relational. Cabrera's role as translator queers the heterosexual dyad of White male colonizer and female of color cultural broker, which has the capacity to disrupt the heteropatriarchal script of decolonization that casts women as currency between colonizer and colonized men. The shift from first-person singular to first-person plural in the last two stanzas illustrates Cabrera's being singular plural for the U.S. Filipinx diaspora. The first line of the last stanza—"We've grown a second skin; the mask"—also gestures to Franz Fanon's *Black Skin, White Masks*, connecting Filipinx colonial critique to Black decolonization (36). Similarly, "Scissor-cut" attends to the dermal, as Suzara takes note of Joy's skin: "The underside was unbearably yellow / against the deep brown of the top of her hand" (69). She goes on to describe Joy: "And her thick braids, closed / with the little balls" (69–70). The end of that stanza ends with "*Joy!*" both as an address to her friend and an expression of joy in Joy's Black female embodiment (70; original italics). By placing Filipinxs in proximity to Blackness, Suzara interrupts the White supremacy of U.S. imperialism and rewrites people of color as subjects worthy of "dignity" (36).[140]

In placing Filipinxs in the middle of the country through elegiac creative texts about the 1904 St. Louis World's Fair, I invite readers to consider how the story of Filipinx America, and the U.S. nation-empire more broadly, might shift if we reconceptualize Cabrera, Markod, John, and the other thousand-plus Filipinxs at the fair as Filipinx Midwesterners. Rather than read *Midwesterner* as a stable referent, I want to emphasize its contingence and possibility for rewriting race, region, nation, empire, and diaspora by Filipinizing it, queering it. Doing so resignifies the middle as dynamic and generative and as a space and place from which melancholic Filipinxs might get unstuck.

2

Tracing the Queer Filipinx Midwest

The Heartland's Archives of U.S. Empire in the Philippines

After living in the Midwest for more than a decade and a half and having traveled to all twelve states that make up the region for research, family, and leisure, I still find myself surprised to see considerable traces of the United States' colonization of the Philippines more than a century ago embedded in the Midwest's public history of itself. Such an affective response indexes the paradox of Filipinx misrecognition and hypervisibility in U.S. national culture that erases the imperial conditions that marry the Philippines to the United States. That is, by displaying the Philippines and its autochthonous inhabitants, hegemonic cultural producers of U.S. history are able to exercise epistemic control and thereby omit the violences (e.g., psychic, physical, material, epistemic) of U.S. empire in the Philippines.[1] At the same time, U.S. coastal and (sub)urban diasporic Filipinxs remain influential in shaping the narrative of Filipinx America and often reinforce the stereotype of the Midwest as flyover country empty of Filipinxs.

Reflecting on the pervasiveness of the Philippines' shadow presence in the heartland's archival repositories, this chapter reveals a constellation of colonial as well as subaltern epistemes that have settled in the middle of the country and that obliquely avow the history and legacy of U.S. empire in the Philippines. It thus presents another alter-narrative point of origin and departure for conceptualizing U.S. empire and diasporic Filipinx American history and culture. Instead of recognizing such material traces of U.S. empire in the Philippines as coincidentally in the Midwest, I argue that they are indicative of the region's central role in administering and documenting the

United States' transpacific imperial forays. By centering the heart(land) of the U.S. metropole in the historical and cultural preservation of U.S. empire in the Philippines, I queer the discursive formations of region, nation, empire, and diaspora that shape Filipinx America, opening a space to reimagine post/colonial intimacies and relationalities.

As I argue in the introduction, the Midwest is a critical but overlooked geography for understanding the mechanisms of U.S. imperial transoceanic expansion at the turn of the twentieth century. While the region may not immediately come to mind as connected to the Southeast Asian archipelago, Midwesterners and the histories they have left behind, some of which are housed and displayed in various institutions in the region, reframe the Midwest as central to U.S.–Philippine relations. The story of U.S. empire in the Philippines cannot be told without the Midwest. This chapter aims to root the Midwest as a critical geography of U.S. empire in the Philippines, but it is not invested in stasis or settlement. Rather, to root the Midwest means to establish a foundation by which the region is no longer removed from transoceanic empire and Filipinx diaspora. Following Gopinath's, Herr's, and Hoganson's engagement with the regional, my archival and museological encounters reveal mobility, transit, and relationality.[2]

My engagement with the Midwestern archive of U.S. empire in the Philippines is self-reflexive. The examples I present reflect my idiosyncratic encounters with ephemera that may seem inconsequential to scholars less interested in the history and placement of the objects of the various archives I have visited, as they narrate a story about region, nation, empire, and diaspora from the vantage of contradictory desiring subjects. I orient to these archives, as I am oriented to queerness, the Midwest, and Filipinx America.[3] I build on feminist, queer, diasporic, postcolonial, and ethno-racial traditions that seek to find the voices of the subaltern while conceptualizing *archive* capaciously.[4] As Manalansan aptly explains, "the archive is a space for dwelling and a quotidian site for marginalized subjects as well as gendered and erotically charged energies, meanings, and other bodily processes."[5] The archive of this chapter is as much about the manuscripts and photographs I analyze as it is about the spaces and places I visit and the psychic resonance activated within me. While I do consider so-called elite figures, whose lives were deemed worthy of documentation, I dwell with more ordinary personal papers donated to public institutions, which give us different accounts of U.S. imperial administration, as they focus less on the stature of the individual person and their contacts and more on their quotidian accounts of U.S. colonial Philippine space-time as they intersect with affect and intimacy. Expectedly, White voices dominate. However, African American and Filipinx voices surprisingly materialize.

Whereas other chapters in this book turn to fiction, this chapter focuses on material traces of lives lived; but the narrative I construct is less concerned with positivist truth and embraces the speculative while respecting real people. Like Suzara's, Fuentes's, and Kercheval's returns to the past to imagine alternative futures discussed in chapter 1, my return to spaces and places of Philippine history in the so-called middle of nowhere serves to ground me, giving me an anchor to counter the sense of disorientation and nonbelonging as a queer Filipinx person living in the Midwest. As Fajardo so elegantly puts it, "sometimes we must *literally revisit and rewrite* [original emphases] sites and spaces of 'nothingness,' or loss, not for the grand project of recreating or naturalizing a utopic indigenous past, but to participate in the powerful act of imagining or reimagining alternative realities and world-views."[6]

The colony and the metropole represent vast geographies. Studying empire requires an acknowledgment that its epistemes are diffuse and partial. As a diasporic U.S. Filipinx subject based in the Midwest, I am more drawn to local and regional histories of U.S.–Philippine relations that enable me to place myself in, and to make tangible, a broader narrative of imperial power and psychic violence. As Gopinath illumines, the regional and the personal are entwined.[7] For various reasons, including financial and emotional, I have yet to travel to the Philippines, to the so-called homeland/motherland. Part of my reluctance aligns with queer diaspora scholarship, which grapples with the ambivalence between home/land / nation and diaspora for queer folx.[8] Also, in queer fashion, I want to unsettle where home is—not to claim America per se but rather to disrupt the Philippines as the default referent for global Filipinxs. Geographic distance imposes inaccessibility. Thus, local and regional cultural objects enable access to global historical phenomena. Living in the Midwest, I can still access the Philippines without having to travel there—a key revelation presented by the chapter's archival materials. Rather than value the local and the regional as less authentic than the national, I argue that the former yields alternative insights foreclosed from the latter. The local and the regional tell different stories, stories that unsettle a singular version of history and reality.[9]

While the stories I share from various university library visits (the content, so to speak) are important for unsettling discursive imaginaries of region, nation, empire, and diaspora, the archival repositories that house such stories (the form) are a key aspect of my analysis of the queer Filipinx Midwest. The locations of these archives trace the intimacies between the Midwest and the Philippines, especially the island of Luzon and its capital region but also, importantly, its nonmetropolitan provinces. Where materials of empire exist matters just as much as what they convey. As Nerissa Balce argues, "the U.S. colonial archive is not merely a source of knowledge but an object of analysis."[10] Similarly, Martinez-Juan observes that the archive's "formal structure not only determines content, it also determines the manner in which content comes into existence and its relationship to the future. In this respect, the process of archivisation produces as much as it records an event."[11] Accordingly, this chapter figures the Midwestern archive of U.S. empire in the Philippines as a subject with a history rather than a mere object to be mined.[12]

As a literary and cultural studies scholar, I recognize *text*, my subject/object of analysis, to be broadly defined as a human creation. Thus, while I use archives as textual evidence to historicize and contextualize literature, performance, and visual media in the other book chapters, archives also function as a media text that communicates information about our culture. This is not a novel leap. However, in historical analyses of U.S. empire in the Philippines, the archive often materializes as the ground rather than as the entire vista upon which we might gaze to imagine the texture of empire.[13] That is, the conditions of acquisition and existence matter just as much as the contents of an archive. Archives are not simply temporal artifacts; they are geographic as well.

Inspired by See's critique of the imperial archive as accumulative, I resist the academic expectation to present a robust, seamless archival constellation.[14] Regardless of how much or little a particular Midwestern archive has pertaining to U.S. empire in the Philippines, the fact that an artifact exists in such seemingly arbitrary locations is worthy of engagement. I resist the pressure to present an archival survey. Accordingly, I do not claim the examples I present are representative of that archival repository nor that they reflect the region as a whole. Rather, these snapshot fragments work to introduce a queer diasporic decolonial regional take of U.S.–Philippine colonial relations and to inspire others to go out and see what they might find about such relations in their own locales.

Transpacific Imperial Tutelage

Midwestern Teachers in Provincial Philippines

Public education was one of the strategies of U.S. imperialism in the Philippines.[15] The Education Act of 1901 (Act No. 74), passed by the second Philippine Commission (helmed by Ohio son William Howard Taft, future U.S. president and chief justice, it was thus also known as the Taft Commission) on January 21, established the Department of Public Instruction and mandated English as the primary language of instruction. This act opened the Philippines to American teachers. On July 23, 1901, well before the end of the Philippine–American War, "an army" of approximately five hundred American teachers left San Francisco on the U.S. Army Transport *Thomas* and arrived in Manila on August 21, 1901, to implement U.S.-style public education on the islands and bridge the "chasm" between the United States and the Philippines via "common schools."[16] Though some of these teachers, dubbed the Thomasites, were U.S. military veterans and had experience teaching in the Philippines in the context of war, most were civilians who hailed from across the country with varying years of teaching experience and no prior contact with Filipinxs. Teachers from the Midwest represented a majority, and Michigan sent the fourth-highest number of teachers.[17]

Among the Thomasites was twenty-seven-year-old Frederick George Behner, an Ohioan who served as inspector of schools in the Philippine Islands from 1901 to 1905 for the U.S. government. Behner returned to the United States and became a Presbyterian minister, serving throughout the Midwest and eventually landing in Michigan. The University of Michigan Bentley Historical Library acquired his papers through his descendants. The Bentley is notable for holding the largest collection of U.S.-Philippine materials after the National Archives. It is a premier repository for the University of Michigan and the State of Michigan history. Its extensive Philippine collection stems from University of Michigan zoology professor Steere's expeditions in the Philippines on behalf of the university museum (which has since split into one public exhibition and four research museums) in 1874 and 1887,[18] the latter of which included Dean Conant Worcester, an undergraduate zoology student.[19] Worcester returned to the Philippines in 1890, sponsored by the Minnesota Academy of Natural Science (further proof of the Midwest's deep entanglement with the Philippines). This led to his publication of *The Philippine Islands and Their People: A Record of Personal Observations and Experience with a Short Summary of the More Important Facts in the History of the Archipelago* (1898), which established him as an American expert on the Philippines.[20] Accordingly, President McKinley included him among four other high-ranking American men in the First Philippine Commission in 1899, charged with assessing the Philippines' capacity for sovereignty.

Worcester went on to serve in the Second Philippine Commission until 1913, also holding positions as secretary of the interior of the Philippine Insular Government and superintendent of Public Instruction.[21] University of Michigan political science professor and Philippine Vice Governor (1933–1935) Joseph Ralston Hayden proclaimed in his 1929 preface to Worcester's two-volume tome, *The Philippines Past and Present* (1914), that Worcester "is the only American who has achieved a secure and important place in history solely as a colonial administrator and statesman."[22] The subject guide to the Bentley's "American-Philippine Relations" emphasizes the scientific and political foundations of Michiganders Steere and Worcester in securing Michigan's prominent relationship to the United States' first and only Asian colony.[23]

I initially learned about the Bentley's vast holdings in conversation with other Filipinx American studies scholars as well as by consulting the references of scholarship on the U.S.-Philippine colonial period. As a Filipinx American studies scholar focusing on the Midwest, I knew I had to visit the archive in person. For me, visiting the Bentley and the University of Michigan's related archives and museum felt like a pilgrimage, akin to my visit of the Missouri History Museum in St. Louis and the former World's Fair site. Without a concrete plan on which materials to consult, I simply desired to see, hear, feel, and smell contents somehow tied to my heritage. My visit was less about a specific archive and more about the archive as a whole, a space and place for accounting the United States' and Midwest's entanglement with the Philippines. Coincidently, during my visit, I met another Filipinx scholar (with ties "east of California") accessing similar material.[24]

Materials that attracted me revealed the presence of Filipinx lives. Tucked among Behner's papers was a collection of nine manila folders containing handwritten essays (and a few pencil-drawn maps of North America) by Filipinx high school students concerning education, folklore, literature, geography, and society. A "Business Letter" by Leoncia Taino from Mauban, Tayabas Province (now Quezon), dated September 3, 1904, indicates Behner was an English teacher in Lucena, Tayabas.[25] (Consolacion Alma's "Literature" essay, dated October 31, 1904, also locates their school in Lucena.)[26] I perused Behner's papers on my third and final day at the Bentley (the fifth and final day of my research trip at the University of Michigan). Students' papers did not appear to be organized in any particular order. As I sifted through various student essays and drawings, I grew excited to be finally engaging with materials by Filipinxs. It felt like I had found a treasure trove of subaltern voices with whom I could identify. Some of the stylized cursive reminded me of mine when I was in elementary and junior high school. I also wondered if my great-grandparents or grandparents had been taught by Americans.

I decided to linger on these files instead of frantically photographing as much as I could in my limited time, as I had been doing all week. This archive of unofficial documents, of various draft stages of student work, seemed important to me, even though most of us likely have parted with our high school homework assignments (or, in the case of instructors, our students' papers). As Malini Johar Schueller's analysis of the Philippines' centennial celebration of the Thomasites notes, "student accounts are rare."[27] This corroborates Marjorie Barritt's introduction to the "American-Philippine Relations" Bentley subject guide, which concedes "the documentation of the Filipino view of the American colonial administration is slight"[28]—giving further weight to this quotidian ephemera. While Behner's students' papers may not provide direct critiques of U.S. imperialism, as their writing appears to be in response to various prompts, they nevertheless give insight into the educational apparatus of empire and how young Filipinxs negotiated their national, colonial, and cultural identities. Such a rare perspective of colonized Filipinxs from the turn of the twentieth century presents an alternative imaginary of 1904, one wherein the subaltern speaks.[29]

Among the sample essays I read, several praise American education, demonstrating the Thomasite army's effectiveness in colonizing Filipinx minds at the local level. One oratory essay emphasizes the regional particularity of U.S. imperial tutelage and advocates for "establishing schools in every province" because of Manila's economic inaccessibility as well as "the lack of . . . distractions," the opportunity for parental support, and the proximity to agriculture the provinces provide.[30] This divide between capital and province, in favor of the latter, unsettles metronormativity and regionalizes colonization while still deferring to U.S. supremacy. The unnamed student exhibits internalized oppression, casting Filipinxs as "intellectual[ly] backward[]," "ignor[ant] [of] the science of the soil" (which apparently accounts for their "poor and undeveloped" agriculture), and not yet capable of being world-class artisans and deferring to U.S. education as the means to uplift Filipinxs' queer temporality.[31] But the student nevertheless honors provincial life as the key to the nation's success.[32]

Andres Rañola's essay arguing for the provincial capital of Tayabas to move from Lucena to Lucban further regionalizes colonial Philippines by addressing the relative differences of rurality, as Lucban's "richer soil" yields abundant crops,[33] including rice, hemp, coconuts, and sugar, whereas Lucena is perceived as more industrialized.[34] Reading both students' essays in tandem, we see varied geographic scales that inform their realities. As colonial subjects, Filipinxs express ambivalence, illustrating their complex subjectivity. While a surface reading may lead to an assumption of Filipinx submission to U.S. imperial tutelage, a queer decolonial Filipinx regional reading reveals simultaneous multiplicities.

Another student, Macaria Allarey, penned two essays on the Americans' so-called gift of public education in the Philippines that lay bare education as a colonial tool of subjection as well as the gendered dynamics of nation building. Both essays forward education as the means to becoming "important in this world."[35] In "The Importance of Education," Allarey casts pre-American Filipinxs as ignorant and "queer" (as in odd, abnormal),[36] which sets up the Americans as saviors who will bring Filipinxs to the straight path of civilization. Filipinx queerness stems from foreigners' aim to position themselves as superior, as the norm toward which the Other must strive. Like the student who wrote the oratory essay previously discussed, Allarey has internalized her inferiority as a Filipinx subject under U.S. occupation but has the capacity to uplift herself through U.S. education, conforming to the progressive sentiment other student essays employ. When she references the First

Philippine Commission's resolve to improve the Philippine nation through public education, she affirms education as part of the U.S. colonial apparatus. On a metatextual level, Behner's editorial corrections, suggestions, and comments further illustrate U.S. education's civilizing mission, as he crosses out unnecessary indefinite articles, wordy phrases, and incorrect verb tenses and rephrases sentences that bolster the American mission.

For example, Allarey writes that those who have not received an American education "have a steady course of life and a self-government is unfit for them"; Behner crosses out "and a" and adds "as long as a stronger mind governs them but," implying the United States is the rightful guide.[37] In the succeeding clause, Allarey writes "while learned ones are those," but Behner crosses out "ones" and writes "men."[38] Earlier in the essay, Allarey does use *men* as a generic placeholder for people, but that is the only time it appears.[39] In another (perhaps later) essay, she uses *men* eleven times (including one as *statesmen*) and includes one sentence unique to women: "A woman who has great education when she is a mother can instruct her children well, can also prepare them to be useful in this world."[40] As a queer-feminist reader, I view this rhetorical move as a subtle act of agency. As a young woman, Allarey does not discount women's roles in nation building. Behner's White masculinity and Allarey's Filipina femininity bear on the colonial teacher-student dynamics at play. Moreover, whereas "Importance" has more of Behner's editorial hand, this second essay, "What Are the Advantages of Being Educated," does not have as many edits, demonstrating Allarey's educational progress. Although a direct link between Behner's insistence on using *men* instead of the genderless *ones* in "Importance" and Allarey's almost excessive use of *men* in "Advantages" may not exist, I see Allarey exercising rhetorical agency over a language and concepts foreign to her. I marvel at Allarey and other students' English fluency and use of varying syntactical styles not to trivialize their colonial education but to honor the struggle of language learning as someone who has struggled to develop basic fluency in Filipino/Tagalog as an adult.

As Behner is an English teacher, his editorial hand is within reason. However, the crossed-out lines, corrections, insertions, rewrites, and comments in fluid ink contrast with the penciled cursive, ranging from neat to barely legible.[41] Behner's marks display the affective force of U.S. empire in the Philippines, as he tutors students in proper grammatical English and guides them to adopt an American mindset. His students' writing and their essay content show the "progress" of U.S. colonization in just "four years."[42] Not only do the students demonstrate English language competency in composing complex sentences, but they also communicate indebted gratitude toward the United States' civilizing mission. However, rather than assume these students support the U.S. regime unquestioningly, I read their sentiments as a negotiation of colonial subjectivity. For example, Allarey writes in "Importance" that education "gives equal opportunities and is [Behner's insertion] the cause of equality."[43] In "Advantages," she similarly writes, "Many of the poor boys have worked their way through school and have become educated and they are great men in the world today."[44] An unattributed essay that prophesizes students' futures likewise proclaims, "It certainly seems impossible that the boy of poorer intelligence would be brighter and more advanced than his fellowmembers [sic], but later on by means of constant patience, application[,] and humility, his name will be seen on the Roll of Honor."[45] Together, they adopt the American notion of equal opportunity that lays a foundation for Philippine sovereignty.

Given the rhetorical nature of these texts as school assignments, they reflect less of what Filipinx youth actually thought and more of what their teacher would have expected as a metric of his lessons' efficacy. A number of essays appeal to teacherly authority. Gregorio Elezler and Rufina Alma praise teachers (presumably American, though Filipinx teachers also taught alongside Thomasites during this period) for educating students on how to be "polite,"[46] calling to mind Louis Dalrymple's racist and ableist *School Begins* (1899) political cartoon, featured as a centerfold in *Puck* magazine, depicting Uncle Sam towering over a row of students adorned with sashes naming the United States' newly acquired territories: Philippines, Hawai'i, Puerto Rico, and Cuba.[47] In transcribing Alma's essay, I noticed several corrections; all four pages have at least three editorial marks, and some have entire lines crossed out—a palpable illustration of colonial discipline. Her last page (which has minimal marks), however, unwittingly articulates the limits of colonial discipline, as she writes, "We know that very few of us have political rights[,] . . . but since our school (has been) [Behner's insertion] established[,] many more pupils are learning, and so, if possible, after a few years . . . more people will have that . . . right."[48] She proclaims the inevitability of Filipinx political power as more Filipinxs gain access to education and use it to their advantage. Still, she exercises deference with the inclusion of the hesitant clause *if possible*, navigating the precarious position of a colonial student. Filipinx self-deprecation figures as humility, while their prophecy of sovereignty holds the United States accountable to its policy of benevolent assimilation. This bilateral relation unsettles the unilaterality of colonialism and resembles the economy of reciprocity See describes in her analysis of Filipinx petition letters to Marguerite Murphy Teahan, sister of the Philippines' last governor-general, Frank Murphy.[49]

Philippine progress under U.S. rule is a predominant theme among Behner's students' essays. V. F. Bertrane's "Progress" and Candida Custodio's "Philippine Government" trace a linear development of Philippine society and politics from pre-Spanish, to Spanish, to American times.[50] Bertrane fawns over the United States, declaring its governance over the islands as "truly . . .

so beneficial" and neglecting to recognize the 1896 Philippine Revolution as Filipinxs' declaration of independence from Spain,[51] instead seeing the United States as "coinciden[tally]"[52] emerging as "protector."[53] Custodio presents a more measured tone that briefly outlines the various forms of governance over four-plus centuries but indicates republican democracy, introduced by the United States, as the most effective form of government. As a historical document, Custodio's essay grants access to Philippine history in this Midwestern archive. C. Lapuio's "America" and Vicente Villavicenind's "If Philippine[s] Had Been Independent" reveal U.S. imperialism as a process of normalization. Lapuio asks, "Countrymen, why can we not make our country similar to theirs[?]," extolling the United States' industriousness and lamenting the Philippines' lack of progress.[54] Villavicenind asks, "If we are less or too poor concerning those principal things that an independent country need [sic] [industrious, educated, moral, and united citizens with a common language], how could we form a good government?" Behner suggests revising this to "if we can not [sic] measure up [to] this standard."[55] Villavicenind presents the Philippines as incapable of self-governance, bolstering the United States' imperial intervention. Through U.S. imperial tutelage, he argues, the Philippines will be able to govern itself.[56] For Lapuio and Villavicenind, the United States is the unquestioned norm toward which the Philippines must aspire.

However, the fact of U.S. education belies the seemingly natural progress narratives these essays present. Bertrane and Lapuio's essays have "3rd time" written on their covers, indicating a repetition of transcription that conditions students to internalize a colonial mentality and contradicts the seemingly commonsense logic of U.S. rule over the islands. Villavicenind struggles to use the conditional verb tense throughout the essay, which Behner corrects. As a hypothetical scenario in which the Philippines is independent instead of under U.S. rule, the essay should use *would have* instead of *will* and *could* instead of *can*.[57] This confusion of reality, possibility, and plausibility unsettles the divinity of U.S. Manifest Destiny undergirding the essay's ideology and figures as a Herring-esque paper cut to U.S. imperial hegemony. The cultural work of imperial tutelage is readily apparent in these essays and others like them, as they emphasize Philippine progress through U.S. intervention and align with the progressivism of the Taft Commission era, which established American-style institutions.[58] Character development signals the mark of progress, an intangible, subjective, and elusive metric. But as See points out, "the agenda of American colonialism" transformed "from settlement [and] resource extraction to one of social and political improvement" in the case of the Philippines,[59] a phenomenon she terms *progressivist imperialism*.[60] Accordingly, students' conception of progress has everything to do with their personal development.

Behner's students' papers are not simply historical documents of student-teacher relations that stage the intimacies of coloniality; they also are cultural artifacts that place students in the role of author with authority. As an English teacher, Behner assigned both composition and creative writing assignments. Consolacion Alma's composition essay, "Literature," advocates for reading and writing instruction, which grants access to worldly cultural capital.[61] She recounts reading the stories of John Henry Gray, Ludovico Ariosto, John Ruskin, and Nathaniel Hawthorne as well as the poems of William Cullen Bryant, Alfred Tennyson, and James T. Fields from their literature textbook.[62] She opens her essay by stating that literary learning grants readers access to "things that should be strange for us" (Behner crosses out "should be" and "for" and writes "are" and "to" instead).[63] In effect, the White male authors she lists figure as "strange," foreign, and thus queer. Although such canonical writers of Anglophone literature may be the norm, Alma queers them and revises the queerness of Filipinxness established by U.S. culture.

The creative writing essays within Behner's archive further queer U.S.–Philippine relations, as they center women's voices and the singular Filipinx subject. Students share folklore about the aswang, shape-shifting mythological creatures who feast on the blood of the sick and the young, which they translate and transmute into English as "the goblin" or "Giant," and why the moon is not as bright as the sun, as well as fables about birds, a monkey, and a fish.[64] In contrast to the White male writers Alma mentions, students recount tales from their Filipina mothers, emphasizing the importance of feminized folk oral traditions. For example, Antonia Evangelista begins her essay as follows: "When I am [sic] a child my mother told me about the goblin."[65] Catalina Delantar similarly opens, "When I was young my mother told me a story about the goblin."[66] Dalmacio Ambalada begins, "When I was a little boy about five or six years old . . . my mother told me in those times there was a large man called Giant,"[67] and Honorio Lopez likewise starts, "When I was a little boy about four or five years old . . . my mother and our family always were telling me and making me afraid that has [sic] a large man in those times in the town called a Giant."[68]

Although slightly varied in detail according to the writer's gender, students' "narratives" (as they refer to their essays) share similar syntax. The repetition suggests a dialogic exchange within their communities, among their peers, or between them and Behner. Though it is possible these narratives could be structured grammar exercises lacking in originality, the subtle variations reveal individual creativity. Additionally, the legibility of folktales lies in their repetitive retellings. These stories also are provincial and local, as one student refers to Atimonan, a provincial town in Tayabas, further highlighting the regional nature of this archive.[69] They remind me of the folktales about *dwende* (dwarves/gnomes) my Bicolana grandmother told me, which I transcribed for an elementary school assignment in the United States. Moreover, H. Allarey shares their fables using *I* and *you*, a shift in tone from the more argumentative essays other students write using *we* and *our*, which creates a sense of intimacy and informality. As the *I* of the essay, Allarey is the storyteller in control of the narrative. Overall, such local tales depart from the propagandistic essays bolstering U.S. education and colonial administration, queering (as in frustrating) Behner's imperial tutelage and revealing the durability of Filipinx culture.

Felisa San Agustin's essay, "What (Is) [Behner's insertion] a Woman Worth," uses literary devices such as analogy and metaphor to argue the importance of women in society, blending creativity and critique. She, too, turns to mothers as a source of inspiration.[70] Such a turn to the domestic shifts value to the subaltern. Prior to her subpoint about mothering, she introduces the metaphor of a sturdy house needing "a roof to cover it," implying woman is the roof, an essential component.[71] At the end of her essay, she proposes "to elevate the lower to the plane of the higher."[72] While they involve gender relations, her ideas also reflect colonial relations. The dominant needs the subaltern, and the subaltern vantage is not concerned with subordinating the dominant but with making space for the subaltern to thrive.[73]

Filipinx Students in the Midwest

Filipinx students also received an American education by traveling to the U.S. metropole. The Pensionado Act of 1903 (Act No. 854), passed by the Taft Commission and the U.S. Congress on August 26, established a scholarship program for mostly elite Filipinxs to study in the United States. These students would eventually make up the Philippine intelligentsia of the early republic.[74] Many attended colleges and universities in the Midwest, a number of which are public land-grant institutions, including Indiana University, Iowa State College of Agriculture and Mechanical Arts (now Iowa State University), Kansas State Agricultural College (now Kansas State University), Oberlin College, The Ohio State University, Purdue University, State Agricultural College (now Michigan State University), the University of Chicago, the University of Illinois, the University of Michigan, the University of Minnesota, the University of Nebraska, and the University of Wisconsin.[75] The irony of U.S. imperial tutelage and democratic principles resulted in Filipinx student calls for Philippine sovereignty.[76]

When I moved to Minneapolis to pursue a Ph.D. at the University of Minnesota, I began to wonder, after reading España-Maram's *Creating Masculinity*, if Filipinx students had attended the university in the early twentieth century. Surely, Filipinxs were not new to a 150-plus-year-old campus. Although I knew Filipinx students currently existed on campus, I felt acutely underrepresented in comparison to my experience in Southern California. By confirming that Filipinxs had a long history at my new institution, I somehow believed I would feel more at home. (Ironically, if I had looked more closely at the framed historical photographs lining one of the hallways in the graduate school building earlier in my time at Minnesota, I would have noticed one of them includes two Filipinxs, Manuel Carreon from San Fernando and Jose Q. Decaney from Binalonan, listed as international students, dated 1922.) A librarian helpfully directed me to University Archives, and the archivist was able to locate a few materials related to Filipinx student organizations over the years. I was pleasantly surprised to discover the inaugural (and only saved) issue of *The Quarterly Philippinesotan*, a journal published in December 1922 by the Filipinx student organization at the time, the Philippinesotans.

"Coined by the members to represent the Filipino spirit in Minnesota and the Minnesota spirit in the Philippines," the term *Philippinesotan* cleverly melds Filipinx Minnesotan students' colonized homeland and local colonial geography.[77] While attuned to their regional particularity, members imagined themselves as part of a broader constellation of Filipinx communities and student organizations across the U.S. nation-metropole-diaspora as well as an international brotherhood as members of the Cosmopolitan Club Minnesota chapter.[78] *The Quarterly Philippinesotan* presents a localized discourse of Filipinx student consciousness-raising that complements national circulating journals such as *The Filipino*, which began publishing in 1906 out of Washington, DC,[79] and *Filipino Student Bulletin*, which began publishing in 1922 out of New York,[80] and figures as a literary heir to U.S. imperial education on the archipelago established two decades prior.

The Quarterly Philippinesotan offers readers a firsthand account of Filipinx perspectives during the 1920s, two decades into the U.S. occupation of the Philippines, from the geographic location of the U.S. Midwest diaspora and the social standpoint of the middle class. "Like all other organizations, Filipino clubs throughout the United States . . . found it necessary to issue to their members and their friends some sort of printed matter of general interest to them," reads the prefatory editorial, reflecting the group's effort to build community while also presenting themselves as "like all other organizations" regardless of racial-ethnic-colonial particularity.[81] Importantly, this opening suggests enough Filipinxs existed in Minnesota to warrant such a publication.[82]

The publication primarily functioned as "an initial attempt . . . to comment on current topics, give a review of quarterly events, offer student contributions, and present a few other miscellaneous facts that are of common interest to Minnesota and the Philippines," highlighting the heterogeneity of Filipinx Minnesotan interests and pointing to Minnesota Filipinxs' positionality as diasporic subjects routed through the heartland.[83] While addressing an urban Filipinx Minnesota audience, contributors also acknowledged the publication's reach beyond their compatriots. Thus, explicit calls for Philippine sovereignty are missing. However, Filipinx Minnesotan college students did engage in local public discourse, authoring op-eds and reader responses in Twin Cities newspapers that champion independence from the United States.[84]

As an example of Filipinx Minnesotanness, the editorial "Our Part in Minnesota's Memorial Drive" reveals how Filipinx students at the University of Minnesota developed a sense of place through pride in their local academic institutional affiliation. The editors write:

> As members of the student body of the University, we feel proud of such a tremendous success scored by Minnesota students [in raising funds to build the Memorial Stadium (football)]. Individually, many of our members subscribed to the best of their paying ability; collectively, we not only hold the distinction of having made the first gift to the memorial fund but also feel the need of giving more.[85]

In positioning the Philippinesotans as "members of the student body of the University," the editors conceptualize Filipinx students as like any other Minnesota student. However, the latter part of the sentence distinguishes the Philippinesotans from "Minnesota students," indicating the liminal status of visiting students as both of and apart from the general student body. The editors' attention to the Philippinesotans "having made the first gift to the memorial fund" and "feel[ing] the need of giving more" also anticipates the model minority myth attached to Asian bodies in the latter half of the twentieth century. The editorial presents Filipinx students at the "U" as model citizens invested in the institution's social and cultural life because they are Minnesota students.

Aside from reporting various social and cultural activities, the editors also published two papers presented at two of their meetings with the theme of "The Philippines, Past and Present," evocative of Worcester's 1914 two-volume book. Both essays reveal how Philippinesotans wrestled with their positionality as students and U.S. nationals, as they were dually invested in the Philippines and the United States, and how U.S. imperialist racism constrained Filipinx nationalism through an emphasis on civilization. The first essay, "The Filipino People Before 1521," written by Jose Gacusana, highlights the ethnic diversity of the Philippines. However, he conceptualizes the various ethnic groups along a hierarchy, where "the real ancestors of the Filipino students you find today in the universities of this wonderful country [the United States]" came from "Indo-Aryan settlements of the Malay Peninsula" and were described as "civilized men . . . taller and braver" than the Igorot who first "invaded" the islands originally inhabited by the Aeta/Negritos.[86] By setting up this linear progress narrative from darkest to lightest complexion, Gacusana dissociates the Filipinx students in the United States from the so-called savage minoritized ethnic groups popularly referenced during the Philippine–American War and displayed at the 1904 St. Louis World's Fair. He also aligns early twentieth-century pensionadxs with the Philippine *ilustrado* class of the late nineteenth century, famously represented by the national hero José Rizal.[87]

Similarly, Eugenio Fonbuena wrote "Filipino Culture in the Pre-Spanish Period" to emphasize how Filipinxs acquired "many civilized ways" through their "contact with other peoples [in Asia (Chinese, Borneans, other Malayans)]."[88] He provides details of Philippine precolonial literacy (reading, writing, literary practices), spirituality, property ownership, farming techniques, industries of weaving and metal working, trading, and law to highlight marks of civilization well before Spanish colonialism. Much like in the writing of Behner's students, a critique of empire only could be made by diminishing Spanish rule. "The Filipinos have their own culture and civilization; have a race of their own; and before 1521 they were already possessed of national traits, customs and tradition that were their own," he concludes, showing that the Philippines is worthy of self-governance, contrary to U.S. imperial rhetoric of the day.[89] Like their counterparts in other parts of the U.S. diaspora, Filipinx Minnesotan students negotiated the politics of race, class, gender, and nationalism to construct a contradictory diasporic Filipinx identity unfortunately premised on anti-Blackness and anti-Indigeneity espoused by dominant Philippine culture and resonant with U.S. hegemony and sentiments of progress set out by U.S. imperialist discourse.

Still, *The Quarterly Philippinesotan* is a unique artifact of the early twentieth-century Filipinx Midwest that simultaneously illustrates local, national, and transnational orientations and counters the assumption that the Midwest is absent of Filipinx history. It reveals a socially, culturally, and politically active Filipinx community in Minnesota with ties to other regional institutions. It also contributes to historical efforts to trace Filipinas' presence in the U.S. nation-metropole-diaspora during this early period, which was marginal (relegated to a note in "Review of the Quarter") but indicative of the Midwest as a point of connection and place of movement.[90] Moreover, unlike their West Coast counterparts, Filipino Minnesotans seemed to freely associate with White women (I presume, with member names such as "Agnes and Florence Pierce" and "Margaret Jackson" also mentioned in "Review of the Quarter") without as much censure; and club chaperone Evelyn Graber Childs, who I also presume is White, wrote a review of "Clauses Three and Four," a play written by Jorge Bocobo and performed by the Philippinesotans, further indicating non-Filipinx participation in the organization.[91] In sum, *The Quarterly Philippinesotan* provides a small glimpse into the seemingly socially well-adjusted lives of primarily male Filipinxs who took pride in both the Philippines and Minnesota and reconfigures the Midwest as a space and place of transnational and cross-cultural exchange.[92]

The (Queer) Imperial Intimacies of the Land-Grant University

As the first operational land-grant college in the United States, Kansas State Agricultural College (now Kansas State University; founded in 1863) can be connected to the Philippines at the turn of the twentieth century. The Morrill Act of 1862 granted states federal lands taken from Indigenous peoples to establish colleges focused on "practical education" in agriculture and mechanical arts, which made higher education more relevant and accessible to the predominantly White U.S. public.[93] One such beneficiary is Franklin "Frank" A. Coffman, a 1914 agronomy graduate and photography hobbyist who served as an experimental station superintendent at La Carlota, Negros Occidental Province, for the Philippine Bureau of Agriculture from August 1914 to August 1916. As a Midwesterner trained at a land-grant institution, he fittingly studied the colony's corn (maize) cultivation (though he later became an oat expert), noting in a letter to his brother that "our little col. [which I interpret as 'colonial'] work seems like play."[94] Despite his relatively brief stay on the islands, the Philippines had a lasting impact on him and his career. Upon his return to the United States, he secured a position with the U.S. Department of Agriculture (USDA). He worked with the organization until his retirement in 1962 and lived in the DC metro area until his death in 1976. From the Midwestern Plains to the Rocky Mountains, Southern Mid-Atlantic, and Northeast, U.S. agronomy has a connection to his work on grain breeding in the Philippines, albeit obliquely and thus queerly.[95] More directly, the detection of a "downy mildew" corn disease at the La Carlota station, which resulted in a U.S. ban on corn imports from Asia, may have preserved U.S. agriculture.[96] And after sixty years, he devoted most of his unpublished memoir to his work, domestic life, and leisure in the Philippines—a memorable sojourn as his first transoceanic travel.

I became familiar with Coffman's archive when I decided to investigate my home institution's potential connection to the Philippines, given my prior findings at Minnesota and my planned visit to the University of Michigan later that summer. Of the few materials I located at my library's special collections, Coffman's was the most extensive in terms of not only print but also visual content. Among his papers donated by his grandson are several loose photographs and a photo album chronicling his voyage to the Philippines as a twenty-one-year-old fresh out of college.⁹⁷ These photographs are impressive in their documentation of a White Kansan young man's excitement traveling abroad for the first time. They also leave a trace of Filipinx bodies in the heartland. Although a few album pages feature photos of Igorot and Ifugao that conform to Worcester's ethnological style, a majority of the photos reflect a traveler's eye, as they depict Coffman's journey between the United States and the Philippines; in situ, seemingly impromptu provincial scenes of villagers and livestock going about their day; various landscapes; Coffman's living arrangements; his leisure activities with other White men; and, of course, his agronomy work. K-State likely does not come to mind as a place to search for the archive of U.S. empire in the Philippines; and yet, Coffman's ephemera yield an alternative vista for exploring the everyday of the United States' colonial administration of the archipelago. Whereas official military or government documents often serve as the basis to tell the story of U.S. empire in the Philippines, an unofficial, agricultural perspective like Coffman's shifts the narrative to the personal, local, and mundane, cultivating new seeds that bring the regional into account.⁹⁸

His fond recollections of his Asia sojourn as a young adult not only give insight into the intimacies of empire but also can be mined for queer relationalities and proximities. Stationed mainly in the western Visayas region, away from Manila, Coffman presents a transregional and translocal take on U.S. empire. His narrative largely focuses on the quotidian rather than the administrative. While corn certainly makes an appearance in his handwritten musings—reflecting his official business on the islands—encounters with native peoples and landscapes form the bulk of his memories, complementing his personal photographic archive. He discusses the complex rural-to-rural journey to the La Carlota Experiment Station from Manhattan, Kansas, which involved multiple rail and boat trips as well as automobile and horse transport across towns, cities, states, countries, and islands.⁹⁹ He describes being "considerably isolated" at the experiment station, with mail arriving only two to three times per month,¹⁰⁰ and recounts to his brother his sense of loneliness, as he had "slept all alone in a house in the tropics where no white man was in a mile."¹⁰¹ While such sentiments may conform to rural tropes, they do not define his memoir, as movement and connection figure throughout—from the "frequent visitors, both official and otherwise," since La Carlota was "one of the more important experiment stations in the Islands at that time," to various business and leisure travels on Negros and Luzon islands, including Manila and Baguio.¹⁰² As a satellite of the Philippine Bureau of Agriculture, La Carlota nevertheless was the center of corn improvement, illustrating the significance of the seemingly minor and provincial.

Homosocial domesticity characterizes the La Carlota Experiment Station, unsettling normative notions of cis-hetero-masculinity but evoking the nonmetronormative homosocialities of Fajardo's contemporary Filipino seafarers, Ryan Murphy and Alex Urquhart's turn-of-the-twentieth-century White lumbermen in Minnesota, and Clare Sears's White California Gold Rushers. While Coffman's descriptions of their station living quarters, which "were considerably improved over those usually occupied by natives in the area"—a clear hierarchy existed between imperial station scientists and colonial locals—lean technical, as he explains the structural framing, wall and roof construction, porch configuration, and water pump setup, they hint at scenes of domesticity, with the pump "suppl[ying] water for shower baths, toilet[,] and kitchen use" and the porch being used for meals during "fair weather."[103]

His photo album features six views of a house with a corrugated metal roof, captioned "Home in Negros." One of the photos, "View [of] Kitchen Door," further highlights the significance of domestic space in Coffman's narrative.[104] He also describes domestic tasks, such as resewing buttons damaged by the laundry process, which was performed by Filipinas, and hanging bedding linens over the porch railing during the rainy season.[105] On occasion, women visited and "were surprised by the clean house; the carefully set table—white cloth and napkins, with food served in courses by obviously scrubbed, white-coated polite and efficient (but usually barefooted) native boy waiters."[106] Coffman's juxtaposed imagery of clothed but barefooted native boys undercuts the women's surprise at encountering a homosocial domestic space, as he frames Filipinxness vis-à-vis primitivism, deflecting the contradiction of White men such as himself also performing domesticity to maintain the station's operations.

Unsurprisingly, Coffman makes several references to "insect pests" that can and do breach the domestic space, metaphorizing the porosity between the colonized tropics and the scientific colonial. Despite the protective measures that were taken—from having an elevated frame on "cre[o]sote-soaked [a tar-based wood preservative] 'legs' set in concrete[-]filled holes," to adorning their beds with mosquito netting, to wearing leather leggings outdoors—insects persisted.[107] However, Coffman and his ilk do not hide inside, as they dine on the unscreened porch with "curious" lizards who "catch the insects attracted by the light" and deal with dengue fever.[108] As they acclimate to tropical provincial life, boundaries become blurred.

Nevertheless, Coffman subtly reinforces the division between colonizer and colonized, as he adopts a White male imperial "porno-tropic" gaze when the narrative shifts from autobiography to colonial travelogue.[109] For example, he describes a *lavendera*, a local Filipina clothes washer, who "partially disrobed and bathed in the stream" after laundering her basket of clothes (a "noisy process" that involved dipping and soaking the clothes in a nearby stream, then bunching them up and pounding them with rocks, and finally spreading them out or draping them over bushes to dry).[110] I cannot help but sense Coffman's titillation in recalling witnessing a seminude native woman and her peculiar laundering and bathing practice without soap.[111] One photo album page is devoted to "'Washer-Wimen [sic]' At La Carlota." Centered is a full-body medium portrait of a young Filipina clad in a white dress sitting on rocks, captioned "Ling." She gazes directly at the camera with a closed-mouth smile. Her right hand rests by the side of her left knee. Four photos shot from a distance, with two close enough for facial features to be deciphered, frame Ling's portrait. Three photos depict a group of mostly women standing in a stream, hair pulled back (save for one who appears to be washing her hair) and torsos covered by fabric wrapped like a towel that conceals their breasts; a few bare-chested Filipino boys appear with them. In one photo, a naked boy runs toward a house, the camera positioned far enough away to make his facial features indecipherable.

On one hand, these images seem benign, but when they are read alongside postcards he sent to his brother, Coffman's porno-tropic gaze materializes.[112] One postcard features a colorized photo of three Filipinas, none of whom look at the camera, donning Maria Clara dresses and flanked by potted tropical vegetation, with the description "Filipina Belles, Philippines." Coffman writes, "How do you like the looks of these? I see lots of things here, some pretty 'fair' ones."[113] Neither *Filipina* nor *women* appears in his message; the literally objectified women, reminiscent of the St. Louis World's Fair playing cards Suzara writes about that I discuss in chapter 1, are simply narrativized by the demonstrative *these* and conceptualized as "pretty" "things." Another colorized postcard presents Japanese women dressed in kimonos in a gated garden setting with the caption "Girls of No. 9 House at Yokohama." While en route to Manila, Coffman briefly writes, "Here's a bunch of good looking one's [sic]. There's lots of them here. I've bought a lot of things here that I'm going to bring back to the states. Frank." Again, Asian women simply are "ones" and "them," though this time *things* refers to Japanese goods, not people; still, the proximity of Asian material objects and people makes palpable Asian subjugation vis-à-vis Coffman's embodied power. A sympathetic reading might attribute this to homosocial fraternal banter. A queer reading might recognize cis-heterosexual performativity.

Sexuality, however, appears as contradiction in Coffman's contemporaneous and recollective accounts of his Philippine trip. In a letter to his brother, he jokes, "As to white beauties as well as colored ones, I don't see no one in these parts[.] I guess 'theys' all vaporated," suggesting the absence of women and reinforcing the trope of provincial isolation.[114] Later in the letter, he intimates abstention from "women and booze" as key to not "regret[ing] my trip over here,"[115] yet he also admits to "wish[ing] I had a girl."[116] In contrast, his memoir implies sexual modesty, as he attributes his nightly refusal to dance with women aboard the various ships he traveled on to his "strict Men[n]onite-Baptist training."[117] He also "politely" declined a Lamao (Bataan Province) mayor's offer to marry one of his daughters, an oblique refusal of compulsory heterosexuality, as the mayor "indicated no young man should be without a female companion."[118] Coffman eventually married in 1919 and had one daughter.

Notwithstanding his apparent heteronormative orientation, Coffman's ethnographic gaze materializes queer relationality. Unique among colonial travelogues, his writing includes a name for one of the colonial Others: "Our cook Esloa," whom he describes as "a Chinese-native" and, at another point, as "Philippine-Chinese native cook mestizo."[119] Esloa's appearance is brief, as Coffman mentions that "meals were carefully prepared by [him]"; he "had been trained by an American woman previous to coming to La Carlota"; "he was resourceful, careful, clean[,] and efficient in preparing and managing special meals which often resulted in American women visitors expressing their pleasure and surprise if not a desire to hire him away from La Carlota"; and "he sometimes did become somewhat 'incapacitated' on residues of beverages he had served during the meal."[120] Albeit a minor presence, Esloa shares intimate space with Coffman and is memorable enough to warrant mention by name.

In orienting to Esloa, I redirect our attention to the Filipinx Other present in the U.S. and Midwestern colonial archive to engender alternative imaginaries that render such figures as simply subservient. While Coffman's use of passive voice disappears the Filipino domestic worker who likely runs the La Carlota house, the act of pausing to reconsider who is serving "dinner wine or possibly gin" as well as "coffee or tea" or obtaining ice to make ice cream brings Esloa to the foreground. This mention of ice cream prompted me to revisit Coffman's album, which includes one image of him churning "Real Ice Cream" (figure 2.1). Upon closer inspection, I see two young Filipinos, one kneeling and another standing, both behind White men. The man kneeling has a darker complexion in comparison to the one standing, which leads me to suspect the latter might be the Chinese mestizo cook Esloa, since Coffman mentions making ice cream after discussing the house's cook. Ironically, a White man stands in front of the person who could be Esloa, thus eclipsing his profile. Such a spectral presence fits with the queer Filipinx Midwestern materializations present throughout the book. Though Esloa is not in the Midwest, his relation to Coffman entangles him with the region.

La Carlota's Filipino houseboys further materialize queerness in U.S. empire.[121] Under a section entitled "House Keeping," Coffman describes how their house's mahogany floors "were kept highly polished." Although he uses passive voice again, the remaining narrative on the page makes clear that the actors are "our native 'house boys" whose "choice chore" was "polishing

Figure 2.1 Franklin A. Coffman (*right*) churning ice cream at the La Carlota house with a young Filipino boy kneeling behind him and another Filipino boy standing behind a White man; all three are watching Coffman. Photo from Coffman's "Philippine Album." (*Courtesy of Richard L. D. and Marjorie J. Morse Department of Archives and Special Collections, Kansas State University Libraries.*)

floors." He explains how they first use "fan[-]shaped brooms . . . [to remove] all debris," which Filipinxs will recognize as the *walis tambo*, and "then [tie] rags to their feet . . . to polish the floors." He impressively notes that the houseboys "put a lively 'dance' record on the phonograph" and "slid[e] strip by strip[,] keeping in time to the music," resulting in "gleaming floors" without the use of wax.[122] I recognize the houseboys' floor-polishing routine as a queer-of-color performative gesture reminiscent of Manalansan's Filipinx diasporic "global divas." A mundane domestic chore transforms into an exuberant choreographed affair. Despite Coffman's imperial gaze, I wonder if he ever desired to join in the dance or if his body unwittingly moved to the beat.

As a technocrat, Coffman nevertheless positions himself in relation to the domestic and thus the feminized and racialized. His private account of empire has all to do with how a home is run, in contrast to his public account, which is based on his administrative duties as agricultural experiment station superintendent and published in scientific journals. Queerness marks the appearance of Filipinxs in his narrative, as practices such as laundering clothes violently against rocks, getting drunk from patrons' leftover drinks, or cleaning through dance figure as novel Philippine quirks. However, Coffman does not necessarily depict such scenes condescendingly. He is a subject of his private archive, as both protagonist/narrator and subject of scholarly analysis, and thus occupies a liminal zone.

Among other White men, Coffman also exhibits homosocial intimacy conditioned by provinciality. As I discuss in chapter 3, U.S. empire in regional contexts fosters queer relationality and intimacy. Despite the masculinist space of the agricultural experiment station, queer potentiality proliferates. As I perused Coffman's "Philippine Album" in the chilly Richard L. D. and Marjorie J. Morse Department of Archives and Special Collections reading room on the top floor of Hale Library during a warm early summer day, I marveled at this young man's global travels to places I only dreamed of visiting. I envied him, for he had traveled to the place of my parents' birth when I have yet to do so. Unlike typical colonial-era photographs taken by Americans in the Philippines (and critiqued by Vicente Rafael, Sharon Delmendo, and Balce) that reinforce a narrative of Filipinx subjugation, Coffman's collection affectively engendered for me not disgust but attraction, for his images forward a relationality between *American* and *Philippine*.[123]

A photo captioned "Tiffin!?!" arrests me (figure 2.2). Five young White men sit around a lakeside picnic, dressed only in their undergarments, muscular skin exposed. I recognize Coffman, with his dark, furrowed eyebrows, from other photos. Mostly blocked by the man in white in the foreground, he is on the left and appears to be the only one looking at the camera. While the relationship between the men is perhaps platonic, I recognize queer intimacy. I wonder why I worry about projecting queerness on a man who

Figure 2.2 Franklin A. Coffman (*second from left*) sharing a daytime meal with four traveling companions next to Taal Lake. Photo from Coffman's "Philippine Album." (*Courtesy of Richard L. D. and Marjorie J. Morse Department of Archives and Special Collections, Kansas State University Libraries.*)

later marries a woman and seems normatively Midwestern, and then I realize my hesitation stems from internalized homophobia, which has ingrained in me that my existence is unworthy of mattering. The veracity of this image matters, but my imagination also matters. Making room for possibility materializes queer abjection, renders it plausible; even if the people in the photo do not identify with queerness, they serve as proxies for bodies who could be queer—and that is affirming.

Coffman recounts this leisure excursion, writing, "Typical of fool hardy young Americans 60 years ago[,] the group stripped and took what was quite obviously the first swim in the lake in the bottom of Taal volcano crater."[124] *Stripped* connotes eroticism, similar to his use of *disrobed* when describing the *lavendera*. As Gopinath explains, "a queer optic . . . allows us to apprehend bodies, desires, and affiliations rendered lost or unthinkable within normative history."[125] The apprehensibility of queerness in this quasi-homoerotic homosocial domestic scene of sharing a meal half naked, following a lake swim, makes room for alter-narratives of White masculinity in the colonial Philippines premised on vulnerability and desire.

Racial Ambivalence

Sherman Allen Harvey's manuscript and memoir provide a local/regional African American perspective on U.S. empire in the Philippines. Born to former-slaves-turned-sharecroppers David and Rebecca (née Brooks) Harvey on October 6, 1864, in Lawrence, Kansas, Sherman became one of the first African American students to graduate from the University of Kansas in 1889.[126] He was elected clerk of the District Court for Douglas County (of which Lawrence is the seat) in 1892 (after an unsuccessful election in 1890) on the Republican Party ticket, was reelected in 1894, and served until January 1897.[127] When the Spanish–American War broke out, he reluctantly enlisted. Fellow African American townsmen wanted him to be their captain, but the mothers of these men eventually convinced him to lead.[128] His motive to serve was a sense of duty more to his local Black community than to nation and empire. He served as captain of the all–African American regiment Company B, Twenty-Third Kansas Volunteer Infantry, in Cuba from September 1, 1898, to March 1, 1899.[129] Although he declined to serve in the Philippine–American War, he traveled to the Philippines at thirty-seven in April 1902 to satiate his "w[a]nderlust" and in response to the "urging" of friends in the Philippines.[130] He stayed in the Philippines for nineteen years, living in the Cagayan River Valley and practicing law with his friend and fellow KU alum Captain William M. Hawkins.[131] With "his w[a]nderlust [satisfied]" and a growing disinterest in the politics of practicing law on the islands, he returned to Lawrence.[132] He died at the Los Angeles Veterans Hospital in September 1934 and was buried in the family plot at the Vinland cemetery (south of Lawrence).[133]

After conducting archival research at my home institution, I decided to look into holdings at the University of Kansas, about a seventy-five-minute drive east from me. I had planned to have lunch with a Filipinx grad student who I had been in contact with virtually after they reached out to me given our overlapping interests in Filipinx gender and sexuality studies and our geographic proximity to each other, so I only allocated the morning to peruse KU's archive. To prepare, I searched "Philippine*" in the Kenneth Spencer Research Library Archival Collections database. I was drawn more to early 1900 materials than to those from the World War II era due to my familiarity with the former period. I found a set of documents authored by Harvey, an African American Kansan, among his family's papers: a c. 1912 manuscript reflecting on the first ten years of his stay in the Philippines and the first fourteen years of U.S. rule on the islands and a typed memoir (as the handwritten original is too fragile to handle) written in 1933 and focusing largely on his time in the Philippines. I was excited to engage a local perspective on the Philippines from a non-White person, a rarity among my archival encounters, so I devoted most of my brief visit to the Harvey Family Papers.

While the Harveys precede the Exodusters and one of Lawrence's most famous African Americans, Langston Hughes, their history entwines racial liberation with Midwestern settlement and transpacific empire.[134] As early Black migrants to the Sunflower State, with three sons graduating from KU (one of whom was involved in county governance and lived abroad and another who worked as a clerk for Republican Congressman Justin De Witt Bowersock),[135] the Harveys are a notable family whose materials would be of interest to the KU archival collection. A grandson (Sherman's nephew) donated materials in 1989.[136] Sherman appears to have never married.

Harvey's manuscript provides an ambivalent ethnographic account of the Philippines under U.S. rule, which is fresh in his mind, whereas his memoir presents him as a protagonist among rural Filipinxs. He writes for an audience who will engage his ideas; these texts are not private. Although he expresses anti-war and anti-imperialist stances, writing in his manuscript that the conflict with Spain "should have been settled without war" and in his memoir that he "refused to take part in the excitement" surrounding the Spanish–American War,[137] he is not necessarily sympathetic to the Filipinx plight. His racialized positionality barely figures in relation to the Philippines, though his allusions to racial inequities in the United States distinguish his views from those expressed in other White historical accounts.

Doubtful of the United States' ability to successfully colonize the islands, he rhetorically asks, "Do you know why, with such bitter race prejudice existing, the U.S. should add to her burdens and further complicate her greatest problem of the day by becoming responsible for the government and welfare of the dark ~~races~~ [original strike-through] people of Hawaii, Porto Rico [sic][,] and the Philippines?"[138] Writing from Kansas, he is connected to national Black discourses that highlight the contradictions of Jim Crow laws and the rise of anti-Black violence vis-à-vis U.S. imperial transoceanic expansion, which Balce discusses in her analysis of Black press coverage of the Philippine–American War.[139] Crossing out *races* and writing *people* instead challenges the dominant U.S. imperial rhetoric and grants people of color dignity, recognizing them as people. However, his writings overall exercise restraint in critiquing U.S. racism and racial imperialism, placing him as more moderate in his views. Though, as Balce argues, "American imperial modernity for some African Americans . . . offered the possibility of cultural citizenship . . . and fighting an unpopular war was the Faustian pact that would allow them to become modern [B]lack American citizens rather than second-class emancipated slaves."[140] Perhaps not fighting in the Philippine–American War immunized Harvey from interracial relationality and solidarity, but his acute awareness of racial inequities experienced in Lawrence and his utopian sentiments of racial transcendence in the Philippines as a civilian reveal his ambivalence toward the U.S. racial imperial project.

Harvey's Midwestern particularity informs his worldview. He recounts "the mutually fair, courteous and helpful treatment of his schoolmates," who were predominantly White; such interracial interactions contrasted with those his parents experienced during their childhoods in Arkansas.[141] Similarly, on his first day of school, January 2, 1883, he feels equal to "three young white men, bent on the same mission" to receive a higher education at the University of Kansas;[142] this differs from "the unjust segregation and discrimination" students of color experienced under Chancellor Ernest Lindley thirty-five years later—against which he protested.[143] Although Harvey does not describe instances of racism in his education, during his time at KU, an 1886 editorial in the student newspaper expresses the incommensurability of Black and White students, suggesting the existence of racial prejudice on campus.[144] The case of *Brown v. Board of Education of Topeka* (1954) further underscores Kansas's racial discord.[145] While perhaps exceptional and/or a refusal to dwell on the negative, Harvey's story adds to the complexities of being Black in Kansas. As a child, he dreamed of becoming a railroad engineer but learned the color of his skin would prevent him from doing so.[146] He circles back to this formative moment to express Black resiliency and ingenuity as a landholder growing wheat, sustaining the family's agricultural legacy.[147] His story resignifies rurality as commensurate with Blackness.

As a Midwesterner, though, he has dreams of escape. Reflecting on his childhood, he writes that "he knew there was a great world beyond[,] filled with people and things that he knew little or nothing about, and of which he longed to know and become a part of."[148] Such sentiment connects to the wanderlust that led him to the Philippines as an adult. When describing his KU peers as "coming from families in all walks of life, from country and town," and his first (April 1902) and second (November 1912) travel to the Philippines, during which he stopped in Honolulu, Yokohama, Tokyo, Kobe, Moji, Shanghai, and Hong Kong, he conveys an attachment to cosmopolitanism.[149] But his Kansas roots are not left behind, as they serve as translocal points of reference and connection. Upon his return "home" to Tuguegarao, Cagayan Province, in January 1913—an indication of his diasporic subjectivity and capacity to conceive of multiple home/lands—he appreciates the "change from barrenness, snow, ice and shivering, to planting crops, flowers, green fields and a tropical sun that makes the most energetic and active lazy."[150] Romanticizing the northern provincial tropics, he celebrates an escape from the harsh Midwest winters. (The latter trope appears in Santos's writing, and I discuss it in the next chapter.) The Cagayan River Valley's fertile land also reminds him of his agricultural roots and makes this part of the Philippines seem more familiar and less disorienting.[151] Bypassing the national, the regional yields an alternate account of American sojourners under U.S. colonization of the Philippines.

Harvey also exemplifies another metaphor of the middle as a diasporic Black American committed to neither the project of White U.S. imperialism in the Philippines nor Filipinx sovereignty. Such a liminal zone places him as structurally queer to American presence on the islands. When he first arrived in Cagayan, he desired to work as a tobacco farmer, which went against custom for "foreigners and white folks."[152] Heeding such advice from non-Filipinxs, however, left him financially insecure, homesick, and lonely.[153] Practicing law with his friend Hawkins, on the other hand, proved satisfying. Not an agent of U.S. empire, Harvey acted as mediator and defended the accused, exercising fairness in the pursuit of justice. For example, he advised two Filipina neighbors and relatives disputing land not to advance their case to court, as the cost of the suit would exceed the land's value.[154] He also defended a thirteen-year-old Kalinga boy sentenced to seventeen years, four months, and one day for killing his wife's lover, obtaining a pardon from General-Governor William Cameron Forbes since the law discriminated against non-Christians.[155] His proudest case involved "saving [an Ilongot man] from serving 11 years and 6 months punishment in prison unlawfully," as the defendant had cause. The latter two cases illustrate Harvey's advocacy against religious discrimination as it intersects with race and class.

Despite his own racial-colonial biases, he remained committed to fairness and honesty.[156] As a mediator, he developed sympathy toward Filipinxs even if he ultimately could not identify with them. Being on the islands placed him in proximity to "all classes of people in their [everyday] life," from rural villagers to colonial statespersons, thus influencing his racial-colonial ambivalence.[157] Writing near the end of his life and in the context of the rise of global fascisms in 1933, he ultimately advocates for a "world safe for humanity" rather than "democracy or any other 'ocracy,'" illustrating a tension between his desire and reality.[158]

Such a tension helps to account for his ambivalence toward the U.S. colonial project in the Philippines. Doubtful of U.S. empire's efficacy, Harvey concludes his 1912 manuscript by setting himself apart from the "American ... stranger in the Orient" who is "selfish, arrogant, [e]gotistical, and about many things ignorant, and insists on doing *his* [emphasis added] own way, ignoring customs, traditions, civilization[,] and even nature itself."[159] But he also does not align with Filipinxs, as some African Americans in the Philippines did, most notably David Fagen, writing, "The Filipino has nothing in common with *us* [emphasis added], and I regret to be forced to say he is ungrateful for the good *we* [emphasis added] have done from him."[160] On one hand, Harvey disidentifies with the American imperialist, using the third-person singular pronoun *he*. On the other hand, he aligns with the United States when conceptualizing Filipinxs, using the exclusive first-person plural pronoun *us* and again using *he* to signify the other to himself, this time the colonized Filipinx. He also expresses hesitation when he says "I regret" and "forced," indicating his ambivalence toward the subaltern whom he has more in common with as subjects under White supremacy. Although reducing both the American imperialist and the colonized Filipinx to singular types, Harvey places both in relation to one another, distinguishing himself as an abstract American citizen from these perverse, and thus queer, others and yet leaving ambiguous what the ideal American–Philippine relation might be.

Much of Harvey's manuscript presents an ambivalent ethnographic account of local Philippine culture not unlike the colonial travelogues of White Midwesterners, such as Coffman's (discussed earlier), Nanon Worcester's 1909 letters to her mother, and Winifred Hubbell's c. 1950 unpublished memoir, "Our Adventure in the Philippine Islands [1907–1913]."[161] Assessing Filipinxs on a national-imperial level, he conforms to racist generalizations, as he characterizes them as "at best . . . but partly civilized," illiterate, "ignorant, child[-]like," and "not very careful about hygiene and sanitation."[162] He discusses domestic customs and praises their hospitality but criticizes their patriarchal familial dynamics.[163] He romanticizes the agricultural economy, often referring to the "simple life" Filipinxs lead,[164] but he sarcastically cautions against foreigners becoming too comfortable on the islands, as it can lead to "Filipinitis," an invented malady to describe "going native," which entails "turn[ing] a cold shoulder to Americans, and discredit[ing] all things American to the advantage of the Filipino."[165]

He looks down on Philippine education under Spanish rule, noting the University of Santo Tomas and José Rizal as exceptions, but expectedly praises the progress instituted by the United States.[166] He critiques the cacique (patronage) system of local governments but concedes that caciques (local bosses) are not unlike American reformers stateside.[167] He devotes several pages to religion, lambasting Filipinx mimetic rituals as impractical and irrelevant to personal and social betterment,[168] but he admires the twilight Easter services. His tone shifts when describing them, moving from the aforementioned generalizations, which are likely observed from his local/regional place in Cagayan, to a thick, poetic description of a local/particular ceremony: "Each star stood out in the heavens only to lose its luster in the halo of silver light of a full moon seldom seen except in the tropics."[169] Altogether, Harvey's ethnographic account is neither completely condescending to nor identificatory with Filipinxs. Instead, his racial ambivalence is entangled with his racialized and regional positionality as someone who is not a White imperialist and is living among—yet apart from, as a foreigner—the people of Cagayan.

Like the other archives I engage with in this chapter, Harvey's observations open a space for Filipinxs to emerge as historical agents. In addition to appearing in the legal cases he describes in his memoir, Filipinxs figure as unruly colonial subjects. Such subaltern performatives are Herring-esque paper cuts to the project of U.S. imperialism. For example, Harvey describes Filipinxs' subterfuge: "The[y] never do today what can be put off until tomorrow.... He will tell you very assuringly [sic] that he is going to do something right away. He may do it tomorrow or [the] day after tomorrow. If you can complain about the loss or inconvenience you have suffered[,] you will be rewarded by his telling you to have patience."[170] Centering the Filipinx laboring body in this scenario reorients notions of normative temporality, unsettling the terms of colonizer and colonized, as Harvey is placed at the mercy of those from whom he needs assistance.[171] In his discussion of caciquism, the Filipinx appears as "not in sympathy with the Americans and what they are trying to do for them[,] and they are not working very well together."[172] Harvey betrays the smoothness of U.S. imperial rule and reveals unexplored Filipinx desires that suggest alternate being under empire. In trying to persuade an American-oriented audience to reimagine Philippine governance, he further presents Filipinx resistance as symptomatic of "wrong[s]" against U.S. presence on the islands, including "flyin[g] their insurrection flag instead of the stars and stripes" and the granting of "chief insurrectos and [the] most radical anti-American Filipinos ... the best official positions."[173] I read such "wrong[s]" as queerness, as Filipinx troubling of U.S. imperial norms and desires.

Despite his racial ambivalence, Harvey returned to the Philippines in 1913, spending another nine years there. Although he does not explicitly discuss the reasons for his return nor overall lengthy stay (almost two decades), clearly the Philippines was good enough for him to call it a second home. The gaps in his manuscript and memoir leave space for queer fabulations; he traveled to the Philippines upon the encouragement of Hawkins, a male friend with whom he partnered in practicing law in a remote part of the country, and he remained unmarried. Regardless of Harvey's sexual orientation, his archive is queer for its regional and racial perspectives. As an African American civilian lawyer from Kansas, he appears as an unlikely figure of U.S. empire in the Philippines. However, his unlikeliness enriches the history and legacy of transpacific imperialism, underscoring the importance of reorienting to the unexpected, such as region.

Unexpected Encounters

Knowing that Filipinxs were central to popular culture at the turn of the twentieth century, as illumined by Balce, and have been migrating to the Midwest since that period, I suspected I could find historical traces at large research universities in the region. Representative of only a portion of the mass of materials I have encountered across multiple states, the four examples featured in this chapter underscore that the Philippines and Filipinxs are everywhere in the so-called nowhere. Although the nonmetropolitan sites that house these archives might suggest the nation's imperial past can remain hidden, their very peripherality indexes the extent to which empire is built into the nation's foundations.

Complementary to their regional resting place, the archival examples in this chapter narrate an alternative story about empire that centers rural-to-rural and regional-to-regional relations that bypass the norm of the urban and national. While colonial relations of power persist, they are not fixed. My turn to the regional and my use of queer decolonial reading practices illustrate how the Philippines, as signifier and place, queers the Midwest. By orienting to Midwesterners in the Philippines and Filipinxs in the Midwest during the colonial period and showing that Philippine (or, more specifically, southern Tagalog mainland, western Visayas, and Cagayan Valley) history is Midwestern history and vice versa, I engender a sense of the queer Filipinx Midwest.

Empire is messy, and so is its archive. Accessing the history of colonized Filipinxs via colonial Midwesterners importantly negates the assumption that the archive absents the colonized but also risks exposure to ontoepistemic violence. Manalansan's embrace of "mess as constitutive of queerness and of a queer immigrant archive" is instructive for conceptualizing the heartland's archive of U.S. empire in the Philippines.[174] The failure of neat distinctions between subject and subjugated, the ambiguity of queerness, and the blurring of place in the archival traces I present resonate with the mode of queering as "messing up" that Manalansan gestures toward. Unsettling region, nation, empire, and diaspora results in mess, enabling multiple entry points to reimagine these analytics.

To close this first part of the book and segue to the bridge that pivots to Filipinx Midwestern cultural producers, I share a final archival snippet. To my surprise, the Bentley Historical Library also houses a recording of Filipino American writer Santos's lecture, "American Influence on Filipino Literature" (likely given during the late 1970s to a presumed Michigan audience), which is part of the University of Michigan Luce Philippine oral history project. Santos's thick Filipino/Tagalog-accented voice struck me uncannily. Although I do not recall hearing his voice prior to listening to this recording, it somehow felt familiar. Augusto Espiritu's description of Santos as self-deprecating palpably vibrated through my headphones.[175] I imagined myself as an audience member fawning over an author I had read so much about and finally had the opportunity to engage live. Despite time and space, audio-recording technology made possible this intimate encounter. Moreover, Michigan's strength in Philippine-area studies, indebted to nineteenth-century professors and students central to the U.S. imperial project in the Philippines, enabled my happenstance encounter with this lone archival trace of Santos at the Bentley. Deviating from my temporal focus (the U.S. colonial period) but remaining steadfast to my spatial focus (the Philippines) allowed me to "discover" this wayward archival trace. As a sonic remnant, this queer artifact is all the more powerful in viscerally placing Filipinxs in the Midwest.

Interlude

3

Sensing the Queer Filipinx Midwest

*Geographic Nostalgia and Melancholia
in Bienvenido Santos's Exile Literature*

Diasporic denizens of the queer Filipinx Midwest know all too well the affective disorientation of inhabiting a space and place not imagined for them. Inhabiting such a geography as a subaltern subject means experiencing a different relation to the environment, attending to the details so-called locals often take for granted. A common Midwestern exchange starts with the weather, as in "How's the weather?" Seemingly benign, discourse about the weather can reveal one's relation to time and place. A sense of climate develops as one occupies a place over a period. But such a sense can be there before one ever relocates to a place.

In literatures of the Midwest, seasonality can signal a sense of place, even as time alters the weather. The Midwest's climate is infamous for tornadoes in the spring and summer and frigid temperatures and snow in the autumn and winter. As a diasporic Filipino writer who spent formative moments in various parts of the Midwest, Santos provides a sense of being Filipinx in the heartland of U.S. empire in his literature of exile. A reassessment of Santos's literature with an attention to setting not only yields new insights to familiar stories but also reveals the geographic structures of feeling that make up queer diaspora.

One of Santos's popular stories, "The Day the Dancers Came," begins with Midwest weather: "As soon as Fil woke up, he noticed a whiteness outside. . . . There was a brightness in the air and Fil knew what it was and he shouted, 'Snow! It's snowing!'"[1] Such a cold backdrop that exudes warmth reflects the ambivalence that clouds the story's two main characters, Filipino old-timers

Fil and Tony. The queer intimacy between Fil and Tony that emerges from their homosocial domesticity ambivalently provides comfort as they work through their nostalgia for the Philippines. The winter weather in this story and others by Santos also set in the Midwest aptly establishes the mood for Filipinx Midwesterners' sense of both isolation and wonder that comes with living in a foreign land. Although snow and cold certainly impact other places in the United States besides the Midwest, in Santos's writings, they especially reflect the particularities of the nation's geographic interior. Rather than relegate setting as incidental to the plot, my reading of Santos's literature recognizes geography as central to diasporic Filipinx affect.

Not unlike Manuel asking Ben, the narrator of the story "And Beyond, More Walls," "How did you live through the [Midwest] winter?" upon his arrival in New York City,[2] Santos's friends and colleagues in the Philippines would jokingly ask, "How was the winter in Chicago? How did you survive the blizzards?" while he anxiously awaited travel to the United States for the first time as a pensionado.[3] Although Santos recalls with fondness his first time touching and feeling snow during his first winter in the United States while studying at the University of Illinois Urbana-Champaign in his memoir *Memory's Fictions*, his later references to winter succumb to its characteristic feelings of hopelessness and isolation: "I used to love winter-time in the States, but in my 70's [sic], my body couldn't take the frigid cold anymore."[4] Such climatological references—a Midwestern idiosyncrasy—portray the Midwest as a complex mixture of novelty and brutality to racial-colonial subjects and point to the ambivalence to place Filipinxs possess in diaspora.[5]

Rereading Santos's exile literature through the prism of region reveals the Midwest's connection to U.S. imperialism in the Philippines, transforming the Midwest from the heartland of the nation to the heartland of U.S. empire. Like other pensionadxs fulfilling the imperialist promise of "benevolent assimilation," Santos arrived in the United States via the Midwest, completing a master of arts (MA) in English at the University of Illinois in 1942. Three decades later, he returned to the Midwest as Distinguished Writer in Residence at Wichita State University in Kansas (with stints in between those years at the Iowa Writers' Workshop, intermittently during the late 1950s through the early 1970s) because he was unable to return to the Philippines due to then-President Marcos's declaration of martial law.

A regional reading of Santos's diasporic literature makes legible the queer Filipinx Midwest. The queer Filipinx Midwest is a geographic trope that remaps the Midwest as a conceivable geography of queerness, race, and empire. Whereas conventional connotations of queerness often point to same-gender sexuality, I deploy queerness to signify other modes of being and desiring that fail to align with the scripts of hetero- and homonormative sociocultural and nationalist formations. Place evokes "identity" and gives meaning to a location.⁶ Attending to place and affect in Santos's life and literature, I show how the exilic queer structures of feeling that propagate throughout his writings are grounded in his literal dislocation in the United States and his specific location in the heartland of U.S. empire, away from the majority of Filipinxs living in California, Washington, and Hawaiʻi.

Although scholars have acknowledged Santos's life and literature in the region, few have foregrounded this geography as a significant factor in shaping his outlook of the United States and his works of fiction that are set in various parts of the Midwest.⁷ That Santos spent a considerable amount of time in the Midwest (nearly two decades in total) while in the United States (as a student in Illinois, writer in Iowa, and faculty member in Kansas) and that some of his most well-known stories take place in the region—from the outskirts of Kalamazoo, Michigan ("Scent of Apples"), to urban Chicago ("The Day the Dancers Came")—suggest that the Midwest figures as a critical lens through which Santos's contributions to diasporic Filipinx and Asian American literatures might be examined. While one way to appraise Santos's work would be to view him as a writer who just so happened to spend most of his time in the Midwest while in the United States, I assert that because of the Midwest's not-so-obvious relationship to Filipinx America, highlighting the importance of the Midwest in relation to Santos's work has the capacity to queerly engender what Melinda de Jesús, in her analysis of Santos's stories, phrases as "new vistas, new lives, and new ways of being."⁸

In support of the book's main argument that place matters in theorizing diasporic Filipinx subjectivity, in this chapter, I argue that the places where Santos lived during his time in the United States played a significant role in shaping his fiction. Unlike the well-renowned Filipino/American author Bulosan, Santos spent most of his time writing in the United States outside of the West Coast, mainly in Iowa City, Iowa, and Wichita, Kansas—places with no considerable Filipinx population. Bulosan's semi-fictional novel *America Is in the Heart* (1946) may offer more rural settings and thus position it to have more commonalities with dominant imaginaries of the Midwest in comparison to Santos's cosmopolitan DC and New York settings, which make up the bulk of *Scent of Apples*, but Santos's lived experience outside the heart of Filipinx America provides another entry point to examine the queer geographies of the U.S. Filipinx diaspora. This is not to argue that Bulosan, by writing from the center of Filipinx America, presents a more authentic representation of Filipinxs in the United States; nor is it to assert that Santos, because he wrote from a queer location with respect to Filipinx America, presents a less authentic depiction of exiled Filipinxs.⁹ Instead, by figuring Santos's location of cultural production as queer, I am critiquing the geographic norms taken for granted within Filipinx American studies (and by extension Asian American, American, Asian, and Philippine studies). Moreover, the novel form, which Bulosan is more known for, tends to align with nation, whereas the short story form, which Santos is more known for, can be interpreted as diasporic, especially with its episodic structure, thereby rendering the latter a locus of normative narrative undoing.[10]

The imagery of snow and cold found in Santos's personal papers and dramatized in his literature illustrates the symbolic meaning of the Midwest in his imaginary. This ever-present though arguably ancillary attention to climate grounds him and his literature in the heartland and illumines the particularities and peculiarities of living apart from most Filipinxs in the United States. Snow engenders excitement as a novelty for Philippine migrants accustomed to the tropics, yet it amplifies sorrow as a symbol of the harsh, cold climate of the metropole these exilic Filipinxs experience as racial-colonial subjects. Foreign to tropical climes, snow is indicative of the American landscape and thus can symbolize U.S. empire.[11] By foregrounding this ambivalence toward snow that Santos attaches to his Filipino characters, I establish a framework for the themes of nostalgia and melancholia that recur throughout his fictional and autobiographical memories of the United States.[12] While such affects may suggest negativity, my close readings of Santos's personal papers; his short stories "Scent of Apples," "The Day the Dancers Came," and "The Contender"; his novel *Robert Taylor*; and his memoir *Memory's Fiction* excavate those fleeting moments of possibility for queer intimacy that being in the Midwest can provide. In other words, an analysis of the ambivalent role of the Midwest in Santos's life and literature lays bare the queer contingencies that at times have magnified Filipinx nonnormativity but also have created opportunities to form alternative socialities in excess of the disciplinary imperatives of both the U.S. and Philippine nation-states.

"Stranded" in the Heartland: Santos's Life and Literature

Santos was a transnational migrant who split his time between the Philippines and the United States for most of his life until his death in 1996.[13] In the fall of 1941, he set sail for the United States as a pensionado and docked in San Francisco on Columbus Day, October 12, 1941.[14] From San Francisco, he boarded a train bound for Chicago, accompanied by a small group of pensionados, two of whom traveled with him to the University of Illinois Urbana-Champaign after their arrival in Chicago.[15] Although he attended Illinois for less than a year, completing an MA in English by the following spring in 1942, the time he spent there left a lasting impression on him due to the outbreak of war in the Philippines following the attack on Pearl Harbor on December 7, 1941. Upon graduation in June 1942, he hopped aboard a train bound for New York City,[16] where he spent the summer learning how to write short stories with writer and *Story* magazine editor Whit Burnett at Columbia University.[17] From there, he spent time "on and off" in Washington, DC, from autumn 1942 through 1946, working for the Philippine Government-in-Exile;[18] when not in DC, he was touring the country, "visiting schools and colleges, including civic and religious clubs and organizations, informing [his] audiences of everything that [he] believed they should know about Filipinos and the Philippines."[19]

Once the war was over, he returned to the Philippines in 1946, reuniting with his wife, Beatriz, and their three daughters, Arme, Lina, and Lily, in the Albay province of Bicol.[20] In 1958, he returned to the Midwest with his wife and son, Tom, enrolling in the prestigious Writers' Workshop at the University of Iowa with support from a Rockefeller creative writing fellowship and staying until 1961.[21] He and his wife returned to Iowa City in 1965. There, he taught as an Exchange Fulbright Professor in the Writers' Workshop, and he stayed until 1969.[22] In 1970, he and Beatriz found themselves back at the University of Iowa, where Beatriz went to complete her Ph.D. in Education.[23] Two years later, they were living with P. C. Morantte, a Filipino writer and "close friend of... Bulosan,"[24] in San Francisco.[25] Although they had planned to return to the Philippines, President Marcos's martial law declaration in September 1972 precluded them from doing so.[26] Fortunately, he obtained what initially was to be a one-year appointment as Distinguished Writer in Residence at Wichita State University in Kansas in June 1973; Beatriz also secured a teaching position in the College of Education.[27] Santos retired from Wichita State in 1982, a few months after Beatriz's death.[28] Thereafter, he split his time between Camarines Sur (another province in Bicol) and Albay, where his daughters and their families were living, and Greeley, Colorado, where Tom and his family were living.[29]

By situating Santos's life and literature within the genealogy of U.S. cultural imperialism manifested through education, I uncover the invisible links that connect U.S. empire and the Midwest. That former Superintendent of Filipino Students in the United States William Sutherland's reflections on the official pensionadx program (1903–1910) simultaneously disavow the United States as empire and celebrate the civilizing effects of U.S. intervention at the turn of the twentieth century is precisely indicative of the ideology of U.S. exceptionalism.[30] As España-Maram points out, the pensionadx program served as a mechanism to bolster U.S. imperialism in the Philippines by training elite Filipinxs in the American way.[31] Similarly, Cruz traces the ascendance of Philippine literature in English to the central role of education in the U.S. imperial enterprise in the Philippines during much of the early twentieth century—which involved both the importation of American teachers to the Philippines and the exportation of Filipinxs, especially the elite, to the

United States via initiatives such as the pensionadx program.[32] However, she rightly argues that U.S. imperial domination is not simply unilateral; rather, transpacific Filipinxs have employed disidentificatory strategies to navigate competing and overlapping imperial conditions and nationalist efforts that have sought to make and remake the Filipinx subject.[33] Accordingly, while writers such as Santos may have been the beneficiaries of U.S. imperial techniques, their "willful disloyalty to the master," as Muñoz puts it to describe critique, acts as a fissure to U.S. imperial power.[34] Through fiction and memoir, Santos reworked his colonial education and training in American literature by laying bare the legacies of U.S. cultural imperialism.

Scent of Apples, a collection of some of Santos's short stories previously published in the Philippines in *You Lovely People* (1955) and *The Day the Dancers Came: Selected Prose Works* (1967), represents the first and only book-length publication of his fiction in the United States. Also, as a book that remains in print, it figures as one of his most well-known texts. Within Asian American studies, it has received considerable critical attention and has become required reading in many introductory courses since its publication in 1979. Similar to how Bulosan's *America* gives insight into the struggles of Filipino farm workers along the West Coast during the Depression, *Scent* provides a window into the lives of mostly middle-class exiled Filipinos living throughout the United States during World War II and the years thereafter. Whereas Bulosan's novel grounds Filipinx migrants to the West Coast, especially California, Santos's short stories move readers away from the heart of Filipinx America and reveal the often-untold experiences of Filipinx sojourners living in the Midwest, America's heartland, and in Washington, DC, the heart of U.S. governance. That most of the stories in *Scent* take place in parts of the country not readily imagined as having a Filipinx population seems to be lost on most scholars analyzing his work. In this way, my analysis of *Scent* foregrounds the relationship between geographic location and exilic subjectivity to highlight how the sparse presence of Filipinxs in places like the Midwest heightens feelings of loneliness but also excitement upon encountering another Filipinx.[35]

Importantly, three of the sixteen stories are set in the Midwest, and two additional stories reference the area. Moreover, the fact that Santos compiled *Scent* while in Wichita is worth consideration. In short, the Midwest is not simply ancillary to the book's production and reception; it also serves as a critical point in the wider constellation of Santos's life and literature. As previously mentioned, the titular story "Scent of Apples" takes place in Kalamazoo, Michigan. The following story, "And Beyond, More Walls," notes that the narrator, Ben, is from the Midwest.[36] In "Of Other Deaths," Ben recounts his college lecture tour, which included many stops throughout the Midwest. Of the last four stories, "The Day the Dancers Came" and "The Contender" are set in Chicago, and both stories are connected by a Philippine dance troupe that comes to the Windy City.[37]

In *Memory's Fictions*, Santos warmly recounts the "two-day celebration of the publication of *Scent of Apples* in 1980" at Wichita State University that "culminated in a grand banquet attended by around 200 Filipino and American guests" and after which he gifted his personal papers to the University (212). In addition to his son's heartfelt speech honoring his work, what he poignantly remembers of the banquet was "the place marks . . . each bearing the name of the guest, planted into the core of a fresh golden apple . . . glowing in candlelight, filling the hall with the unmistakable scent of apples" (212). Like the unnamed narrator in "Scent of Apples," who "immediately . . . was aware of the familiar scent of apples" when he entered Celestino Fabia's home—an event that left an indelible impression on his memory of Kalamazoo a few years later (26)—Santos vividly recalls that night in Wichita through the scent of apples. As Tuan points out, "Odors lend character to objects and places, making them distinctive, easier to identify and remember."[38] For both the unnamed narrator of "Scent of Apples" (presumably Santos) and Santos himself, the scent of apples reminds them of not only a memory in time but more specifically a memory in place and time. In the short story and in Santos's memoir, the smell of apples takes them back not simply to the United States but more specifically to the Midwest—to rural Michigan and to Wichita, respectively.

Whereas *Scent of Apples* largely focuses on the experiences of Santos and other Filipinx exiles during the 1940s, Santos's novel *The Man Who (Thought He) Looked Like Robert Taylor* depicts the experiences of this earlier generation of Filipinx expatriates, now elderly persons living during the late 1960s and early 1970s, estranged from the younger post-1965 professional class of Filipinxs. One of the chapters appeared as "Immigration Blues" in *Scent*, a story about two elderly Filipina sisters who tactfully proposition an elderly Filipino man to marry one of them so that she may avoid deportation. However, *Robert Taylor*'s plot centers on Solomon "Sol" King, an elderly Filipino man who lives alone in Chicago and believes his looks and life resemble those of the actor Robert Taylor. As such, *Robert Taylor* is not unlike Kercheval's "The Dogeater" in its attention to an aging Filipino man who leads a lonely life (see chapter 1); Santos's novel also resonates with Noël Alumit's *Letters to Montgomery Clift* (2002), with each narrative anchored by the protagonist's identification with a leading male Hollywood actor.[39]

Written while Santos was living in Iowa City, San Francisco, and Wichita, the novel shares *Scent*'s themes of disorientation, liminal subjectivity, and unfulfilled dreams resulting from living in diaspora. And like *Scent*, the novel's setting outside the capital of Filipinx America not only makes palpable Sol's solitary life but also offers an alternative, and arguably understudied, route for tracing Filipinx migration to the United States. Despite the civilizing efforts of the United States, particularly via education but also through popular culture, Filipinxs fail to fulfill their destiny of becoming American, which in fact reinforces U.S. imperial dominance. But it is exactly this failure that loosens exilic Filipinxs like Sol from the grasp of both the United States and the Philippines. For Sol, as for so many of his diasporic compatriots, dreams become an alternative to reality; and in the dream world, he can live out that which has been foreclosed due to his race, class, and age—a recurring theme in *Memory's Fictions*.

Remapping Santos's Exile Literature

While Santos is a diasporic Filipinx writer, he also is a Midwestern writer. If one's geographic base determines their literary categorization, then Santos's binational life in the Philippines and the United States and translocal life in Bicol and the Midwest mark him as a Philippine, American, Filipino American, Bicolano, and Midwestern author. A diasporic approach to Filipinx cultural production already affords such a porous notion of identity, but it does not always account for the regional specificities that inform the senses. Elaine Kim, Eleanor Ty, and Augusto Espiritu use exile as a frame to interpret Santos's work, illustrating how diaspora connects Filipinxs in the United States to the Philippines. Whereas Kim focuses on the structural racism that forced Filipinos into menial jobs, preventing them from "develop[ing] a full life" in the United States and often leaving them with the desire for "a fleeting dream of the [Philippine] homeland,"[40] Ty focuses on the U.S. imperial dynamics that structure the Filipinx American exilic condition.[41] Like Kim, Ty notes the exclusion of Filipinxs from accessing White hetero-patriarchal power,[42] which left them disfranchised, "dislocat[ed]," and alone in the United States—a place that is both home and not.[43] Alternatively, Espiritu focuses on Santos's shame stemming from a sense of being unable to live up to self-imposed expectations as a cultural ambassador of the Philippine nation, which Kim notes of Filipino old-timers more generally. Certainly, this ambivalence in diaspora reflects the feeling of being in exile from one's place of birth. However, this sense of dislocation and isolation is not an abstract universal feeling in diaspora but a geographically tempered one.

As Tuan's exploration of the relationship between human experience and geography suggests, the archive of human feeling housed in "literature ... humanistic psychology, philosophy, anthropology, and geography" reflects a catalog of space and place,[44] and "the different modes of experience (sensorimotor [sic], tactile, visual, conceptual)" make palpable one's place in the world.[45] From scents that waft through the pages of Santos's fiction and memoir to the imagery of snow that sets the mood for the narrative arc of his stories and personal letters, such sensory references function to (con)textualize Santos's imaginary as an exile inhabiting the U.S. interior during much of his life. That the title of his most famous short story "Scent of Apples" refers to the smell of unsold apples in the home of a Filipino farmer living in the outskirts of Kalamazoo, Michigan, stitches sensory experience to the unnamed narrator's experience of traveling throughout the United States for the U.S. Office of Education to educate the White American public "on the work and stamina of Filipinos as allies" during World War II.[46] Such a connection between sense and place reflects Paul Rodaway's concept of sensuous geography, or "geography of the senses."[47]

According to Rodaway, sensuous geography "refers to a study of the geographical understanding which arises out of the stimulation of, or apprehension by, the senses."[48] In the case of olfactory experience, or "the geography of the nose,"[49] "the association of odours with particular things, organisms, situations[,] and emotions... contribute to a sense of space and the character to places."[50] So, "the familiar scent of apples" the narrator of "Scent of Apples" encounters not only draws attention to the intimacy of Celestino Fabia's living space but also becomes a reference point for the narrator's travels around the United States—from Oneonta, New York; to Muncie, Indiana; to Higgins Lake, Michigan; to Terre Haute, Indiana; to Emporia, Kansas; to Troy, Alabama; to Kentucky; to Bloomington, Illinois; to New Mexico; to San Francisco and Oakland; to St. Louis; to Stockton, California; to Detroit; to Chicago; to Shippensburg, Pennsylvania—which are "all sensation, all feeling."[51] Reading *Scent* through sensuous geography enables a remapping of the U.S. Filipinx diaspora, making space for the alternative pathways Filipinxs have charted as they bypass the normative locations of Filipinx America.[52]

"Snow! It's Snowing!": Climatic Symbolism in Santos's Exile Literature

For Filipinx migrants accustomed to the tropical conditions of the Philippines, the United States' climatic differences, particularly in places such as the Midwest, the Mid-Atlantic, and New England, present some cause for concern.[53] According to Sutherland, pensionadxs were selected based on "mental fitness and physical, as well"—the latter "doubly important... because of the fact that being a tropical race, and going for instance to Boston or St. Paul, constituted a marked change from Philippine climatic conditions, where not even a frost has ever been recorded."[54] Notwithstanding his racial essentialist overtones, Sutherland's point regarding the severe weather distinctions between the Philippines and the United States is not too far from reality. For those who have not had to brave the subzero temperatures of such places as the Upper

Midwest and Great Lakes states, transplanting (t)here may come with a bit of both culture and climate shock. Even diasporic Filipinxs who have only lived in California, such as my family, find the Midwest climatologically disorienting, which can have the effect of the region being imagined as a whole other country.

The literal climate shock of the snowy and cold Midwest also has its metaphoric counterpart, as illustrated by Santos's diary entries during his first few months as an exile in the United States. Considering the uncertain fate of his wife and three daughters in the Philippines weeks after the attack on Pearl Harbor, Santos's entries in late December 1941 and early January 1942 reveal an implicit link between the bitter cold weather and the heaviness of his heart. For example, he begins one entry with, "Discovery on Christmas Day: I am not the only lonely man in Chicago to-day [sic]." He ends it with, "Even you, Chicago, you are a lonely city, with all these lonely souls seeking solace in the coldness of your bosom."[55] Here, physical temperature serves as imagery for the loneliness and homesickness Santos experiences on what is supposed to be a day spent with family. In another entry, the second clause reads, "still sub-zero [sic] temperature," setting the tone for the anguish of still not knowing the fate of his family and the future of his country; he closes the entry with "but out here in sub-zero [sic] weather, even the big American heart cannot help being cold."[56] Two days later, his continued agony is apparent, as he writes, "There is no let up in the cold, it's still sub zero [sic] temperature; and there's no snow."[57] Such references to the physical and symbolic coldness of the United States are less related to the nation being unfriendly to exilic Filipinxs such as Santos than to his being away from his loved ones back in his homeland.[58]

In Santos's fiction, the snowy and cold Midwest evokes the complex emotions exilic Filipinxs possess living in the colonial metropole. For Fil, the protagonist of "The Day the Dancers Came," snow brings about excitement—he proclaims, "Snow! It's snowing!"—and represents a unique feature of the Midwest that allows him to feel emboldened as a resident of Chicago who might serve as a credible guide for the touring Filipinx dancers (113).[59] In "The Contender," snow and cold set the somber tone of the story, which centers on an argument between two friends, Bernie and Felix:

> Winter came early that year in Chicago. The mild autumn had become increasingly violent, the trees shedding their leaves before they had turned deep gold. By October the flurries of wind raking the dead leaves on the twilight streets and parks bore the snow-dusts of winter. Now in November there was slush and ice on the avenues and the lake winds bit into the covered flesh like thrusts of pain into the naked body. (129)

And yet, like the story, this image of winter possesses a calming quality. The darkness of winter parallels the gradual darkness Bernie experiences as the health of his eyes deteriorates, due in no small part to his former career as a flyweight boxer; but, likening it to the beauty of "the twilight streets and parks," he basks in the "perpetual twilight" of his "compromise[d]" vision (138). For him, going blind opened new views of the world hitherto taken for granted: "Now he understood a lot of things that were not clear to him before. In the long night, the voices were not only clearer but kinder" (138). Angered at first by Felix's constant nagging to go see an eye doctor, by the story's end, marked by the seasonal change from winter to spring, Bernie, too, undergoes a change of heart and realizes Felix's actions stem from deep affection.

For *Robert Taylor*'s protagonist, Sol, the wintry Midwest figures as home, and as such, it is both familiar and uninspiring.[60] When he finally musters the courage to leave Chicago and start his terminal vacation, he decides to drive to New York City to reconnect with long-lost friends. However, holiday weekend traffic stops him in his tracks: "The more he thought of New York, the less interested he was in going there. Who were still in that city among his friends?"[61] In line with the views of the early twentieth-century anti-urbanist writers that Herring analyzes, Sol's impression of New York disrupts the ascendancy of the Eastern metropolis over the Second City and its adjacent hinterlands.[62] Nevertheless, the narrator reinforces the dominant cultural imaginary of the Midwest as ambivalently plain, ordinary, and frigid: "He was going to turn back to Chicago. It was no problem. A different route, but the scenes looked the same, familiar, drab, and cold."[63]

Though winter is often associated with bleakness, in Santos's recollections of his time in the United States in *Memory's Fictions*, it signifies youthfulness and joy. With time, however, it becomes linked to the characteristic feelings of hopelessness and isolation.[64] As a pensionado visiting the United States for the first time in 1941, he "saw [his] first snow, far away in the distance, on the peaks of the Rocky Mountains" en route to Chicago but experienced the touch and feel of it while at Urbana-Champaign (77, 118). In both instances, he was filled with excitement, describing the former as "thrill[ing]" with "[v]apor [coming] from our mouths as in the movies" and the latter as a "happy" occasion that warranted having a photograph taken (77, 118). Later, he writes of his time in Washington, DC, after completing his MA, as follows:

> My favorite memories of Washington are winter memories, warmth by the fireside, alone or in company, idle talk and subdued laughter, while outside the glass windows the wind howled noiselessly as in a silent picture show, shaking the bare branches of trees laden with snow and more snow falling, silently, like it was a different world far away.

Those are the times when I felt farthest away from my true home and quite often forgot where I'd come from, as if this had been the only life I had ever known. (173)

Here, Santos expresses happiness but also guilt. On one hand, this memory of living in the United States' capital, with snow falling, is like a movie scene of his youth, and it reveals the carefree life he once had. However, in the context of both his exile from his wife and three daughters and the realization of his class difference from the "Pinoys"—those of the "laboring class"—this memory betrays the sadness he is supposed to have felt away from his homeland (172).[65] As Espiritu argues, "Santos experienced expatriation neither as affirmation nor as negation but through intense feelings of guilt, or more properly, shame (*hiya, supog*) [original italics], brought about by his perceived inability to meet the demands of family, community, and nation for authentic subjectivity."[66]

Whereas these flashbacks to his earlier years in the United States portray winter as comforting, Santos's references to this season in his later years in diaspora prove less positive. He recalls elsewhere in *Memory's Fictions*, "I wrote *Villa Magdalena* with what sometimes seemed like insurmountable hardships, especially in winter. Only Tom seemed to enjoy the Iowa winter. . . . Each year winter stayed too long and there seemed to be no hope of ever seeing spring and summer, which made us long for our home in Albay" (87). While the discomfort of "the inadequate heating system in [their] Quonset hut" during the winter made it difficult for him to type, since he could not wear gloves while typing (83), and the "sub-zero [sic] temperature[s]" made it less enticing to go outside (87), Santos's memories of Iowa and its winters in the end were more pleasant. He notes, "Iowa City to which we kept returning, is one American city we will never forget, Beatriz and I [sic]. The people were genuinely caring and simple. They made us forget our size, our stature, our complexion. We were not interlopers; we were people" (197–198). In this way, the snow and cold of Santos's memories reflect the multiple, ambivalent, complex feelings exilic subjects can possess for a place that is not of their birth but is nevertheless a home. That Santos and his Filipino characters do not find themselves completely alienated in the Midwest suggests that the heartland is not necessarily antithetical to Asian Americans.[67]

Spatializing Loneliness

If Filipinx exilic structures of feeling are geographic, as I have been arguing, then expressions of loneliness that characterize much of Santos's oeuvre must be understood less as an emotion tied to living as an exile in the United States in general and more as rooted in a particular place and time. Most of the "hurt men" of Santos's literature experience alienation as exiles "east of California," especially in the Midwest, and as part of the old-timer generation, those mostly unmarried men who immigrated prior to 1965. In the case of Santos, his loneliness as a pensionado stems from his enforced exile from the Philippines during World War II; however, as his diary reveals, the particularities of living in Illinois make palpable his sense of being cut off from his familiars. Even when joined by his wife and son later in the postwar decades, he still experienced "isolation . . . as resident author on Midwest campuses."[68]

Despite the small Filipinx communities that they were a part of in places like Iowa City and Wichita, Santos and Beatriz did not have the sizable Filipinx populations of places like San Francisco or Los Angeles to quell their enforced exile now as a result of the Marcos dictatorship. Nevertheless, loneliness in Santos's writings is not simply about being alone, without another diasporic Filipinx to commiserate with, as evidenced by his wife's companionship as well as all his stories' depictions of Filipinx communities outside the capital of Filipinx America. Rather than asserting that the Midwest is isolating in a negative sense, I argue that the lack of critical mass in the Midwest makes being a Filipinx feel isolating; however, the demographic specificities of this diasporic periphery have the potential to facilitate alternative socialities that exceed the mandates of compulsory heterosexuality.

"The Day the Dancers Came" illumines the intersection of geographic isolation and the feeling of loneliness. Set in early postwar Chicago, the story centers on Filemon "Fil" Acayan, an unmarried Filipino old-timer and U.S. Army veteran who anticipates the arrival of a Philippine dance troupe in the city.[69] Fil shares an apartment on West Sheridan Road with another unmarried Filipino old-timer, Antonio "Tony" Bataller, "a retired Pullman Porter" (120, 114). Together, they resemble an old married couple—each relying on the other for companionship for better or worse. On the day the dancers arrive, Fil wakes up with excitement, as "he notice[s] a whiteness outside, quite unusual for the November mornings they had been having" (113). In contrast to the unfriendly skyscrapers of the city, the snow brings "a brightness in the air" (113). Fil gleefully announces to Tony, "'They'll walk in the snow and love it. Their first snow, I'm sure" (113). While Fil's excitement may seem outlandish to those accustomed to the harsh climatological realities of the Great Lakes region, his status as a Filipino exile provides the necessary context for rendering such emotion legible. The novelty of snowfall brings into relief Fil's, and by extension Filipinxs', tropical dissonance from the United States, which the Midwest—as synecdoche for America—makes palpable. Although Fil resides in Chicago, which enables him to assume the authority of local tour guide for the traveling troupe, he does not belong there.

As his encounter with the dancers makes clear, neither does Fil belong in the Philippines. When he goes to meet the dancers at the Hamilton Hotel, he tries to muster up the courage to engage his compatriots, but he soon discovers himself "wander[ing] about the mezzanine, among the dancers, but alone" (121). Later, in a dream scene, Fil imagines himself telling the dancers, "I shall listen to your voices with my eyes closed and you'll be here again and I won't ever be alone, no, not anymore, after this" (124). Such moments reveal Fil's loneliness as an exile in America; however, I argue that his location in Chicago, despite Tony's companionship, particularly dramatizes his sense of dislocation in diaspora. Like Celestino Fabia, "a Filipino farmer" who travels "thirty miles" from his farm to Kalamazoo, Michigan, to fulfill his desire to see another Filipino, in "Scent of Apples," Fil goes out of his way to connect with the Filipinxs passing through his city (21). Whereas larger Filipinx communities have thrived in places like California and Washington and continue to do so today, Filipinxs in the Midwest have not always had the same scale of social and cultural support. Hence, the possibility to connect with another compatriot is made even more significant in stories such as these.

Santos continues this theme of isolation years later in his fourth novel, *Robert Taylor*, set in Chicago in the summer of 1969. The narrator reveals that the story's protagonist, Sol, lives alone on Honore Street, "which . . . was part of an extensive area covering several blocks of a Polish colony where, as far as he [Sol] knew, he was the only Filipino" (8). Like Fil,[70] he no longer has kinship ties to the Philippines (6). However, as a resident of Chicago, Sol is really not alone, as there are other Filipinxs, both "new" and "old," living in the Second City.[71] He connects with them informally and sees them at an annual anniversary celebration of the Republic of the Philippines' independence. Moreover, he communicates with Filipinxs on both coasts via letters. Nevertheless, he exhibits the loneliness characteristic of Santos's "hurt men" in *Scent* as he wallows in the past long gone, nostalgic for "the old country" yet "making no move to return" (8). While his loneliness can be attributed to his being a Filipino old-timer, it also stems from "his enforced aloneness" resulting from a series of failed relationships (168). As the narrator reveals more than midway through the novel, "It was not easy deciding, in the last few years, to live a life alone without companionship, involvements, love affairs, but the price in heart-break [sic] was too much" (126).

During his last attendance at the annual Philippine independence celebration, Sol reflects on his unmarried status:

One or two [of the Filipino old-timers also in attendance] were like him. Alone. Perhaps he should have married. The price of loving was too high. And too painful. He did not wish to dwell on it, but there had been times when he felt that nobody had any right to impose such aloneness on one's self [sic]. It was not normal. It was not right. Better perhaps that he had chosen the other way, a continuing involvement with people, enduring the vicissitudes, the pains of separation and betrayal, a gradual dying of the fires of love, passion, lust, whatever, the violence, the wounds.... But he was a coward. He could have found one willing to share her life with his, be the mother of his children. (41–42)

Here, the pull of compulsory heterosexuality weighs on Sol's psyche. Although he questions the normalcy of his decision to remain sexually and romantically unattached, his words belie the benefits of achieving heterosexual coupling via marriage, as he describes that path as leading to pain and death. When viewed from a heteronormative vantage, Sol deviates from the straight path by both failing to be in a procreative heterosexual marriage and facing backward and contemplating his diasporic life as a Filipinx island in America's heartland.[72] However, reading Sol's unattachment through archipelagic queerness reveals a different way to interpret his aloneness. His solitary life in Chicago is part of an archipelago of Filipino old-timers in the Midwest that transcends time, thereby situating him as part of a constellation of "hurt men." This homosocial plurality defies the logic of heteronormative diasporic isolation. Like Fil and Tony, Sol has the companionship of the "one or two ... like him" (41).

"Miss[ing] You and the Wonderful Mild Climate of S.F.": Diasporic Longings for Elsewhere from the Heartland

Whereas popular understandings of diasporic nostalgia often cast one nation-state as the homeland for which the diasporic subject longs, in Santos's life and literature, exilic Filipinxs' longing for homeland is not exclusive to the Philippines but rather encompasses places that have been made home, however temporary, via the intimate connections made with other Filipinxs.[73] A regional sensitivity to diaspora enables the notion of home to be within the diaspora itself, depriviledging the nation as the primary scale of home.

In Santos's writing, a place carries multiple—and at times contradictory—meanings; place is subjectively dynamic. During the initial months in what he later called their "'second wind' in America ... in a quiet Kansas town in the middle of the continent presumably not too far from the Yellow Brick Road,"[74] he described to Morantte his and Beatriz's sense of alienation as elderly Filipinx transplants who could not immediately identify with the professional class of Filipinx Wichitans who most likely arrived in the United States post-1965.[75] Yet, after nearly a decade, Wichita became a formative and memorable place much like Iowa City years earlier, as the small Filipinx community welcomed him as a respected elder, despite not being familiar with his literary accomplishments.[76] After Beatriz's death, however, his feelings toward place once again transformed, now as a reminder of his love no longer there in the flesh, thus prompting him to seek refuge with daughters in Bicol and a son in Colorado.

Perhaps surprisingly, Santos notes in his recollection of San Francisco and its considerable Filipinx population that he also felt alienated from the latter due to the generational divide between pre- and post-1965 immigrants. For example, in *Memory's Fictions*, he mentions how "in our loneliness, we [he and Beatriz] would try to start a conversation [with the younger generation of Filipinxs], but they simply stared at us and turned away" (217–218). He also recalls a time when a Filipino man "continued to water his yard and the sidewalk," fully aware that he and Beatriz were unable to pass carrying groceries (218).[77] Despite the temperate climate of San Francisco, his memories in the early 1990s portray it as cold and isolating, whereas in Wichita in the early 1970s, "the temperature has never been lower than 95 and most of the time it's over 100," which caused him to miss the "wonderful mild climate of S.F."[78]

Instances such as these show how longing for elsewhere is always relative and contingent; it is bound in place and time. Ideas about home and homeland, diaspora and nation, alienation and belonging are never absolute; however, their context mediates understanding. Santos's shifting attitudes toward various diasporic locations within the United States developed out of broader contextual realities. In the case of San Francisco, it served as a familiar point of reference, a sort of temporary home base, both when he was interviewing at Wichita State and immediately after his and Beatriz's relocation to Wichita.[79] However, years later, it reminded him of their inability to return to the Philippines as they had intended and thus endowed the place with unpleasant memories.[80] In the case of Wichita, it initially brought into relief his generational estrangement from the Filipinx professional class made palpable by the lack of similarly aged exiles in the land of Oz. But as their sojourn unintentionally turned into settlement lasting a decade, its foreignness transformed into familiarity. As a "country boy," Santos found solace in rural America, for it reminded him of the Philippines' provincial charm.[81] Such an intersubjective connection with White Midwesterners and Filipinx immigrants did not quell his longing for his Philippine homeland but made it bearable. In short, California is not always the promised land, nor is the Midwest always the hinterland of Filipinx America.

In *Robert Taylor*, Sol similarly longs for elsewhere, as he feels stuck in the middle. His determination to go on an extended vacation, see the rest of the country, and renew old connections with other Filipinx exiles before dying ironically leaves him nowhere. Craving human connection in his cold Chicago, he goes to the Greyhound bus depot to soak in the anonymous crowd. However, a young woman, Blanche, catches his attention, and they have the following exchange:

> "Where's this place you're going?"
> She gave him the name again, adding, "That's in Michigan."
> "What are you going to do now?"
> "Wait. What else?" Then as if the thought had just struck her, she asked, "And you, where you [sic] going?"
> "Nowhere," he said.
> "I thought so. You have a car out there. You're meeting someone."
> "No, I'm not. I came to ask for some information."
> "You're going some place [sic]."
> "Yes. But not now." (133)

In his quest to leave Chicago for greener pastures, when put to the test, Sol actually has no place to go. However, going nowhere for Sol leaves open alternative possibilities. His lack of definite planning allows him a chance to connect with another human being—in fact two, Blanche and her toddler son, Jerry. Together, the three form a temporary, nonheteronormative family, thereby providing Sol respite from his self-imposed celibacy. Although this brief relationship also ends in failure, it nevertheless propels him to put his grand plans of leaving Chicago into action.

In one of the interludes that pepper the novel, Santos makes another reference to nowhere, further illustrating the particular conditions of Filipinx exiles who do not quite belong in either the homeland or the diaspora:

> *You leave home and country, seek sanctuary in an alien land, refuge in another idiom, but you remain on the outside, you are neither called nor chosen; and you keep running, stumbling along the road over a snag of rocks, a net of thread at the feet, a clouding over in the mind, but it is only the surging forward that is momentarily checked, the motion continues, circular into nowhere; backward to what had been the native land, its warmth, its horrid climate, the farce of its form of government, the kindness of the poor, their hunger, their sentimentality; and forward, again into a glut of strangeness that never becomes familiar, an embarrassment of colors, a negative in black and white blown out of proportion.* (152; original italics)

Here, Santos expresses the ambivalence diasporic Filipinxs exhibit toward homeland and diaspora. He also launches an implicit critique of U.S. imperialism in the Philippines, which had resulted in the Marcos regime as well as his past and current fate as an exile. Placed immediately after Blanche and Jerry depart for Dowagiac, Michigan, and before Sol travels via bus to Washington, DC, to finally begin his extended vacation, this interlude clarifies the Filipinx diasporic condition. Rather than settle for either homeland or diaspora, the Philippines and Chicago, respectively, Sol suggests that his constant yearnings for a place that exists only in one's imaginary, in between past and future, is all the exile really has. The realization of this reality is what allows him to become unstuck. The literal middle, Chicago, the Midwest, becomes a metaphor for diasporic Filipinx American ontology, remapping the so-called nowhere as a geography that makes possible an elsewhere.

Diasporic longings for home expressed by Santos and his "hurt men" remind us of the unstable meaning of home. Although the search for home always seems to orient toward an elsewhere, in the end, such quests, usually tied to a desire to belong somewhere, often ironically lead to nowhere. Seeking a better place than their current conditions, such men end up discovering that they belong right where they are—which in most narrative contexts is in the Midwest. According to philosopher José Medina, "situated meanings always point *elsewhere* [original emphasis], that is, they point to other contexts in which they are further delineated, elaborated, extended, or simply transformed," and this suggests that meaning depends on multiple, overlapping frames of reference beyond the immediate context.[82] In the case of Filipinx exiles, their desires for elsewhere reflect not only their dissatisfaction with the present as racial-colonial subjects but also their disorientation wrought by constant travel. As Avery Gordon provocatively puts it, "We need to know where we live in order to imagine living elsewhere. We need to imagine living elsewhere before we can live there."[83]

The desire for a better world emerges out of an acute awareness that the past and the present are not enough, which resonates with Muñoz's utopian vision of queerness.[84] Likewise, Gopinath argues that "the queer diasporic body is the medium through which home is remapped and its various narratives are displaced, uprooted, and infused with alternative forms of desire."[85] She further states that "nostalgia as deployed by queer diasporic subjects is a means by which to imagine oneself within those spaces from which one is perpetually excluded or denied existence."[86] Despite not being gay- or queer-identified, as Filipino exiles situated in the heartland, Santos and his "hurt men" nevertheless figure both as queer diasporic subjects who are barred from their normative homeland, the Philippines, and "impossible" subjects—as Gopinath puts it to describe queer diasporic people—for living in the hinterlands of the U.S. Filipinx diaspora.

Inhabiting Loss

Loss figures prominently in both Santos's fiction and nonfiction writings. In many of his stories, the lead characters ambivalently face the reality of their mortality, especially as elderly persons. For instance, the first chapter of *Robert Taylor* opens with the following: "Sunday, June 8, 1969, Robert Taylor died in Hollywood of lung cancer" (2). Whereas June 1969 signifies a pivotal moment in U.S. LGBTQ+ civil rights history, in Santos's novel, it marks a turning point for the protagonist Sol that prompts him to liberate himself from the banality of his lonely existence. It also becomes a harbinger of death. As the narrator illumines:

> Soon after Robert Taylor, Judy Garland went, a hag at forty-seven. . . . In the fall, his favorite person because he liked the way he spoke and looked, like one of the venerable uncles of his childhood, died, too. But Senator [Everett] Dirksen had lived a full life. There was no beating Mister Death. (106)[87]

Rather than casting the end of the 1960s as instantiating a new dawn for civil rights, Santos frames this moment as one of impending loss—and rightly so, as law enforcement systemically worked to disarm the U.S. civil rights movement and authoritarianism began to develop in the Philippines under Marcos. While the narrator's mention of Garland's death and the reference to her as a "hag" might imply a queer sensibility (given her status as a gay icon and the usage of *hag* among some gay men as a term of endearment for female intimates [i.e., "f—hag"], though not without contention) and therefore align with the 1969 Stonewall Riots and its struggle for queer and trans* liberation, that Garland's passing signaled "the end of the old gay world and the beginning of a new one" reinforces the sentiment of loss as opposed to hope.[88] In other words, the end of the 1960s may have ushered in a new era of possibility for some social actors; however, for others, such as the Filipino old-timers whose lives Santos documents and the older generation of gay men who identified with Garland, the end of the decade coincided with the end of the world as they knew it. Indeed, for Sol, much of the tension between him and other Filipinxs who populate the novel derives from the latter's status as professionals who migrated to the United States with the passage of the Hart-Cellar Act in 1965. However, the loss in *Robert Taylor* is not simply temporal but spatial as well, as Chicago serves as both a place of departure and an origin point for return for Sol.

The spatialization of loss in Santos's work underscores the geographic dimensions of diasporic identity, home, and belonging. For example, Sol's lack of kinship ties to either the Philippines or the United States "was always a problem" for him when he had to name beneficiaries or emergency contacts on U.S. forms (32). In "The Day the Dancers Came," when Tony minimizes Fil's concern about the potential bombing of the Philippines in the context of the early Cold War, remarking, "'What's that to you?'... 'You got no more folks ove'der, right?'" Fil is overcome with sadness (116). Tony's rhetorical questions reveal that the loss of home coincides with the passage of time away from home and the resultant severing of kinship ties. Because a new sense of home does not materialize in diaspora for such hurt men, the loss of the so-called original home and kin is made even more palpable.

However, all is not lost in the face of such perpetual mourning in regional diasporas without a critical mass of compatriots. As sexually unreproductive exilic subjects, characters like Sol, Fil, and Tony cannot readily claim home based on normative kinship structures. Instead, they create fictive kinships unlimited by imagination. For example, Sol "invent[s] relationships and addresses or copie[s] actual names that [sound] Filipino and their addresses from the telephone directory" to produce "'ghost' beneficiaries" (33). Similarly, Fil recreates kinship ties to the Philippines through his de facto marriage with Filipino old-timer Tony and his "magic sound mirror" that records the sounds of the Philippine dance troupe's Chicago performance (117). Despite being in the middle of the country and away from concentrated diasporic Filipinx enclaves, Sol and Fil manage to find hope amid loss, thus revealing the fecundity of regional diasporas.

Nevertheless, the loss of home, be it the Philippines or the Midwest, becomes tied to one's sense of identity and makes palpable one's sense of nonbelonging. Such nonbelonging is not simply psychic but also somatic. Desai's theorization of homesickness as literally producing sickness in diasporic subjects clarifies the sense of being out of place in a locale that is now home yet not. For her, homesickness functions as a "concept-metaphor" that denotes "the gendered embodiment and subjective experience of nostalgia," specifically "located in racism and heteropatriarchy."[89] By focusing on embodiment rather than the body, she orients our attention toward process as opposed to stasis.[90] In tracing the linkage between nostalgia and homesickness, she reveals how, "during the colonialism and imperialism of the eighteenth and nineteenth centuries," both concepts "became intertwined in the English language, and nostalgia became understood as an illness that linked spatial displacement with the experience of loss, which resulted in physical and psychological pain."[91] As such, nostalgia names the psychosomatic experience of homesickness—the loss of one's attachment to home, both literal and metaphoric—and is thus also geographic.[92] As Desai's analysis reveals, diasporic homesickness is a structural phenomenon linked to imperial practices and is racialized, gendered, and sexualized in form.

Such somatic manifestations of homesickness can be observed in "The Day the Dancers Came." As the narrator describes, Tony "suffer[ed] from a kind of wasting disease that had frustrated doctors" and had left him "bedridden most of the time for the last two years" (114). While Tony's pains are real, Fil, frustrated over not knowing what exactly the friend he "worshipped" suffers from (118), complains to Tony, "You don't care for nothing but your pain, your imaginary pain" (115). To cope, Fil masks his concern for Tony's failing health by fixating on the Philippine dance troupe visiting their city. However, by the story's end, the tape that recorded the performance so that he could replay the memory of his homeland come to life one night in a Chicago theater unravels, and he sadly exclaims, "Tony! Tony! ... I've lost them all" (128). Although Tony's deteriorating health may not be a direct result of his living in Chicago, his sickness nevertheless metaphorizes the uncanny sense of disorientation and alienation Filipino exiles experience in a place that is not quite home, which Fil's anticipation for the dancers makes clear. The loss of the tape recording further reinforces Fil's loss of homeland; and with Tony serving as a surrogate for a home no longer accessible, his illness further compounds Fil's sense of loss.

Like Tony, *Robert Taylor*'s Sol experiences chronic pains. He describes to a doctor, "All over my body. They travel. On the arms, the joints. Feel my knees. On the chest, at the back, the neck. It's not just pain, but worse, painspainspainspains. I wonder how I survive" (29–30). U.S. doctors are unable to diagnose his ailments and instead assume they are just part of being elderly. Sol's staccato syntax mirrors his disjointed being in diaspora, while his blurring of multiple pains ironically spells *Spain*, thereby implicating the Philippines' palimpsestic legacies of multiple colonialisms. Sol meets Artemio Banda, a Filipino transient "suffering from recurring stomachaches," and reluctantly feeds him (88). Sol views Banda's homesickness as a sickness that forced Banda to remain in the United States starving or else face the shame of not amounting to much while abroad and stemmed from the sustained U.S. occupation of the Philippines (100), which did nothing to improve hunger after the Japanese occupation during World War II (98–99).

In addition to physical maladies, homesickness manifests as a kind of mental illness (in an expansive sense of the phrase). In *Memory's Fictions*, Santos makes a reference to "a disease, with a name [he has] never learned to spell, that afflicts the minds of the aging" and causes "brownouts"; and yet, "as if to compensate for [his] erratic memory, [he is] still capable of instant, almost apocalyptic, recall of things long buried in the past" (6). Again, while his sickness may not necessarily be attributed to his living as a Filipino Midwestern diasporic subject, what interests me is the resonance between nostalgia for one's homeland and disease—or, more fittingly, dis-ease. Besides Filipinizing what most likely is Alzheimer's disease by referring to episodes as "brownouts"—though the specific illness matters less than the experiencing of the symptoms of illness themselves—he views his mental illness less as an impediment and more as a fact of life. More importantly, he calls attention to this unreliability of memory to posit that memories are always fictions, thus the title of his memoir (6).

Alternatively, for some of his characters, the potential to experience or the actual experience of mental illness plays out in various ways. In "And Beyond, More Walls," Manual tells Ben, "I looked at them [photographs of his dad, mom, and brother] when I was feeling kind of homesick, but heck, a man can't keep doing that for sixteen years without going nuts" (33). In "The Day the Dancers Came," Tony comments on Fil's excitement by saying, "Ever since you heard of those dancers from the Philippines, you've been acting nuts. Loco. As if they're coming here just for you" (113). These two stories illumine the psychic effects of homesickness on Filipino exiles longing for a homeland to which they cannot and most likely will not return, but in *Robert Taylor*, Sol's obsession with being recognized as the actor Robert Taylor drives him to the point of near insanity and perhaps costs him some of his romantic relationships, bringing into relief the slippage between the Filipinx Other and the American self. Despite the promise of "benevolent assimilation," Sol's schizoid subjectivity lays bare the realities of U.S. imperialism. As a post/colonial subject, Sol can approximate but never actually stand in for the Hollywood actor who metonymically figures as the United States.

Noli and Bart, two Filipino old-timers from Sol's younger days in Washington, DC, further illustrate this psycho-ontological tension. For Noli, performing yo-yo tricks in a drugstore window "five hours a day" (160) during the 1940s begins to unhinge him: "'I really felt like a monkey,' he confided to Sol, 'and I was afraid I was beginning to look like one and thinking like one. . . . I was getting crazy. Perhaps I was, already'" (161). Of Bart, whose "job during the war" was "hauling T.N.T.," Noli tells Sol, "He survived all right. But he's nuts now. . . . He says he's making 'em bombs to drop on the oppressors of our country"—though which oppressors, "he didn't say" (164).

The aforementioned examples of diasporic loss as an embodied, cognitive, and geographic inhabitation of diaspora are a reminder that diaspora is not an abstract universal referent for homelessness but rather a pointer to particular places in time. Recognizing that the nostalgia of these stranded Filipinx Midwesterners (Sol, Tony, Santos, Fil, Noli, and Bart) for a home that no longer exists, if it ever did, coincides with melancholic, inexplicable psychosomatic ailments is a provocation to reimagine diaspora queerly.

Reading Santos's literature psychoanalytically provides a critical vocabulary to articulate the experience of loneliness, longing, and loss woven throughout his writings. As I discuss in chapter 1, Freud's theories on mourning, melancholia, and unconscious desire present a useful framework for unraveling the ambivalent psychic dispositions—from sadness to affiliation and from contentment to nostalgia—performed by Santos and the characters who embody fragments of himself. However, aligned with See, I use Freud not simply as an authority but rather as a refracted mirror of normativity's anxieties and inability to fully capture the subjugated.[93] Rather than posit melancholia as a structure of feeling that casts exilic Filipinos as wounded, I position it as an entry point for enabling previously hidden, repressed, unthought affects to surface, albeit fleetingly. While characterized by Freud as the pathological mourning of a lost love-object, melancholia also allows desire to live on, even if only in the unconscious.[94] In this way, melancholia refers not simply to extreme grief but also to the barring of desire. Critical of Freud's racialized humanism, See asserts that "the racially marked, colonized subject completely exceeds the bounds of humanity" and thus poses a threat to the normal order of things.[95] Accordingly, "the colonized subject has nothing left but the body to articulate loss."[96] That bodily articulation of loss, however, is rooted in a particular place and time.

The Queer Potentialities of Diasporic Loss

Along with the loss of homeland and the ethno-racial-national self that Santos and his characters experience as homesick post/colonial, exilic subjects, the melancholic loss that haunts his stories is also tied to the ambivalent queer potentialities that momentarily emerge ironically out of U.S. imperialism but quickly dissipate due to the homosexual taboo of heteropatriarchal nationalisms.[97] Whereas scholars such as Bascara and de Jesús have recognized the queer socialities that populate Santos's fiction, they have paid less attention to the geographical dimensions that contribute to such social relations.[98] This is not to reify the problematic binary that casts homeland as sexually conservative and diaspora as sexually liberating but rather to examine how alternative socialities beyond heteropatriarchy are made possible by living in the peripheries of both nation and diaspora. Put differently, Santos's "hurt men" are able to form nonnormative social relationships—including cross-class, homoerotic, and interracial—because they are in the post/colonial metropole-cum-diaspora; and as inhabitants of the U.S. Filipinx diaspora "east of California," or what I have been conceptualizing as the queer diaspora of Filipinx America, those living in the Midwest bring into relief this reality.[99] As Leonard Casper notes in his introduction to *Scent*, "His [Santos's] enforced separation from his wife and three young daughters [during World War II] brought him closer to fellow 'exiles.'"[100] Although his following paragraph downplays the significance of homosocial bonding by casting early twentieth-century diasporic Filipinos as alone and isolated due to the "unnatural conditions imposed on" them, thereby rehearsing the hackneyed heteronormative bias that dominates the social history of these men, Santos's stories reveal otherwise.

Amid the longing and sadness Santos's "hurt men" exude, readers are also presented with intense homosocial bonds that, at times, exceed the bounds of friendship. It is these kinds of relationships that I argue also contribute to the feelings of loss found throughout *Scent*. Celestino Fabia, who "[had] seen no Filipino for so many years now" living on "a farm about thirty miles east of Kalamazoo," immediately decides to come "all that way . . . just to hear [the story's narrator] talk" (21). Despite their brief encounter, Fabia and the narrator develop a deep connection stitched together by Fabia's concern for the status of the Filipina. Whereas Cruz views this moment as an illustration of the centrality of the Filipina during the early twentieth century, I read the Filipina more as a conduit that links these two Filipino men. In other words, drawing from the insights of Eve Sedgwick, I view the Filipina as a veil for the homoerotic relationship between Fabia and the narrator.[101]

Although the spectral appearance of the Filipina interrupts her overwhelming absence in much of early twentieth-century diasporic cultural production and history, her status as object in Santos's story should give us pause on how queer recovery may be at cross purposes with feminist agency.[102] The fact that "after this [Fabia's question and the narrator's answer], everything that was said and done in that hall that night seemed like an anti-climax," and that "all night [the narrator] had been watching his face and . . . wondered when he was going to smile" belies the narrator's attraction toward Fabia and places the narrative focus on both men (23). Perhaps like Fabia, the narrator is drawn to him because each is a familiar Brown face in a sea of White, and each provides comfort for the other as exiles. At the story's end, Fabia "extend[s] his hand" and the narrator "grip[s] it" (29). However, Fabia "drop[s] [his] hand quickly" after the narrator tells Fabia to send his regards to Fabia's wife and son (29). The narrator's reminder of Fabia's present—that he has a nuclear family to return to but not a homeland—cuts the fantasy of their dreaming of an unchanged Philippines, despite the ravages of war. However, the unspoken eroticism between the two men also abruptly dissipates as Fabia lets go of the narrator's hand and the narrator resolves to prepare for his next speaking engagement in Muncie, Indiana.

In "The Contender," Bernie's blindness might be understood as a physical manifestation of his inability to mourn the loss of his intimate connection with Felix, since to name that loss would avow the homoeroticism of their relationship. When Bernie visits the first doctor, the doctor tells him,

"Your eyes are okay.... Those blackout spells must be due to something else" (134). While four other doctors later confirm that "something else" to be his boxing career, other seemingly benign clues provided throughout the story suggest otherwise. First, the story casts Felix as a kind of "nagging" spouse whose actions are ultimately tied to his concern for Bernie (129, 133). Second, the narrator notes how "[Bernie] and Felix were always together in those days [when they were both younger]. True, they had occasional quarrels, but this was different. There was no sense to it" (131). Third, whereas Felix eventually marries, Bernie "never got around to it. There was always an impediment: no money, no time, or just any old excuse—no gut perhaps" (133). Fourth, Bernie only feels comfortable with Felix in the barbershop that he took over from Felix when Felix left for the Philippines to find a wife; Bernie does not interact with Felix's nuclear family (135).

Together, these points suggest more than friendship exists between Bernie and Felix; however, that excess is never uttered. Such silence is a familiar trope of queerness. When seen in this light, Bernie's loss of sight becomes a metaphor of the lost intimacy between the two. Although the Midwest may have initially been a place where they decided to build their lives together—thereby resisting the compulsory heterosexuality demanded by both the Philippine and U.S. nation-states—that reality faded when Felix left for the Philippines and eventually returned with a wife (133). However, the cane Felix gifts to Bernie at the end of the story, a phallic object to be sure, allows Bernie to work through his grief and move forward by accepting Felix's literal and symbolic support.

When Celestino and the narrator of "Scent of Apples," Bernie and Felix in "The Contender," and Fil and Tony in "The Day the Dancers Came" are recognized as queer pairs—in terms of not only their platonic excess but also their same-gender romantic-sexual attraction—the plausibility of same-gender sexuality in diaspora and region becomes clear. While I share the same ambivalence as Bascara toward labeling the intimacies between old-timers as gay, I am inspired by de Jesús's critique of Asian American epistemologies as heterosexist.[103] I also am inspired by Muñoz's provocation to consider potentiality as "a certain mode of nonbeing that is eminent, a thing that is present but not actually existing in the present tense," which makes space (and time) for queer desire in the past, present, and future.[104] Rereading Santos's characters as erotically queer unleashes them from the restraints projected onto them by a phobic society and engenders validation for queer diasporic Filipinxs inhabiting the Midwest. Reworking loss—the loss of home, access to the densities of the U.S. Filipinx diaspora on the West and East Coasts, and queer erotic intimacies—as an entry point into queer regional spatialities of diaspora is my attempt to name what could have been as well as what is yet to come for diasporic Filipinxs of the heartland.

Santo's View from the Middle

As this chapter illustrates, Santos's literature is not simply about the loneliness, longing, and loss of U.S. Filipinx exiles; it is also a window into the particularities of those living in the peripheries of the U.S. Filipinx diaspora during and several decades after World War II, a period that transformed the Philippines from a colony into an independent, though arguably neocolonial, nation and that witnessed a dramatic shift in the demographic makeup of the U.S. Filipinx population. By rereading Santos's oeuvre with geography in mind, we can obtain a better sense of how isolation and alienation vary according to one's relation to place. However, while the Midwest's lack of a Filipinx critical mass may amplify one's sense of exilic disorientation, it also affords such subjects the opportunity to imagine community and social belonging differently. As Santos's life and literature reveal, Filipinxs in the heartland find ways to obfuscate the disciplinary logics of nation and empire by forming nonheteronormative socialities, resorting to the fictive, and unsettling the meaning of home.

As a pensionado who fictionalized the lives of other pensionadxs and early Filipinx migrants, Santos is a direct product of the U.S. imperial regime; however, as his stories of fiction and nonfiction illumine, such a fact did not necessarily translate into acceptance of the "benevolence" of the United States with open arms. Instead, his exile in the metropole was fraught with ambivalence. Regarding the first generation of pensionados, Celia Bocobo Olivar, daughter of Bocobo (fifth president of the University of the Philippines), writes,

> All the new things they [the pensionadxs] did appeared queer and artificial [to Filipinxs and Americans upon their return to the Philippines]. They were looked upon with distrust, even to the extent of ridicule. They were mockingly referred to as "Americanized" or "American Boys." The mode of dressing appeared queer. Their manner of speech too, was criticized. People jokingly said they spoke English like a Spaniard and Spanish like an American.[105]

Although Santos was not part of this early generation of scholars studying on several campuses throughout the Midwest, his experiences closely resemble such liminal subjectivity. Whereas Bocobo Olivar's statement positions pensionadxs as between the Philippines and the United States, in my reading of Santos and his "hurt men," I situate them as also outside the Filipinx American nation, centralized as it is in California. As queer subjects who exceed the boundaries of nation, pensionadxs, as well as those later-turned exiles in the heartland, occupy a unique vantage point that offers glimpses of another world beyond the present. Geographically in between but also neither culturally of the Philippines or the dominant United States, Santos and his exiles present alternative ways to imagine Filipinx America. Whereas theories of diaspora often present middleness as a metaphor of nonbelonging and transnation, and thus ambivalence as a mode of queer un/becoming, engaging the literal middle of diaspora involves reconsidering where we speak from when articulating colonial-cum-diasporic racial-ethnic subjectivity.[106] This is a provocation to decenter the centered margins and make space for other views.

Despite my emphasis on spatiality throughout this chapter, temporality figures as just as important to the analysis of Santos's oeuvre. As Casper points out, the arrangement of Santos's collection of stories in *Scent* "is chronic, rather than chronological"; this suggests a nonlinearity and circularity to the Filipinx exilic condition.[107] In this way, *Scent* plays with both space and time, presenting a mosaic of diasporic experience. Likewise, *Robert Taylor* refuses a linear temporality, opting instead to shuffle back and forth between the present of the novel and its protagonist's past. Moreover, the interludes between various chapters often include no introduction as to who is speaking and reveal the heterogeneity of the U.S. Filipinx diaspora. Furthermore, Sol's enigmatic phrase, "*Time was of the important* [original emphasis]" (5), which repeats throughout the novel, enjoins the reader to pause and attempt to make sense of a seemingly ungrammatical phrase. If *important* is being used to describe time, the presumed subject of the sentence, then the preposition *of* and the article *the* are grammatically excessive; however, *important* might also function as a noun referring to people who are important and worthy of study and thus history. In this way, Sol's words present a Filipinx critique that emanates from the particularity of Midwest diaspora. Such alternative, utopian world making—of bending space and time, of creating space-time—is not exclusive to Santos and his view from the middle of the country. As the following chapters featuring contemporary diasporic Filipinx Midwestern cultural production and representation illustrate, imaginative revisions of Filipinx American history, culture, and experience from the heartland continue to challenge and cultivate the idea of a queer Filipinx America.

II

The Midwest Queering Filipinx Diaspora

4

Filipinas in the Wild West

Filipinas in the Wild West connotes the following: Girls and women of Philippine descent in the American frontier; girls and women of Philippine descent perceived as wild, unruly because they live in the West, America; pioneering Filipinas; the Philippines, Pilipinas, Filipinas, the nation feminized, transported to the Old West, Wild West, Middle West at the turn of the twentieth century, on display for White Americans who savor the latest spoils of U.S. imperialism.[1]

This turn of phrase—*Filipinas in the Wild West*—activates multiple registers: gender, sexuality, race, nation, diaspora, empire, temporality, and region. To utter this phrase is to put in proximity seemingly opposing constructs: Filipina, the Philippines, West, the Wild West, the United States. However, as I have been arguing, the Philippines and the Midwestern United States have been entangled since at least the late nineteenth century via empire. And while the West often signifies the United States and Europe, geography is relative, and the Philippines and what we imagine as Asia actually could be considered the Far West, as opposed to always the East. But I digress. In this chapter, I situate the West as a metaphor of spatialized unruliness that recognizes the origins of the Midwest as wilderness and frontier in the U.S. imaginary. Hence, even though *Wild West* might connote the desert climes of the Plains, Rockies, and Pacific Coast—impressed by the Western literary, televisual, and cinematic genre—Frederick Jackson Turner's (in)famous frontier thesis delivered at the 1893 Chicago World's Fair reminds us that the frontier also includes the Midwest.[2] The confrontations between Native Americans and White settlers that we associate with the Wild West took (and continue to take) place in what we now know as the Midwest; the Midwest as America's heartland is only made possible by violent Indigenous removal.

In the same way that acknowledging that Indigenous removal and African American migration are not simply national phenomena but rather take place in specific parts of the country, my focus on the regional dynamics of empire and diaspora functions to take stock of the pervasiveness of U.S. imperial cultures. A focus on the regional scale gives insight into material geographies *within* (as opposed to *of*) the metropole. Such a move operates as a type of anti-abstraction that homogenizes postcolonial diasporic experience. As I have argued thus far, region is a critical framework for reimagining our understanding of identity, history, and geography, tempered as they are by gender, sexuality, race, and empire.

To illustrate the power of region as a lens to gain new insights into the gendered, sexual, and racialized modes of postcolonial diasporic subjectivity, I turn to Galang's debut collection of stories, *Her Wild American Self* (*HWAS*; 1996), and Pamatmat's play *Edith Can Shoot Things and Hit Them*, which premiered across four U.S. cities "east of California" in 2011 and 2012.[3] Whereas part I of this book focuses on the historical presence of Filipinxs in the Midwest to queer our discursive imaginary of region, part II, ushered in by this chapter, focuses on the modern-day presence of Filipinxs in the Midwest to queer our discursive imaginary of U.S. Filipinx diaspora. *HWAS* and *Edith* are fitting entry points to illustrate how contemporary diasporic Filipinx Midwesterners revise how we conceptualize diaspora and nation. Both texts start from the place that Filipinxs in Midwest are unexceptional, and neither desire an elsewhere beyond the heartland. However, I engage these texts in part because of my happenstance encounter with them.

I first read *HWAS* as an undergraduate student in California for a comparative ethnic studies course on Filipinx and Mexican identities and communities.[4] I was a gender studies major, and Galang's stories resonated with my salient sense of gender and sexuality informing what it meant to be Filipinx in the United States as a queer Pinoy, even though the stories themselves focus on heterosexual girls' and women's lives. It was only later, when I moved to the Midwest for graduate school, that I recognized Galang's stories as not simply Filipina American but specifically Filipina Upper Midwestern.

I learned about *Edith* as a regular patron of Twin Cities–based Mu Performing Arts (now Theater Mu), the premier Asian American theater company in the Midwest and one of the largest Asian American performing arts companies in the nation. The Filipino playwright drew me to this show, and it was only when I was reading the program that I realized that the story was set in Middle America and had a queer storyline. As a queer Filipinx living in Minneapolis at the time, seeing a play about an adolescent Filipina tomboy whose older teen brother also happens to be gay and in an interracial relationship resonated with me. I remembered the powerful feeling of seeing one's particular narrative represented to a larger audience, some of whom could identify with the character's particularities.

I read these two texts in tandem, since they illumine the specifically feminine perspective of the queer diasporic Filipinx Midwest. Suarez's conception of "gender difference as a politics rather than an identity" is instructive for my focus on the feminine of the queer diasporic Filipinx Midwest.[5] Analyzing narratives of overseas Filipinx care work, which is largely embodied by women, Suarez dissociates gender from strict embodiment and recasts it as a structural position that highlights the uneven relations of power between colonizer and colonized. While girls and women are central to Suarez's analyses and mine as well (though I do not focus on labor per se), our foci are less about revealing some kind of essential understanding of gender through such embodiment and more about the systemic relations that materialize through such identifications.

What interests me is how Galang's short stories and Pamatmat's play render possible the Midwest as origin for Filipinxs. Through their gendered and sexualized narratives of growing up and living in the middle of the country as not-quite-White but nevertheless refusing the assimilation imperative, the protagonists present another way to be.[6] Moreover, these texts complicate the trope of isolation that often informs Asian Midwestern narratives by depicting a sense of Filipinx community within domestic spaces.[7] And while the Philippines haunts some of the girls in Galang's stories, it fails to appear in Pamatmat's play. That the Philippines is not always a referent for Filipinxs in the United States is not so much a rejection of the foreign in favor of the domestic as it is an opening for other origin stories that are not steeped in normative nationalisms. To assert, "I'm from Brookfield, Wisconsin," as the narrator of Galang's "Mix Like Stir Fry" does,[8] or to place two Filipinx youth "on a non-working farm, in the remotest Middle America" (in the "boondocks," as it were, a fitting transposition given that the origin of that word is *bundok*, meaning "mountain" in Filipino/Tagalog, and it was brought to the United States by the military) without explanation or apology, as Pamatmat does,[9] disrupts the heteropatriarchal and normative diasporic tendency of lineage in favor of inheritance and palimpsest.[10] Whereas lineage prioritizes biological relations and conflates national origin with racial-ethnic identity, thereby locking *Filipinx* and *Philippines* in the case of diasporic Filipinxs, inheritance and palimpsest loosen the grip of consanguinity and nation and allow for multiple genealogies that may originate in diaspora. Both texts' presentations of queer diaspora and queered Filipina and Filipinx wildness provide a glimpse into the liberating potential of spatial socialities in between and beyond the national and global.

HWAS is an important contribution to contemporary Filipinx American literatures. While few scholars have critically engaged it since its mid-1990s publication, it remains indicative of the emergence of a postcolonial U.S. Filipinx diaspora coming of age and a particular peminist sensibility rooted in U.S. women of color feminisms and Third World feminisms.[11] I revisit Galang's debut book to foreground its regional specificity and to reconsider Filipinx and Filipina peminist politics. Whereas critics and community members view *HWAS* as a window into Filipinx and Filipina American life, I recognize the stories as also regional representations of U.S. Filipinx and Filipina diasporic experience.[12] Though it is admittedly a subtle interpretive shift, reorienting the marginal center as the centered margin works to generate narratives of diaspora, nation, and empire that address the micropolitical scale that undergirds the macropolitical.

Reading *HWAS* and *Edith*, two peminist texts, alongside each other reorients us toward their world making and remaking potential. Feminism is not simply an orientation; it is also a practice, a way of being, an imagining of a different kind of dwelling. Ahmed recognizes feminism in action as "that sort of girl or woman, the wrong sort, or bad sort, the one who speaks her mind, who writes her name, who raises her arm in protest."[13] She is the wild one, the unruly one, the one who refuses the status quo. She is the one who dares to see the world differently, a world that is habitable for those lost in empire's shadow. She paves a path that departs from the norm and engenders a different sense of knowing and being.

Wild as Metaphor

Galang's stories and Pamatmat's play feature representations of strong, unruly Filipinas from the American heartland, and wildness is a thematic thread that runs through these narratives. By using *wild* as a metaphor for diasporic Filipina Midwestern cultural formations, I situate both texts' portrayal of young women's gender transgression vis-à-vis Midwestern aesthetics. I also resignify the Filipinx-as-wild-savage trope rampant in U.S. popular culture at the turn of the twentieth century. By disidentifying with *wild* in relation to regional Filipinx America, I rewrite the term as a concept of possibility. In establishing the connections among place, racialized gender and sexuality, and feminist and queer sensibilities, I reveal how the U.S. heartland activates alternative ways of living and being for minoritized subjects that are geographically informed, exist under the radar of U.S. postimperial regimes of knowledge, and relate to but nevertheless are distinct from hegemonic diasporic Filipinx social and cultural formations.

Whereas chapter 3 illustrates how Filipinx Midwestern literary production simultaneously queers dominant perceptions of Midwestern character and diasporic Filipinx culture, with a particular emphasis on the masculine homosocial as a byproduct of U.S. empire, this chapter redirects the gaze toward the feminine and overtly queer. This move, in part, heeds Cruz's critique of Santos's objectification of the Filipina and Gopinath's critique of masculinity as the default of queer analysis.[14] My explicit focus on girls, women, and the feminine in this chapter is not meant to be an additive correction to the preceding chapters' focus on queer(ed) diasporic Filipinos (as Filipinas appear throughout). Rather, it is an opportunity to highlight the gendered dynamics of region, nation, and diaspora as they intersect with other sociocultural formations (such as race, class, and sexuality) that yield particular interiorities and socialities. By recognizing Filipinas and the feminine as they relate to queerness in the Midwest, I am reworking the heteropatriarchal settler-colonialist mentality of conflating and subordinating the feminine with and to the land.[15]

Even as this chapter plays with the homonyms *Filipinas*, referring to girls and women of Philippine descent, and *Filipinas*, as in Las Islas Filipinas, the Hispanic name for the Philippines, I refrain from framing Filipina Midwesterners as pure embodiments of nation and instead position them as exceeding the Philippine nation and diasporic U.S. Filipinx nationalism. Nevertheless, if Filipinas are referents for the Philippines, then locating them in the Midwest unsettles the normative geographies of nation and diaspora, the latter of which often operates at the scale of the national. Notwithstanding Filipina Midwesterners as settlers on Indigenous lands, foregrounding a regional dimension to ethno-raciality shifts the terms of national belonging in relation to the Philippines, the United States, and Filipinx America.

Focusing on wildness functions both to foreground feminist-queer ways of knowing and being that exceed the heteronormative scripts of nation and diaspora and reimagine regionalized tropes of Filipinx savagery. As I argue in chapter 1, the primal scene of U.S. Filipinx subjection, the 1904 St. Louis World's Fair, is not simply a national event but rather a localized one that then is scaled up to the national and the global. I transpose Balce's corporally fragmented approach to U.S. imperialism in the Philippines onto geography, focusing on the regional epistemes of Filipinas to re-present a narrative of Filipinx subjectivity that is more robust.[16] See's engagement with the notion of primitivism in two Michigan museum exhibitions of the Philippines to reconsider post/colonial American obsessions with the Filipinx Other further illumines the promise of a regional approach to diasporic Filipinx subjectivity.[17] In foregrounding the regional, I reveal how the Filipinx fragments that U.S. empire makes seem out of place are a discursive construction with material consequences. The recognition of this epistemological formation enables another geography to come into view. While Filipinx Midwestern culture may be distinctive, it is not disconnected from diasporic U.S. Filipinx culture writ large per se. My point is to shift our frame of reference to see anew.

Wild *Americanxs*

The Midwest is at once a stifling place and a place of possibility. These motifs are readily apparent in the literatures of the Midwest that center on girl and women protagonists. These Midwestern girls and women—from Dorothy Gale in Baum's *The Wonderful Wizard of Oz* (1900), to Ántonia Shimerda in Willa Cather's *My Ántonia* (1918), to Laura Ingalls Wilder in Wilder's *Little House* series (1932–1971), to Esperanza Cordero in Sandra Cisneros's *The House on Mango Street* (1984), to Tita Augustina in Galang's *HWAS*, to Jane Takagi-Little in Ruth Ozeki's *My Year of Meats* (1998), to Edith Tolentino in Pamatmat's *Edith*, to Lee Lien in Bich Minh Nguyen's *Pioneer Girl* (2014), to Lydia Lee in Celeste Ng's *Everything I Never Told You* (2014)—embody the wild spirit of the frontier Middle West ushered in by the Northwest Ordinance of 1787. Rather than reinforce sexist and colonialist tropes of the feminine as closer to nature or settler tropes of pioneers who displace Indigenous peoples, I reread the Midwestern feminine in these narratives as sites of rupture in these characters' unruliness and refusal to be tamed by hetero-national and -imperial patriarchies.

For the young Filipinas in Galang's stories, the Midwest is either the only home they have ever known or a new home wherein burdens from the homeland can be shed, if only because of physical distance, but nevertheless loom. Most of the stories are set in Chicago, Milwaukee, or their surrounding suburbs. Although the all-American suburban backdrop might reflect an assimilationist investment by these post-1965 immigrants, in contrast to the urban pre-1965 generation featured in Santos's stories (see chapter 3), starting with the Midwest reveals alter-narratives of diaspora. Interestingly, four of the stories are narrated in the second person, interpellating the reader and assuming a Filipina Midwestern audience who can identify with the narrated experiences.[18]

The titular story, "Her Wild American Self," presents the United States as a place that transforms dutiful Filipina girls into wild *Americanas*. However, by noting the context in which the narrator intimates her aunt's story—1960s/1970s, Chicago's North Side—the story becomes more about the peculiarities of region as it intersects with gender, race, and nation than simply about nation alone. The premise of the story lies in disciplining the narrator's alleged proclivities toward mischief.

The narrator opens the story by stating, "My grandmother, *Lola* Mona, says that I'm as wild as *Tita* Augustina [original italics]. That I have that same look in my eye. A stubbornness. And if I'm not careful I will be more trouble than she ever was. She says her daughter was a hard-headed *Americana* [original italics] who never learned how to obey, never listened" (67). Immediately, the narrator establishes the story's conflict of young Filipina rebelliousness, which Lola Mona attributes to geography. Lola Mona understands this geography to be America writ large, but their location in the middle of the country factors into what this America means.

The Midwest historically was the frontier, a space of unruliness significantly associated with youth and vitality, as cultural geographer Shortridge notes.[19] While separated by a century, Tita Augustina and the narrator evoke the spirit of the Midwest frontier. This Filipina wildness also is a corrective to, and a reappropriation of, the wild savagery associated with the first Filipinxs brought to the region for the 1904 St. Louis World's Fair, coinciding with the closure of the nation's continental frontier at the turn of the twentieth century.[20]

Wild appears multiple times in the story to signal a specifically feminized unruliness associated with geography and sexuality. As previously mentioned, it is first used to describe the narrator and her similarity to her estranged aunt, both of whom are reared in the United States (67). The narrator uses it again to elaborate the signification of *wild* as associated with being "stubborn" and "opinionated" due to the cultural influences of White America (68). Teenage Tita Augustina utters the word when referring to a White classmate's lipstick at the all-girls Catholic school her parents send her to "to tame her" (69, 68). In this moment, *wild* is a referent to both American femininity and budding sexuality, as the use of makeup for girls marks their transition into normative young womanhood. As the story continues, Tita Augustina's wildness becomes more associated with sexuality than geographic location (and nationality); the next reference is to "her cousin Gabriel [being] in love with her" as the cause of her wildness (70). However, the source of unbridled feminine sexuality in the story is always connected to diaspora, to America, and, as I read it, to the Upper Midwest.

Similar to the narrator, Augustina receives a lecture from her parents about a family friend's daughter, Emmy Nolando, who became pregnant presumably as an unmarried teen. The admonishment "Better not be wild, better not embarrass the family like that girl. Better not, better not, better not" frames *wild* as both an undesirable trait for young Filipinas and an irresistible temptation toward a life free of the restrictive gaze of hetero-national family (73). The final instance when *wild* appears occurs on the last page of the story: "Some of the relatives say it was to have a baby, others it was to discipline her wild American self.... Even my mother thinks her older sister was a bad girl" (81).

While the narrator recounts the familiar story of her Tita Augustina that Lola Mona often has told, her tone toward Tita Augustina's alleged wildness is less contemptuous and more curious, if not suspect and identificatory. The narrator seems unconvinced by the idea of America as morally degenerate. The transfer of the Virgin Mary necklace, which Tita Augustina had taken from her mother's jewelry box many years ago, before her cryptic return to the Philippines, from Tita Augustina to the narrator, emphasizes the story's peminist and queer investments (80–81). Tita Augustina's "wild American self" is a model of courage and strength, symbolized through the Virgin Mary whom she venerates and the necklace she passes on to her niece. Such a material and symbolic transfer between kin women, but in excess of the nuclear family, challenges heteropatriarchal generational transmission.

Region in this story functions as a critique of the nation. On one hand, it dramatizes the predominant Whiteness of the United States, wherein "the row of milk-white faces, faces so pure and fresh," oppressively renders the Brownness of Filipina skin as a liability and cause for social exclusion (69). In this scene, Tita Augustina's racial-ethnic difference from her high school classmates manifested through food (her peers comment that her lunch is "smell[y]") is akin to other Asian Midwestern narratives of nonbelonging (69).[21] At the same time, the narrator's distrust of her family's admonishment to be obedient reveals the disciplining logics of racial-ethnic nationalisms. As erin Khuê Ninh reveals, the family unit is not isolated from the social, political, and economic imperatives of the model minority discourse that haunts Asian American life but rather constitutes it.[22] The family unit, as micro-unit of the nation, functions as the disciplining apparatus through which societal norms propagate. The narrator's regional location in diaspora works to disrupt the heteropatriarchal hegemonies that buttress Philippine, U.S., and Filipinx American national cultures. What is more, Galang's collection of stories offers a composite of various Filipinas located in America's heartland who ambivalently find strength in their extended kin, indicating a constellation of diasporic Filipinxs in the Midwest that challenges the discourse of anomaly and isolation.

Wildness is symptomatic of Filipina *American*-ness, and thus the Philippines is used as a threat by Filipinx immigrant parents to keep their daughters in line. While feminine (hetero)sexuality primarily is what parents police, feminine agency generally is more apt, as young Tita Augustina's desire to carry the crucifix as a Catholic Mass altar server is discouraged by her mother (67). And when Tita Augustina refuses to attend Mass in rebellion, her father threatens to "send her to the Philippines for lessons in obedience" (68). Later in the story, Tita Augustina's mother casually asks if she wants her father to send her to the Philippines for not behaving properly in the United States, which is related to her ditching school to be with Gabriel (78). Her mother is matter-of-fact. In this way, the Philippines is less the home of U.S.-born diasporic Filipinxs than it is the home of their parents.

The specifically gendered nature of the threat reveals how nation is not a space of freedom. Region as an alternative space operates as a liminal geography that enables freedom of expression. Instead of conceptualizing this threat within Filipinx America as international, between the Philippines and the United States, we might pivot to region to recognize the heterogeneities, as well as commonalities, *within* diaspora that do not privilege the national. Moreover, if hegemonic U.S. Filipinx diaspora figures as a form of cultural nationalism, then Filipinx Midwesterners as not hegemonic because of geography further illumine the limits of a national frame for understanding ethnic identity and community formations.[23] Certainly, Augustina's story finds resonance with other children of immigrants; however, neglecting its geographic specificity homogenizes diasporic subjectivity. Diaspora is not simply spatial but place-bound as well. To be a Midwestern girl, standing out among "the row of milk-white faces," highlights the quintessential American backdrop Augustina inhabits and brings into stark relief how far removed she is from the Philippines, the home of her parents.

In Pamatmat's play, wildness materializes through the Tolentino siblings, Edith and Kenny, who are latchkey kids living on a farm without parental supervision. The play opens with Edith humming "Ein Männlein steht im Walde" from Engelbert Humperdinck's opera *Hänsel Und Gretel*. Sitting on a barn rafter, she is wearing "a stained T-shirt, ratty shorts, and is barefoot" (7). The sonic intertext that adapts the German fairy tale of the young siblings Hansel and Gretel lost in the woods along with Edith's seemingly ungirly presentation illustrate Herring's anti-urban aesthetics, inviting audiences into the nonnormative racial-gender-sexual worlds created by the characters and the play as metatext itself. Edith's tomboyishness; commitment to defending her home and family (composed of her older brother, Kenny, and her) with a BB gun; refusal to take on the role of dutiful daughter and obedient, pretty little girl (symbolized by a frilly dress); and acceptance and promotion of queer love (manifested in Kenny and Benji's budding romance) indicate her wild spirit.

Kenny likewise calls to mind wildness in a pivotal scene titled "Wild and Free," wherein he stands up to his father:

LISTEN TO ME. IF YOU WON'T TELL US [Edith and him] WHAT TO DO SO THINGS GO RIGHT, THEN YOU CANNOT TELL US WHAT TO DO WHEN THINGS GO WRONG.

. . .

You made us. You raised us to need nothing except the money in the bank. We used to want you to come back. But now when you're here all we want is for you to leave. I took what you left us and made a home. Our home. We don't need your supervision or your new girlfriend or your decisions about reform school. I can get us everything we need. Without you. You left us wild and free. You can't cage us now. (76)

Kenny's monologue culminates in an affirmation of Edith's and his rural, unsupervised domesticity and the sense of freedom it engenders. Although a lack of parental supervision is not uncommon among immigrant as well as working- and lower-middle-class families, heteronormative societal values deem such a domestic setup as improper. The play's domestic and regional setting, focus on Edith's unconventional femininity, and support of queer rurality combine to showcase the peminist-queer possibilities of the diasporic Filipinx Midwest.

By orienting to region, and the Midwest specifically, in diasporic Filipinx literatures, I mine for alter-narratives of being and belonging that tell us different stories of Filipinx America. In so doing, I discover that texts that are not even grounded in America's heartland still manage to relate. Such free association signifies another form of wildness as undisciplined relationality. My peminist-queer regional reading practice engenders connectivity across texts that is reminiscent of the connections among biologically unrelated Filipinas and between non-immediate family members in Galang's stories and among femininity, queerness, and interraciality in Pamatmat's play.

For example, Hagedorn's *Dogeaters* materializes the diasporic feminine-queer that predates Galang and Pamatmat's narratives. Rio Gonzaga, one of the novel's protagonists, recounts her coming of age in Manila during the late 1950s/early 1960s as an adult living in the United States. Hagedorn's choice to title her novel accordingly aims to rework the derogatory term used by (White) Americans in reference to Filipinxs.[24] The novel unapologetically engages with the trope of Filipinxs as wild and savage in the colonial imaginary, especially as a legacy of American occupation. However, the Midwest as the quintessential American referent obliquely appears and actually is foundational to Rio's wild diasporic resistance—a detail yet to be remarked on by scholars of the text. As a "*rebellious* [original emphasis]" and "*precocious* [original emphasis]" daughter who seems to be unable to get her cousin Pucha's "damn history straight," Rio embodies the wild spirit of the diasporic Filipinas I chart in Galang and Pamatmat's work.[25] Incidentally, Rio's genealogy can be traced back to the Midwest: "And where was my maternal grandfather from? Somewhere in the Midwest, my mother shrugs and tells me. I am ashamed at having to invent my own history" (239).

Earlier in the novel, Rio describes her American grandfather, Whitman Logan, as one of the "leftovers from recent wars, voluntary exiles whose fair skin is tinged a blotchy red from the tropical sun or too much alcohol" (14). When he lies dying in the American Hospital in Manila, "he groans *Chicago, Chicago, Chicago* [original emphases], with such longing [Rio shuts her] eyes and the movie projector goes off in [her] head" (16). Although Hagedorn's postmodern narrative intentionally casts doubt on the veracity of her characters' stories, Rio's literal origins in the Midwest via Whitman make palpable the importance of America's heartland in one of Filipinx America's beloved texts. To recognize the Midwest in Filipinx America is to reorient to an un-straight mode of being presented by characters like Rio Gonzaga, Edith Tolentino, Tita Augustina, and the narrator of "Her Wild American Self" and to see beyond the horizon of social, cultural, and national normativities.

Wild as *Willful*

Reading Galang's stories and Pamatmat's play as peminist underscores the Filipina particularity that buttresses these narratives of resistance, refusal, and resignation. The *wildness* that cathects onto these Filipina American characters is geographic. Surely, I am not claiming that all Midwest regional narratives are inherently wild, unruly, and socially, culturally, and politically transformative; rather, in mining for moments when the Midwest appears in Filipinx America, I am pointing to registers that render diaspora heterogeneously. Such a rhetorical move resonates with Ahmed's notion of willfulness.

According to Ahmed, willfulness is symptomatic of feminism, for willfulness is often a character flaw ascribed to girls and women: "The word *willfulness* [original emphasis] exists in close relation to other words, such as stubborn, obstinate, and contrary. . . . If feminists speak of wrongs, this speech is understood not only as unreasonable, but as a product of having an obstinate and unyielding nature. . . . Feminism is diagnosed as a symptom of failed subjectivity, assumed as a consequence of immature will, a will that has yet to be disciplined or straightened out."[26] For Ahmed, willfulness is a mark of determination against the status quo; the willful girl or woman is a subject who says no to heteropatriarchy, and because of her willing refusal, she is deemed a threat. However, when read as an affirmation, willfulness might be understood aptly as "not being willing to be owned."[27] Willfulness points to feminist, queer, and anti-racist movements to eradicate social injustice and to engender pathways for freedom.[28] She explains how willfulness might be reclaimed as a charge that enables us to find each other, to find those cast outside the norm: Being called willful "can be a connection: a way of relating to others similarly charged."[29] Such a notion of proximity via negative affect resonates with the protagonist's affinity with Tita Augustina in "Her Wild American Self." Like the proto-feminist girls who endure the charge of willfulness, the diasporic Filipinas in Galang's stories and Pamatmat's play are negatively labeled as wild by their elders; and yet, the charge of wildness is that which enables these Filipinas to find each other (and me to connect them).

Willfulness not only describes the wildness of Galang's and Pamatmat's protagonists; it also describes my refusal to dismiss the Midwest as marginal, and thus not inherent, to how we might interpret these texts (or other texts set in the Midwest more generally). My willfulness to connect the Midwest to peminist cultural production aims to disrupt the hegemony of coastal narratives and to inspire more nuanced analyses of the Filipinx American diaspora. An orientation toward the Midwest is the means through which alter-narratives of diaspora that are not rooted in nationalist (or even transnationalist) sentiment can emerge. In this case, Galang's Midwest and Pamatmat's Middle America bring willful girls and women to the fore. Their stories defy the stereotype of the Midwest as being only banal, staid, and White.

Placing Filipinas in the Heartland

You. Not many stories use the English second-person personal pronoun as the subject. Unlike Filipino/Tagalog, which uses *ikaw* (placed at beginning of a sentence) and *ka* (placed after a verb) for the singular second-person personal pronoun and *kayo* for the plural second-person personal pronoun and to demonstrate respect for a singular person, often an elder, English uses the same personal pronoun for both. Such a mode of address thus can function simultaneously as an intimate and collective interpellation. Its ambiguity fittingly aligns with the metaphor of the middle the Midwest evokes. In *HWAS*, the subject *you* is used in four stories: "The Look-Alike Women," "Lectures on How You Never Lived Back Home," "Filming Sausage," and "Mix Like Stir Fry." Except for "Filming Sausage," these stories are much shorter in length than the other nine stories that make up the volume, ranging from two to four pages; their titles are also set off by italics in the table of contents and in the book itself.[30]

Galang's choice of *you* invites readers to imagine themselves as part of the narrative. It also renders possible a Filipina Midwestern subject. This tension between universal and particular is characteristic of minoritarian cultural production. However, Galang nuances this bifurcation by indicating a diversity of gendered and geographic experiences *within* minoritarian communities. Certainly, we can read Galang's stories as capturing the experiences of diasporic Filipinas in the United States. And yet, the specificity of places like Peoria, Illinois, or Brookfield, Wisconsin, that Galang mentions are indicative of a Filipina Midwestern sensibility.[31] Universalizing Galang's stories as simply Filipina American erases the "smallness and specificity," as See puts it, of the diasporic Midwest in relation to Filipinx America.[32] Hence, the *you* that leads the more polemical stories is a political act that says "I see you; I affirm your existence" to the Filipina Midwesterner who may or may not fit the dominant experiences of Filipinx Americans concentrated along the urban and suburban coasts.

The three shorter stories ("The Look-Alike Women," "Lectures on How You Never Lived Back Home," and "Mix Like Stir Fry") read less as fiction and more as autobiographical creative nonfiction. The *you* in these stories interpellates both an imagined and real Filipina Midwestern subject reading them but also refers back to the author, whose experiences as a second-generation Filipina American from suburban Milwaukee are refracted throughout the entire book. Galang's biographical imprint on her creative writing places her in a literary tradition of ethnic American authors and women of color feminists whose writing is a testament to their own experiences and those of marginalized peoples who are often written out of official histories.[33] In this way, Galang invokes a collective individuality that finds relationality in the face of U.S. imperial-racist-sexist capitalism.

In her contribution to *Pinay Power*, Galang explains,

> The "you" in this creative nonfiction essay ["Deflowering the Sampaguita"] represents the collective "you." The experience in this essay is neither biographical nor autobiographical to any particular woman but is a conglomeration of various anonymous interviews with young women from New York, Illinois, Wisconsin, Ohio, and Virginia. Yes, these are your daughters speaking.[34]

The essay is a meditation on the parallels between Catholic First Communion and girls' and women's first encounter with heterosexual sex. Its tone and themes resonate with those of *HWAS*, and the motif of wildness appears in the essay's last paragraph: "Wild and fresh, little white star with fragrant petals . . . you are left clinging to the vine that is the family you were born to."[35] The sampaguita is a jasmine flower and the national flower of the Philippines. The obvious metaphor of flower and feminine sexuality is apparent. Less apparent in the text and only revealed in Galang's author note is the referent *you* as generated from the voices of women, presumably of Philippine descent, living "east of California." While the essay interpellates a collective diasporic Filipina *we*, its second-person mode of address is intimate, individual, personal. It simultaneously materializes a universal diasporic Filipina and a particular Filipina American whose sociocultural geographic context is not situated in the center of Filipinx American diaspora (i.e., California).

Galang describes her upbringing in Brookfield, Wisconsin, a suburb of Milwaukee, as involving "two worlds": the school world, wherein she was "a minority American watching the majority American experience," and the home world, wherein she learned the customs of her Filipina ethnic heritage routed through her Philippine-born parents.[36] Her bicultural identity certainly reflects the experiences of American-born Filipinxs—and children of immigrants more generally—who must navigate the dominant American culture and the minoritarian culture of their kin. However, Galang's experience fittingly aligns with her Midwestern upbringing, for the region is not only quintessentially American but also a geographic and metaphoric middle zone. And while she and her characters did not grow up without a Filipinx cultural context, with the presence of extended kin, unlike their coastal counterparts, they often remain "the only" Filipinx in their everyday social worlds, namely school and work. In this sense, Filipinx Midwesterners (and non–West Coast Filipinxs more broadly) are Filipinx American, "but not quite."[37] Such liminality can be unsettling in its ambiguity, but such amorphousness can enable alternative sociocultural formations to emerge.

In their dialogue via email, poet Nick Carbó and Galang note the polyvocal nature of Filipinx/American literatures. As multiply colonized peoples, Filipinxs embody split subjectivity. For Carbó, that ontology translates into form: "Depending on where you are coming FROM your stories can be linear or circular—resolved or never ending—character driven, plot driven, image driven, politically driven."[38] The content is the form. See similarly illustrates how form has everything to do with Filipinx art.[39] Such observations are responses to critics who fail to recognize the formal qualities of Filipinx and ethnic cultural productions more broadly, instead denigrating them to pseudo-autobiography. The form of Galang's stories is just as important as the content they reveal. Their narration style, episodic structure, and cinematic aesthetics reflect the fractured, hybrid subjectivity Filipinxs embody.

In reflecting on her upbringing, Galang notes that overt anti-Asian racism did not color her experience growing up in Brookfield; rather, being "the new girl in school" was more salient in feeling out of place.[40] Nevertheless, being "new" was entangled with "always being the only brown girl," thus illumining the gendered raciality of region.[41] Galang's sense of being the only one of her kind, so to speak, resonates with other Asian Midwestern narratives, where a lack of critical mass makes the sense of isolation palpable.[42] This sense of isolation also is gendered; girls and women paradoxically are invisible and hyper-visible, as they are confined to the domestic sphere and expected to perform as dutiful daughters, yet their Orientalized bodies are publicly scrutinized by classmates, coworkers, and strangers.

While Galang rightly imagines the dominant culture to be White, I also want to have us think about the dominant culture as being coastal Filipinx America; there can be multiple forms of dominance. As Lowe cogently articulates in her call to recognize *Asian American* as a heterogenous assemblage born from historical material conditions, focusing on the sameness of Asian Americans risks homogenizing a race made up of a range of ethnicities and histories and subordinates them to a unified norm.[43] While Asian American sociocultural identity may stem from race, gender and region factor into its heterogeneity.[44] Whereas Lowe points to regional differences of the homeland for immigrants, regional differences of the diaspora also apply. A micro-focus on Filipinx cultural identity likewise works to discourage the homogenizing tendencies from without and within that attempt to simplify the intersectional nature of identity and experience. If "the point of writing," as Galang reflects, "is to communicate a world outside of the reader's experience," then her regional narratives of gender, sexuality, race, and empire address audiences within and beyond Filipinx America.[45]

Reading the *you* in "The Look-Alike Women," "Lectures on How You Never Lived Back Home," and "Mix Like Stir Fry" as Galang referencing herself is both typical and unique. Most people tend to refer to themselves and others in the second person when describing experiences and perspectives (e.g., "You know when you do this...") to an intimate audience. Alternatively, the choice of *you* instead of *I* could be interpreted as a distancing from the traumas of sexual racism and psychic imperial violence. Such an out-of-body experience, metaphorically speaking, reflects the split subjectivity colonized people endure. This fragmentation protects the subject (ego) while shining a light on the horrors of misrecognition the subject has faced; Galang's tone is both rage and lament for experiences that have occurred and will continue to occur for women of Asian descent, the so-called "look-alike women."

"The Look-Alike Women" is the first story in *HWAS* and begins as follows: "Because you are all beautiful—but in different ways. Your skin, yellow and light as the moon; and other times, the color of the earth, of clay from the red rocks, from the mountains; or baked golden-brown like the crust of honey bread" (11). The *you* in this story operates in the plural mode, interpellating various ethnic women under the singular racial and racist marker "women of the Orient" (12). Galang uses a blazon style in the first three paragraphs, describing skin; hair "like the silk from milkweed, or coarse like hemp and black like a sleeping universe" (11); and mien that flitters from "sensual," to "crafty," to "obedient" (11). As Rachel Lee observes, the body is central to Asian American racial formation—a corrective to discourses of the socially constructed nature of race that aims to decouple it from pseudo-scientific racism that fixes it as inherently biological.[46] Galang's imagery emphasizes the embodied sense of sexual racism. The third paragraph's listing of "Mount Fuji and Pinatubo," "Olongapo," and "Saigon" geographically orients readers to East and Southeast Asia, with Pinatubo, Olongapo, and Saigon serving as oblique references to U.S. military occupation and the feminized and sexualized forms of Asian/American racialization. In this way, Galang tethers gender, race, and sexuality to place. Although each paragraph begins with *be-*

cause, creating a cadence that explains gendered racialization, the third paragraph's repetition of *husbands* in the last sentence ("please your husbands—always your husbands first") signals a shift in tone, conveying the narrator's critique of Asian/American women as being perceived as all the same by dominant culture (11).

The litany of attributes, both positive and negative, renders Asian/American women as complex persons; yet, in the end, they are reduced to being a synecdoche for the faceless "look-alike women, the beautiful women. The women of the Orient" (12). Galang uses *Orient* ironically to signal how Asian/American women are simply Other. While the *you* can refer to Asian/American women in general, given the rest of the stories in the collection, the pronoun can be read as particularly signifying Filipina/Americans. In a multiethnic society like the Philippines, with legacies of varying colonialisms and interethnic migrations beyond the archipelago, Filipina/Americans do not all look the same.[47] In beginning *HWAS* accordingly, Galang invites readers to reconsider the heterogeneity of Asian and Filipina American women's experiences in terms of phenotype and nationality but also, I argue, in terms of geography.

Whereas the subject in the title "The Look-Alike Women" is plural and the *you* of the essay is not geographically specific, thereby presenting a more universal story, the *you* of "Lectures on How You Never Lived Back Home" is more particular. The essay's *you* "grew up hearing two languages" and "pouring chicken soy sauce dishes over beds of steamed rice" (83, 85); "[is] the first born. First generation. First American. First cousin. First hope" (83); "never had to obey a curfew because of war" (84); and "[has] always had one foot planted in the Midwest, one foot floating on the [Philippine] islands" (86). This *you* is she: Galang. "Lectures" is a condensed life story of the author, but the choice of *you* over *I* works to complicate notions of subjectivity and objectivity. The narrative form renders the story's subject as an object of both the author's and reader's gaze, presenting a cinematic account of the Filipina Midwestern *you* who navigates both Philippine and American cultures. This distancing enables the author to develop a metacognitive recognition of her peminist and queer (as in nonnormative) diasporic existence. And yet, the *you* also functions as an interpellation, which ironically creates intimacy between author and reader. *You* in "Lectures" materializes not only the singular figure of the Filipina Midwesterner embodied by Galang as both author and character but also the possibility of a plural Filipina Midwesterner who might relate to Galang's particularity. "Lectures" suggests the Filipina Midwestern is more than one; she is a plural pronoun—she is both *ka* and *kayo*.[48]

Akin to "Her Wild American Self," "Lectures" illustrates the disciplinary regimes of nation and diaspora mediated through the family. To be lectured to is to occupy a subordinate position; in the context of family, the lecturer typically is an adult parent, and the person being lectured is typically a child. The power relation between parent and child often is unilateral, in favor of the former—the parent lectures, the child listens.[49] For the narrator, to be lectured "on how you never lived back home" is to be reminded of your place—where you do (and do not) belong and how you should (and should not) behave. Place is both geographic and cultural. For the narrator, back home is the Philippines, the home of "one of [her] grandmothers [who] sewed children's clothing by hand and sold them in an open-air market. The other grandmother [who] raised seven children on her own, gathering them up, hiding them away in the provinces along the sea, away from Japanese soldiers, away from American fighters" (83).

The homeland is abstract, a fantasy elsewhere intangible to the diasporic subject who has never actually lived there. But, as the narrator indicates, the homeland is not simply amorphous: "The provinces" of the Philippines, similar to region in the United States, provide momentary refuge from urbanity and empire, or at least a different experience of them. *Back home* also is a tropic disciplinary device the narrator's parents use to admonish her for deviating from proper feminine domesticity and sexuality: "Back home, a young girl serves her parents, lives to please them, fetches her father's slippers and her mother's cups of tea. Back home a young girl learns to embroider stitches, learns parlor dances, wears white uniforms at all-girl schools, convent schools . . . back home a girl does not date. She is courted" (84). Back home, the Philippines, is an ambivalent place for the narrator. It is both a place where women have inspired independence and courage, as demonstrated by her grandmothers, and a place where so-called traditional gender norms run counter to her attitudes and beliefs, as her parents remind her.

As a specifically Filipina Midwestern narrative, "Lectures" also reveals how Midwest regional diaspora is a metaphor of middle-ness. Certainly, the stories of second-generation immigrants often focus on the theme of bicultural ambivalence.[50] However, the Midwest particularity of Galang's essay nuances that trope. Like Tita Augustina in "Her Wild American Self," the narrator recounts being out of place in suburban Milwaukee as the only Filipina girl at school: "From the start, you were a piece that did not fit, never given the chance to be like the rest—the ones with blond hair and red hair . . . the ones with eyes that change like the ocean. . . . To the kids at school, you were no different from the other Oriental girl" (85). However, from the perspective of her immigrant aunts and uncles, she was "turning into a *bratty Americana* [original emphases] . . . mouthy like the kids who ran the streets wild" (85). Caught between normative America and the Philippines, she is neither American nor Filipina. Instead, she is "the hyphen in American-born" (86).

As the embodiment of the punctuation between *American* and *born*, the narrator unsettles the idea of Filipinx Americans simply being American in the eyes of their Philippine-born kin.[51] Rather than putting the hyphen between *Filipinx* and *American*, as it often appears, Galang places it within America.[52] I read this as her complicating America as a homogeneous abstraction and pointing to the particularly of her Filipina Midwestern sensibility. Moreover, as someone who lives in the geographic middle of the United States, the narrator figures as an outlier to her White Midwestern peers, her Filipinx kin who did not grow up in the United States, and her U.S. diasporic Filipinx co-ethnics who live in urban coastal places with a considerable density of Filipinxs. And while the essay ends in a lament—"And somehow, when you stand in the center of a room, and the others look on, you find yourself acting out your role. Smart American girl, beautiful Filipina, dutiful daughter"—I want us to reconsider what it means to "stand in the center," to look at and from the middle, to reimagine the dynamics of diaspora (86).

"Mix Like Stir Fry" is the third and final short essay that uses second-person narration. It also is the last story in Galang's collection. As a bookend, it interpellates the reader, similar to "The Look-Alike Women"; however, it does so by narrating a regionalized account of racial-gender nonbelonging. While the opening places the narrator-reader "on the very edge of the east coast of the United States of America," it quickly turns to "many places," describing experiences of growing up with American fast food and American Chinese food familiar to children of immigrants (181). Such a rhetorical move works to make the author's particular experience more universal but also points to the dynamic nature of diaspora. However, Galang then grounds the narrative focus in the regional—where "your parents planted you in the heartland, among wheat and corn" (181). Here, Brookfield, Wisconsin, becomes a point of origin for diasporic Filipina/x formation. And yet, living in America's heartland transforms the narrator from being a misrecognized Asian into an "All-American" "typical teen" (182). Nevertheless, growing up in the Midwest does not make "you" any less susceptible to being perceived as a perpetual foreigner or as an exotic Asian woman (183). The regional becomes a pivot that balances the universalities and particularities of diasporic racializations, genderings, and sexualizations. Inhabiting and embodying the interstices of diaspora, the regional diasporic subject is rendered as "one of a kind. An anomaly" (183).

As a response to the question *Where are you from?* Asian Americans often get asked, Galang proclaims, "It is enough for you to know you are not white, you are not from China or Japan or even, you're not even from the Philippines, the place where your parents are from. You are from the Midwest. You are an American. You're what they call American-born-Filipina" (184). As tempting as it might be to read this as Galang's desire to claim America, to call for ethno-racial assimilation, such an interpretation dismisses the powerful revelation that the Midwest is an overlooked point of origin for Filipinx and

Asian America. Moreover, her mode of address in the second person "speaks to you, guides you, brings you to this place where you can find your wild American self, a woman who speaks out with nasal twang, drinks beer with brats and rice, and dances when no one's looking" (184). As the culmination of her collection of stories, these final lines present Galang's singular anomalous experience as a Filipina Midwesterner while engendering a reading subject with similar identificatory origins. *You* becomes a collective *we*, which rewrites the Midwest as not simply an anomalous hinterland on the way to more populous communities along the coasts but rather a constellation of alter-narratives of grit in the face of temporary isolation.

A Filipina in the Middle of Nowhere

If *HWAS* orients us toward the wild, *Edith* materializes what that alternative world might look like. Much as Galang's collection of short stories does, Pamatmat's play assumes Filipinxs in the Midwest are in place—not out of place as hegemonic American and diasporic Filipinx cultures often perceive. It also proffers same-gender romance and parentless domesticity as viable in rural Middle America. Together, these play themes present the queer Filipinx Midwest not as an anomaly but rather as an important but underexamined sociocultural-spatial formation in queer diasporic and Asian American studies.

Inspired by the playwright's queer Filipino coming of age "on a non-working farm outside of Port Huron [Michigan],"[53] the play centers on the queer affective kinship that an unconventional twelve-year-old Filipina American, Edith Tolentino; her sixteen-year-old brother, Kenny; and her brother's sixteen-year-old non-Filipino friend/lover, Benji, form in the absence of parental supervision on "a remote non-working farm outside of a remote town in remotest Middle America" during "the early [1990s]" (6).[54] Staging queer Filipinx Midwestern domesticity as viable, the play challenges the idea of queerness as both unproductive and un-*re*productive and positions the Midwest as a fecund site not only for queer desire but also for rethinking Asian American identity and national belonging.[55]

The play's protagonist, Edith, or Ed or Eddie, as Kenny affectionately calls her, is a precocious adolescent tomboy who refuses the scripts of normative femininity. However, as she is a resident of rural Middle America, her gender expression is consonant with her geography.[56] Wielding a BB gun, sitting up in barn rafters, donning overall shorts over frilly dresses, Ed is a literary successor to Cather's Ántonia Shimerda, a Bohemian immigrant who also goes by a masculine abbreviated name: Tony. This tween protagonist is a straight shooter, so to speak; sure, she wields a BB gun and a toy bow and arrow to protect her kin and property from outsiders (appropriating weapons of the Wild West), but more importantly, she is direct and honest. She says what

Kenny and adults in general are afraid to say. In her opening monologue, she speaks to her stuffed-animal frog, Fergie: "I am very mature for my age.... I look twelve, but I'm really much, much older.... The truth is true. Our kind mature at a different speed than stupid, little human girls. On my planet, I'm a full-grown grown up, and I have my own apartment where I live without my twenty parents. Who needs them?" (7). Her fantasy escapist mentality might align with Baum's land of Oz; however, much like Dorothy, who desires to return home to Kansas, Ed is a realist.

As the play unfolds, Ed becomes the sound of reason, refusing to follow decorum in favor of what is right. A major source of conflict occurs between her and Kenny, who desires to follow the rules and be the responsible older brother and dutiful son in the absence of parental supervision. After Ed accidentally shoots her future stepmother, Chloë, in the shoulder with a BB gun, mistaking her for Benji's homophobic mother (end of act 1), her absentee father resolves to send her to Catholic reform school—a motif also present in Galang's stories. And, like Galang's stories do, the play indexes the oppressiveness of parental power over children.[57] The very reason why Ed accidentally shoots Chloë stems from Benji's mom kicking him out of their house after she discovers a mix tape and love letter from Kenny to Benji. The Tolentino kids' father's financial (and, in Kenny's case, emotional/psychological) dominance enjoins them to obey his whims despite his failure to appear on stage. Benji's mother allows him to return home under the condition that he has no contact with Kenny, thereby blocking his romantic and sexual activities with his boyfriend. Whereas Ed and Benji work to resist their respective parents' disciplinary regimes, Kenny remains steadfast in following his father's orders.

Desiring to forge another reality beyond heteropatriarchal parental supervision, Ed attempts to persuade Kenny to save her from being sent away and being split apart from him (as well as from Benji) by suggesting that they run away. Kenny reasons that it is better for them to stay put than escape their father's clutches. Ed pleads, "Let's get out of here. We'll get in the car, but we'll do it right this time. We'll drive and drive and drive until we never have to see him again" (61). In response, Kenny recounts the lesson from a parable their mother once shared about a turtle and a monkey: "Because he's a slow turtle, too little to break free. But he's clever and patient, so he just waits for the monkey to set him free" (62). Ed is unconvinced by such a passive act that defers to the future and threatens, "If you don't do something, I will" (63). Kenny responds, "No. The things you do have consequences," clearly referring to her accidental shooting. Ed replies, "The things you don't do have consequences, too" (63). Here, Ed calls out inaction and maintaining the status quo, which can result in the disciplining of the feminized and queered body.

Even though the pull of heteronormative time may preclude Kenny from initially embracing the potentiality of their queer refusal to adult supervision—he reminds Ed, "we're kids. We're just kids!" while they are on the run after her accidental shooting—other ways of living and loving prevail (60). In a pivotal scene, Kenny stands up to his father and asserts (over the phone), "I took what you left us and made a home. Our home. . . . You left us wild and free. You can't cage us now" (76). Prior to this scene, Benji jokingly offers Kenny some words of encouragement: "You take it up the butt, remember? You can do anything" (74). Here, feminized queerness is not an abject subject position; it serves as a source of empowerment.[58] Although Kenny stands up to his father, his general demeanor may appear as regressive, the opposite of Ed. However, as Ponce's concept of "Pinoy posteriority" proffers, the Filipino bottom simultaneously illumines an alternate way of being apart from the disciplinary and normative progressive mandate to decolonize and reflects anxieties of diasporic and neocolonial investments in White supremacy and Euro-American imperialisms.[59] Certainly, Kenny's act of defiance aligns with progressive politics, but his desire to maintain the status quo—in this case, unsupervised youth domesticity—is both normative and queer. That is, his investments are not about changing the world but about maintaining the queer world he has inadvertently built with Ed and Benji away from adults and urbanity. That Kenny retreats from the pull of heteropatriarchal power through Ed's wildness and Benji's unapologetic queerness—both of which embrace the feminine—clears the way for a queer diasporic Filipinx Midwestern futurity in the present, which takes the form of the trio's queer, adolescent domesticity that has already come into being. In short, *Edith* illustrates that a queer diasporic Filipinx Midwest already exists if we allow ourselves to refuse the normative scripts that restrict our ways of being, knowing, seeing, feeling, and inhabiting.

The Fecundity of Queer Filipinx Midwestern Domesticity

The play's setting in Middle America deemphasizes its geographic particularity on one hand, as the regional and socioeconomic middle of the United States often is interpellated as the so-called real America, further propelling this story as generic. On the other hand, its rural backdrop is all the more significant considering its featuring of nondominant racial and sexual subjectivities.[60] The play is remarkable in its rendering of Filipinxs and queerness in the Midwest as *not* out of place. Such a utopian vision seems unreal when accounting for the material reality that normalizes the geographies of queerness, Asian America, and the Midwest as incommensurate, in contradistinction to the play. As a creative endeavor, however, the play produces—but also gestures toward—a future that is viable and certainly real in the present.[61]

The play's portrayal of queer Filipinx Midwestern domesticity as remarkable is not so much a denial of the heartland's Whiteness and straightness as it is a provocation to imagine otherwise in the future present. Certainly, in the heterosexist and racist society in which we (and they) live, Kenny and Benji's budding interracial romance figures as queer, not the norm; however, the play's round portrayal of young, queer love presents a queer orientation as a possible way of life. Instead of the characters' identities serving as a basis for their sociocultural difference, their nonnuclear familial formations do. Concerned about an upcoming recital, Ed proclaims to Kenny, "Everyone will have a mom and a dad. So I'll have you and a Benji. It'll be more fun" (36). The parents' absence at Ed's recital underscores that the siblings survive on their own. As latchkey kids, Ed and Kenny find alternative ways to manage without parental supervision—from cooking, to cleaning, to loving. Interestingly, for Ed, Kenny and Benji figure as the equivalent of her recital peers' moms and dads. In Ed's cosmology, a family composed of Kenny, Benji, Fergie, and her proves sufficient.

The play's staging of racial-sexual nonnormativity in the context of Middle America seamlessly weaves these aspects of identity into the plot, making Filipinxness and queerness in the Midwest more mundane and imaginable. For example, while Benji initially calls attention to Kenny's Filipinx difference—stating, "You're Filipino, and you live in the boondocks"—Filipinxness figures less through direct articulation and more through cultural references embedded in Ed and Kenny's quotidian routines (37), such as having fried rice for breakfast (52), mongo and spaghetti with ketchup for lunch (45), and chicken afritada for dinner (86).[62] Still, Benji's attempt to place his lover's ethnic identity alongside U.S. rurality smooths over the seeming disjuncture between queerness, Filipinxness, and the Midwest. As Benji notes, *boondocks* comes from the Filipino/Tagalog word *bundok* (mountain) and refers to remote, sparsely populated areas. Benji's declaration that Kenny "live[s] in the boondocks" appropriately blurs the boundaries between an imagined Philippine elsewhere and a derided Midwestern nowhere, revealing the translocal intimacies between the two geographies stitched together via U.S. imperial expansion.

While the Tolentino kids' financial dependence on their father makes possible Kenny's homemaking (as their father regularly transfers money into a bank account so they can maintain the house and put food on the table), capital is not what makes the Tolentino farm a diasporic queer interracial rural home; rather, the affective bonds among Eddie, Kenny, and Benji engender this domestic space. More specifically, Ed does not subscribe to the "it gets better" mantra of queer futurity popularized by journalist Dan Savage in the 2010s, and it is her persistence in the present that enables the three youths to live in a peminist and queer space-time. As Lee Edelman cautions, "the future is mere repetition and just as lethal as the past."[63] Whereas Kenny initially waits for the future, Ed knows the future will be no different from the past—that both she and Kenny will remain stuck under the patriarchal authority of their absent father; thus, she desires to act in the here and now.

Whereas Edelman favors the present over futurity given the latter's investment in the figure of the Child, which heteronormativity bolsters and against whom the queer subject has been set up, my investment in the fictional children in *Edith* revises the relationship between queerness, temporality, and the Child. That the play features racialized youth and same-gender interracial adolescent romance and sex suggests Eddie, Kenny, and Benji are not the idealized children hetero-repro-normativity desires. As Muñoz cogently highlights in response to Edelman's polemic, "all children are not the privileged white babies to whom contemporary society caters."[64] In fact, "the future is only the stuff of *some* [emphasis added] kids. Racialized kids, queer kids, are not the sovereign princes of futurity."[65] Muñoz's observations reveal how some bodies are marked for life, while others are marked for death, and that race and sexuality are key vectors that influence such a bio-necropolitical outcome.

Edelman sees the future as thoroughly captured by hetero-repro-normativity, but Muñoz revises the province of the future as open to more than one trajectory. When he writes, "Straight time tells us that there is no future but the here and now of our everyday life," Muñoz is referring to a future where queers continue to be consigned to abject status.[66] Thus, in proffering queer futurity, he gestures toward an alternative way of living and being that has yet to materialize wherein hetero-repro-normativity no longer is the order of the day. In the case of Pamatmat's play, however, the future is some time and place yet to be determined and already in motion in the present. That is, the play provides clues to another world in the future present where "racialized kids, queer kids" can be and already are.

The play's plot conflict illustrates the different realities the Tolentino siblings inhabit by contrasting them with Benji's. Act 2 begins with Ed, Kenny, and Benji trying to enjoy a cup of ice cream after being on the run for two days following Ed's shooting of Chloë. Whereas Ed seems unfazed by her action, rationalizing it as defense against a threat to her chosen family, and Benji attempts to lighten the mood by making puns about nuts, reflecting his preoccupation with sex, Kenny begins to realize the futility of their impromptu escape. To comfort Kenny, Benji points out all the things the Tolentino siblings can do: Ed knows how to use a gun, and Kenny knows how to plan "what groceries to get so [he] can make dinner and lunch and all the food for the week" (58). He "take[s] Ed to school and extra-curriculars" and still earns good grades (58). Benji adds, "You and Edith. You're all alone in that house and sometimes it's creepy and sometimes you're running out of money, but you can take care of yourselves. I would just be helpless. Or scared" (58). Unlike Benji, whose mother takes care of him, Kenny has had to grow up and take on responsibilities typically reserved for adults. Such domestic labor is not only gendered but also racialized and classed. Although the play does not focus on the specifics of the adults, Benji's parents are present in their home, while the Tolentino patriarch's work in health care keeps him away from the farm. The Tolentinos' familial setup, however, is not uncommon among global Filipinxs.[67]

This scene lays a foundation for the play's climax. Ed instills in Benji the idea of queer kinship when she says that Benji's mom is "sitting at home right now with no idea whether you're eating, whether there's a roof over your head, whether you're even alive. You think someone capable of that could never shoot you, just because she gave birth to you?" (56). Ed's rhetorical question evokes the image of families who disown their children once they come out as LGBTQ+. Her sentiment also deprivileges biological family in favor of chosen families. In turn, Benji helps Kenny overcome his internalized homophobia as well as his desire for order by challenging him to hold hands in public, albeit under a table. When Benji says, "Be scared," inviting Kenny to let go of his will to control things, Kenny acquiesces (59). Benji promises, "And then we'll figure out what to do. And I'll help, I can help. You won't have to do it by yourself" (59). The play notes indicate that "Benji squeezes his [Kenny's] hand, and after a moment the fear starts to fade" (59). At the end of the scene, "Kenny takes Edith's hand. Edith reaches out to Benji, who takes her other hand" (60). The Tolentino patriarch finds them at the ice cream parlor, but the trio's linked hands show that a new familial bond has developed. Ed's proto-peminism and Benji and Kenny's courage to embrace queerness set them on a path for a more livable life.

The Wild Roots and Routes of Peminist-Queer Midwestern Space-Time

Rurality and the Midwest are often seen as backward or frozen in time.[68] And Galang and Pamatmat's 1990s aesthetic and settings may appear as anachronistic to contemporary Filipinx cultural critique, which tends to focus on the macro and the global. Yet, as Ahmed points out, framing something as passé functions to distract from the status quo.[69] That is, while a progressive understanding of time might suggest only recent events are of import and that the past is that which has been resolved, a f/peminist and queer notion of time reveals otherwise. Hence, (re)turning to Galang's 1990s publication and Pamatmat's production set in the 1990s opens the enduring force of sexism and homophobia in a postimperial context. In fact, Carbó hails Galang as "the first U.S. born [sic] Filipina writer to publish a book with a Filipino American perspective"; an accolade like this should prompt us to give attention to such a cultural producer.[70] While the burden of representation and "firsts" unevenly falls to writers of color and is further delineated by gender and sexuality (and thus should not be the primary reason an author is worthy of study), recognizing the impact such writers can have on an audience whose lives typically are not the center of narratives is critical in assembling an alter-archive.

While Galang's stories may rehearse the immigrant generational conflict reflected in early Asian American literatures and now viewed as trite, they nevertheless present a vantage atypical in such a body of work: the Midwest regional. They perform important cultural work in documenting the experiences of Filipinxs in the interior metropole.[71] In her reading of Galang's "Miss Teenage Sampaguita," one of the stories in *HWAS*, Marie-Therese C. Sulit concludes that the literary can function as an allegorical space for working through national and transnational traumas.[72] However, as I argue in this chapter, the regional is more appropriate in reading Galang's work. While Galang's regional perspective revises our understanding of diaspora as not simply national in scale and scope, unfortunately, its dyadic counterpart, the homeland, remains largely intact. In Galang's stories, the Philippines is more of a phantom, an abstract geography "over there," than it is an actual place that registers for the protagonists; though in facing away from the homeland, these girls and women also face away from normative scripts bolstered by the nation.

Ultimately, Galang's short stories and Pamatmat's play present an alternative space-time to hegemonic Filipinx diaspora that shifts the discursive periphery to the center. In both texts, diasporic Filipinx Midwesterners are the protagonists; their stories matter. More specifically, Filipin*a* Midwestern girls and women lead the way in narrating a different account of diaspora, nation, empire, and region. They guide us to recognize possible desires and to revel in queerness, in the wild, interstitial excesses of empire, nation, and diaspora.[73] The regional becomes a scale that enables alternative roots and routes for home and belonging.

Peminist-queer diasporic Filipinx Midwestern domesticity links Galang's stories and Pamatmat's play, but these works' interpellative modes of address through form enables them to be intertextual and intersubjective. In the case of the play, the live performance of actors and the ephemeral community of the theater audience creates a sense of intimacy and identification between individual audience members and actors and among audiences and actors.[74] Similarly, Galang's use of second-person narration brings readers into the story, making them part of the action. Both texts render their audiences as active, encouraging identification; they also move audiences to act. Here, action begins with a different mindset, one in which the Midwest, from its urban centers to its rural hinterlands, becomes a plausible point of origin for Asian America, queerness, and U.S. empire. Transforming minds can transform discourse, and discourse, as we know, has the power to shape knowledge, policy, and cultural practices.

Whereas queer Filipinx Midwesterners appear in the pages of Santos and Galang's fiction, they materialize as three-dimensional plausibilities in Pamatmat's stage production. Live performance makes palpable the affective and embodied particularities of racial-sexual regionality. The next chapter's turn to television, with its presentation of recorded live performance, further illustrates the power of peopling the Midwest with queer Filipinxs.

5

"See[ing] the World Not as It Is, but as It *Should* Be"

Queer Filipinx Midwesterners and Postracial-Postimperial Televisuality

The final shot of Fox's hit high school dramedy *Glee* (2009–2015) begins with a close-up of a plaque inscription marking the renaming of the William McKinley High School auditorium in honor of deceased New Directions glee club cocaptain Finn Hudson (played by White Canadian actor Cory Monteith): "See the world not as it is, but as it *should* [original emphasis] be" (season 6, episode 13, "Dreams Come True").[1] This sentiment not only summarizes what the prime-time television show was able to accomplish during its six-season run, with its campy celebration of the musical format, diverse casting, and engagement with multiculturalism; it also invites viewers to imagine other possibilities and plausibilities that exceed the proper scripts of the show. While the series is notable for not shying away from identity and difference, featuring episodes and narrative arcs that focus on characters' struggles with race, ethnicity, class, gender, sexuality, and ability, it is in no way comprehensive, nor can it be. It is in such moments of failure and rupture that I find glee.

Glee's musical dramedy format certainly makes it an enjoyable show to watch, as its immense following across the globe from all age groups attests. However, the glee I find on the show also emerges from minor moments of uncanny imperial (dis)avowal that escape most viewers' awareness. That the show takes place in a fictionalized Lima, Ohio, at a high school named after one of the state's sons, President McKinley, infamous for authorizing the colonization of the Philippines in 1898, following the Spanish–American War, lays bare the Midwest as a critical nodal point in the circuits of U.S. empire in the Philippines. That its Filipinx characters—Howard Bamboo, Sunshine Corazon, Blaine Anderson, and Frida Romero—are abstracted from this local-global imperial history is all the more telling of the imperial amnesia that pervades its contemporary, supposedly postracial context.

NBC's workplace sitcom *Superstore* (2015–2021) is another television show that allegorically conjures the specters of the Midwest's entanglement with U.S. empire in the Philippines. Returning to the primal scene of Filipinx subjugation in the United States—St. Louis, Missouri—the show takes place in a big-box store in contemporary suburban St. Louis. Like *Glee*, *Superstore* features a multicultural ensemble cast and episodes that engage contemporary U.S. political issues tied to race, ethnicity, class, gender, sexuality, and ability and often uses camp to defuse tension. And like the Filipinx characters on *Glee*, its primary Filipinx character, Mateo Fernando Aquino Liwanag, is abstracted from U.S. empire in the Philippines. In fact, Mateo's citizenship status figures as one of his narrative arcs, positioning him less as an imperial subject and more as a precarious migrant, which aligns with the show's contemporary setting. Nevertheless, the history of St. Louis and Filipinxs addressed in chapter 1 provides the necessary context for interpreting a character like Mateo in the present day. The Midwest is a palimpsest of U.S. empire in the Philippines, and the Filipinx apparitions on twenty-first-century television shows such as *Glee* and *Superstore* use indirection and relationality to reveal these veiled traces. A queer decolonial Filipinx Midwestern eye and ear enable us to see and hear these oblique references to envision alternative archipelagic landscapes and soundscapes that affirm queer Filipinx Midwestern being.[2]

If the Filipinx characters on *Glee* and *Superstore* engender surprise, either because of their location in Middle America or because Filipinxs, and Asians more broadly, are underrepresented on mainstream U.S. television (and film), such a sentiment should be interrogated. The appearance of Filipinxs on a prime-time U.S. television show set in the Midwest is uncanny because it bolsters Hollywood's multicultural trend yet (re)opens the wound of U.S. empire. Although not the norm by any means, Filipinx characters played by Filipinx actors have garnered presence on U.S.-based television shows since at least the turn of the twenty-first century.[3] While perhaps coincidental, the confluence of Ohio and McKinley on *Glee* and St. Louis on *Superstore* with modern-day Filipinx performing bodies illustrates the durability of empire, even in a supposed postimperial moment. Whereas both shows expectedly refrain from tying Filipinxs to U.S. empire in the Philippines, I approach these contemporary popular cultural archival flashes,[4] following Balce's early twenty-first-century treatment of fin de siècle American popular culture, via anamnesia, or the act of remembering by analyzing the cultures of empire.[5]

Heeding the directive to "see the world not as it is, but as it *should* be," this chapter reads the oblique appearance of the queer Filipinx Midwest on *Glee* and *Superstore*, as manifested through Filipinx characters and the actors who portray them, to frustrate U.S. imperial amnesia as well as U.S. diasporic Filipinx abjections of the Midwest. To see the world as it should be is to recognize the palimpsestic nature of Filipinx presence in the United States on local, regional, national, and global scales; it is to acknowledge the complexity of Filipinx identity and experience. This chapter reckons with the unexpectedness of seeing queer(ed) Filipinx characters in a Midwest setting to account for the workings of what I am calling postimperiality, a form of imperial amnesia that coincides with postracialism. This reckoning also further challenges the implausibility that coastal Filipinxs ascribe to the interior United States. As characters like Howard, Sunshine, Blaine, Frida, and Mateo intimate, inhabiting sites of subjection forces an engagement with the regional (settler) colonial past and inspires alternative performances that exceed the dominant scripts for racial-colonial-diasporic being that emanate from both the colonial metropole and the diasporic center.[6]

Televising the Heartland

The Midwest and Middle America tend to be synonymous. Thus, television shows that aspire to represent the average American family—imagined to be White, middle class, able-bodied, heterosexual, and procreative—are often set in the region.[7] Although shows like ABC's *Modern Family* (2009–2020), *Black-ish* (2014–2022), and *Fresh Off the Boat* (2015–2020) challenge normative ideas that constitute the so-called ideal average American family by featuring multigenerational families, blended families, gay families, and families of color as American families, their coastal suburban settings (Los Angeles for the first two shows and Orlando for the latter) inadvertently maintain the Whiteness of the Midwest.[8] While *Glee* and *Superstore* are not American family sitcoms, their characters' private lives spill into public spaces, thereby unsettling what average American families look like.[9] And instead of focusing on one family unit, these shows feature multiple families who inhabit the same space, thereby depicting a more realistic representation of Middle America. Granted, racial and class segregation exist across the country, and people of different races and classes often collide; so, screening such collisions means acknowledging what the country is really like. Such an acknowledgment is less about casting these two shows as authentically representative of the Midwest and America more broadly—far from it, given the musical format of the former and the black comedy of the latter. Instead, these two shows stage the complex intimacies and relationalities that define the Midwest but are often whitewashed and conveniently ignored.[10]

Notwithstanding *Glee* and *Superstore*'s Hollywood production, their respective fictionalized settings in Lima, Ohio, and St. Louis, Missouri, paradoxically work to emphasize their representativeness of Middle America and dramatize their celebrations of social and cultural diversity.[11] The former mode reflects Victoria Johnson's observations of U.S. prime-time television, wherein executives and producers summon the averageness of the Midwest to appeal to a broad national market.[12] For Johnson, the heartland myth particularly is evoked "in times of cultural transition or perceived cultural threat or tension," as it "provides a short-hand cultural common sense framework for 'all-American' identification, redeeming goodness, face-to-face community, sanctity, and emplaced ideals to which a desirous and nostalgic public discourse repeatedly returns."[13] In other words, while contemporary television programs may offer a range of diverse perspectives in terms of form and content, the Midwest continues to function as an anchor point for portraying, in Benedict Anderson's words, an "imagined community" of the U.S. nation.

In the wake of the 2008 global financial crisis, *Glee*'s emphasis on Midwesternness appealed to "Main Street" rather than "Wall Street."[14] For example, the pilot's close-up of McKinley High's soon-to-be glee club director Will Schuester's (played by White American actor Matthew Morrison) Ohio license plate during the second scene works to frame the series as Midwestern and thus representative of the so-called average American high school (and appealing to the so-called average American household). The immediate effects of the Great Recession appear in the second episode ("Showmance"): Will mentions to his wife, Terri, (played by Jewish Canadian actor Jessalyn Gilsig) the availability of foreclosed homes on their street as they look into buying their first home, and Principal Figgins (played by Pakistani American actor Iqbal Theba) refers to the number of janitors he has had to fire as a result of the school's reduced budget.

Season 2's (2010–2011) introduction of the blond-haired, blue-eyed Sam Evans (played by White American actor Chord Overstreet) and his family's financial hardships captures the struggles many Americans had to endure in an austere economic climate.[15] Burt Hummel's (played by White American actor Mike O'Malley) congressional campaign during season 3 (2011–2012) emphasizes his blue-collar values as a local tire shop owner who takes a voluntary pay cut to avoid firing his employees (episode 6, "Mash Off"). Accordingly, the show's Ohio setting centrally informs its revised version of Midwestern populist values characteristic of the region during the early twentieth century.[16] That is, while the show may seem atypical of the discursive Midwest—in its unabashed display of queer sexuality, people of color, transgender identities, and various disabilities—such a move in the context of the 2010s postracial, liberal multiculturalist United States actually reflects a "new normal" based on diversity and inclusion and thus positions the Midwest as once again representative of the nation's core ideals.[17]

If progressivism is one of the legacies of turn-of-the-twentieth-century Midwestern politics and values (though not without its shortcomings, as discussed in chapter 2), then *Glee* celebrates that legacy through its emphasis on inclusion in terms of race, gender, sexuality, and ability. The series' particular emphasis on anti-bullying makes clear that LGBTQ+ inclusion figures as one of its signature agendas.[18] And in the final season (2015), the epitome of inclusion results in a double queer (and interracial) wedding: Brittana (Brittany S. Pierce, played by White American actor and dancer Heather Morris, and Santana Lopez, played by multiracial Afro–Puerto Rican American actor Naya Rivera) and Klaine (Kurt Hummel, played by White American actor and author Chris Colfer, and Blaine Anderson, played by multiracial Filipinx actor and singer-songwriter Darren Criss). In "A Wedding" (season 6, episode 8), Santana and Brittany wed in the Indiana barn where Brittany was birthed because same-gender marriage at the time was not legal in Ohio but was in neighboring Indiana.[19] Blaine and Kurt wed in a surprise plot twist at the behest of Brittany. Coach Sue Sylvester (played by White American actor and comedian Jane Lynch), the show's sometimes villain, also chimes in that their wedding would give Gleeks (show fans) what they want. The wedding ceremonies of these couples are touching and empowering, especially for queer youth (of color), whose futures are not always certain, and they also challenge negative attitudes toward the Midwest and rurality.

However, progressivism ultimately is about narrow, linear progress. While the legalization of same-gender marriage is important, it should not be the (only) marker that equality has been achieved as activists, critics, and scholars have asserted.[20] At the same time that marriage equality was making its way through various legislative systems in the Midwest and the nation as a whole, the epidemic of Black deaths at the hands of the state gained national attention in the form of the Black Lives Matter movement.[21] Michael Brown's murder in August 2014 in Ferguson, Missouri, a suburb of St. Louis, in particular galvanized social protest of police brutality against Black bodies. George Floyd's murder by a White Minneapolis officer in May 2020 reignited social protest across the region, nation, and globe in major cities and notably in small towns. The Ferguson and Minneapolis uprisings provide stark reminders that the Midwest is a battleground of racial inequity and structural violence.[22] They also remind us that people of color do exist in the region. This is obvious yet often needs to be explicitly stated given the powerful discursive imaginaries of the region that paint it as bucolic and White.[23]

Like *Glee*, *Superstore* presents an atypical representation of the heartland with its inclusive casting and characterizations. Its main characters include a daughter of Honduran immigrants (Amy Dubanowski/Sosa, played by Honduran-Lencan American actor America Ferrera), a gay Filipino man who is undocumented (Mateo Fernando Aquino Liwanag, played by Filipinx American actor Nico Santos), a Black man with Norwegian and Swedish heritage who uses a wheelchair (Garrett McNeil, played by multiracial Black American actor Colton Dunn), a Native Hawaiian woman (Sandra Kaluiokalani, played by Native Hawaiian American actor Kaliko Kauahi), a multiracial Asian American woman who is a teen mom (Cheyenne Lee/Thompson, played by multiracial Japanese American actor Nichole Sakura), and a Jewish man (Jonah Simms, played by Jewish American actor Ben Feldman). Throughout the series, employees also interact with ethno-racially diverse customers. The show is notable for its direct address of racial and gender inequity, with characters unapologetically calling out White supremacy and unconscious bias. A White character (Bo Derek Thompson, Cheyenne's boyfriend/husband, played by White American actor Johnny Pemberton) aspiring to be a rapper ends his flash mob performance with a shout-out to #BlackLivesMatter near the end of the pilot, immediately establishing the show's willingness to engage contemporary social issues.

At the same time, *Superstore* also is like *Glee* in using its Midwestern setting to establish a heartland aesthetic. The pilot opens with a sunny morning high-angle crane shot of the Cloud 9 storefront and parking lot with a voice-over by Garrett, the store's public-address system announcer: "The American superstore. One-stop shopping for everything you could ever want or need." As he narrates, the camera cuts to different interior shots of the store, from checkout lanes with blue-vested employees to quirky customers from disparate social groups. The tone is both uplifting and depressing, as anyone who has ever shopped or worked at a big-box store knows. Evocative of Walmart, Cloud 9 gives viewers a look into the workings of Middle America. While the show focuses on working-class employees who do not earn a living wage, it also features cutaways to customers performing odd yet humorous acts, from a woman in athletic attire running on a raised treadmill to a man in his underwear using a display washing machine. Although unflattering, such portrayals seem honest, albeit exaggerated.

Shortly after Garrett's voice-over, Dina, the store's assistant manager (played by White Canadian actor Lauren Ash), instructs the staff to limit the sales of "garden variety generic decongestant," as it can be used to make crystal meth. This serves as an acknowledgment of the meth epidemic plaguing the region.[24] The pilot opens with "American" rather than "Midwestern" set props, but a sign in the break room marks the location as St. Louis, serving to subtly orient viewers. The conflation of American and Midwestern reinforces Johnson's observations regarding television shows using a Midwest setting to represent average America.

Whereas *Glee* evokes the Midwest through naming, as characters reference their location in Lima, *Superstore* integrates place in its episode plots. As I pointed out in chapter 3, weather is a distinctive feature of the heartland, and *Superstore* reinforces this association with a tornado destroying the store at the end of season 2 (episode 22, "Tornado") and a blizzard forcing employees and customers to camp out in the store during season 4 (episode 12, "Blizzard"). Less benign remarks also appear, linking the show's fictional Ozark Highlands store to rurality, even though the store is in suburban St. Louis, with the skyline visible from the rooftop. For example, a shoplifter snidely refers to the employees as "back country idiots" (season 1, episode 5, "Shoplifter"). When Mateo is about to transfer to a Cloud 9 Signature Store, he makes a tribute video of himself, which includes a self-interview: "What am I gonna miss the most [about the store]? Uh, the people? They're salt of the Earth. Simple, basic. Just sort of harmless" (season 2, episode 18, "Mateo's Last Day"). Mateo's attitude positions him as cosmopolitan and in contrast to the rural, which is ironic, since he, too, is of the store. Such moments reveal the ambivalence toward the Midwest—at once wholesome and abject. Rather than disavow the heartland's abject status, the show uses it to critique an array of intersecting sociocultural inequities perpetrated by the collusion of the nation-state and corporate entities.

Queer Filipinx Visuality in the Context of Postracialism and Postimperiality

Glee and *Superstore* are complementary television programs that help us to unpack the racial and colonial legacies of the U.S. nation through a regional frame. *Glee*'s on-air run coincided with Obama's presidency and *Superstore*'s coincided with Trump's first term, enabling us to witness the false reality of postracialism and postimperiality and the mercurial nature of social justice in the face of White supremacy but also the power of media to instill hope in creativity. While both shows cater to a popular audience as prime-time network television productions, they also reach niche audiences through streaming and online fandoms. As media studies scholars point out, meaning is co-constructed through audience reception.[25] Hence, even if both shows are not directed at the queer Filipinx Midwest, my sensitivity allows for such an interpretive scheme to materialize nevertheless. Whereas *Glee* appears to capitalize on the aura of postracialism in the wake of the nation electing its first biracial Black president and *Superstore* traffics similar sentiments about racial equality through a multiracial ensemble cast and the stories it tells, the latter's context post-Ferguson and amid the Trump administration's racist, sexist, homophobic, transphobic, anti-immigrant, anti-science, isolationist politics pulls the curtain of postracialism.[26]

As critics of postracial discourses have illumined, the celebration of multiculturalism in media reflects but also shapes early twenty-first century discourses of race, revealing "race and its intersectional orders of difference have neither moved off nor been replaced so much as they now emerge rearticulated into new forms."[27] Ralina Joseph argues that the presence of the term *race* in *postrace* "highlights the continued centrality of race in this ideology" and betrays the ideology's supposed departure from race.[28] She explains that *post* rhetorics essentially are attempts to mask power.[29] The postracial era marks new forms of racialized visibility, especially beyond the Black-White racial paradigm, that suggest the problem of race has been solved yet enables White supremacy and systemic racism to remain invisible. As Roderick Ferguson observes, the postracial marks a shift in the state and capital's "suspicion of difference and particularity toward a qualified retooling of those elements," resulting in the incorporation and thus domestication of minority difference in the service of the state and capital.[30] Hence, while diverse casting and storytelling in early twenty-first-century television may seem progressive, they do not necessarily signal a structural commitment to antiracism and decolonization. Moreover, as Catherine Squires rightly points out, the re-entrenchment of racism, sexism, and other systems of inequity in our contemporary moment—a moment when we are supposed to be over past injustices, according to postrace rhetoric—should serve as a caution against the false hope/relief that postracialism ushers.[31]

As popular cultural texts, *Glee* and *Superstore* bolster postracial sentiment as they forward palatable diversity; yet, they obliquely present echoes, fractures, and fissures that give rise to contradiction, enjoining viewers to disidentify and recognize the minor histories and realities embedded in dominant culture. In *Racism Postrace*, Roopali Mukherjee, Sarah Banet-Wiser, and Herman Gray note that "media representations and discourses . . . have helped to consolidate the operations of postracial power and naturalize the aesthetic and analytic gaze it engenders"—emphasizing the importance of culture in tracing postracialism.[32] Although popular culture may be "the arena in which we imagine ourselves," which, for Joseph, often yields sanitized representations of identity and difference,[33] Kent Ono argues that "by taking into account strategies for forgetting racism that work in complicated and often perhaps unconscious ways . . . it is possible to disrupt and challenge postracism."[34] Ono also connects postracialism to colonial and neocolonial preoccupations with representation and racial surveillance.[35] Thus, my queer diasporic Filipinx Midwestern reading of popular cultural texts like *Glee* and

Superstore in the context of postracialism and postimperiality demonstrates how U.S. empire in the Philippines at the turn of the twentieth century and Filipinx Midwestern misrecognition at the turn of the twenty-first century are linked phenomena.

My focus on Filipinx characters and actors on *Glee* and *Superstore*, as it intersects with both programs' geographic setting, necessitates an engagement with empire; therefore, I use postimperiality as a critical frame that nuances U.S. notions of race and postrace. Ohio and Missouri as we know them today (from a U.S. perspective) are the ancestral lands of various Native nations as well as the homes of contemporary Native peoples who have returned and/or have been displaced. Ohio and Missouri also are states that came into being because of U.S. imperial desires—the former through the Northwest Ordinance of 1787; the latter through the Louisiana Purchase of 1803. And, as I discuss in chapter 1, St. Louis for the Philippines and Filipinx America is a referent for U.S. empire; that the 1904 St. Louis Fair featured an Indian Reservation adjacent to the Philippine Reservation weaves together continental and transpacific empire building, illustrating the intimacies of racialized violence.

Like postracialism, postimperiality names a desire to disavow the United States' continuing imperial reach across the globe and history of conquest as imperial in the first place. It also works to conjure the afterlives of U.S. empire. In reading *Glee* and *Superstore* as instances of postracial postimperiality, I make sense of Filipinx remarkable unremarkability and unremarkable remarkability. On one hand, Filipinx characters on both shows may not stand out among other characters of color; however, given the general paucity of Filipinx characters on U.S. television, they stand out all the more, especially from the perspective of Filipinx viewers.[36] While migration may explain their contemporary presence, considering the landmark 1965 Immigration Act reopened the United States to Asian immigration, the legacy of U.S. empire in the Philippines nevertheless influences such geographic movement. In not addressing this history, both shows train viewers not to see empire and suggest the nation has moved on from its imperial past. Naming these shows as postimperial also redirects us toward oblique moments that unwittingly lay bare the nation's ongoing wrestling with race and empire as being intrinsic to its ontology.

If anything, postracialism and postimperiality are provocations to remain vigilant against sanitized narratives that suggest that parity among various sociocultural formations has been achieved or that the past is in the past. As postcolonial scholars have argued, the past permanently haunts the present.[37] Contemporary television presents a unique opportunity to engage postimperiality because it is an audiovisual medium that reaches a mass audience. While the aesthetic in general makes possible the recognition of submerged histories and realities subordinate to colonial modernity,[38] popular culture, as a form of colonial culture, both encompasses the colonial repressed and enables the colonized to access and rework dominant culture.[39]

Balce's work on turn-of-the-twentieth-century U.S. visual and print cultures draws our attention to the "subtle or implied" forms of U.S. imperial abjection toward the Filipinx body to illustrate how colonial violence became rationalized and taken for granted by the mainly White American public.[40] Acknowledging the Filipinx body as a haunting clarifies the uncanny and often unintelligible Filipinx presence in our contemporary moment. Balce focuses on the visual and popular for their emergence as modern technologies that coincided with the United States' expansion to Asia-Pacific.[41] As quotidian objects, they also mask the violence of cultural imperialism. However, by looking awry,[42] we can recognize abject Filipinx bodies in the U.S. popular archive as "icons and indices of the U.S. nation's institutionalized acts of forgetting, repressing, and revising the violent occupation of its first colony in Asia."[43] In this way, Filipinxs on contemporary prime-time television shows like *Glee* and *Superstore* are not simply complementary pieces in the multicultural mosaic of the nation; instead, they are allegorical remainders and reminders of the Asia-Pacific empire that the American public desires to forget. As hauntings, they are simultaneously alluring in their uncanny presence and threatening in their capacity to unravel the myth of American exceptionalism.

Visuality is important here, as empire has used the visual to surveil its subjects. Moreover, racial formation has hinged on phenotypic variance, utilizing the visual field to falsely determine human difference. Hence, the visually embodied presence of Filipinx characters who stand out of place forces the American public to confront their denial of racism and empire. As See argues, echoing Balce, to consider the visuality of the Filipinx body in U.S. culture is to encounter the United States' imperial past, a past the American public largely forgets.[44] Accordingly, even when empire is not explicitly part of the narrative, the presence of Filipinxs conjures the specter of U.S. empire. Thus, recognizing Howard, Sunshine, Blaine, Frida, and Mateo as subjects of U.S. empire and as the return of the U.S. colonial repressed, despite the Philippines no longer being an official colony of the United States, is not unwarranted. In fact, the very denial of that link reinforces U.S. imperial amnesia, for "the violence and romance of empire haunts the representation of the Filipino in the American imaginary."[45] Television is ephemeral in that it is a form of popular culture that most viewers simply consume and move on from. By pausing, returning to, capturing, and meditating on those fleeting moments when Filipinxness appears on screen, we begin to re-member what was lost.

Legible Gay, Elusive Filipinx

Glee's Blaine Anderson is Filipinx. Even though, or perhaps because, the show does not confirm his racial-ethnic identity, it can be attached to the actor who portrays him. Criss, whose father is White and mother is Filipina, proudly identifies as Filipino.[46] Criss's racial-ethnic heritage makes plausible Blaine's Filipinxness; as an embodied form, acting presents a visual register to see race. As a mestizo Filipino, Criss, and by extension Blaine, may pass as White; however, the possibility of non-Whiteness is not completely foreclosed. By interpellating Blaine as Filipinx, I forward a subaltern, disidentificatory reading practice that capitalizes on the excesses of the show's script to make space for queer postcolonial Filipinx Midwestern imaginaries.

Blaine's plausible Filipinxness via Criss's embodied raciality, however, is only an entry point to seeing colonial raciality on a show that celebrates U.S. multiculturalism. Blaine's Filipinxness materializes via his performative and aesthetic embodiment. By reading his mesmerizing stage presence queerly, and with a Filipinx sensibility, I position Blaine in relation to Filipinx subjectivity. Lucy Burns's discussion of the Filipino/Tagalog idiom *puro arte* is instructive here. *Puro arte* refers to excessive performance. Its literal translation from Spanish and Filipino/Tagalog to English is "pure art," but its connotative meaning "gestur[es] ... to the labor of overacting, histrionics, playfulness, and purely over-the-top dramatics."[47] *Puro arte* names a mode of being that plays with normative performative scripts and thus can be interpreted as a Filipinized version of Muñoz's theory of disidentification.[48] Importantly, "*puro arte* [original italics] functions as an episteme, as a way of approaching the Filipina/o performing body at key moments in U.S.-Philippine imperial relations."[49]

Blaine's deliciously histrionic performances are not enough to suggest he is Filipinx. Rather, the form of his performance particularly underscores his relation to colonial raciality. Much of *Glee*'s musical numbers are covers of popular songs from a wide range of genres, including Broadway, pop, hip-hop, country, R&B, soul, and funk. As one of the vocal leads, Blaine performs songs and dances that straddle these musical forms, and he performs them well. His performative adaptability, coupled with his plausible non-White raciality, is what makes his Filipinxness conceivable. See refers to this as mimetic aesthetics, which she argues "is a recurrent cultural and socioeconomic phenomenon in Filipino/American studies and other interdisciplines with which it overlaps or abuts, such as queer of color studies."[50] If Filipinxs are "widely regarded as consummate mimics both in Asia and Asian America," as she suggests, then characters like Blaine can be interpellated and interpreted as Filipinx.[51] The mimetic aesthetic Filipinizes Homi Bhabha's thesis on colonial mimicry and reparatively reads the Filipinx ability to reproduce so-called originals both faithfully and with a flourish.[52]

Despite the potential for viewers to see Blaine as a racial-colonial subject, the show narratively constructs him primarily as a sexual subject. For example, in "The Substitute" (season 2, episode 7), the episode following his debut performance of Katy Perry's "Teenage Dream"—which clearly establishes his gaze as gay via close-up shot/reverse shots between him and Kurt—Blaine's gayness is further established as his most salient identity. Conversing about gay rights issues, from California's Proposition 8 to the U.S. military's "Don't Ask, Don't Tell" policy, Kurt and Blaine try to encourage fellow glee club member Mercedes Jones (played by Black American actor and singer Amber Riley) to share her thoughts as they wait to order food at McKinley High's favorite restaurant, Breadstix.[53] Unable to follow the conversation, Mercedes hallucinates (signaled by the scene slowing down) that all the words coming out of Kurt's and Blaine's mouths are "gay." Through Mercedes's eyes, Blaine is interpellated as simply gay. What is more, Blaine's physical proximity to Kurt in this scene, as they sit next to each other opposite Mercedes but also more generally throughout the series, works to mediate viewers' understanding of Blaine along the lines of sexuality rather than race.

The series initially created Blaine to serve as the love interest of the show's resident gay, Kurt, in season 2; however, Blaine's charisma eventually eclipsed Kurt's queerness, which gave viewers multiple representations of gay identity. Whereas Blaine is "the alpha gay" who inadvertently gets the male solos that used to go to Kurt (season 3, episode 17, "Dance with Somebody"), he is a "gay bro" to his best friend, Sam, in part because he presents as more normatively masculine in comparison to femme Kurt (season 4, episode 3, "Makeover"). Once Kurt moves to New York and Blaine remains in Lima during season 4, enabling both characters' identities to be reimagined as not exclusively tied to their romantic-sexual relationship, Blaine continues to be interpellated primarily as gay rather than also as a racial subject.

For example, when Blaine and Tina Cohen-Chang (played by Korean American adoptee actor and producer Jenna Ushkowitz) approach Coach Sue Sylvester to join the Cheerios, Sue regards Blaine as "a handsome, nonflammable gay" but only looks to Tina when she says, "My squad is looking a little pale these days. Wouldn't hurt to add a dash of yellow number four to my championship cheer batter" (season 4, episode 9, "Swan Song"). This is clearly a reference to Tina's Asianness but not Blaine's, foreclosing the proximate raciality between the two. Later in the season, Blaine self-identifies as a "sexually non-threatening gay," and Sue describes him as a "gay Clark Kent from season 1's *Smallville*" (season 4, episode 16, "Feud"). By repeatedly marking Blaine as a gay subject, the show frames how audiences ought to see him. While presenting Blaine as unapologetically gay in the context of the Midwest works to challenge normative myths of the region, the failure to present plausible intersectional subjectivities is a missed opportunity that oversimplifies difference and reinforces cosmetic diversity.

If Blaine's queerness is both relational to and distinct from Kurt's, I argue that his raciality figures similarly.[54] In fact, Kurt's raciality materializes a proximate raciality for Blaine that enables the latter to be read as a racial-colonial subject. During most of season 2, Blaine wears his navy-blue, red-piped Dalton Academy uniform. Blending in with his schoolmates, he can be read as the assimilated racial-ethnic. That is, Blaine's racial-ethnic identity goes unmarked, as his sexual identity surfaces as his mark of difference. However, when Kurt and Blaine first encounter each other on the grand staircase of Dalton in "Never Been Kissed" (season 2, episode 6), Blaine's raciality subtly materializes as the camera switches back and forth between their faces (figure 5.1). Although Blaine may initially appear as White with his light skin, he seems slightly tanned in comparison to Kurt, whose "porcelain" skin resembles the popular M. I. Hummel collectible figurines, which the lighting enhances.[55] Moreover, Blaine's slightly flat nose and dark brown hair stand out against Kurt's more pointed nose and lighter brown hair.

As LeiLani Nishime argues, "If race does not have an existential reality, then it follows that race only becomes evident in difference, difference to and difference from some agreed upon norm."[56] While these phenotypic differences between Blaine and Kurt certainly do not reveal the so-called truth of each person's race, the scene's use of medium-close reverse shots encourages viewers to make comparisons between them; and if race appears through such juxtaposition, then these minute visual contrasts illustrate how race is relational and subjective. What is more, this scene reveals how race is affective and invites us to take up Rachel Lee's turn to embodiment in theorizing Asian American racial formations. What prompts me to recognize Blaine as Filipinx is rooted in biology—his nose—and this activates an affective kinship as a fellow Filipinx and the biological kinship between my mother, who taught me to see race accordingly, and me.

Yet this moment of racial difference quickly fades as the focus returns to the emerging sexual tension between Blaine and Kurt. Immediately following their exchange on the staircase, we see them running in slow motion through a hallway, with Blaine holding Kurt's hand, even though they just met seconds ago. And once Blaine performs "Teenage Dream," the camera's close reverse shots between him and Kurt and the lyrics' expression of teen love encourage viewers to recognize a budding romance between the two. In viewing this scene, I become distracted from seeing racial difference and more focused on their commonality as gay male teens. Indeed, most of the episode emphasizes gender and sexual nonconformity, thereby eclipsing racial difference. From Kurt's experiences with homophobia from a school bully and heterosexism from Mr. Schuester's glee club assignment to sev-

Figure 5.1 Blaine (*top*) and Kurt (*bottom*) meeting for the first time. (*Bradley Buecker, Glee, "Never Been Kissed," 2010.*)

eral characters repressing their (hetero)sexual drives, sexuality is prioritized as the episode's thematic arc, which deters viewers from seeing the visuality of race.[57]

Declaration is the primary mode of confirming identity on the show, overriding viewers' contextual gleanings. Given the show's explicit production and reception based on diversity and inclusion, alongside industry attempts to cast diversely in response to consumer demand, marking identity matters. My preoccupation with tracing Blaine's identity has more to do with opening possibilities than pinning down who he is supposed to be. Thus, when lead female character Rachel Berry (played by Jewish American actor and singer Lea Michele) randomly references Blaine's raciality, it is unremarkably surprising. That is, marking Blaine's racial identity should not be surprising on a show invested in racial diversity, but it nevertheless comes as a surprise because it does not confirm nor deny his racial-ethnic identity. After Rachel and Blaine share a passionate, drunken kiss during a game of spin the bottle, she and Kurt question Blaine's sexuality (season 2, episode 14, "Blame It on the Alcohol"). A few days later, they both wait for Blaine at the Lima Bean coffee shop. Ignoring Kurt's caution that Blaine might not be romantically and sexually interested in her, Rachel replies, "I may get a new boyfriend out of this who can keep up with me vocally and, in the future, give me vaguely Eurasian-looking children." When Blaine arrives, Rachel walks up to him and lays a big kiss on his luscious lips. Afterward, Blaine slowly nods his head, displays a look of clarity, and says, "Huh. Yup. I'm gay. 100 percent gay. Thank you so much for clearing that up for me, Rachel." Blaine leaves for the restroom, and Rachel turns to Kurt and exclaims, "That was amazing. I am speechless. I just had a relationship with a guy who turned out to be gay." Through this scene, Blaine's sexual orientation becomes solidified as "100 percent gay." Oddly enough, Rachel fixates on experiencing a brief relationship with a gay guy and forgets that this relationship may have also been interracial.[58]

Although the show's emphasis on Blaine's sexuality eclipses his (multi)raciality and allows Whiteness to remain unmarked, casting Blaine as exclusively Filipinx would forego the possibilities of alternative racializations, namely multiraciality or transracial adoption.[59] While Blaine's last name, Anderson, moves him closer to Whiteness, it remains unclear whether the offspring Rachel refers to would be Eurasian due to Blain being exclusively Asian and her being of European descent or because Blaine himself is Eurasian. As Josephine Lee suggests, analyzing how staged passing unsettles normative ideas about the stability of race allows for more capacious and tentative imaginings of race, ethnicity, identity, and the body.[60] Thus, while Blaine may appear White, the show's reluctance to explicitly pin down his racial-ethnic identity, Criss's biracial self-identification, and fans' desire to see Blaine as not White destabilize the fixity of race that the show attempts to present.[61] Unlike other characters throughout the series' run, Blaine occupies an ambiguous status as possibly White but also possibly Asian. This racial indeterminacy inadvertently runs counter to the show's postracial celebration of difference based on discrete racial types. In this way, Blaine disrupts the facile yet powerful association between phenotype and race by failing to conform to existing racial categories, thereby revealing the limits of conceptualizing race based on the logic of White supremacy.

After Rachel's vague pronouncement in the middle of season 2, the series does not directly reference Blaine's racial-ethnic identity again; instead, it does so through proximity, free association, and affect. Whereas the introduction of Blaine's brother, Cooper Anderson (played by White American actor Matt Bomer), in season 3 and mother, Pam Anderson (played by Jewish American actor Gina Gershon), in season 6 reinforces Blaine's Whiteness, uncanny connections between Blaine and non-White raciality nevertheless surface throughout the series.[62] Such references function to queer racial formation in the context of region, nation, and diaspora and figure as the return of the U.S. colonial repressed. Blaine's hair especially illustrates this point.

When senior class president and fellow glee club member Brittany institutes an outlandish ban against hair gel at the prom, Blaine is the only one affected, even though other members obviously use hair gel, such as Mike Chang (played by Chinese American actor and dancer Harry Shum Jr.), whom the camera also cuts to (season 3, episode 19, "Prom-asaurus"). In defiance, Blaine shows up to the prom with Kurt and with his signature shiny, slicked-back hair. Brittany immediately blocks the couple from proceeding to the dance floor, saying, "No. Sorry, Blaine. I said no hair gel, remember? I can totally smell it." As she is the embodiment of McKinley High's student government, her personal attack on him obliquely symbolizes the disciplinary logics of U.S. imperial domination over the Filipinx body. Blaine reluctantly complies by washing out his hair, even though Brittany exerts no physical force. To establish drama, earlier in the episode, Blaine had explained to Kurt that his natural hair is "baby-hair fine" and that he will "look like Medusa." When Blaine returns, the camera is positioned from Blaine's point of view, and students awkwardly look at the camera/Blaine, building suspense for his big reveal. Kurt, the final person the camera pans to, blurts out "Oh, my dear God," covering his mouth with a look of shock/horror. The camera then cuts to a medium close-up of Blaine with dark, curly locks (figure 5.2).

Brittany appears to Kurt's right and ironically admonishes, "Don't make fun of the new kid with the bad 'fro. It's hair bullying." Insecure, Blaine asks, "Is it really that bad?" And Brittany unsympathetically replies, "Yeah, you're Mr. Broccoli Head." But then, despite her own bullying of Blaine, she concedes, "I abused my power as president. But to help save the prom, and to keep people from turning to stone when they look at you, I'll give you special permission to wear hair gel—immediately." Brittany's dry humor defuses the racially coded dynamics at play in this scene, and this is a common plot device used throughout the show, particularly with respect to racial issues.[63] However, when read through a queer postcolonial Filipinx critical lens, Brittany's change of heart calls to mind President McKinley's policy of "benevolent assimilation."[64] Oscillating between repression and acceptance,

Figure 5.2 Blaine revealing his natural hair. (*Eric Stoltz*, Glee, *"Prom-asaurus," 2012.*)

Brittany's disciplinary attitude toward Blaine similarly enacts U.S. ambivalence toward Filipinxs.[65]

As if Blaine's visual coming out as also a vaguely not-exclusively White racial subject during the prom was not enough to establish him as likely a queer Pinxy, his face-off with incumbent Brittany for senior class president in "Makeover" (season 4, episode 3) clarifies this point.[66] As a prominent citizen of the high school of U.S. empire,[67] Blaine decides to run for senior class president so he can "shine" during his senior year out of Kurt's shadow and make McKinley High a better place. He enters the race while singing Tears for Fears' "Everybody Wants to Rule the World," a fitting performance that evokes President McKinley's desire to make Filipinxs in the image of the United States through imperial domination. However, Bhabha's theory of colonial mimicry reminds us of the limitations of racial-colonial assimilation, which manifests when Brittany questions Blaine's citizenship status. Coinciding with the 2012 U.S. presidential election, the episode attempts to satirize the racist and xenophobic "birther" movement against then-President Obama with Brittany's offhand comment.[68] In the process, Blaine's Whiteness is called into question, given the connotations of non-nativity with non-Whiteness in immigration rhetoric. Despite his upstanding social citizenship at McKinley, emphasized in this episode by his signature bowtie aesthetic, Blaine remains an outsider; Brittany's reference to him as "Blaine Warbler" is a reminder that he immigrated to McKinley from Dalton, which casts doubt on his loyalty.

This episode not only raises questions about Blaine's Whiteness but also enables us to connect him to Filipinxness. When Brittany and Artie Abrams (played by White American actor and singer Kevin McHale) prepare for their debate against Blaine and Sam, Artie asks, "What is your favorite color?" She responds, "Filipino. They're very hard workers and family is important to them." Though we can read such a response as simply another Brittanyism attributed to her "dumb blonde" characterization, this statement comes after she accuses Blaine of not being born in the United States. Such a paradox illustrates the unconscious ambivalence expressed by the United States toward its post/colonial Filipinx subjects. White women often mediate U.S. imperial sentiment, and Brittany is no different here.[69] Moreover, Brittany's shout-out to Filipinxs intersects with fans' knowledge of Criss's mixed-race Filipinx background, which positions Blaine as not only a marked racialized subject but also as a specifically Filipinx one.[70]

Even though the episode ends with Sam comforting Blaine by saying, "You're McKinley's first gay guy president," I resist the resolution that Blaine is just a gay character. By insisting on Blaine's plausible Filipinxness, I uncover the imperial repression that lives deep in America's heartland. I also challenge postracial representations that are unable to foreground intersectional subjectivities. And yet, Blaine's elusive Filipinxness provides an opening to imagine identity differently. In a DVD bonus clip, Blaine records a video tribute for his fiftieth high school reunion and states, "I . . . was . . . just an ordinary kid, in 2013. I didn't save the world or change history. But I was here. And I sang my heart out with my friends."[71] In his eyes, he is "just an ordinary kid," and simply existing—"I was here"—in a specific place and time is enough to be remarkable. While identification marks someone, refusing to be marked as a marginalized someone enacts a queer-of-color mode of resistance. Knowing that Blaine well indeed may be gay and Filipinx, what might it mean to see him as "just an ordinary kid" from Lima, Ohio? His time capsule functions as an archive that documents the queer Filipinx Midwest, that a gay Filipinx who could pass as "just an ordinary kid . . . was here."

Other Filipinxs

Blaine is not the only Filipinx on *Glee*. As a recurring character in season 2 and a main character from seasons 3 to 6, he certainly is the most notable. However, at least three additional characters warrant our attention: Howard, Sunshine, and Frida.[72] Although Sunshine is the only character who explicitly is identified as Filipinx, Howard and Frida's embodied performative presence enables them to be read as Filipinx. As other Filipinxs, they not only lend credence to Blaine's Filipinxness but also render alternative modes of Filipinx embodiment, the latter of which challenges the colonial tendency to flatten colonized subjectivity. In this section, I focus on Howard Bamboo to illustrate further the postcolonial Filipinx unconscious that pervades the show. Appearing in the very first episode and dubbed "the real first Filipino on 'Glee'" by the Philippine-based *Inquirer.net*, Howard, played by Filipino American actor Kent Avenido, aptly symbolizes how Filipinxs indeed are everywhere in nowhere.[73]

With a minor fan base and appearing as a recurring character in the first two seasons and a guest character in season 6, Howard is worth considering.[74] Whereas Blaine passes as White, Howard's Brown skin makes him more legible as a potential Filipinx subject. However, he is never interpellated as Filipinx and instead appears as the nondescript, deferential Asian. Asian/American racialization eclipses his ethnic particularity; that is, for most viewers, it does not really matter that an actor of Filipinx descent, who understands his character as Filipinx, plays Howard; for them, it is enough that Howard phenotypically looks Asian.[75] In addition, Howard's deference to powerful White women—namely, Terri and Sue—conforms to the stereotype of the feminized Asian man.[76] His deviation from hetero-masculinity leaves open the possibility that he could also be read as ambiguously gay. By emphasizing Howard's plausible Filipinxness, however, I reveal that his Asian performance more accurately exemplifies the U.S.–Philippine colonial dynamics of what Rafael terms "white love."

In each of the four episodes that Howard appears in during season 1, his Sheets-N-Things supervisor, Terri, is not far behind, thus implying that he only exists because of her tutelage. In the pilot, viewers first encounter Howard through Terri as she explains how to fold a fitted sheet. As a supporting character, Howard appears in this scene only to bolster Terri's characterization as Will's overly demanding wife. Although she works outside the home, she nevertheless figures in domestic space by working at a home furnishings store. In this way, Terri's reign extends from the domestic sphere to the public sphere. As mistress of the Sheets-N-Things household, Terri occupies a position of power, and the camera works to place her higher than her subordinate Howard, even though they are practically the same height (figure 5.3). And while Howard is an adult, his self-doubt, dyslexia, and submissiveness combine to characterize him as infantile. When Terri curtly sends him to deal with a customer return, admonishing him to make sure the customer has a receipt, Howard returns with soiled bed sheets, looking uncertain as to what he should do. In response, she turns to Will, who stopped by with lunch, and sighs, "Do you see what I have to deal with here, hmm?" She storms off, with Howard following behind. This exchange between Terri and Howard stages the colonial dynamics of White love/ambivalence exhibited by White women who traveled to the Philippines during the early twentieth century, either as teachers or as the wives of colonial authorities, toward Filipinxs on the archipelago.[77] Howard's relational position also evokes the figure of the Filipino houseboy.[78] Such scenes of domesticity unsettle the region's remove

Figure 5.3 Terri (*left*) berating Howard (*right*). (*Ryan Murphy*, Glee, *"Pilot," 2009.*)

from transpacific empire, as the contemporary heartland fictionalized on the show contains this trace.

Despite the appearance of a domesticated, and thus repressed, palimpsest of U.S. empire in the Philippines in Howard's subjugated relation to Terri, Howard's fleeting presence presents an alternate way to think about interpellation and agency. After Will and Terri divorce at the end of season 1, Terri disappears from the show along with Howard; however, he reappears when Terri does—once in season 2 (episode 21, "Funeral") and finally in the penultimate flashback episode "2009" (season 6, episode 12)—reinforcing the colonial "white love" dynamic that defines their relation.[79] His brief performance in "Funeral," though, suggests other ways of being beyond the dominant frame of subjugation. In her plot to foil the glee club, Sue enlists Terri, as Will's ex-wife, and asks her to "recruit an expert computer hacker" to reroute the New Directions' nationals competition flight itinerary. Terri offers Howard, which is ironic, since the show established him as dyslexic and unable to count past thirty. Disappointed, Sue nevertheless allows Howard to join her team of barely undercover "super villains" and dubs him "Panda Express." Howard protests, "But I'm not Chinese," and Sue wittily replies, "Neither is the food at Panda Express." Instead of clarifying Howard's ethnic identity, the scene leaves it ambiguously Asian. But when Howard says, "We don't know his [Principal Figgins's] password," a Filipino/Tagalog accent is audible when he pronounces the *a* in *password* with a short *o* sound.

This moment exemplifies Shilpa Davé's concept of "brown voice," an accented English performed by South Asians and non–South Asians in brown-face that focuses more on pronunciation than on syntax, recognizes the colonial context that enables South Asians' relative facility with English, and reveals that South Asian racial representation materializes sonically in public culture.[80] While Filipinxs and South Asians have different histories of Anglophone colonization, both racial-ethnic groups similarly do not experience Orientalism in the same way as their East Asian counterparts; the visual cues used to read Asians do not readily apply to Brown Asians. Instead, "accent racializes a group that has been historically difficult to categorize."[81]

But just as the visual is subjective, so, too, is the sonic. Tongson's queer listening reminds us that "how we *hear* [original emphasis] . . . is just as conditioned by our own contextualization, our own bodies, our own material conditions, and our own visceral archives."[82] Hence, whether Howard actually pronounces *password* with a Filipino/Tagalog accent is beside the point; his utterance resonates with my aural register of Filipinx sound and provides an alternate pathway to make sense of his character. Moreover, Avenido's understanding of his character as Filipinx and Howard's refusal to be interpellated as Chinese by Sue in this episode unsettle Howard's ambiguous Asianness throughout the series—challenging the show's reification of the "Asians are all the same" trope. That he protests but does not correct is a form of minoritarian disengagement with dominant culture, calling on us all to do the work of disarticulating racial formation. In holding out the plausibility of Howard being Filipinx without confirmation, the program unconsciously leaves room for other voices to be heard that jam the signals of postracialism and postimperiality.

Howard teaches us to see and hear the world differently. Like Blaine, his identity is flexible, but since he has less of a backstory and recurring role, viewers are left to imagine both his past and his future. His dyslexia symbolically points to other ways of reading him. Appearing in the very first episode as a Sheet-N-Things store associate, he seems firmly planted in the Midwest, which subtly challenges the notion of the heartland as the province of Whiteness. And while his disappearance after season 2 may reinforce the absence of Filipinxs in the heartland, his reappearance, albeit via flashback, in season 6 indicates he has been (t)here all along. With his literal inability to read, Howard metaphorically embodies See's illiterate Filipinx subject who is not invested in capitalist accumulation and hetero-nationalism.[83] Unlike Blaine, he is not invested in belonging in Lima, Ohio. He also does not need to accumulate ample screen time for us to recognize the presence of Filipinxs in the Midwest; his existence—akin to Blaine's desire for us to simply know that he "was here"—is enough. His fleeting presence, his present absence, gestures toward a mode of minoritarian unsettlement that turns away from settler colonial claims to space.[84]

McKinley's Ambivalence toward Filipinas

Howard's Filipinx spectrality orients us toward other fleeting Filipinx figurations on *Glee*. Although I read Blaine and Howard as examples of the U.S. colonial repressed, in this final close reading of the show, I discuss how Sunshine Corazon and Frida Romero clarify U.S. ambivalence toward the Filipinx body and the haunting it thus engenders. Like the wild Filipinas of chapter 4, Sunshine and Frida further illustrate national-imperial anxieties concerning the unruly feminine; as embodiments of nation, these feminine characters allegorize U.S.–Philippine relations. Their contemporary presence at a high school named after the U.S. president responsible for annexing the Philippines more than a century ago fittingly illustrates how the show stages the afterlife of U.S. empire.

In Freudian psychoanalysis, the return of the repressed is a particular phenomenon of the uncanny. The uncanny "is that class of the terrifying which leads back to something long known to us, once very familiar";[85] it "is nothing else than a hidden, familiar thing that has undergone repression and then emerged from it."[86] Analyzing the various connotative meanings of the uncanny through its German equivalent *unheimlich*, Freud highlights the slippage between *unheimlich* and *heimlich*. While *heimlich* "means that which is familiar and congenial," it can also refer to "that which is concealed and kept out of sight."[87] As a word tied to the home, *heimlich* at once suggests familiarity and comfort as well as privacy and concealment. In this way, "what is *heimlich* thus comes to be *unheimlich*."[88] This slippage reveals how the uncanny is paradoxically homely and familiar yet also un-homely and unfamiliar;[89] the *un-* in *uncanny/unheimlich* signals the mark of repression.[90] In other words, the uncanny points to that which does not belong; however, as M. Jacqui Alexander rightly suggests, for something to be excised, it must first exist within that which it is to be excised from.[91] Thus, the uncanny renders legible one's ambivalence toward aspects that are a part of oneself but undesirable. In the context of coloniality, Freud's theory calls into question the line between self and Other. Unsurprisingly, the fear of one's double is a notable feature of the uncanny.[92] As Bhabha illumines, the menace of colonial mimicry lies in the colonized double's ability to unsettle the arbitrary nature of colonial power.[93]

Whereas Blaine initially appears as a threat to the New Directions' male vocal leads (Finn and Kurt) but eventually is incorporated into the high school of U.S. empire, Sunshine and Frida threaten to undo the glee club itself and thus remain beyond the grasp of McKinley High. Such Filipinx figures belie the ideals of postracialism and postimperiality, as the ambivalence engendered by their embodied presence suggests racial difference and the legacies of U.S. empire still matter. Their ability to effectively perform popular U.S. songs in the style of their so-called original illustrates their supposed success in becoming assimilated into dominant U.S. culture; however, their performative repetition of U.S. popular culture becomes unsettling, as their performance destabilizes the hierarchy between original and copy.[94] The captivating performances of Filipinxs on *Glee* slip into excess as they surpass the normative boundaries of mimicry. Made in the image of America, Filipinxs not only reinforce U.S. hegemony but also efface it through unfaithful appropriation.

As a migrant student from the Philippines, Sunshine unambiguously is Filipinx; however, she is elusive as a postcolonial subject. A queer postcolonial Filipinx Midwestern reading practice allows us to register her as a subject of empire, as the return of the U.S. colonial repressed that betrays the fiction of postimperiality. Emblematic of See's "foreign in a domestic space,"[95] Sunshine (played by transgender Filipinx international recording artist Jake Zyrus) simply appears at McKinley High as a new foreign student who Rachel assumes is unable to speak English (season 2, episode 1, "Audition").[96] Her duet of Lady Gaga and Beyoncé's "Telephone" with Rachel in the girls' bathroom aptly conveys the unconscious sapphic tension between the two characters but also the uneven desires between the Philippines and the United States. Right before they burst out in song and dance, Rachel excitedly approaches Sunshine, who does not realize she is talking to her, as she is listening to "Telephone" through her earbuds. Whereas Sunshine attempts to listen to Rachel, who speaks loudly and in broken English, Rachel is focused on simply recruiting another chorus member who will "stand behind [her] and stare at [her] with wet-moved eyes while [she] sing[s] solos"; she fails to hear Sunshine's protests. The camera establishes Rachel's dominance over Sunshine, as the former is shot at a slight low angle in contrast to the latter. Rachel also pats Sunshine's shoulder in a condescending manner. Sunshine commences singing, which commands a response from Rachel, thereby reversing the power dynamic of the dialogic scene (figure 5.4). In repeating the lyric "stop callin'," Sunshine symbolically rejects Rachel's insincere benevolence and retains her agency.[97]

Disarmed by Sunshine's powerful vocals, Rachel attempts to shift course. As the de facto leader of the New Directions, Rachel wields power and profits from White supremacy, even if, as a young brunette Jewish woman, she is not quite White.[98] She attempts to enlist Kurt and Mercedes—both of whom embody difference in terms of sexuality and race, respectively—by announcing, "Ladies, we have a problem. There's a new student at this school named Sunshine, who is a *Filipino* [original emphasis] and is shorter than me . . . and is very unnerving." She uses the logic of White supremacy to pit the glee club's marginalized vocal members against another marginalized body. Disingenuously remarking, "I'm just, I'm very worried. You know, not for myself, but for my lesser glee clubbers who don't get as many solos," she ignores the structural inequities based on meritocracy that favor her over

Figure 5.4 Rachel (*foreground*) stunned by Sunshine's (*background*) vocals. (*Brad Falchuk, Glee, "Audition," 2010.*)

others, in true postracial fashion. Mercedes and Kurt, however, see through her ploy, signaling a moment of intersectional solidarity.

Rachel's ambivalence toward Sunshine mirrors the United States' ambivalence toward the return of its repressed imperial past. Whereas Rachel desires Sunshine only when she can be put in the service of her vision, Rachel abhors her when she discovers her "remarkable voice," illustrating "the *menace* [original emphasis] of mimicry" that Bhabha describes when the colonized, "in disclosing the ambivalence of colonial discourse[,] also disrupts its authority."⁹⁹ Thus, Sunshine's mimicry of U.S. popular culture, a requirement for her to become legible to Rachel and by extension to U.S. audiences, also becomes Rachel's moment of undoing and exposes the racialized contradictions of U.S. imperialism. Her name, Sunshine Corazon, appropriately symbolizes the light she sheds on McKinley High's postimperial failures occurring in the contemporary heartland of U.S. empire.

Likewise, Frida (played by *American Idol* season 11 runner-up Jessica Sanchez, who is of Filipinx and Mexican descent) is met with ambivalence. Her on-screen debut toward the end of season 4 (episode 20, "Lights Out") is a cutaway of her singing a cappella two lines of "The Star-Spangled Banner" while sitting at a piano. Mr. Schuester sets up this scene by announcing to his students, "Guys, we got a problem. Her name is Frida Romero. With Regionals only a few weeks away, I went to scout out the competition." After this disconcerting announcement, we see the back of Frida's head as she belts out the lyrics to the U.S. national anthem from the perspective of Mr. Schue, which the following shot establishes with Frida now in the foreground facing the camera and him secretly watching her while standing in a doorway. The camera quickly zooms to a shocked, awed, and concerned Mr. Schue; he is literally stunned, with his jaw dropped. Frida, on the other hand, is completely enveloped in the song. After this brief flashback, the scene returns to Mr. Schue reporting what he saw and heard: "The Hoosierdaddies [of North Central High School in Indianapolis] have a secret weapon. She's a tiny little sophomore, never competed before, but her voice could fill an arena. I mean, it's big." While lasting only a few seconds to set up an impending conflict for the season finale's regionals competition, the scene itself shines a spotlight on Frida's arena-filling voice and captivates viewers. In short, Frida's debut figures as a sample for what is yet to come—aural pleasure for viewers but also ontological anxiety for the New Directions.

Two episodes later (season 4, episode 22, "All or Nothing"), Frida reappears and takes to the stage as the Hoosierdaddies' female vocal lead. Prior to her performance, Mr. Schue once again reminds the New Directions (and viewers) that their main competition is "a tiny juggernaut of talent." This oxymoronic statement further builds up the anticipation in witnessing firsthand Frida's powerhouse vocals, which Sanchez was known for on *American Idol*. As the glee club's coach, Mr. Schue represents McKinley's institutional power. His ambivalence, similar to Rachel's toward Sunshine, engenders a conflict in viewers who are supposed to root for the New Directions and yet desire to experience Frida's/Sanchez's commanding stage presence. Frida's two performances deliver on Mr. Schue's promise. During her first number, Zedd's "Clarity," she struts all over the stage, evoking sensuality in true diva fashion; and while seven mostly White young male dancers flank her, the camera remains focused on her (figure 5.5). Her second number, Little Mix's "Wings," immediately follows, and the crowd once again cheers at the sound of her soulful voice while four young Black women dance around her. Despite the Hoosierdaddies' show-stopping performance, due in large part to Frida's remarkable vocal range, the New Directions predictably win regionals.

Frida's performance of "Clarity" and "Wings" appropriately stages the racial-colonial dynamics between the United States and the Philippines. As a song about ambivalent love, "Clarity" has Frida singing "you are the piece of me I wish I didn't need" and repeatedly asking, "If our love's insanity, why are you my clarity?" Reading Frida as a postcolonial Filipinx subject, we can interpret the first line as a desire to excise the traumas of U.S. imperial violence in the Philippines that imprint on the Filipinx body and psyche and the second line as the postcolonial subject's exposure of the farce of "benevolent assimilation." Frida's vocals clarify how "white love" does not serve the colonized. "Wings" is a response to the pull of "white love," as Frida symbolically "spread[s] [her] wings" and "fl[ies]" away, rejecting the love-hate of U.S. imperial culture. Although Frida disappears from the show after this spell-

Figure 5.5 The Hoosierdaddies diva, Frida Romero (*center*). (*Bradley Buecker*, Glee, "All or Nothing," 2013.)

binding performance, much in the same way as Sunshine does at the end of season 2, she leaves an indelible mark.

Sunshine and Frida both figure as a "problem" for the high school of U.S. empire because of their powerful (singing) voices, and their physical smallness confounds their rivals. These racist-sexist projections of colonial ambivalence at the heart of U.S. empire reveal the fallacy of underestimating the creative capacities of the colonized, of the marginalized—those deemed by the dominant as small and therefore insignificant. For queer diasporic Filipinx Midwestern viewers, both women problematize the postracial and postimperial politics of *Glee*. Whereas Sunshine's migratory route from the Philippines to Lima, Ohio, symbolizes the effect of President McKinley's overseas annexation, Frida's rootedness in the heartland as a Filipinx Hoosier resonates with Howard's lack of a solid backstory; both trajectories make plausible a queer Filipinx Midwest. Rather than viewing such characters as mere supporters of the main cast, I redirect us to consider them on their own terms.

Unapologetically Filipinx and Gay

"Sorry, not sorry. I'm not here to make friends," says Mateo to Garrett as they vie for the attention of a customer whom they mistakenly believe is a secret shopper (*Superstore*, season 1, episode 6, "Secret Shopper").[100] Mateo's ruthlessness in this example is what audiences have come to expect of him. Immediately established as a perky force to be reckoned with in the pilot episode, Mateo regularly utters pithy remarks and offers barbs and quips that simultaneously function as humor and overt criticism of the structures of inequality that not only inform the show's reality but also refract the world of (U.S.) viewers.

Introduced in the pilot as one of Cloud 9's newest Angels—what store associates of the big-box retailer are called—alongside Jonah, who embodies the stereotypical White straight cisgender man who leans politically liberal, Mateo figures as a shady shadow to Jonah. And yet, his refusal to align with either end of the political spectrum poses a bright alternative to the status quo. When he proudly recites his full name to his new coworkers, viewers, especially those versed in Filipinx culture, can immediately read him as Filipinx. Although his first name and first middle name, *Mateo Fernando*, coupled with the length of his total name, might suggest he is Latinx, *Aquino* evokes Corazón "Cory" Aquino, the first woman president of the Philippines (1986–1992) and widow of Senator Beningo "Ninoy" Aquino Jr., whose assassination sparked the end of President Marcos's dictatorial regime.[101] His last name, *Liwanag*, is the Filipino/Tagalog word for light. The show establishes Mateo's racial-ethnic identity through naming. It also hints at his queer identity: He sits upright and attentive at the front of the room during his first staff meeting and is the only store associate wearing a dress shirt and necktie (under a V-neck sweater) besides the store manager. When he stands up to introduce himself, he speaks with a singsong cadence, bounces when he moves his body, and belts out a soulful line. Unlike *Glee*'s Blaine, Mateo can be plausibly identified as Filipinx and gay within the first few minutes of his screen time, and later episodes only confirm that. Additionally, though both Mateo and Howard are retail workers, the show featuring Mateo spotlights laborers who typically figure in the background.

As a series regular, Mateo often is central to the half-hour episode plots, which sometimes engage his intersectional identities. *Superstore* recognizes Mateo as embodying queerness, Filipinxness, and Midwesternness simultaneously, indicating that other models of representation that do not reduce minoritarian characters to a singular being nor foreclose what Gordon calls "complex personhood" are possible.[102] I certainly am drawn to Mateo because he self-identifies as Filipino, gay, and undocumented and lives in the Midwest; however, my sustained interest in him derives from his character as an unapologetic bitchy queen who also expresses vulnerable emotions with his coworkers. Although his persona is what makes him distinct from other characters, the show reminds us that identity still matters, particularly when it comes to his undocumented status—revealing the illusion of postracialism and postimperiality.

Store-manager-turned-floor-worker Glenn Sturgis's (played by White Canadian actor and comedian Mark McKinney) introduction of Mateo to his pastor is fitting: "Mateo is gay, but not in a way that defines him" (season

4, episode 18, "Cloud Green"). This is not to say that Mateo is a more compelling representation of the queer Filipinx Midwest than Blaine, whom I analyze as primarily reading as gay at the expense of Filipinxness/Asianness. Rather, I recognize both characters as occupying shared ontoepistemological space, which debunks the myth of the gay Filipino Midwesterner as a unicorn. Santos, the actor who plays Mateo, echoes this sentiment: "There are very, very few queer Filipino characters on TV. But I'm out there, I exist. . . . We are part of the workforce[,] and you will find us in the [M]idwest, I promise!"[103] By drawing attention to how our mediascapes reckon with sociocultural-geographic difference, I present such figurations less as singular dots and more as part of a constellation that assembles another vision of reality.

Coming Out as Undocumented

In a postrace and postgay America, with the nation's election of its first non-White president and the legalization of same-gender marriage, Mateo coming out as Filipino (season 1, episode 3, "Shots and Salsa") and gay (season 1, episode 8, "Wedding Day Sale") in 2015/2016 seems unremarkable. When he comes out as an undocumented immigrant in season 2, however, we begin to see the ruse of postracialism. Mateo's narrative arc concerning his undocumented status coincides with Trump's rise to power and presidency, highlighting the durability of White supremacy and xenophobia in the United States. Mateo actually does not come out of his own accord but rather learns it from Jonah in the special episode "Olympics" (season 2, episode 1), in honor of the 2016 Summer Olympics in Rio de Janeiro.[104] As an event that brings most of the world's nations together, the Olympics also reignites localized nationalism.

When Glenn notices Mateo wearing a pin of the Philippine flag, he questions Mateo's U.S. patriotism, but Mateo is unfazed. Later, Glenn attempts to persuade Mateo of the United States' greatness by showing off "a good old pair of American blue jeans pants" he found in the men's department and saying, "Good luck getting a pair of these babies in, Ma-nai-la"—mispronouncing the capital city of Mateo's homeland while looking down and reading his palm. As Glenn walks away, Jonah tries to dismiss Glenn's behavior, and again Mateo is unfazed. However, when Mateo expresses his belief that Asian Americans cannot vote, pointing to it as evidence of U.S. racial injustice, Jonah corrects him and questions his citizenship status out of concern. Mateo explains how he obtained his documents from the "green card store," and Jonah slowly shakes his head *no*; Mateo then realizes his citizenship may be invalid. The scene cuts to Mateo on his cell phone in the back of the store. He speaks the following at a rapid pace: "Grandma, na alala mo kung binilihin natin date para sa akin? So, yung green card ngayon counterfeit? So, ibig

Figure 5.6 Mateo realizing he is undocumented. (*Ruben Fleischer*, Superstore, "Olympics," 2016.)

sabihin 'di ako American citizen? At pwede din natin pinanuod ng *Spider-man* legally sa Netflix?" (figure 5.6).

Viewers can pick up that Mateo is in fact not a so-called legal U.S. citizen by his concerned facial expressions, animated dialogue, the fragments of English, the close-ups on his face when he says "green card" and "counterfeit," and the editing. However, the untranslated Taglish is a subtle nod to Filipinx viewers who identify with Mateo's diasporic identity. Again, Davé's concept of "brown voice" is instructive here in considering the performative and sonic dimensions of racialization. Whereas a Filipino/Tagalog accent and dialogue may play into stereotypes of minoritarian subjects as foreign, such a perspective holds if we privilege the White spectator; for the Filipinx viewer, such a sound engenders recognition and affinity.

As Dorinne Kondo argues, "Minoritarian art can allow minoritized subjects the pleasure of being mirrored, conferring existence in a significant domain in the public sphere, despite the inevitable (mis)recognition that inaugurates the founding of any subject."[105] Although she writes in the context of theater, her point about minoritarian spectatorship still applies to my reading of network television. Santos's performance demands that viewers work out the drama that unfolds for his character, unsettling who an American viewer is. Moreover, the lack of resolution of his citizenship status in this and subsequent episodes works to portray a more realistic representation of living as an undocumented immigrant in the United States: a mix of complexity, precarity, and ordinariness. As a gay Filipino undocumented immigrant, Mateo expands the image of what undocumented looks like, not unlike gay

Filipino journalist, filmmaker, and immigrant rights advocate Jose Antonio Vargas, who came out as undocumented in 2011.[106] Technically a fugitive, Mateo resists capture, and the support of his coworkers provides an alternarrative to anti-immigrant sentiment present in the Midwest, especially pervasive in the era of Trumpism.[107]

A Dream Deferred

For most of season 2, Mateo's undocumented status does not affect his work life; instead, his secret romantic-sexual relationship with Cloud 9 District Manager Jeff Sutin (played by White American actor Michael Bunin) creates narrative tension. However, in the eighteenth episode, "Mateo's Last Day," these two plotlines intersect. Once Jeff discloses their relationship to his bosses, he tells Mateo that for them to stay together, Mateo will have to transfer stores (season 2, episode 17, "Integrity Award"). Given that Jeff is White and part of the managerial class of the Cloud 9 corporate structure, the racial and class dynamics of this exchange is palpable. Nevertheless, Mateo gladly obliges, as he will be transferring to a Cloud 9 Signature store, an upgrade from his current store. During the first part of the episode, Mateo bids good riddance to his coworkers, illustrating the desire for upward mobility that late capitalism inspires. However, when Jeff asks for his Social Security card to process the store transfer, Mateo tries to deflect, giving an uncomfortable laugh and saying, "I didn't realize this store [the new one] was like Nazi Germany." He follows this up with an awkwardly comedic Nazi salute and march. Mateo assures Jeff that providing his actual Social Security card should not be a problem, but as Jeff walks away, Mateo's face changes from cheerful to concerned, emphasized by a cut to a low-angle close-up of Mateo with furrowed eyebrows. To cut the dramatic tension, Cheyenne, who is standing behind him and arranging a display with Jonah, asks confusedly, "Do undocumented people have documents?" Mateo curtly responds under his breath, "No, no we don't." She follows up by asking, "So like won't that be an issue?" Mateo hisses, "Yes!"

This scene is followed by Mateo, Cheyenne, and Jonah trying to come up with ways for Mateo to obtain proper U.S. citizenship documents. Cheyenne regrets her inability to marry Mateo, which would grant him citizenship, because she already is marrying her boyfriend, Bo. Jonah offers himself up, even though he is straight, to which Mateo responds, "Eww." Later, they review different criteria on a U.S. immigration website that could make Mateo eligible for citizenship. Whereas Mateo rejects Jonah's suggestion to serve in the military because he "would like killing too much" and another marriage proposition from Jonah, he is amenable to Cheyenne's suggestion of being "a victim of a violent crime, such as an assault." Mateo provokes his warehouse coworkers, who perform normative masculinity, but that proves unsuccessful, so he begs Jonah to physically assault him. Jonah finally relents, and they go outside to the back of the store with Cheyenne. Jonah cannot bring himself to punch Mateo. Cheyenne fairs no better; in hopes of becoming enraged, she begs Mateo to "say something mean about Beyoncé." Disgusted by such a request, Mateo quips, "I'd rather be deported." Mateo's refusal to marry Jonah suggests that he views marriage as a significant institution but also that it does not completely solve the problem of navigating anti-immigrant systems.[108] His veneration for Queen Bey further reveals the queer economies with which he is invested.

In the final minutes of the episode, Mateo finds Jeff getting ready to drive away from the store. Mateo tells Jeff he is unable to transfer, but instead of disclosing his undocumented status as the reason, he unexpectedly tells Jeff that he is not in love with him and thus is ending their romantic-sexual relationship. This scene is serious in tone, as indicated by the diegetic sound of traffic, the slow pacing of the dialogue, and the subtle nondiegetic sound of somber piano. This contrasts with previous scenes, which appear more humorous and ironic. As the credits roll, viewers see Mateo crying and walking back into the store, where Cheyenne is ready to comfort him. Out of the blue, Jonah punches Mateo in the face, and the scene ends with Mateo crouched and groaning on the floor, thereby resolving the drama through comedy. This moment marks a turn in Mateo's character arc, as it begins to lay bare the costs of being undocumented in the United States. However, Cheyenne and Jonah's willingness to protect Mateo from state apparatuses aligns with the progressive politics Ozark Highlands Angels espouse as they challenge corporate capitalism. Moreover, although Mateo's personal sacrifice to remain in place might be an act of self-preservation, it also suggests that the homonormative "good life" that Jeff and the bougie Cloud 9 Signature store proffer are not enough to secure happiness.[109] Such quotidian acts by low-wage workers unsettle the American dream and encourage us to recognize the value of queer kinship and anti-capitalist economies.

To further emphasize the economic and emotional effects of living undocumented, "Safety Training" (season 3, episode 14) features Mateo refusing to sign off on a $50,000 settlement after a workplace injury (a pot-of-gold sign falls on him as he tries to flirt with a customer), as it would involve a background check. As district manager, Jeff attempts to mediate between Mateo and Corporate and interprets Mateo's refusal as greed and spite. However, when Mateo realizes Jeff still cares about him months after their breakup, he reluctantly comes out as undocumented, and Jeff is stunned. To emphasize the drama, their conversation is edited as a series of shot/reverse shots. When the camera cuts to Jeff, only he is in the frame; but when the camera cuts to Mateo, Jeff's profile is on the left edge of the frame. The cinematography and editing together render the scene from the perspective of Mateo, encouraging viewers to empathize with his precarious legal status.

Both these episodes present a local/regional and thus more intimate take on federal/national law. While immigration often is couched as a national issue, its everyday realities tend to be felt locally and regionally. Recognizing this scalar shift yields specificity and puts a human face to the political rhetoric that eclipses the on-the-ground struggles of a precarious population. At first glance, the Midwest might seem like an unlikely place where U.S. immigration battles occur. Although three states in the region border Canada (Michigan, Minnesota, and North Dakota), most Americans do not associate the Midwest as a borderland; rather, the Midwest is the heartland, the core of the nation. It is "the quintessential home referenced by 'homeland security,'"[110] was "a psychic fallout shelter in which to seek refuge from a changing and dangerous world" during the Cold War,[111] and is, in the early twenty-first century, a place that must be protected from Middle Eastern and Latin American refugees and migrants. According to Hoganson, "the heartland myth draws the nation together around a shared sense of vulnerability."[112] As the geographic and psychic center of the nation, the Midwest figures in the American imaginary as a fort that must be protected at all costs. However, as she rightly points out, securing the Midwest as the national home is a White nationalist endeavor. Homeland security is a project invested in securing White supremacy and casting Native peoples, people of color, and migrants as outsiders.[113]

As with other U.S. regions, the Midwest relies on migrant labor to keep its economy running. For Midwestern immigrants of color, the specter of the U.S.–Mexico borderlands is at once distant and salient. On one hand, the Midwest's geographic distance from the border buffers immigrants of color from heavy surveillance. Because immigration discourse is racialized, however, their/our skin color makes them/us a target in the predominantly White heartland. Still, the dominant framing of immigration as a largely U.S. Southwest issue affords Midwestern immigrants of color some sense of unparalleled relief.

Mateo's Filipinx identity unsettles this notion of the Midwest as refuge from the militarized border, since Filipinxs are not readily imagined as the figure of U.S. immigration and undocumentation.[114] Certainly, Mateo experiences the anxiety and fear of living as an undocumented immigrant in St. Louis; however, his racial-ethnic identity and geographic location do not make him an immediate target of surveillance. Nevertheless, as the series demonstrates, the Midwest is not isolated from national discourses, nor is it removed from global technologies (if it ever was). A simple phone call to Immigration and Customs Enforcement (ICE), which has field offices throughout the United States, is a sober reminder that immigration enforcement is not confined to the U.S. Southwest, as we see at the end of season 4.[115]

Both these episodes also remind viewers that Mateo is undocumented, yet these narrative moments appear as the exception rather than the rule in Store 1217's universe. That is, Mateo's undocumented status certainly circumscribes his movement within the store, but it does not predetermine much of his day-to-day interactions with customers, coworkers, supervisors, and lovers. Nevertheless, from soliciting bodily harm from others to rejecting significant compensation for an accidental workplace injury, Mateo exhibits the extent of his determination to preserve his relation to the state. Such actions mask the structural forces that limit his social mobility, presenting them as personal and voluntary choices. As a neoliberal subject, Mateo is forced to become entrepreneurial to remain hidden from state surveillance. Still, we also can read his actions as a form of queer diasporic refusal to invest in capitalist accumulation; but since there is no outside to power, such refusals are difficult to negotiate.

Perpetual Precarity

In emphasizing Mateo's undocumented status, I risk centering an aspect of his identity that does not necessarily reflect his salient sense of self; however, I draw attention to it, as it presents an atypical representation of Filipinxness and undocumentation. To forget Mateo's undocumented status, along with his Filipino and gay identities, is to allow him to be a round character. Yet, completely ignoring it reeks of postracialism and postimperiality.[116] As the show illustrates, his undocumented status positions him in a state of perpetual precarity, as labor, economics, and politics are intertwined. The choice to present Mateo as the face of undocumented immigration to millions of viewers nuances the discourse, engendering opportunities for cross-racial-ethnic solidarity and exploring the limits of such mutuality under the duress of the state. In the eighth episode of season 4 ("Managers' Conference"), we see Mateo as a flawed character, as he willingly sacrifices a fellow Brown migrant to once again preserve his livelihood.

When Glenn reports during a staff meeting that Corporate has asked him to run all employees through E-Verify, a U.S. Department of Homeland Security website that employers use to verify an employee's eligibility to work in the country, Mateo becomes nervous and makes eye contact with Cheyenne, who is also concerned. Sitting closest to Glenn, Mateo feels interpellated. As the discussion continues, Mateo grows hysterical and tries to deflect to Sayid (played by Iranian American actor Amir M. Korangy), a new Angel who has been working for a few weeks and is sitting behind Mateo.

When Glenn identifies Sayid as the problem in E-Verify, Mateo immediately is relieved and turns his head to tell Sayid unsympathetically, "I think you're getting deported." Sayid protests that he is not undocumented, and Dina clarifies that he is a refugee. Sayid goes on to explain that he "was fleeing the civil war in Syria." Good-hearted Glenn reassures Sayid, "you're home now." Mateo's attitude toward Sayid can be attributed to his bitchy persona as well as his fear of being deported himself.

Later in the episode, Mateo grows jealous of Sayid's special treatment from Glenn. Having just returned from the store parking lot, Mateo stands near the store entrance and complains to Cheyenne: "It's so unfair. I'm stuck outside shoveling snow, while Sayid gets treated like he's part of Janet Jackson's entourage, or something." Cheyenne sympathetically quips, "I know, he's safe and sound now. If anyone deserves special treatment, it's you." She continues, "I mean, you could be deported literally at any moment, just taken back to the Philippines on some sex trafficker's yacht." When she says this, the camera cuts from a medium-long to a medium shot. Mateo responds, "What? I'm undocumented, not Liam Neeson's daughter," pointing out that Cheyenne is describing the plot of the film *Taken* (2008), which stars Neeson. As Mateo declares that he is undocumented, Sayid enters through the sliding doors, out of focus. The camera does a quick cut to Cheyenne, who coughs to alert Mateo. This is followed by a long shot of Sayid walking into the store, seemingly unaware of the conversation between Mateo and Cheyenne. Mateo tries to engage Sayid in small talk, transforming his bitter frown into a bubbly smile. This scene creates a new plot conflict between Mateo and Sayid, which unfolds as the episode progresses, now with Mateo ingratiating himself to Sayid.

At first, Mateo plays dumb with Sayid, saying that he often confuses "documented" and "undocumented immigrant" and tries to convince Sayid that he is "definitely the legal kind" of immigrant. Afraid that Sayid will report him, Mateo escalates the situation by spreading lies about Sayid and getting Cheyenne to introduce the racist phrase "lying like a Syrian" in hopes that his coworkers will doubt Sayid's integrity should he report Mateo. While folding clothes in the women's department, Sayid confronts Mateo about spreading the racist phrase. Mateo lets his guard down and admits he spread the lie. Despite Mateo continuing to use the racist phrase even when speaking softly to Sayid, Sayid is sympathetic to Mateo's situation, explaining, "And why would I wanna turn you in? It's none of my business."

In classic comedic fashion, Mateo makes it worse by outlining reasons why Sayid would want to turn Mateo in, and Sayid realizes his own precarity as an "innocent bystander" who nevertheless could be interpellated as an "accomplice." The scene ends with Sayid backing away from Mateo and lying that he has "work to do" in the back, but when Mateo insists on following,

Sayid says that he has "to go to the men's room first." Presumably, Sayid leaves to report Mateo. Like Mateo, who was willing to preserve his tenuous security by sacrificing Sayid at the beginning of the episode, Sayid is not above such actions, especially as a means of avoiding returning to the violence in Syria. While this plotline functions as comedy, it also reveals the structural forces of White supremacy and neoliberal capitalism that pit minoritarian subjects against each other. Although instances of solidarity based on economic status have appeared on the show, in this episode, there is no interethnic immigrant-refugee solidarity.

However, cross-racial sympathy and empathy do prevail. When Mateo ends up in Glenn's office upon Sayid reporting him, Glenn confronts him with skepticism and concern and gives him an opportunity to provide the correct Social Security number after learning that the one he had given belongs to a Polish woman from Buffalo, New York. Mateo hesitates, and Glenn reluctantly insists. When Mateo slowly dictates the last four digits, Glenn's facial expression indicates his realization that Mateo is undocumented. As a manager, Glenn knows his legal duties. But his character throughout the series shows his humanity supersedes his job. When the end credits roll, Glenn tells Mateo that the new Social Security number "checked out" in E-Verify. Mateo is surprised, but Glenn's eye contact reassures an unspoken understanding. To confirm all is well, Glenn says, "Merry Christmas, Mateo."

Glenn's actions demonstrate how people in positions of power can use their status to protect the disenfranchised. While verifying his employees' legality is part of his job, it is more a directive from Corporate than his volition; his acknowledgment that undocumented immigrants are "human beings" at the beginning of the episode is affirmed at the episode's end. Surely, we could read Glenn's actions as part of a White Christian savior mentality; but doing so would reduce the complexities the series offers to us as viewers. Episode after episode shows us that these characters are both flat caricatures and round characters with complex emotional depth, pushing the genre of workplace sitcoms. Glenn's generosity is less about quid pro quo than it is about caring for another human being—not despite their difference but because of their differential relations to power; this is an example of "seeing the world not as it is, but as it *should* be."

Although *Superstore* traffics in progressive politics—advocating for unions, cultural diversity and inclusion, universal health care, and gender equity—and thus attempts to debunk the postracial myth, it remains tethered to postimperial racial formation. Hence, while Mateo's Filipinxness may remix the trope of being undocumented in the United States, which is typically tied to Mexicans, and Latinxs more generally, his ethno-racial connections to the region and nation are not explicitly understood as colonial in form. Whereas over a thousand people from the Philippines arrived in St. Louis at the turn of the twentieth century under the aegis of displaying U.S. imperial power, Mateo's arrival in the same city over a century later is met without pomp. Instead, he is but one of many ethno-racially diverse inhabitants who fulfill the trope of the United States as a melting pot. Aside from knowing he is an undocumented immigrant, his peers and, by extension, viewers are unclear how he arrived in the United States and in St. Louis. The United States is a plausible destination for Mateo and his family, as the nation is a global economic driver; however, its colonial ties to the Philippines unsurprisingly are left undisclosed. Perhaps more surprising is Mateo and his family settling in St. Louis, as it is not readily imagined as a global city, nor is it a coastal metropolis that Filipinx immigrants might readily occupy.[117] And yet, the show places Mateo and other Filipinxs as perfectly plausible in a Midwestern city like St. Louis.[118]

Anti–Model Minority

Whereas Blaine figures as an assimilated minoritarian subject whose raciality disappears and whose sexuality appears as palatable, Mateo figures as an anti–model minority subject. Asian Americans are the model minority par excellence in U.S. racial discourses.[119] However, the dominant image of Asian Americans continues to skew toward East Asians. Hence, while Mateo strives to be the best worker, consistently earning employee of the month, his ethnic, sexual, and national identities complicate his model minority status. In fact, Mateo's hard work is often self-serving and not necessarily about uplifting any one sociocultural group. Reading Mateo as Asian with a difference reorients us toward other modes of interpreting televisual representations of race and other ways of being that divest from inclusion within existing structures.

As a queer subject, Mateo challenges the heteronormativity of race and the homonormativity of gay identity. After he comes out as undocumented to Jeff, Jeff resigns from his position as regional manager rather than report Mateo. They also resume their romantic-sexual relationship. However, the possibility that Mateo could marry Jeff, as Jeff presumably is a U.S. citizen, never crosses their minds, despite Jonah's platonic proposal. Accordingly, Mateo and Jeff enact a form of bad gay citizenship in their refusal to aspire to marriage and secure Mateo's legal status. This is not to denigrate same-gender marriage as a pathway to legal and social citizenship; for some queers, accessing normative modes of state recognition is the only way to survive. Mateo's circuitous navigation through labor and love resists the straight path to U.S. citizenship and national belonging—in this way, Mateo is queer. And though the penultimate scene of the series finale (season 6, episode 15, "All Sales Final") shows him married to Amy's brother, Eric (played by Filipino Ecuadorian American actor George Salazar), his citizenship status remains decoupled from his romantic-sexual relationship.

Moreover, Mateo's resolve to live and work as he always has, despite an expanding pool of people in the know about his citizenship status, enacts the aesthetics of queer diaspora that Gopinath describes. As a complex subject, Mateo may aspire to recognition within the local Cloud 9 corporate apparatus, but his invisibility from the juridical state apparatus until the season 4 finale symbolizes a mode of precarious queer diasporic resistance that "may be inaudible or unintelligible because they ... are unspectacular and banal, woven into the fabric of everyday life."[120] As a scripted television show, *Superstore* could construct a progressive narrative that results in the "good life" for Mateo: a promotion and/or pay raise, a husband, and legal citizenship. Instead, the writers have opted to present a more realistic portrayal of living "TNT" (*tago ng tago*, a Filipinx idiom in reference to undocumented immigrants).[121] Surely, Mateo experiences moments of uncertainty that could result in deportation prior to, as well as after, his apprehension by ICE, revealing the psychic effects of legal precarity; however, much of his narrative arc centers on his bitchiness—even after he is out on bond during season 5.[122] As such, Mateo exceeds the scripts of undocumentation.

As a queer figure in terms of race and ethnicity, sexuality, nationality, and regionality, Mateo models a mode of queerness that revels in the here and now and is less invested in some progressive future predicated on hard work and hetero- and homonormative conformity. This aligns with Gopinath's sense of queerness that "allows for an alternative form of suspension that resists the forward and upward directionality of normative visions of aspirational success. Unlike the stuck or stalled temporality that marks the state of being undocumented, queerness offers another pathway ... that may be contingent, momentary[,] and tentative, but that nevertheless opens up a different vista of what constitutes success and 'making it.'"[123] So, while Mateo is prevented from upgrading to a Cloud 9 Signature Store and living happily ever after with Jeff due to his undocumented status, placing him in a state of suspension, "apprehend[ing]" his queer world-making capacities as a form of what Kondo terms "reparative creativity" enables us to recognize that being undocumented is a powerful yet non-absolute, socio-juridically constructed state of being that effaces one's humanity.[124]

Mateo's Filipinx identity and the colonial baggage it carries further complicate his relation to Asian America and undocumentation. As Balce explains, "because Filipino Americans constitute the largest Asian immigrant group in the United States, the history and culture of Filipinos cannot be understood as just another variant of the Asian immigrant narrative, but as one that is uniquely scarred by colonization and codependence."[125] As several Filipinx/American studies scholars have argued, Filipinxs exceed the discursive boundaries of Asian American racial formations because they are colonial subjects.[126] I point this out not to sever Filipinxs from Asian America but to acknowledge the particularity of Filipinx difference.[127] Recognizing Filipinx difference as colonial in form works against the flattening impulse of U.S. racial formations. Moreover, Filipinxs were not always restricted from traveling between the Philippines and the United States, since the Philippines was formally—and continues today informally as—an extension of U.S. sovereignty.[128] Thus, although Mateo technically may be undocumented as a post-1946 Filipinx person living in St. Louis, as a Filipinx subject, he is heir to U.S. empire.

What is more, Mateo is another example of See's foolish illiterate, whom I discussed in relation to *Glee*'s Howard. But unlike Howard, Mateo does not completely divest from capitalist accumulation, as evidenced by his determination to consecutively be the store's employee of the month as well as his penchant for expensive brands. Arguably, though, his materialism is self-(pre)serving and thus not wholly invested in the normative scripts of neoliberal capitalism. And his loyalty to the store, as evidenced by his decision to reject an upgraded store transfer (season 2, episode 18, "Mateo's Last Day") and his dissolution of his relationship to Jeff when Jeff takes Corporate's offer of a promotion instead of exposing Corporate's firing of Myrtle (played by White American actor Linda Porter) as ageism (season 3, episode 22, "Town Hall"), reveals his investment in collective support structures.

As he is an undocumented immigrant living in suburban St. Louis, Mateo's social and economic mobility is limited, but he does not go out of his way to gain legal citizenship to access the mythic "good life." The retail work he does as a Cloud 9 employee places him in the same space as other Filipinx laboring bodies overrepresented in low-wage service industries. To be sure, Mateo finds value in earning a wage as a Cloud 9 employee, but his motivation throughout the series has less to do with financial earning power and more to do with the sociality fostered by the store. See's explanation of the unique status of Filipinxs' relation to U.S. capitalism is instructive for understanding Mateo's precarious and paradoxical position as a laboring undocumented immigrant. As noncitizen nonaliens in their historical status as American "nationals," Filipinxs conveniently have fulfilled "the role of the outside constantly being incorporated" that capitalism demands at a time when Asians were barred from entering the United States.[129] In the postimperial era, Filipinxs become simply another foreigner decoupled from the history of U.S. colonial occupation of the Philippines. Such an occlusion has violent psychic and material consequences.[130] However, See argues that the Filipinx subject can then "symbolize and embody the positioning of the noncapitalist *within* the capitalist and the foreign *within* the domestic [original emphases]. Thus, any threat posed to the nation-empire by the Filipino comes from both within and without."[131] This excessive ontology of the Filipinx subject in U.S. culture engenders a rupture of resistance.

For See, the foolish Filipinx illiterate is not simply a dupe of colonial modernity but rather the conduit for "literalizing and exposing both capitalist exploitation and other ways of being."[132] Such anti-capitalist modes of ontological alterity include the "index[ing] . . . of an *other* [original emphasis] economy of debt that is based on assumptions of reciprocity, generosity, and collective survival."[133] Mateo exhibits such forms of indebtedness with his coworkers who know about his precarious status, not simply because he worries they will turn him into the authorities, but because he has developed an intimate bond with people who care about him. Recognizing Mateo's ethno-racial-juridical status as extrinsic as opposed to some kind of intrinsic deviance provides an alternative humanization that runs counter to Euro-American humanisms, which are embedded in the colonial-imperial-capitalist project of human domination.

Seeing the World as It Is *and* as It *Should* Be

Superstore's season 4 finale presents a twist that forces viewers to simultaneously see the world as it is *and* as it *should* be. When Amy (who now is store manager) learns from Jeff (now a regional manager) that Corporate has called in ICE to bust Sandra's union organizing, the store rallies together to help Mateo escape (episode 22, "Employee Appreciation Day"). To Amy's surprise, Jonah, Marcus (played by Jewish American actor and comedian Jon Barinholtz), Cheyenne, Glenn, and Sayid each reveal that they have known about Mateo's precarious status. The camera cut to ICE fanning out from the store entrance forces her to focus on a plan of action. This assault on the store pushes her to discontinue her efforts to quell unionization per Corporate's pressure. In the warehouse section of the building, she leads a strategizing meeting to help Mateo. Marcus offers to shelter Mateo, revealing to his coworkers that he has been living within the walls of the store. Dina, always following the rules, points out, "I mean no offense to Mateo, but technically, he did commit a crime," at which the others grumble. Glenn chimes in: "Let's not forget that Jesus was an immigrant from heaven." Sayid explains the long and violent process of waiting to emigrate to the United States as a refugee. Finally, Amy resolves to fill the store with as many people as they can to distract ICE.

Despite their differing views on undocumented immigrants, the store employees rally together to sneak Mateo out of the store. Mateo dresses in plain clothes, wearing a gray hoodie and a tan baseball cap. Dina serves as the eyes for Amy, Cheyenne, and Mateo, using the surveillance cameras to identify a pathway around the ICE agents. The tone is tense, with fast pans across the aisles, quick cuts to multiple ICE agents zeroing in on them, and upbeat nondiegetic percussion. To temper the drama, the camera also cuts to different characters distracting an ICE agent to humorous effect for viewers. Unfortunately, Dina is unable to identify a clear pathway, as the ICE agents are "everywhere." Unwilling to give up, Amy and Cheyenne try to come up with solutions. Mateo, tired of running, tells them, "It's okay. It's over." The melodic yet somber song "Homegrown" by Haux begins to play nondiegetically, and the scene cuts to a close-up of Mateo frowning. His face is obstructed by the black metal grate of the Homeland Security van. As the van drives out of the rainy store parking lot, we see a crowd of customers standing in front of the store showing signs of solidarity and store employees sadly waving at their fellow comrade. Mateo, wearing a forced smile, waves back with his hands in plastic cuffs. The camera cuts to Glenn, who somberly asks, "What do we do now?" Jonah responds, "I mean, we have to fight this." Cheyenne asks, "How?" The camera cuts back to Mateo, who looks forlorn, and then back to Amy, who asks Jonah, "Wanna start a union?"

After three years of Mateo being out as undocumented to a few coworkers, his ever-present fear of deportation ends with a dramatic arrest by ICE. The series also returns to the issue of labor organizing that coincided with Mateo coming out to Jonah at the beginning of season 2. As previously mentioned, Mateo's undocumented status is a narrative focus only a handful of times during seasons 2 through 4; most of his narrative arc centers on being a sassy, mean queen for comedy. However, the season 4 finale visualizes the sobering reality of ICE raids in the region and across the nation. The creators' decision to feature this plot poignantly enlightens its viewers on the violence of homeland security, especially as migrants continue to be locked up in cages for simply seeking refuge in a country where they do not have citizenship.[134] Citizenship, however, does not confer protection, as witnessed by the incarceration of Japanese Americans during World War II, the conflation of Latinx people with illegality, the racial profiling of Middle Eastern and South Asian men, especially after September 11, the murders of Black people at the hands of police, and the disproportionate violence against Indigenous women.[135]

At the same time, this episode returns to its roots in anti-capitalist collaboration. To the Cloud 9 Angels, Mateo is not just a lawbreaker; he is their friend and coworker—he is a human being. As naïve as the latter statement might be, to see Mateo as a human being is powerful, especially considering the systemic dehumanization of people like Mateo: non-White, queer, working class, and undocumented. That his coworkers band together to help him escape and continue to rally together after his arrest reveals that other ways of living and being are possible in the face of White supremacist imperialist capitalist heteropatriarchy.

Glee and *Superstore* present delightful escapes from reality, but they also invite us to recognize the harsh realities of our present. On one hand, both shows offer a new representation of the Midwest that celebrates its cultural diversity. Their focus on the lives of people of color, LGBTQ+ people, and immigrants is a refreshing counter to the heartland myth that paints the region as overwhelmingly White, straight, and "native"-born. However, television is fantasy. High school is not a place where diverse students spontaneously break out in song and dance, nor do big-box stores foster cross-cultural mutual aid. But fantasy is not frivolous. As the previous chapters illustrate, cultural production simultaneously reflects and refracts the world in which we live and provides blueprints for another world that is more capacious and just. In this chapter, region admittedly recedes as an analytic to show what else is conceivable once we start acknowledging the regional forms that inform cultural production. By now, queer Filipinxs in the Midwest should not come as a surprise.

A queer Filipinx Midwestern reading of the Filipinx characters on both programs reveals how the return of the U.S. colonial repressed televisually manifests and points us toward subversive potentialities transpiring in the future present. Contrary to President McKinley's infamous phrase, "They [Filipinxs] are unfit for self-government," it turns out that neither is the United States capable of governing the Philippines and its peoples.[136] Characters like Blaine, Howard, Sunshine, Frida, and Mateo figure as corporeal specters of the United States' inability to effectively govern its transpacific colony. As ungovernable and thus unruly subjects inhabiting America's heartland, these heterogenous characters work to subvert monolithic conceptualizations of Filipinx America from within and without. Notwithstanding the postracial and postimperial contexts that inform both shows' narratives, the appearance of ethnically and sexually diverse characters and actors in these fictionalized locales enables moments of disidentification and transgression within hegemonic systems, presenting a luminous glimpse of the utopian possibilities that embracing a racialized queer regionality affords.[137]

Such a reparative gesture makes space for the queer diasporic Filipinx Midwestern viewer who recognizes wayward glances, gestures, utterances, and sounds as interpellating an alternative register. Characters like Blaine, Howard, Sunshine, Frida, and Mateo fill me, as that viewer, with glee and inspire me to have a "heavenly day" as they challenge dominant discourses that render their and my existence unimaginable. They offer a momentary address, an affirmation of Othered existence. However, this is not so much a claim to occupation or assimilation; rather, it is an accounting of palimpsestic histories and realities of nonbelonging in the middle of nowhere/somewhere.[138] Seeing the world as it is serves as an acknowledgment of the limits of televisual representation, national discourses, and minoritarian cultural politics; seeing the world as it *should* be enacts a refusal to cede the spectatorial pleasures and imagination of the marginalized. Holding both these visions in tension allows us to be creative in our critiques.

Conclusion

"Looking Back at Looking Forward": Toward a Queer Cartography of the U.S. Filipinx Diaspora

Mapping is an ontoepistemic project. A map creates a sense of space and place. It is an example of Ahmed's orientation device.[1] The map I offer in *The Heartland of U.S. Empire* is conceptual, a provocation to imagine region, nation, empire, and diaspora alternatively. Whereas historical, demographic, and novelty maps tend to characterize the Midwest as the province of White settlers and their descendants as well as of normative Americana, this book's map charts palimpsestic, intersectional, and relational minoritarian histories and realities. In her survey of motifs in Great Plains literatures, Diane Dufva Quantic, a K-State English alum who incidentally taught in Wichita State University's English Department while Santos was there, emphasizes the relationship between White European settlement and physical geography. Although the region she focuses on only represents a part of the broader Midwest, the American mythos of open spaces in need of cultivation is a through line that relates her work to this book. In particular, she relates the creation of place, which domesticates the openness of space, to the building of houses, which signifies "the enclosure that acknowledges the presence of men and women" and which I interpret as the sign of White settler coloniality.[2] In conceptualizing the Midwest as the heartland of U.S. empire, as the house that builds and shelters U.S. empire transcontinentally and transpacifically, I resignify the White pioneer spirit of Midwestern settlement to become the structure that also has room for minoritarian subjectivities. Resignifying the Midwest as queer and Filipinx also invites Filipinx and queer people from without to imagine the Midwest as a viable space and place.

Three final waypoints on the "yellow brick road" to the queer Filipinx Midwest illustrate this book's cartographic gestures. The first is an illuminated map of the world that fills a large wall in a building that houses Indiana University's Geography Department. I encountered this map by happenstance as I roamed the building's hallways during my first Asian American studies–centered conference as a second-year graduate student. At that point, I had not developed this project on the Midwest. What struck me about the map was its myopic presentation of modern global European empires in the wake of Cold War decolonization. Gravitating toward the Philippines and the broader East and Southeast Asian regions where much of the U.S. Cold War battles were fought, I was surprised the map failed to name Spanish empire in demarcating the Philippines' colonial history—though I was not surprised the United States was not identified anywhere as an imperial power.

The map is an assemblage of square panels that illustrate "Newly Independent States, 1945–1973." The map's legend indicates which countries were formerly under British (white), French (green), or "Other" (yellow) rule. Malaysia and Singapore are colored white; Laos, Cambodia, and Vietnam are colored green; and Indonesia, the Philippines, Taiwan, and Korea are colored yellow. I have always been fascinated by how maps visually illustrate space and place (which perhaps explains my collection of Disneyland souvenir maps as a child). In its exclusive focus on former British and French colonies, the Indiana Geography Department map papers over other Western European empires as well as Japanese colonization in East and Southeast Asia (a reckoning of the latter is emerging in Asian American studies).[3] Appropriate to my focus on queer Filipinx Midwestern diaspora, the Philippines' "Other" designation figures U.S. imperial disavowal as symptomatic not only of U.S. epistemologies but also of Midwestern cartographies; it also metaphorizes the island nation's minoritarian status in post/colonial studies and Filipinx Americans' distinctive colonial history, which sets them apart from Asian immigration discourses (but is more aligned with Southeast Asian refugee resettlement).[4] Although *Other* may signify a failure to engage complex histories and realities, I view it as an opportunity to embrace Filipinx nonnormativity.

A second final example of my queer Filipinx Midwestern cartography brings us back to St. Louis. My position as a queer Filipinx Midwesterner queers scenes of the queer Filipinx Midwest wherein Filipinxs appear as objects of display. Whereas chapters 1 and 5 present entertaining Filipinxs who appear boxed in, as either colonial natives confined to the grounds of an international exhibition and performing living tableaus or a postcolonial immigrant television character working in a big-box store and broadcasted or streamed on screens, only apprehending such figures as subjected and objectified negates their potentiality as complex persons.⁵ Despite our differing contextual subject positions, I recognize such figures as queer kin. This is not simply a settlement for limited Filipinx Midwestern representations; it is an unsettlement of the sentiment that exploitative representations have no plausible value to be imagined Otherwise. My disidentificatory apprehension of queer Filipinx Midwestern being aims to place subjects often seen as unmoored.

Thus, as I move through the Missouri History Museum's *The 1904 World's Fair: Looking Back at Looking Forward* exhibit, I imagine that my status as patron (rather than as displayed object) reworks the meaning of the fair for the U.S. Filipinx diaspora. Looking at glass cases filled with Philippine artifacts and commercial souvenirs and framed portraits that transform Filipinxs from so-called savages to civilized citizens, as poet Suzara does in *Souvenir* (discussed in chapter 1), I reflect on the uncanniness of a Filipinx person looking at themselves. The museum attempts to critique its imperial legacy by emphasizing education, but it is arguably no more successful than the fair's reliance on edutainment.⁶

Stereographs were popular at the time of the fair, as their three-dimensional imagery created a sense of realism for viewers. The exhibit provided a sample stereoscope to view such images. Looking at a non-ethnological scene, I become the looker as opposed to the looked at, akin to Fuentes's Markod in *Bontoc Eulogy* (discussed in chapter 1). What does it mean for the colonized to return the gaze? The queer diasporic Filipinx Midwestern lens refracts colonial scenes of subjection, opening up spaces for different realities to exist that exceed normative conceptions of people and places. Despite the sense of alienation and hesitation I often experience in the Midwest as a queer-of-color body, those feelings did not emerge during my visit to the museum. Instead, it felt like a homecoming, a confrontation with a mythical past now made visceral. And just like visits home can be ambivalent for folx, especially those who are queer, I experienced sadness, anger, awe, and wonder as I tried to imagine the sights and sounds of a grand fair tied to Filipinx and American histories.

A final example of my queer Filipinx Midwestern cartography can be found in Kansas, where I began this book. The Dwight D. Eisenhower Presidential Library, Museum, and Boyhood Home is located in Abilene, Kansas, a small town about forty minutes west of where I live and "about 100 miles from the geographic center of the contiguous 48 states," according to one of the museum displays. Given Eisenhower's decorated military career and national service, I suspected his museum would have some representation of the Philippines, especially after my unexpected discoveries at the U.S. Cavalry Museum (discussed in the introduction). Even if I did not find anything related to the Philippines, I still wanted to visit a museum of national (and arguably transnational) significance in a regional locale. I visited the museum with no prior knowledge about Eisenhower.

To my surprise, the Philippines garnered its own display, albeit small, in the World War II exhibit section. Unsurprisingly, signage and accession tags failed to explain the colonial relationship between the United States and the Philippines; one panel simply reads, "Preparing the Philippines for independence," without stating from whom. On one hand, such an omission might suggest the colonial relationship is common knowledge, rendering explicit mention redundant. More likely, U.S. imperial disavowal drives rhetorical absence. Nevertheless, such a public display in the so-called middle of nowhere confirms a direct link between the regional and transnational, unsettling the notion that the Midwest is removed from transpacific empire. Notwithstanding the discursive substance of such displays, the fact that the Philippines appears in seemingly random places throughout the region engenders a different conceptualization of place and national belonging.

The spatial arrangement of the Eisenhower Museum tells visitors that we are in "the heart of America," with opening and closing exhibits using such phrasing in their overview posters. While the normative heartland motif aims to present the former president as "ordinary," "humble," and "hard work[ing]," as the embodiment of Middle American values, the heart of the museum, so to speak, focuses on his military career during World War II and his presidential career (1953–1961) during the Cold War and the U.S. civil rights movement. A radical reading of the heartland vis-à-vis the museum's geography indicates the local and regional as imbricated with the national and imperial, aligning with this book's provocation. Fittingly, at the center of the World War II area are a tall glass display case and an array of photos of Eisenhower's tenure in Manila from September 1935 to December 1939, which I had not been aware of. Eisenhower served as an assistant military advisor to General Douglas MacArthur to aid the Philippine government in the development of "a viable Filipino Army."[7] The displays neglect to contextualize why Eisenhower or MacArthur would need to help the Philippine government in the first place, as this was during the Commonwealth period, when the United States and the Philippines were developing strategies to transform the latter from colony into independent nation (though this moment of U.S. dependence ironically reflects the Philippine condition post-1946).

The Philippine displays are simple (figure C.1). A pillar in between the glass case and enlarged photograph reads "1935 / 1939" and "Gaining a Global View," with "Manila, Philippines" underneath. In the glass case, two scrolls feature an enlarged map of South and Southeast Asia. The left scroll features the word *Recognition* in large font with the following information underneath: "At a farewell banquet, Philippine President Manuel Quezon awarded Ike [Eisenhower] the Philippine Distinguished Service Star. Recognizing

Figure C.1 Partial display of President Eisenhower's time in the Philippines in the Dwight D. Eisenhower Presidential Museum. (*Photo by Thomas Xavier Sarmiento, August 2022.*)

that Ike would have left sooner had Mamie [Eisenhower's wife] not joined him, Quezon asked Mamie to pin the medal on Ike." The right scroll features an enlarged photo of Mamie pinning the medal on Ike, with Quezon smiling and clapping behind her. The medal, "the third highest award of the Armed Forces of the Philippines," sits in the case below the photo. Other items in the case include a bamboo model house to remind the couple of their time in Manila, a private pilot's license Eisenhower earned from the Philippine Bureau of Aeronautics, and a Shaeffer pen desk set gifted from officers of the Philippine Air Corps, a military branch Eisenhower advocated for to MacArthur.

The display next to the glass one features a giant sepia photo of the Philippine Army Headquarters building with soldiers standing in front of it. One of the interpretive details explains how Eisenhower benefited from this post: "He had deep experience with military planning in the United States and familiarity with European battlefields. Ike now added awareness of military affairs across the Pacific and East Asia." While the Philippine military and government benefited from Eisenhower's expertise, the museological narrative reinforces an accumulative and extractive relationship between the United States and the Philippines. Next to this text is a photo of Eisenhower with Filipino soldiers at Camp Murphy (named after Michigander Frank Murphy, last governor-general and first high commissioner to the

Philippines; it was later renamed Camp Aguinaldo in 1965, in honor of the first president of the Philippines), c. 1938.

Known for his "Middle Way" governing philosophy, "balanc[ing] political extremes, public and private power, investment and spending, security and liberty," and his critique of the rising military industrial complex mentioned in his 1961 presidential farewell speech, Eisenhower and his museum invite us to reimagine the middle. Certainly, the political middle connotes moderation and compromise. However, the notion of middle I have been proposing throughout this book aims to conceptualize it as a space not of normativity but of queerness, of messiness, non-singularity, multiplicity, and contradiction.[8] Learning about Philippine history as a queer diasporic Filipinx Midwesterner in a museum at the almost geographic center of the contiguous United States is an uncanny, queer experience. The fact that I can find connections to the Philippines by visiting Midwestern public institutions contradicts the notion that Filipinxs are out of place in the heartland.

Heartland of U.S. Empire provokes a queer cartography of the U.S. Filipinx diaspora that unsettles both American exceptionalist and hegemonic Asian American discourses that imagine the interior United States as empty land. Susan Naramore Maher's turn to deep mapping, inspired by William Least Heat-Moon's *PrairyErth: (a deep map)* (1991), to engender an alter-narrative of the Great Plains resonates with this book's investment in reimagining place Otherwise. A deep map "presents the multiple histories of place, the cross-sectional stories of natural and human history as traced through eons and generations," that "artful[ly] braid . . . deep past, scientific knowledge, cultural history, and personal participation in a spatial milieu."[9] Naramore Maher explains that the deep map "insist[s] on capturing a plethora of interconnected stories from a particular location, a distinctive place, and framing the landscape within this indeterminate complexity. Deep maps present many kinds of tales in an effort to capture the quintessence of place, but the place itself remains elusive and incompletely limned."[10] For her, a deep map of the Great Plains unsettles the master narrative of White settler colonials who aim to conquer the inhospitable lands of the U.S. West and makes space for Indigenous cosmologies.[11] Similarly, this book desires to unsettle the notion that the Midwest is an inhospitable place for queer people and people of Asian descent. While not necessarily engaged with the region's physical geography, my peopling of the Midwest with queerness and Filipinxness unsettles the myth of the region as a geography of nowhere indicative only of White cis-heteronormativity.

As the preceding chapters illustrate, *Heartland of U.S. Empire* is not simply a project of unsettlement, of critique; it also is a project of creation, of new mapmaking. Katherine McKittrick's work on Black feminist geographies has influenced my thinking of the queer Filipinx Midwest. For her, "The history of black subjects in the diaspora is a geographic story" that "maps the ties and tensions between material and ideological dominations and oppositional spatial practices. Black geographies and black women's geographies, then, signal alternative patterns that work alongside and across traditional geographies."[12] Geographic tropes of "placements and displacements, segregations and integrations, margins and centers, and migrations and settlements" that constitute Black diasporic history also are indicative of queer Filipinx diasporic history.[13] Centering the dialectic Other of normative geography works to materialize submerged narratives that "illustrate the ways in which human geographies are, as a result of connections, made alterable."[14] The Other is already (t)here. We simply need to reorient to them, to open ourselves up to the possibilities and plausibilities they proffer to engender more livable geographies.

Whereas each chapter focuses on a set of site-specific literary and cultural texts, together they form an assemblage of queer diasporic acts that interrupt the normative narratives of the Midwest and Filipinx diaspora and map waypoints for queer Filipinx Midwesterners to locate themselves. Like Lowe's framing of immigrant acts as not simply U.S. immigration policies but also subtle (and not so subtle) resistive acts performed by immigrants and Herring's "paper cut politics" in which small acts accrue to become considerable forces with which to reckon, this book's tracing of Midwesterners in the Philippines and Filipinxs in the Midwest charts how the heartland is an imperial space and place wherein the presence of U.S. imperial subjects transform the hegemonic discourses of the region to affirm the queer diasporic Filipinx ontoepistemes that exist under the shadow of the normative myths of the Midwest.[15] By Filipinizing the Midwest and queering Filipinx diaspora, this book reorients us toward "new vistas, new lives, and new ways of being."[16] Ahmed writes of "the promise of reorientation" as a byproduct of queering: "Those lodged as particular can dislodge the general"; "to be in question is to question being."[17] Here, Ahmed speaks of bodies out of place as being made to be out of place by discursive norms; however, when we pay attention to those bodies, we see the world anew.

The vantage of the marginalized particular opens up a different conceptual map of sociality and culture. Nevertheless, the power of normativity makes it difficult to recognize this alternative. As Muñoz advises, "to access queer visuality[,] we may need to squint, to strain our vision and force it to see otherwise, beyond the limited vista of the here and now."[18] But once we reorient to the particular, the marginal, the peripheral—that which is queer because it has been queered—our field perception is able to accommodate the impossible.[19] Filipinx people, queer people, and queer Filipinx people are not new to the Midwest; however, because they do not represent a population majority, they typically are not associated with the region. Moreover, their counted and perceived population majorities in urban coastal regions reify where they should belong and eclipse where they could belong. As numerical minorities, their unrepresentativeness in and of the region discursively casts them as statistical anomalies. However, the heart of queer theory is to orient toward and engage the anomalous to imagine a different sense of space and time wherein that which is counter-normative is granted dignity. Ultimately, the queer Filipinx Midwest emergent in these pages is a love letter to all of us who have felt like we do not belong and a reminder that we do.

Notes

INTRODUCTION

1. Throughout the book, I use *Filipinx* (singular) and *Filipinxs* (plural) as inclusive terms for people of various gender identities and expressions with ethno-racial ties to the Philippines. Whereas *Filipina/o* (and *Filipin@*) intervenes in the decidedly masculinist *Filipino*, an indicator of the Spanish language's colonial history on the Southeast Asian archipelago, it nevertheless presents gender as binary. *Filipinxs* makes room for nonbinary gender–identified people. This linguistic move aligns with activists and scholars who deploy *Latinx* (and *Latine*) rather than *Latina/o*, though it is not without contention.

2. I define the Midwest region geographically according to the U.S. Census Bureau's twelve-state designation: Illinois, Indiana, Iowa, Kansas, Michigan, Minnesota, Missouri, Nebraska, North Dakota, Ohio, South Dakota, and Wisconsin. "Census Regions and Divisions of the United States," U.S. Census Bureau, accessed March 6, 2023, https://www2.census.gov/geo/pdfs/maps-data/maps/reference/us_regdiv.pdf. While geographic boundaries demarcate the Midwest, culture also plays a role in defining as well as unsettling the region. For example, the Big Ten Conference of intercollegiate athletics—historically made up of institutions in the Census-defined Midwest (University of Chicago [Illinois], University of Illinois Urbana-Champaign, Indiana University, University of Iowa, University of Michigan, Michigan State University, University of Minnesota, University of Nebraska–Lincoln, Northwestern University [Illinois], The Ohio State University, Purdue University [Indiana], and University of Wisconsin–Madison)—now includes the University of California, Los Angeles; Johns Hopkins University (Maryland); Pennsylvania State University; Rutgers University (New Jersey); the University of Maryland, College Park; the University of Oregon; the University of Southern California; and the University of Washington in its membership. "About the Conference," Big Ten Conference, last updated December 3, 2024, https://bigten.org/about/general/about-big-ten-conference/. Like-

wise, other universities in the Census-defined Midwest belong to intercollegiate athletic conferences that exceed the region; the University of Kansas, Kansas State University, and Iowa State University belong to the Big 12 Conference, which is composed of institutions heavily in the Southwest and West, whereas the University of Missouri belongs to the Southeastern Conference, which includes institutions mainly in the South. "Big 12 Biography," Big 12 Conference, June 30, 2024, https://big12sports.com/news/2019/7/31/big-12-conference.aspx; and "History of the Southeastern Conference," Southeastern Conference, accessed December 19, 2024, https://www.secsports.com/history.

3. "History of Fort Riley and 1st Infantry Division," U.S. Army Fort Riley, last updated October 2, 2024, https://home.army.mil/riley/about/history. Janette writes about Fort Riley's sonic and material influence in our town and on our teaching. Incidentally, one of the camps at Fort Riley is named after Kansan U.S. General Frederick Funston, whose troops, with the aid of the Filipinx Macabebe Scouts, captured Generalissimo and President Emilio Aguinaldo on March 23, 1901, in Palanan, Isabela Province, which brought an end to the First Philippine Republic.

4. "Fort Riley Museums," U.S. Army Fort Riley, last updated September 16, 2025, https://home.army.mil/riley/about/museums; "History of Fort Riley"; "Context and Story of the Battle," Little Bighorn Battlefield National Monument, National Park Service, last updated April 23, 2025, https://www.nps.gov/libi/learn/historyculture/battle-story.htm; and Kristin Moore, dir., "The Battle of the Greasy Grass," posted March 23, 2017, Smithsonian Magazine, YouTube, 3 min., 25 sec., https://www.youtube.com/watch?v=SCl_oeOk_Yo.

5. Ahmed, *Queer Phenomenology*, 135.

6. See, *Filipino Primitive*, 59.

7. During the "American Empire: The State of the Field" Symposium at the University of Notre Dame in March 2014, a conversation between Harrod Suarez and me yielded the phrase the heartland of empire to describe my work on the Philippines, Filipinx diaspora, and the Midwest.

8. "History of Fort Riley."

9. Alidio; Bascara, *Model-Minority*; Campomanes, "New Empire's"; Cordova; Isaac, *American Tropics*; Kaplan; Kaplan and Pease; Mendoza; Rafael, *White Love*; and See, *Decolonized Eye*.

10. I borrow the notion of unexpectedness from Deloria.

11. Bascara, *Model-Minority*, 45.

12. Ibid., 34.

13. Baum, 24.

14. Ibid., 159.

15. Oler, "Introduction," xv–xvi; emphasis omitted. I use *U.S. Filipinx* following Campomanes, who uses *U.S. Filipino* to signal the illegibility of Filipinxs in the context of U.S. empire ("New Empire's," 150–152). Writing in the Cold War context, Diaz uses *configuration* to reconceptualize the Philippines and the U.S. Filipinx diaspora.

16. Sumida.

17. Gopinath, *Unruly Visions*, 25–26.

18. Scholarship on queer nonmetronormativities includes Halberstam, *In a Queer Time and Place*; Herring; C. Johnson; and Tongson, *Relocations*. Asian American studies "east of California" include Bow; Dhingra, "Introduction"; Dhingra, *Life Behind*; Galura and Lawsin; Gupta-Carlson; Joshi and Desai; E. Lee; Ling, *Chinese Americans*; Ling, *Chinese Chicago*; Ling, *Chinese St. Louis*; Ling, *Voices of the Heart*; See, *Filipino Primitive*; Sumida; Trieu; and Wilkinson and Jew. Critical studies of the Midwest include Allegro

and Wood; Campney, *Hostile Heartland*; Campney, *This Is Not Dixie*; Curtis; Edmunds; Halvorson and Reno; Oler, *Pieces*; Valerio-Jiménez, Vaquera-Vásquez, and Fox; Vega; and Williamson. Campomanes provocatively notes, "'East of California' as a formulation uncommendably dissolves the middle of the United States outright while privileging the 'East' as the sole locus of ferment" ("New Formations," 524).

19. Balance, 14.

20. Barillas, 18. See also Cantrell; Cayton and Gray; Cayton and Onuf; Halvorson and Reno; and Shortridge.

21. "U.S. Census Bureau Releases Key Stats in Honor of 2023 Asian American, Native Hawaiian, and Pacific Islander Heritage Month," U.S. Department of Commerce, May 1, 2023, https://www.commerce.gov/news/blog/2023/05/us-census-bureau-releases-key-stats-honor-2023-asian-american-native-hawaiian-and. Hoganson; and Oler, "Introduction," frame the Midwest as a space of connection.

22. See, *Decolonized Eye*, xvi.

23. LeRoy, 4–5. On the evening of February 4, 1899, Private William W. Grayson of the Nebraska Volunteer Infantry Regiment was guarding the Santa Mesa barrio in Manila when he fired his gun. See also Chaput.

24. Trinidad Rojo quoted in Baldoz, 196; Mercer, 7; Stuart Hall quoted in Morley, 2; and R. Rodriguez, "Toward a Critical Filipino Studies," 51.

25. "The Life of Mateo Francisco," "'Michigan Men' in the Philippines," *The Philippines and the University of Michigan, 1870–1935*, Michigan in the World exhibit, University of Michigan, accessed February 14, 2023, https://philippines.michiganintheworld.history.lsa.umich.edu/s/exhibit/page/the-life-of-mateo-francisco.

26. "Pensionado Profile: Santiago Artiaga," "Filipino Students Stateside," *The Philippines and the University of Michigan, 1870–1935*, Michigan in the World exhibit, University of Michigan, accessed February 4, 2023, https://philippines.michiganintheworld.history.lsa.umich.edu/s/exhibit/page/pensionado-profile-santiago-artiaga.

27. Mason, 547.

28. Lillian Pardo, "Filipinos in Kansas City Through the Years: A Historical Perspective," Filipino Association of Greater Kansas City, accessed February 4, 2023, http://www.filipino-association.org/about/history.asp.

29. Balance; Clutario; Coráñez Bolton, *Crip Colony*; Cruz, *Transpacific Femininities*; Diaz; Fajardo, "Decolonizing"; Fajardo, *Filipino Crosscurrents*; Fajardo, "Queering"; Isaac, *American Tropics*; Suarez; Velasco; and Winkelmann.

30. Manalansan's *Global Divas* is notable for transnationalizing Asian American studies.

31. Desai; and Ponce, *Beyond the Nation*, influence my thinking of "beyond the nation."

32. Zarsadiaz's *Resisting Change in Suburbia* traces Southern California's East San Gabriel Valley's Asian suburbanization in the late twentieth century, which includes a large concentration of Filipinxs.

33. Muñoz, *Cruising Utopia*, 1. In tracing *queer*'s etymology from "the 'Middle French *querir* to seek, to ask, request, to inquire' and the 'Spanish *querer* to seek, to ask, inquire, to like, prefer,'" Ponce similarly casts *queer* as indicative of "both desire and inquiry" (*Beyond the Nation*, 27). Ferguson coins "queer of color critique" in *Aberrations*, building upon the works of Reddy, "Home," and Muñoz, *Disidentifications*.

34. Chakrabarty; and Rafael, "Regionalism." Barillas distinguishes provincialism from regionalism, the former being associated with "local chauvinism, contempt for other places and cultures, racism, sexism, homophobia—a whole host of prejudices" (16), while the latter is "concerned with the mutual influence of place and humanity" (17).

35. Choy; Dhingra, *Life Behind*; Fu; Galura and Lawsin; Lee and Miller; Ling, *Chinese Chicago*; Ling, *Chinese St. Louis*; Ling, *Voices of the Heart*; Park Nelson; Pate; Posadas and Guyotte; and Vang. The *Journal of Asian American Studies* special issue on the Midwest (Dhingra); Wilkinson and Jew's edited collection on Michigan; Ling's *Chinese Americans*; Trieu; D. Anderson's; Kinney's; Nguyen-Dien's; Pha's; Woodcock's; and Yin's contributions to the *American Studies* double special issue "Unsettling Global Midwests" (Perreira et al. and Sarmiento et al.); D. Anderson's dissertation; and Kinney's *Mapping AsiaTown Cleveland*, however, place the Midwest as a central analytic.

36. Dr. Jennifer Bacani McKenney, Wilson County (Kansas) health officer, wife of Fredonia (Kansas) Mayor Bob McKenney, and daughter of Filipinx immigrants, who was born and raised in Fredonia, experienced harassment by community members in response to mask mandates and public health measures to mitigate the spread of COVID-19 that she speculates was compounded by her racial-ethnic identity. People of Asian descent in the United States have been targets of violence in the wake of COVID-19, reigniting anti-Asian racism, as China has been linked to the novel coronavirus's origin. Antonia Hylton and Emily Berk, "Health Official in Kansas Target of Anger, Harassment over Proposed Covid Measures," *NBC News*, December 4, 2020, https://www.nbcnews.com/news/us-news/health-official-kansas-target-anger-harassment-over-proposed-covid-measures-n1249961.

37. Dhingra, "Introduction," 239, 244, 245; and E. Lee, 254.

38. In her study of Asian Americans in the Midwest, Trieu argues that "space must be considered if we are to more fully understand the racialization of Asian Americans" (3). See Lipsitz for a discussion of the spatialization of race (and the racialization of space). See also Ahmed, *Queer Phenomenology*, 24; and See, *Decolonized Eye*, 64.

39. Sarmiento, "Diasporic Filipinx Queerness"; Sarmiento, "Peminist"; Sarmiento, "PhilippinExcess"; and Sarmiento, "To Return to St. Louis."

40. Quiray Tagle importantly frames California as a regional space of Asian and Filipinx diaspora, intervening in its often-abstracted status as the locus of Asian and Filipinx America (1113).

41. Additional critical scholarship on Filipinxs that centers California includes Y. Espiritu; Ocampo; and Zarsadiaz, *Resisting Change*. In terms of Filipinx literary representations that center the West Coast, R. Zamora Linmark's *Rolling the R's* is set in Kalihi, Hawai'i; Noël Alumit's *Letters to Montgomery Clift* and *Talking to the Moon* are set in Southern California, as is Brian Ascalon Roley's *American Son*; and Elaine Castillo's *America Is Not the Heart* is set in the San Francisco Bay Area.

42. Ahmed, *Queer Phenomenology*, 67.

43. Ahmed describes queer phenomenology as "a disorientation device . . . [that] allow[s] the oblique to open up another angle on the world" (*Queer Phenomenology*, 172). Building on this scholarship, Gopinath forwards queerness as "a state of being out of place and disoriented in the landscape of heteronormativity" (*Unruly Visions*, 61). Tongson also illustrates the spatiality of queerness in *Relocations*.

44. Gopinath, *Unruly Visions*, 5.

45. Gopinath, "Queer Regions," 351.

46. Gopinath, *Unruly Visions*, 20.

47. Ibid., 21, 29, 50, 52.

48. See, *Decolonized Eye*, xxx.

49. Gopinath, *Unruly Visions*, 4.

50. Ibid., 8. See also Khubchandani.

51. Percentages calculated from "Profile of General Population and Housing Characteristics," U.S. Census Bureau, Decennial Census, DEC Demographic Profile, Table DP1, 2020, accessed June 21, 2024, https://data.census.gov/table/DECENNIALDP2020.DP1?g=010XX00US_040XX00US06,17,18,19,20,26,27,29,31,38,39,46,55&d=DEC%20Demographic%20Profile; and "Total Population," U.S. Census Bureau, Decennial Census, DEC Detailed Demographic and Housing Characteristics File A, Table T01001, 2020, accessed June 21, 2024, https://data.census.gov/table/DECENNIALDDHCA2020.T01001?t=038:3854:Race%20and%20Ethnicity&g=010XX00US_040XX00US06,17,18,19,20,26,27,29,31,38,39,46,55&d=DEC%20Detailed%20Demographic%20and%20Housing%20Characteristics%20File%20A. Data includes multiracial Asians and Filipinxs.

52. Herring, introduction.

53. Balance and Burns's edited collection, *California Dreaming*, indicates California's prominence in the Asian American discursive imaginary.

54. On regional nostalgia and fictive innocence, see Cantrell.

55. I use *plausible* instead of *possible* as a subtle shift from Gopinath's theorization of queerness as an impossible desire (*Impossible Desires*).

56. Tuan, "Place," 158.

57. Ibid., 159.

58. I borrow "imagine Otherwise" from Chuh, *Imagine Otherwise*; and Gordon, 5.

59. Herring, introduction; and Tongson, *Relocations*, chap. 3. Oler's "pieces" to represent the Midwest heartland also resonate here (*Pieces*).

60. In their introduction to the *GLQ* special issue "Queering the Middle," Manalansan, Nadeau, Rodríguez, and Somerville caution against an outright rejection of the metronormative, and thus urban, which unwittingly can erase QTBIPOC Midwestern narratives located in cities (9).

61. Herring, introduction.

62. Rice Paper Collective of the Madison Asian Union, quoted in Wei, 30.

63. I borrow *metroimperial* from Mendoza.

64. Tongson, *Relocations*, chap. 1.

65. Ibid.

66. Ibid.

67. Herring, introduction. Certainly, the Midwest, like the rural in Herring and the suburban in Tongson, is not without its shortcomings as a habitable space and place for queer/Filipinx people. My focus here is more on the normative frames through which we create knowledge about diasporic identity, community, and experience.

68. Tongson, *Relocations*, chap. 1; and Herring, introduction. Byrd informs my thinking of "transits of empire."

69. Balce; Isaac, *American Tropics*; Kaplan and Pease; See, *Decolonized Eye*; and See, *Filipino Primitive*.

70. "Land Acknowledgement Statement," Office of the Chancellor, University of Illinois Urbana-Champaign, July 26, 2018, https://chancellor.illinois.edu/land_acknowledgement.html; "Land Acknowledgment," First Nations Educational and Cultural Center, Indiana University Bloomington, accessed March 4, 2023, https://firstnations.indiana.edu/land-acknowledgement/index.html; "Provisional Land Acknowledgement," American Indian and Indigenous Studies, Michigan State University, accessed March 4, 2023, https://aiis.msu.edu/land/; "University Origins," American Culture, University of Michigan, accessed March 4, 2023, https://lsa.umich.edu/ac; "IAS Land Acknowledgement," Institute for Advanced Study, University of Minnesota, accessed March 4, 2023,

https://ias.umn.edu/about/ias-land-acknowledgement; "Land Acknowledgement," Earthworks, The Ohio State University, accessed March 4, 2023, https://earthworks.osu.edu/land; and "Tribal Lands Map," Wisconsin First Nations, accessed March 4, 2023, https://wisconsinfirstnations.org/map/. For more on the history of the Midwest, see Cayton and Gray; Cayton and Onuf; Edmunds; Halvorson and Reno; Hoganson; and Shortridge.

71. "Land Acknowledgement," Diversity, Equity, and Inclusion, Iowa State University, February 18, 2020, https://www.diversity.iastate.edu/dei-resources/land-acknowledgement; Indigenous Faculty Staff Alliance, "Land Acknowledgement," About K-State, Kansas State University, last updated October 8, 2025, https://www.k-state.edu/about/our-culture/land-acknowledgment/; "Tribes of Missouri," Native American/Indigenous Studies: MO Indigenous Nations, University of Missouri Libraries, last updated February 17, 2023, https://libraryguides.missouri.edu/nativeamericanstudies/motribes; "History," The Otoe-Missouria Tribe, accessed March 4, 2023, https://www.omtribe.org/who-we-are/history/; "Land Acknowledgement Statement," Native American Coalition, University of Nebraska–Lincoln, accessed October 16, 2025, https://nativecoalition.unl.edu/; "NDSU Land Acknowledgement," Center for Community and Belonging, North Dakota State University, accessed October 16, 2025, https://www.ndsu.edu/community-belonging; "Land Acknowledgement," Student Diversity and Inclusion, University of North Dakota, accessed March 4, 2023, https://und.edu/student-life/diversity/multicultural/land-acknowledgement.html; and "Land Acknowledgement," Wokini Initiative, South Dakota State University, accessed March 4, 2023, https://www.sdstate.edu/wokini-initiative/land-acknowledgement.

72. Shortridge, 17.

73. "Freedom, Slavery & the Midwest Slavery Bans," African American Midwest, accessed March 4, 2023, https://africanamericanmidwest.com/history-slavery/slavery-the-midwest-slavery-bans/.

74. Shortridge, chap. 3. Sundown towns in the region also have shaped the region's predominantly White demographic. Campney, *Hostile Heartland*; Campney, *This Is Not Dixie*; and Loewen.

75. Cantrell, 58, 61.

76. V. Johnson, introduction.

77. Hoganson, xvi–xvii. Cantrell offers a similar argument.

78. I thank Lisa Tatonetti for helping me to foreground the violence of settler colonialism discussed in these last two paragraphs.

79. Bow; and Justice inspire my use of *anomalous*. Joshi and Desai; and Rafael, *Discrepant*, inspire my use of *discrepant*.

80. See also Curtis; De Genova; Edmunds; Valdés; Valerio-Jiménez, Vaquera-Vásquez, and Fox; Vega; and Williamson. Ling's oral histories of Asian American women in *Voices of the Heart* implicitly does this work as well. The movement for Black lives, especially in response to the deaths of Michael Brown in Ferguson, Missouri, in 2014 and George Floyd in Minneapolis, Minnesota, in 2020, brings into relief the Midwest's (and the nation's) racial reckoning. As Campney's historiography of anti-Black racism in the region illumines, America's heartland is not exempt from racial strife.

81. Reddy writes, "Unaccounted for within both Marxist and liberal pluralist discussions of the home and the nation, queers of color *as people of color* [original emphasis], I argue, take up the critical task of both remembering and rejecting the model of the 'home' offered in the United States in two ways: first, by attending to the ways in which it was defined over and against people of color, and second, by expanding the locations and

moments of that critique of the home to interrogate processes of group and self-formation from the experience of being expelled from their own dwelling and families for not conforming to the dictation of and demand for uniform gendered and sexual types" ("Home," 356–357).

82. In *Filipino Crosscurrents*, Fajardo uses *Filipino-ize* and *Filipino-ization* to describe Filipino seamen's cultural practices that resignify spatial and temporal aspects of seafaring (148).

83. Reddy, "Home," 357.

84. Muñoz, *Disidentifications*.

85. Reddy, "Home," 357.

86. Cayton, "Anti-Region." See Cayton and Gray; Cayton and Onuf; and Shortridge. Herr's comparative study of the American Midwest and rural Ireland is consistent with other studies of the Midwest as a region that carries national symbolism; however, Herr is ultimately concerned with the value of comparing regions across the globe and the agrarian rural rather than with unsettling the particularities of the Midwest as synecdoche for America.

87. Barillas, 19.

88. For more on critical regionalism, see Ayers et al.; Hoganson; Herr; and Powell.

89. Herr, 18.

90. For more on the Great Lakes, see Fajardo, "Queering." Michigan is the only Midwestern state that does not have a river that feeds into the Mississippi River basin.

91. Ayers et al.; Gopinath; and Hoganson.

92. Gopinath, *Unruly Visions*, 7.

93. Ibid., 30.

94. Debunking the U.S. heartland mythology, Hoganson notes: "To be local . . . has meant to be left behind: close-minded, isolated, ignorant, backward looking, peasant-like, and probably rural" (3). Clampitt's history of maize/corn and the Midwest likewise emphasizes the region's global connectivity.

95. Manalansan et al., 5.

96. Gopinath, *Unruly Visions*, 7. See also Lowe, *Intimacies*.

97. Hoganson, iv.

98. See, *Filipino Primitive*, 62.

99. Ibid., 53, 79.

100. Isaac, *American Tropics*, 7.

101. See, *Filipino Primitive*, 54.

102. Fajardo, *Filipino Crosscurrents*, 28. See also Fajardo, "Queering."

103. Suarez, 16.

104. Ibid., 18.

105. Eng, *Feeling of Kinship*, 13–14.

106. Ibid., 58.

107. Gopinath, *Unruly Visions*, 13.

108. Fajardo, *Filipino Crosscurrents*, 160–161.

109. Desai, ix; and Ponce, *Beyond the Nation*, 1.

110. For more on queer diasporas, see Khubchandani; La Fountain-Stokes; Manalansan, *Global Divas*; Tongson, *Relocations*; and Velasco.

111. See writes "I am dissatisfied with both scholarly and everyday practices of identifying the Philippines as 'home' or 'homeland' and everywhere else as the 'diaspora'" and asks "what if California is home?" to trouble the false dichotomy between *Filipinx* and *Filipinx American* (*Decolonized Eye*, 168n13).

112. Isaac, *American Tropics*, xxiii. Campomanes's "New Empire's" is foundational in conceptualizing U.S. imperial amnesia with respect to the Philippines and its U.S. diaspora. See also Balce; Mendoza; See, *Decolonized Eye*; and See, *Filipino Primitive*.

113. Manalansan et al., 1.

114. Cruz, *Transpacific Femininities*, 33.

115. Tongson similarly transforms *nowhere* into *somewhere* (*Relocations*, chap. 1). Toward the end of *Another Country*, Herring acknowledges *nowhere* as "a dead end, a cul-de-sac" for some as well as "a much-needed detour" (chap. 5).

116. See, *Filipino Primitive*, 104.

117. Ponce, *Beyond the Nation*, 232.

118. Tongson, *Relocations*, chap. 1.

119. Certainly, exclusion mars Midwestern Asian American experiences, but it is not necessarily the dominant narrative. In her introduction to *Asian American Plays for a New Generation*, Josephine Lee remarks on Asian American isolation and singularity in the context of the Midwest (4). In Trieu's contemporary study of Asian Midwesterners, isolation is one of the key themes that inform her participants' lived realities (1–5).

120. Governor's Interracial Commission, 7, 8; and Ling, *Chinese Americans*, 44, 193.

121. Houston; and Mitchell.

122. Lee and Miller; McKee; Park Nelson; and Pate.

123. Nguyen-Dien; Pha, "Minnesota"; Smalkoski; Vang; and Xaykaothao.

124. Gupta-Carlson, 51, 136.

125. Moua is "the first Asian woman chosen to serve in the Minnesota Legislature and the first Hmong American elected to any state legislature" (Tiffany Vang, "Election of Mee Moua to the Minnesota Senate, 2002," *MNopedia*, March 5, 2015, https://www.mnopedia.org/event/election-mee-moua-minnesota-senate-2002).

126. See, *Decolonized Eye*, 66–67.

127. Gopinath, *Unruly Visions*, 3, 4.

128. Tongson, *Relocations*, chap. 1.

129. See, *Decolonized Eye*, 65.

130. My "eye" reference is an homage to See's *Decolonized Eye*.

131. Takaki.

CHAPTER 1

1. A part of this chapter has been revised from "To Return to St. Louis: Reading the Intimacies of the Heartland of U.S. Empire through 'The Dogeater,'" Thomas Xavier Sarmiento, *Amerasia Journal* (2020), Taylor and Francis, reprinted by permission of the publisher (Taylor and Francis, http://www.tandfonline.com).

2. Fajardo's "Decolonizing" intervenes in the impulse to subsume this local story under the national.

3. Blanco.

4. Tajima-Peña.

5. Ibid.

6. Ibid.

7. The Philippine "Reservation" also was referred to as the Philippine Exhibit, Philippine Exposition, and Philippine Village.

8. Gilbert; and Rydell.

9. Balance; Balce; Burns; Delmendo; and Fermin.

10. See, *Decolonized Eye*; and Tiongson et al.

11. I appreciate Hey-Colón's work on Afro-Latinx cultural production, which links the Caribbean to the United States. She cites Baptist's chapter, "Hidden in Plain View," to trace the United States' acquisition of New Orleans and the broader French Louisiana territory to the Haitian Revolution. In *Intimacies of Four Continents*, Lowe also links the Haitian Revolution to U.S. settler colonial expansion.

12. *Sights, Scenes and Wonders at the World's Fair: Official Book of Views of the Louisiana Purchase Exposition* (Official Photographic Company, 1904), Washington University Archives, St. Louis.

13. Herbert S. Stone, *Philippine Exposition: World's Fair, St. Louis, 1904*, guidebook, Missouri History Museum Archives, St. Louis.

14. See notes that "the derogatory term 'dogeater' . . . is particular to Filipino American history" (*Filipino Primitive*, 116), though racist stereotypes associate East and Southeast Asians with dogeating as well.

15. Patajo-Legasto. My argument that the St. Louis World's Fair is the primal scene of U.S. imperialist subjection for Filipinxs draws influence from Hartman's work on Black subjection in the United States during slavery and its afterlife. While the *Oxford American Dictionaries* defines *primal scene* in the strict Freudian sense as "the occasion on which a child becomes aware of its parents' sexual intercourse, the timing of which is thought to be crucial in determining predisposition to future neuroses," I use the concept more expansively by construing the Filipinx subject as the progeny of the imperial union between the Philippines and the United States. Eng and Han's engagement with psychoanalysis through critical race theory further supports the transposition of psychoanalysis's emphasis on familial dynamics to the realm of the social and racial.

16. Balance; Balce; Burns; Delmendo; and See, *Decolonized Eye*. Gonzalez offers a comparative regional analysis of Filipinx primitivism, citing the 1904 St. Louis World's Fair as an originary event in U.S.–Philippine relations and connecting the Cordillera Mountain region with the U.S. South. She cites Missouri's slaveholding past as aligning the state with the South rather than the Midwest (150).

17. I appreciate Tanya González, who inspired me to contemplate the diasporic Filipinx cultures of the St. Louis World's Fair in terms of elegy. Following See, I use *post/colonial* rather than *postcolonial* to signal the continuing conditions and effects of colonialism despite the so-called formal end of Euro-American colonialisms after World War II (*Decolonized Eye*, xvii).

18. Weisman's introduction to *The Oxford Handbook of the Elegy* notes *elegy* lacks scholarly consensus; instead, she offers a more expansive definition that considers change over time and geographical context.

19. Formally, *elegy* is poetic and mournful, whereas *eulogy* is prose that praises the life of the deceased.

20. Weisman, 1.
21. See, *Decolonized Eye*, 6.
22. Weisman, 7.
23. Ibid., 3, 6, 8.
24. Ibid., 9.
25. Ibid., 2, 3, 5, 7.
26. Ibid., 1.
27. Freud, "Mourning and Melancholia."
28. Isaac, *American Tropics*; and See, *Decolonized Eye*, discuss the Philippines as "foreign in a domestic sense" during the official U.S. colonial period, revealing the unique case of Filipinxs as ontoepistemically liminal subjects.

29. J. Kim, 11, 22.

30. Gordon; Hu Pegues; Isaac, *American Tropics*; Lowe, *Intimacies*; Mendoza; See, *Filipino Primitive*; and Stoler, *Haunted*. Balce's focus on abjection provides a compelling approach to understanding U.S. imperial amnesia and the illegible Filipinx body in American culture. Whereas abjection underlies her view of international expositions / world's fairs (24), prominent at the turn of the twentieth century, I forward attraction as the missing but necessary counterpoint to the scholarship on imperial exhibition.

31. Chang, 17–18.

32. Isaac, *American Tropics*, 2. Baldoz; Isaac, *American Tropics*; and See, *Decolonized Eye*, address the paradox of Filipinxs being "U.S. nationals" during the U.S. colonial period, which juridically figured Filipinxs as neither alien nor citizen.

33. Mendoza, 129.

34. Balce analyzes the fetish of the Filipina breast. Fairgoers also often remarked on Igorot men wearing G-strings, implicitly drawing attention to their Brown bare buttocks.

35. Mumford; and Gilbert, 151.

36. Lowe, "Intimacies," 193.

37. Ibid., 195.

38. Ibid., 203.

39. While the *primitive* contextually refers to colonized Filipinxs, as See's work in *Filipino Primitive* indicates, I want to avoid flattening the various Indigenous and ethnic Philippine peoples present at the fair, instead recognizing *primitive* as constitutive of Philippine plurality.

40. I use *phantasies* instead of *fantasies* to signal the psychic dimensions of coloniality.

41. During the U.S. colonial period, Filipinxs and Americans freely traveled between the Philippines and the United States, calling into question the geographical borders of nation under empire.

42. Ria Unson's art and criticism and Al Evangelista's dance performances likewise illustrate twenty-first century preoccupations with the fair. Ria Unson, "Interrogating the Colonized Mind Through Contemporary Art Practices," presentation at the annual Association for Asian American Studies conference, Seattle, WA, April 26, 2024. Al Evangelista, "places i can't dance," accessed December 20, 2024, https://alevangelista.com/index places%20(1).html.

43. "The 1904 World's Fair: Looking Back at Looking Forward Centennial Exhibition Opens May 2, 2004, at the Missouri History Museum," Missouri Historical Society, April 12, 2004, https://mohistory.org/legacy-exhibits/fair/NewsEvents/press/Press7.html.

44. The Filipinx experience of the fair is discussed in Quizon and Afable. Afable's and Buangan's essays, which draw on archival sources and oral histories, particularly focus on the fair's Philippine ethnological displays.

45. Manalansan and Espiritu.

46. For further formal analyses of Suzara's *Souvenir*, see Pascual; and Vallarta.

47. Suzara, 9.

48. See's epilogue to her concluding chapter in *Decolonized Eye* also recounts her pilgrimage to St. Louis during the fair's centennial celebration, which coincided with the Filipino American National Historical Society annual conference.

49. Tadiar's concept of remaindered life for Filipinxs influences my thinking here. See also Derrida.

50. Suzara's "Oral History" also employs second-person narration.

51. While Filipinxs from the Philippines may be more accustomed to humidity, Filipinxs from the West Coast (including Suzara and myself) may be less so.
52. Balance, 4.
53. Ibid., 27.
54. I am responding to Spivak's "Can the Subaltern Speak?"
55. Craig Santos Perez's praise for Suzara's collection printed on the back of the book.
56. Eng and Han define racial melancholia as "histories of racial loss that are condensed into a forfeited object whose significance must be deciphered and unraveled for its social meanings" (1).
57. Eng and Han, 11–12.
58. Clutario, 14.
59. Evangelista uses augmented reality in *somewhere good* (performed at Oberlin College on May 20 and 21, 2022) to feature the names of the displayed at the fair. See also Al Evangelista (@professor.evangelista), "What day is it? Screenshots from act II. Spoiler alert: audience members get to see the invisible text the dancers have been moving with the entirety of act I through augmented reality. The text includes the names of participants from the 1904 world's fair and descriptions about them," series of two Instagram photos, May 18, 2022, https://www.instagram.com/p/CdtDsdyriBT/?img_index=1. Naming has been a minoritarian practice to account for those who have been disavowed and forgotten by majoritarian culture. For example, trans* activists have called on us to "say her name" in response to the disproportionate murders of transwomen, especially those who are Indigenous and of color.
60. "World's Fair Official Souvenir Playing Cards," "Shopping at the Fair," *The 1904 World's Fair: Looking Back at Looking Forward*, Missouri Historical Society, accessed September 16, 2022, https://mohistory.org/legacy-exhibits/fair/Artifacts/shopping/image2.html.
61. Eng and Han discuss how the melancholic subject through reparation can transform their lost object from a fixed ideal into a "living racial subject" (97).
62. I appreciate Sony Coráñez Bolton's help with analyzing the poem's linguistic structure.
63. Suzara's "Norms" and "Good Boy" likewise narrate from the perspective of the Igorot to counter their objectification.
64. "MHM LRC" refers to the Missouri History Museum Library and Research Center at 225 South Skinker Boulevard in St. Louis. The first call number that Suzara lists is "St.L. 711 F76eg," "Meet Me in St. Louis: Viewing Historic Integrity in a Continuum of Change through an Analysis of Forest Park," a 2006 master's thesis by Katherine Lynn Egan from Goucher College (Maryland). The second call number is "St.L. 606.02 W177s," "Savage to Civilized: The Imperial Agenda on Display at the St. Louis World's Fair of 1904," a 2005 master's thesis by Alicia Shannon Walker from the University of Missouri, Kansas City. The third call number is "St.L. 811 Ig24s," *Souvenirs of a Shrunken World*, a collection of poems published in 2008 by Holly Iglesias. Finally, the fourth call number is "907.4 En56," *Encyclopedia of World's Fairs and Expositions*, a coedited collection published in 2008 by John E. Finding and Kimberly D. Pelle.
65. Bauman.
66. "Our History," Kennewick, Washington, accessed September 17, 2022, https://www.go2kennewick.com/646/Our-History. Suzara's "Manifest Destiny 1980" presents text from a letter from President Thomas Jefferson to Meriwether Lewis juxtaposed against Suzara's family's westward journey to Kennewick.

67. "Population," Tri-City Development Council, accessed October 21, 2025, https://tridec.org/population/.

68. "Columbia Center," Kennewick, Washington, accessed September 17, 2022, https://www.go2kennewick.com/764/Columbia-Center.

69. In "Downwind: A Timeline," Suzara draws attention to the environmental racism local Native nations experience because of the U.S. imperial-military industrial complex that materializes in nearby Hanford, the site of the Manhattan Project, where the United States first developed nuclear weapons.

70. Yoneyama inspires my phrasing "the ruins of U.S. Cold War military imperialism."

71. Balance; Bernabe; Homiak; Martinez-Juan; and Rony.

72. Blumentritt, 86.

73. Ibid.

74. My desire to avow Filipinxs claims to the Midwest is not meant to bolster settler coloniality. Rather, to recognize Filipinxs as part of the Midwest is to challenge where Filipinx America is and can be and relatedly who can be seen as belonging to a place.

75. Blumentritt, 87.

76. Ibid., 87–88. Bernabe indicates Fuentes also visited the University of Pennsylvania (732), likely given Fuentes's proximity as a master of fine arts student at Temple University in 1991 (753n2), and notes the University of Michigan and Missouri History Museum archives house considerable relevant collections that Fuentes could have used but did not (755n19).

77. Blumentritt, 76.

78. Ibid., 85.

79. Ibid., 78. Bernabe reveals the Blumentritt *Amerasia Journal* interview actually is a conversation Fuentes has with himself, which Fuentes confirmed (757n56).

80. *Merriam-Webster Dictionary*, "in situ," accessed September 23, 2025, https://www.merriam-webster.com/dictionary/in%20situ.

81. Blumentritt, 85.

82. Martinez-Juan notes, "The archival footage of [Igorot] dances and rituals, and even the mourning women, are mostly taken from the Hilman Footage of the Northern Luzon Tribes held at the Smithsonian's Human Studies Film Archives. The only footage from 1904 that Fuentes was able to use were the panoramic shots of the exposition grounds and parade scenes, as well as footage of the Filipino Scouts marching and exercising at the Fair" (125–126).

83. Blumentritt, 88.

84. Ibid., 88–89.

85. Fermin, 42; Gilbert, 39; and Delmendo, chaps. 1 and 2.

86. Balance; Bernabe; Feng, chap. 1; Homiak; and Rony. Martinez-Juan does not address the prologue but instead focuses on the archival footage featured in the body of the film and lays bare its source material.

87. For more on how Fuentes complicates the ethnographic gaze, see Bernabe; and Rony.

88. I reference images from the "Structures" page of *The 1904 World's Fair: Looking Back at Looking Forward* online exhibit (accessed September 23, 2022, https://mohistory.org/legacy-exhibits/fair/Overview/page3.html#) and the Pharus map of the fairgrounds from the Library of Congress (accessed September 23, 2022, https://www.loc.gov/item/99466762/) to determine the building images in the film.

89. See Gilbert, 165–166, for a discussion of the Orientalism on the Pike.

90. Gilbert includes an image of an Igorot family as audience members for a parade, which illustrates the multiple positions displayed Filipinxs could occupy on the fair-

grounds (133). A close-up shot of this same image appears toward the end of the film. Earlier in the film, the narrator states that some of the Bontoc Igorot decided to travel to St. Louis, as "many of the men in Markod's clan wanted to see what was beyond the mountains."

91. Obusan also served as an associate producer, still photographer, and gaffer for the film.

92. Balance, 4.

93. Ibid.

94. Ibid., 5.

95. Rony also engages sound in her analysis of *Bontoc Eulogy* (137, 144).

96. For further discussion of *Bontoc Eulogy*'s play with form as a mode of authentic unsettlement, see Balance, 2–4.

97. Balance, 6.

98. Ibid.

99. Bernabe, 728.

100. Martinez-Juan also attends to cinematic form, providing rich details about the audiovisual materiality of the film.

101. Rony, 139.

102. Martinez-Juan, 122, 123.

103. Focusing on mise-en-scène, Palis provides a spatial analysis of three Thomas Edison Biograph short films (shot in West Orange County, New Jersey) that reenact the Philippine–American War and that Fuentes includes in his film. Santos Aquino also considers the spatiality of Edison's films to illustrate how coloniality is performed through such cinematic reenactments.

104. The St. Louis and San Diego Fairs' architectural styles differ, with the former conforming to Beaux-Arts and the latter introducing Spanish Colonial Revival, though the Spreckels Organ Pavilion, where Fuentes filmed, reflects Italian Renaissance architecture. Richard Amero, "The Spreckels Organ Pavilion in Balboa Park," San Diego History Center, accessed September 22, 2022, https://sandiegohistory.org/archives/amero/organ/.

105. Bernabe, 739. The narrator provides his own translation in the film: "He who does not look back from whence he came from will never ever reach his destination."

106. Hoorn analyzes the scene right after this sequence, wherein Filipino men self-flagellate and are flagellated by another Filipino man, as expressive of Freud's theory of melancholia, which states that the melancholic subject resorts to punishment to overcome guilt derived from a parental figure's death (199).

107. See Bhabha; Butler; and Reddy, "Home," for a discussion of the origin-copy dyad foundational to post/colonial and queer theories.

108. Gopinath, *Unruly Visions*, 128.

109. Informed by Fuss, and as my close readings in this chapter hopefully illustrate, I am not arguing that elegies are unproductive.

110. Bernabe, 730.

111. Muñoz, *Cruising Utopia*, 10.

112. Viego's concept of dead subjectivity as a critique of ego psychology, which posits the capacity to restore the wholeness of the subject, is instructive for understanding subjects as never fully knowable.

113. Kercheval's story has not received scholarly attention in American and Asian American literary studies.

114. I thank Michele Janette for this insight.

115. The Igorot represented about 10 percent of displayed Filipinxs at the fair, but they often stand in as *the* Filipinxs at the fair. As Cruz asserts, "To many who attended the fair in St. Louis, *Filipina* and *Filipino* were synonymous with the fascinating spectacle of Igorots or Negritos rather than with the smartly dressed officers of the Philippine Scouts" (*Transpacific Femininities*, 38). Moreover, the Igorot Village's occupation of more space and its higher visitation levels than any other village on the Philippine Reservation (based on various maps I consulted) further solidify the conflation of Igorotness and Filipinxness within the popular imaginary.

116. Kercheval, *Building Fiction*, 7. Coincidentally, I chanced upon *The Dogeater* in the Minneapolis Central Library online catalog when searching for texts concerning the Filipinx-as-dogeater trope while I was a graduate student at the University of Minnesota.

117. *The Dogeater* won the 1986 Associated Writing Programs (AWP) Award in Short Fiction. "Other Previous Winners," "Grace Paley Prize for Short Fiction," Association of Writers and Writing Programs, accessed October 22, 2025, https://www.awpwriter.org/AWP/Contests/AWP-Award-Series/Grace-Paley/Overview.aspx?733e92e66382=6#733e92e66382.

118. Fajardo's attention to waterways in the U.S. Filipinx diaspora recognizes the link between St. Louis and New Orleans/St. Maló ("Decolonizing," 230). Gonzalez also links St. Louis and St. Maló (148).

119. Kercheval, *Dogeater*, 82.

120. Some of the excerpts from *The Book* in Kercheval's story are slightly modified from Marshall Everett's *The Book of the Fair* (Philadelphia: P. W. Ziegler, 1904), which Kercheval does not cite. Also, contrary to Kercheval's fictionalized tale, there actually were a few children in the Igorot Village.

121. Brattain. For Filipino men in California, see also Baldoz, chap. 3.

122. For an analysis of photography in relation to Filipinxs during the fair, see Breitbart; Delmendo, chap. 2; and Vergara, *Displaying Filipinos*, chap. 6. For an analysis of photography in relation to Filipinxs more generally, see Rafael, *White Love*, chap. 3.

123. Chang, 8. Chuh's concept of illiberal humanisms (*Difference Aesthetics Makes*) resonates with Chang's inhuman citizenship.

124. Chang, 14.

125. Ibid.

126. Ibid., 9.

127. Ibid., 2–4.

128. Ibid., 13.

129. Ibid., 4.

130. Aging is a recurrent theme in *The Dogeater*, with several story protagonists being elderly (and likely White, as they are racially unmarked).

131. Deloria.

132. Edwards; and Kniffen.

133. Fajardo, "Decolonizing."

134. Cruz presents irreconcilabilities as a concept that illumines "the uneasy, the troubling, and the disruptive within representational practices" ("Jose Garcia Villa's Collection," 14).

135. Fuss, 5.

136. Ibid.

137. Ibid., 7; and Viego.

138. Baldoz mentions that a St. Louis family wanted to adopt "an Igorotte boy named Antaero" (spelling variation *Antero*) (40). Emily Grant Hutchings, "Igorrote Interviewed," *Los Angeles Times (1886–1922)*, October 15, 1904, https://search.proquest.com/docview/164259658, features Antero (spelled *Antaero* in the article).

139. Seattle arguably is another capital of Filipinx America. See Fujita-Rony. Even though Suzara's family lives in Washington state, they are peripheral to Seattle's Filipinx community.

140. See Pascual for further analysis of Suzara's relational reading of Filipinxness and Blackness.

CHAPTER 2

1. See, *Filipino Primitive*, 52–54. See also San Juan, "One Hundred Years." J. Kim understands the colonial archive as "not a disinterested organizing of the past and present; it is a site through which colonialism attempts to gain control over the future of human relations and knowledge production. Thus, if the colonial archive functions to measure and assign place to the colonial subject, then the postcolonial archive has the double duty of unmooring and unsettling colonial common sense and making the future an a priori, contested project" (19).

2. Gopinath, *Unruly Visions*.

3. Ahmed's meditation on "orientation" in *Queer Phenomenology* informs my thinking here.

4. Yale, 348.

5. Manalansan, "'Stuff' of Archives," 94.

6. Fajardo, "Decolonizing," 245.

7. Gopinath, *Unruly Visions*, 25–26.

8. Eng, "Out Here"; Gopinath, *Impossible Desires*; La Fountain-Stokes; Manalansan, *Global Divas*; and Velasco.

9. I appreciate Jigna Desai's affirmation of what the local and the regional avail to diasporic subjects.

10. Balce, 10.

11. Martinez-Juan, 126.

12. Arondekar; and Stoler, "Colonial Archives."

13. See's *Filipino Primitive* is a notable exception.

14. See, *Filipino Primitive*, 2.

15. Steinbock-Pratt.

16. Knapp, 11, 12. Notable Thomasite Mary Fee (who actually preceded the teachers on the *Thomas*, arriving on the *Buford*) described the American teacher presence in the Philippines as a "pedagogic invasion," further reinforcing the coloniality of U.S. education on the islands. Roma-Sianturi uses Fee's perspective to critique the benevolence of U.S. education, revealing the gendered racialized logic that governed American attitudes toward Filipinxs in (and out of) the classroom.

17. According to *The Log of the "Thomas,"* a "souvenir of the [Thomasites'] voyage to Manila" (7), under the "Notes of the Voyage" section, 72 teachers hailed from New England, 112 from the Mid-Atlantic, 51 from the South, 182 from the "Central states" (which I presume aligns with the Midwest, though in the "Directory of Teachers and Passengers on Board" section, I count 180 from the twelve states that define the Midwest), 20 from the "Mountain and Plateau states," 59 from the Pacific Coast, and 7 from the Territory

of Hawai'i (49). Of the states representing the most teachers, New York came in first with 63, followed by California with 41, Massachusetts with 35, and Michigan with 30 (49).

18. "History," Museum of Natural History, University of Michigan, accessed February 1, 2023, https://lsa.umich.edu/ummnh/about/history.html.

19. Powers, 5. See also See, *Filipino Primitive*, chap. 1, for more on Steere. The University of Michigan's Museum of Anthropological Archaeology holds one of the largest collections of Philippine archaeological objects in the United States as well as D. Worcester's photographic collection, boasting "nearly 5000 glass negatives and lantern slides." "The Dean C. Worcester Photographic Collection," Online Collections, University of Michigan Museum of Anthropological Archaeology, accessed February 14, 2023, https://lsa.umich.edu/ummaa/collections/online-collections/worcester-photograph-collection.html. Although I viewed part of the museum's D. Worcester collection as well as print materials related to the Carl E. Guthe 1922–1925 Philippine Expedition (the museum was in the process of moving to a new building, so actual artifacts were inaccessible, as they had already been packed), which led to the establishment of the Department of Anthropology at Michigan, I focus in this chapter less on "great White men" narratives to make space for subaltern perspectives and lesser-known archives. At the time of my visit, the Museum of Natural History shared the same building, so I also viewed the Philippine exhibit that See analyzes in *Filipino Primitive*, chap. 1. While the Bentley's Philippine archive is vast, the University of Michigan's libraries and museums combined present an unparalleled collection. The ReConnect/ReCollect: Reparative Connections to Philippine Collections at the University of Michigan project (https://www.reconnect-recollect.com/) and *The Philippines and the University of Michigan, 1870–1935*, online exhibit (https://philippines.michiganintheworld.history.lsa.umich.edu/s/exhibit/page/home) are two notable examples of efforts to decolonize Michigan's Philippine collection.

20. Barritt, 2.

21. Powers, 6. For more on D. Worcester, see Rice.

22. Worcester and Hayden, v.

23. Additional prominent Michiganders in the Philippines include Harry Bandholtz, head of the Philippine Constabulary (1907–1913), "the chief peacekeeping force on the islands" (Powers, 6), and Frank Murphy, the last Philippine governor-general (1933–1935), former mayor of Detroit (1930–1933), future governor of Michigan (1937–1939), U.S. attorney general (1939–1940), and associate justice of the U.S. Supreme Court (1940–1949). For more on Murphy, consult See, *Filipino Primitive*, chap. 2. Kirkwood also traces the history of University of Michigan alums from the Progressive Era and their legacy.

24. Several Filipinx American studies scholars, including Balce; Clutario; Coráñez Bolton, *Crip Colony*; Mendoza; See, *Filipino Primitive*; and Winkelmann utilize the Bentley's collection in their work.

25. Leoncia Taino, "Business Letter," September 3, 1904, Behner Students' Papers, folder 4 of 9. Incidentally, Lucena was a site of horrific violence in 1902 (just two years prior to these student essays) during the Philippine–American War. Records at the University of Michigan document this event. "Transcriptions of Violence," "The Philippine–American War," *The Philippines and the University of Michigan, 1870–1935*, Michigan in the World exhibit, University of Michigan, accessed February 14, 2023, https://philippines.michiganintheworld.history.lsa.umich.edu/s/exhibit/page/transcriptions-of-violence.

26. Consolacion Alma, "Literature," October 31, 1904, Behner Students' Papers, folder 1 of 9.

27. Schueller, 947.

28. Barritt, 3.

29. This turn of phrase plays with Spivak's "Can the Subaltern Speak?" For more on Behner's experience in the Philippines, see Eittreim.
30. "Necessity of Establishing High Schools in Every Province of the Philippine Islands," 2–3, Behner Students' Papers, folder 6 of 9.
31. Ibid., 1–4.
32. Ibid., 3. Another unnamed student writes, "The society of farmers is the most quiet and happy life," further supporting a rural/agricultural orientation. "Society," 3, Behner Students' Papers, folder 3 of 9.
33. Andres Rañola, "Lucban Is a Better Place to Be (the Capital of the Province)," 3, Behner Students' Papers, folder 8 of 9.
34. Ibid., 6.
35. Macaria Allarey, "The Importance of Education," 1, Behner Students' Papers, folder 5 of 9. In "What Are the Advantages of Being Educated," she writes, "in this world in order to become useful and important" (1); Behner Students' Papers, folder 8 of 9.
36. M. Allarey, "Importance," 1, 3, 4. M. Allarey writes, "People who did not receive instructions, usually are those who have the simplest forms of life; those who have queer customs and ideas." Behner writes in the margin concerning the first clause, "Here I think you mean uneducated or uncivilized people" ("Importance," 4).
37. M. Allarey, "Importance," 5.
38. Ibid.
39. Ibid., 3.
40. M. Allarey, "Advantages," 4. Although Behner's Students' Papers did not appear to have a clear order, this essay is in folder 8 of 9, whereas "Importance" is in folder 5 of 9.
41. See provides an insightful discussion on the politics of penmanship in *Filipino Primitive* (9–12).
42. V. F. Bertrane, "Progress," 1, Behner Students' Papers, folder 5 of 9.
43. M. Allarey, "Importance," 1.
44. M. Allarey, "Advantages," 3–4.
45. "History & Prophecy," 2, Behner Students' Papers, folder 6 of 9.
46. Gregorio Elezler, "The Best Kind of School," 2, Behner Students' Papers, folder 4 of 9; and Rufina Alma, "Our School," Behner Students' Papers, folder 1 of 9.
47. Louis Dalrymple, *School Begins*, 1899, chromolithograph, published in *Puck* 44, no. 1142 (January 25, 1899), https://www.loc.gov/pictures/item/2012647459/. Coráñez Bolton offers a provocative reading of this cartoon in *Crip Colony*, chap. 1.
48. R. Alma, "Our School," 4.
49. See, *Filipino Primitive*, 86–96.
50. Bertrane; and Candida Custodio, "Philippine Government," Behner Students' Papers, folder 6 of 9.
51. Bertrane, 1.
52. Ibid., 2.
53. Ibid., 7.
54. C. Lapuio, "America," Behner Students' Papers, folder 7 of 9.
55. Vicente Villavicenind, "If Philippine[s] Had Been Independent," Behner Students' Papers, folder 5 of 9.
56. Ibid., 5.
57. Ibid., 1
58. Cullinane, 16.
59. See, *Filipino Primitive*, 66.
60. Ibid., 60.

61. C. Alma, "Literature," 2–3.
62. Ibid., 4–5.
63. Ibid., 1.
64. Antonia Evangelista, "Narratives," Behner Students' Papers, folder 6 of 9; Catalina Delantar, "Narraatives" [sic], Behner Students' Papers, folder 6 of 9; Dalmacio Ambalada, "Narrative of Dalmacio Ambalada's Life," Behner Students' Papers, folder 2 of 9; Honorio A. Lopez, "Narratives—Honorio's Life," Behner Students' Papers, folder 2 of 9; and H. Allarey, "Folk Lore," Behner Students' Papers, folder 5 of 9.
65. Evangelista, 1.
66. Delantar, 1.
67. Ambalada, 1.
68. Lopez, 1.
69. Delantar, 3.
70. Felisa San Agustin, "What (Is) a Woman Worth," 2–3, Behner Students' Papers, folder 3 of 9.
71. Ibid., 2.
72. Ibid., 5.
73. *The Philippines and the University of Michigan, 1870–1935*, online exhibit presents an alternative interpretation of San Agustin's essay that emphasizes Behner's Christian-oriented teaching and maintains a gender hierarchy. "Gender in Behner's Christian Lessons," "Frederick G. Behner's 'Thomasite Adventure,'" "Empire and Education," *The Philippines and the University of Michigan, 1870–1935*, Michigan in the World exhibit, University of Michigan, accessed February 10, 2023, https://philippines.michiganintheworld.history.lsa.umich.edu/s/exhibit/page/frederick-g-behner-thomasite-adventure.
74. *Pensionados* officially referred to U.S.-sponsored students, though scholars also have referred to nonsponsored Filipinx students studying in the United States during the early twentieth century as pensionados. I follow the latter convention.
75. Sutherland; and Posadas and Guyotte. In August 1904, pensionadxs "served as guides in the exhibition halls and as waiters in the mess halls" at the Louisiana Purchase Exposition in contradistinction to the Indigenous Filipinxs on display (Sutherland, 31).
76. For more on pensionadxs, see Cruz, *Transpacific Femininities*; Delmendo; España-Maram; and Posadas and Guyotte. Importantly, Cruz draws attention to Filipina students, who, while a numerical minority, counter the historical narrative that focuses primarily on Filipino men.
77. "The Quarterly Philippinesotan," *Quarterly Philippinesotan* 1, no. 1 (December 1922): 1. The 1910 U.S. Census recorded 2 Filipinxs living in Minnesota; in 1920, the population rose to 20, and by 1930, 236 Filipinxs resided in the state (Mason, 547).
78. According to Carlos Del Plaine, president of the University of Minnesota's Cosmopolitan Club in 1922, "The membership of the club is composed of the foreigners who come to us for education and of the finest American students and faculty members. The membership is restricted to not more than 50 per cent [sic] Americans and not more than 50 per cent [sic] women. In this way, a representative group is maintained with ideal opportunities for international friendships." Del Plaine explains the objectives of the organization: "The Minnesota chapter of the Corda Fratres Association of Cosmopolitan Clubs is an organization working for world peace and *brotherhood* [emphasis added] by means of close association and friendship between college students of the different nationalities." Carlos Del Plaine, "Minnesota Chapter of Corda Fratres Active in Working for World Peace," *Minnesota Daily*, April 26, 1922, https://hdl.handle.net/11299

/232379. Cosmopolitan Clubs were present at other U.S. college and university campuses during this period. Santos (who is the focus of chapter 3) was a member of the Illinois chapter when he first arrived in the United States in fall 1941 as a non-government-sponsored scholar at the University of Illinois.

79. "The Pensionados and the Image of the Filipino 'Primitive,'" "Filipino Students Stateside," *The Philippines and the University of Michigan, 1870–1935*, Michigan in the World exhibit, University of Michigan, accessed February 10, 2023, https://philippines.michiganintheworld.history.lsa.umich.edu/s/exhibit/page/pensionados-and-the-image-of-the-filipino-primitive.

80. The Young Men's Christian Association sponsored the journal. For analyses of *Filipino Student Bulletin*, see Lawsin; Peralta; and Posadas and Guyotte.

81. "Quarterly Philippinesotan," *Quarterly Philippinesotan*, 1.

82. In their "Review of the Quarter," the editors list the club having 27 active members (3).

83. "Review of the Quarter," *Quarterly Philippinesotan*, 3.

84. Dedimo M. Fonbuena, "The Public Pulse: In Defense of the Filipinos," *Minneapolis Morning Tribune* (1909–1922), July 14, 1921, ProQuest; D. Fonbuena, "The Public Pulse: Who Is a Filipino?," *Minneapolis Morning Tribune* (1909–1922), July 16, 1921, ProQuest; D. Fonbuena, "The Public Pulse: Moonlight and Liberty," *Minneapolis Morning Tribune* (1909–1922), August 5, 1921, ProQuest; Julian P. Bacalzo, "The Public Pulse: Filipino Independence," *Minneapolis Morning Tribune* (1909–1922), September 5, 1921, ProQuest; Numeriano Rojas, "The Public Pulse: Challenges Statements About Philippines," *Minneapolis Morning Tribune* (1909–1922), January 24, 1922, ProQuest; and D. Fonbuena, "The Public Pulse: Regarding the Filipinos," *Minneapolis Morning Tribune* (1909–1922), January 26, 1922, ProQuest. D. Fonbuena and Rojas attended the University of Minnesota, whereas Bacalzo attended Hamline University in St. Paul.

85. "Our Part in Minnesota's Memorial Drive," *Quarterly Philippinesotan*, 1.

86. Jose Gacusana, "The Filipino People Before 1521," *Quarterly Philippinesotan*, 7, 6.

87. "Rizal Day" is another article that appears in *The Quarterly Philippinesotan* (2), reinforcing the significance of Rizal in the political consciousness of early twentieth-century U.S. diasporic Filipinxs. Historians Posadas and Guyotte discuss Rizal Day celebrations among Filipinx Chicagoans, and writer Santos fictionalizes such an event in *The Man Who (Thought He) Looked Like Robert Taylor*.

88. Eugenio Fonbuena, "Filipino Culture in the Pre-Spanish Period," *Quarterly Philippinesotan*, 10.

89. Ibid., 11.

90. The editors write, "Dr. Cruz, and Misses Manongdo, Abary, and Sapao, Filipino girls, passed through Minnesota and visited their countrymen in the Twin Cities on their way east to study" (4). For an analysis of the underrepresentation of Filipina students during this period, see Cruz, *Transpacific Femininities*.

91. "Impressions of the Play, 'Clauses Three and Four,'" *Quarterly Philippinesotan*, 8–9. Bocobo, a famous pensionado, was dean of the University of the Philippines College of Law at the time. He graduated from Indiana University in 1907, matriculating in 1903, and infamously attended an anti-imperialist rally featuring future Secretary of State William Jennings Bryan while at Indiana.

92. Shin highlights "the significant role that colleges played in U.S. foreign relations in the nineteenth century" (196). Such "collegiate cosmopolitanism" simultaneously engendered localized transnational exchange and implicated institutions of higher learning in U.S. imperialism (197).

93. "First in Service," Kansas State University, updated January 28, 2019, https://www.k-state.edu/wildcatway/land-grant/; and Robert Lee and Tristan Ahtone, "How They Did It: Exposing How U.S. Universities Profited from Indigenous Land," Pulitzer Center, May 19, 2020, https://pulitzercenter.org/stories/how-they-did-it-exposing-how-us-universities-profited-indigenous-land.

94. Coffman to William B. Coffman, August 6, 1915, 3, Coffman Papers, box 1, folder 14. See Clampitt for corn's association with the Midwest as well as the significance of land-grant institutions in the development of modern agriculture. Clampitt notes that Ferdinand Magellan brought maize seeds to the Philippines in the sixteenth century, which introduced the Indigenous North American crop to the Asian archipelago (10).

95. The Coffman Papers finding aid notes, "In 1957, he became the principal agronomist in charge of winter oats and was responsible for 120 experiment stations in 44 states." He also "published approximately 200 articles and several books" pertaining to agronomy (4). Jane Schillie, "Franklin A. Coffman papers, 1884–1978," finding aid, Richard L. D. and Marjorie J. Morse Department of Archives and Special Collections, Kansas State University Libraries, April 24, 2013, https://archivaldescriptions.lib.k-state.edu/catalog/franklin-a-coffman-papers.

96. "Philippine Service," Coffman Papers, box 1, folder 4; and "Philippine Service," Coffman Papers, box 1, folder 5.

97. Since Coffman was an alumnus of K-State, along with his parents and siblings, I suspect his papers, which include early photos of the campus, are of import to the institution.

98. At the same time Coffman was in the Philippines, K-State President Henry Waters (1909–1917) visited the Philippines (May–September 1914), which culminated in the 1915 publication *The Development of the Philippines: A Summary of the Results of Special Investigations made by Henry Jackson Waters, President of the Kansas State Agricultural College, by authority of an Act of the Legislature of the Philippine Islands*—further indicating the role of land-grant institutions in administering U.S. empire in the Philippines.

99. "Philippine Service," box 1, folder 4.

100. Ibid.

101. Coffman to William B. Coffman, August 6, 1915, 1.

102. "Philippine Service," box 1, folder 4.

103. Ibid.

104. "Philippine Album," Coffman Papers, box 9.

105. "Philippine Service," box 1, folder 4.

106. Ibid.

107. Ibid.

108. Ibid.

109. McClintock.

110. "Philippine Service," box 1, folder 4.

111. Ibid.

112. Gopinath writes, "The postcard as a genre has both temporal and spatial valences: it is the most mundane form of memorialization of places, people, events, or objects, and is meant to be read quickly and then either discarded, or perhaps stuck on a fridge with a magnet, instantiating a brief moment of connection between the sender and the recipient, between 'here' and 'there'" (*Unruly Visions*, 115–116).

113. Coffman to William B. Coffman, postcard, December 31, 1914, Coffman Papers, box 1, folder 14.

114. Coffman to William B. Coffman, August 6, 1915, 1.

115. Ibid., 2.
116. Ibid., 3.
117. "Philippine Service," box 1, folder 4.
118. "Philippine Service," box 1, folder 5.
119. "Philippine Service," box 1, folder 4. His photo album also provides names for some Filipinxs with whom he interacted.
120. "Philippine Service," box 1, folder 4.
121. España-Maram; and See, *Decolonized Eye*, discuss the Filipino houseboy figure in the U.S. diasporic context.
122. "Philippine Service," box 1, folder 4.
123. Rafael, *White Love*.
124. "Philippine Service," box 1, folder 5.
125. Gopinath, *Unruly Visions*, 8.
126. "Harvey Family Papers" finding aid, Kenneth Spencer Research Library Archival Collections, University of Kansas, 2008, updated 2019, https://archives.lib.ku.edu/repositories/3/resources/2234; "The Harvey Family" history, 1, 4–5, Harvey Family Papers, box 1, folder 4; and Sherman Allen Harvey, "Story of My Life," July 20, 1933, 1, Harvey Family Papers, box 1, folder 7. Although Sherman claims to be the first African American to receive a diploma from the University of Kansas (Harvey, "Story," 5), Blanche Ketene Bruce of Brunswick, Missouri, received his diploma in 1885 (Slater, 78). Sherman also describes his heritage as a mixture of African, Indigenous North American, and European (Harvey, "Story," 1).
127. Harvey, "Story," 6.
128. Ibid., 7–8.
129. Ibid., 8. His younger brother, Grant, served in the same company as a surgeon ("Harvey Family," 2).
130. Harvey, "Story," 9.
131. Ibid., 9–10; and "Harvey Family," 2.
132. Harvey, "Story," 17.
133. "Harvey Family," 2.
134. Exodusters were African Americans from the U.S. South who migrated to Kansas in 1879; "Exodusters," Homestead National Historical Park, Nicodemus National Historic Site, National Park Service, last updated November 9, 2022, https://www.nps.gov/articles/exodusters.htm. Nicodemus, Kansas, founded in 1877, is notable as "the longest-lasting [B]lack homesteader colony in America"; "Nicodemus Kansas," Homestead National Historical Park, Nicodemus National Historic Site, National Park Service, last updated January 24, 2022, https://www.nps.gov/places/nicodemus-kansas.htm. Hughes's semi-autobiographical debut novel, *Not Without Laughter*, is set in 1910s Stanton, Kansas, a fictional small town based on his upbringing in Lawrence.
135. "Harvey Family," 3.
136. The nephew (Dean) is the son of KU's first Black football player and Sherman's youngest brother, Ed(ward) Harvey. John P. Tharp, "Grandsons of Slaves Made Kaw Valley Home," newspaper photocopy, undated, Harvey Family Papers, box 1, folder 1.
137. Harvey, manuscript, c. 1912, 1, Harvey Family Papers, box 1, folder 3; and Harvey, "Story," 7.
138. Harvey, manuscript, 4.
139. Balce, chap. 3.
140. Ibid., 95.
141. Harvey, "Story," 1–2.

142. Ibid., 3.
143. Ibid., 4.
144. Slater, 78.
145. Campney's *This Is Not Dixie* reveals Kansas's violent racist history against African Americans.
146. Harvey, "Story," 2.
147. Ibid., 25–26.
148. Ibid., 2.
149. Ibid., 4, 20–24.
150. Ibid., 24. Harvey published an extended version of his second travel to the Philippines, including this sentiment, in "More of the Philippines," newspaper photocopy, 1913, Harvey Family Papers, box 1, folder 5.
151. Harvey, "Story," 9.
152. Ibid.
153. Ibid., 10.
154. Ibid., 11–12.
155. Ibid., 13.
156. Ibid., 11, 16.
157. Ibid., 16.
158. Ibid., 19.
159. Harvey, manuscript, 30.
160. Ibid., 31. See Balce, 97–98, for more on Fagen.
161. Nanon Fay Leas Worcester, diary, 1909, Bentley Historical Library, University of Michigan; and Winifred W. Hubbell, "Our Adventure in the Philippine Islands," c. 1950, Theodore H. Hubbell Papers, box 3, Bentley Historical Library, University of Michigan. See Rafael, *White Love*, chap. 2, for more on White American women's travel writing, including that of N. Worcester and Hubbell.
162. Harvey, manuscript, 5–6.
163. Ibid., 5–7.
164. Ibid., 5, 9.
165. Ibid., 11.
166. Ibid., 12–15.
167. Ibid., 16–17. See Owen for American criticism of caciquism.
168. Harvey, manuscript, 25.
169. Ibid., 22.
170. Ibid., 8.
171. For more on Filipinx temporality, see Isaac, *Filipino Time*.
172. Harvey, manuscript, 18.
173. Ibid., 32.
174. Manalansan, "'Stuff' of Archives," 97.
175. A. Espiritu, chap. 5.

CHAPTER 3

1. Santos, *Scent*, 113.
2. Ibid., 32.
3. Santos, *Memory's Fictions*, 72. Sentence edited from Thomas Xavier Sarmiento, "Literary Perspectives on Asian Americans in the Midwest," © Oxford University Press

USA, 2019; reproduced with permission of the Licensor through PLSclear. Similarly, my parents, who live in California, regularly ask me during the colder months of the year since I have lived in the Midwest if it is snowing whenever we talk on the phone or on Zoom.

4. Santos, *Memory's Fictions*, 215.

5. Sentence edited and expanded from Thomas Xavier Sarmiento, "Literary Perspectives on Asian Americans in the Midwest," © Oxford University Press USA, 2019; reproduced with permission of the Licensor through PLSclear.

6. Tuan, *Space and Place*, 4.

7. Cruz mentions the "frozen Midwest" of "Scent of Apples" (*Transpacific Femininities*, 185), de Jesús notes the "chilly Midwest" of "The Day the Dancers Came" ("Rereading History," 100), and A. Espiritu simply mentions Santos being in the Midwest (138). Bresnahan, on the other hand, substantively takes up the Midwest in Santos's life and literature ("Can These" and "Midwestern Fiction").

8. de Jesús, "Rereading History," 109.

9. Such distinctions between "original" and "copy," "authentic" and "inauthentic," as Butler argues, are futile (41).

10. I appreciate MT Vallarta's insight on this point.

11. Again, I appreciate MT Vallarta's insight on this point.

12. Queen Lili'uokalani's recollection of experiencing snow in the Rocky Mountains during her journey across the United States similarly illustrates the excitement and wonder Santos's characters exhibit toward snow (119).

13. Santos describes his wartime exile (1941–1946) as him being "stranded" (*Memory's Fictions*, 104). A. Espiritu, chap. 5.

14. Santos, *Memory's Fictions*, 77.

15. Ibid., 78.

16. Ibid., 122.

17. Ibid., 100.

18. Ibid.

19. Ibid., 95.

20. Santos, preface to *Scent*, xvii.

21. Ibid. During his tenure at the Iowa Writers' Workshop, he completed his first novel, *Villa Magdalena*, and a draft of his second novel, *The Volcano*, both published in the Philippines in 1965.

22. Santos, preface to *Scent*, xviii. Although Santos lists 1966 as the year of his return to Iowa City, his papers at Wichita State University and his memoir both list 1965. See Fulbright 1 and personal papers, 1965–1966, letters, Santos Papers, box 4, folder 2; and Santos, *Memory's Fictions*, 88.

23. Santos, *Memory's Fictions*, 88.

24. Ibid., 102.

25. Personal correspondences with P. C. Morantte I, Santos Papers, box 1, folder 3.

26. At this time, Santos was working on *Robert Taylor* and began *What the Hell For You Left Your Heart in San Francisco* (1987).

27. Santos, *Memory's Fictions*, 200.

28. Ibid., 34.

29. Ibid., 26, 110; and A. Espiritu, xviii, 142.

30. Sutherland, 8. Other sources list 1943 as the end of the pensionadx program. See, for example, Panganiban and Bonus, 360. Sutherland, 7, 43, 53.

31. España-Maram, 75.

32. Cruz, *Transpacific Femininities*, 10, 11.
33. Ibid., 22–23.
34. Muñoz, *Cruising Utopia*, 17.
35. In a diary entry, dated January 15, 1942, Santos makes note of Remedios, a pensionada in Bloomington, Indiana, who is rumored to be in a sanatorium "with a nervous breakdown which is due to the war." He expresses compassion for Remedios, whom he speculates is "so alone in Indiana" without the company of other Filipinxs like him in Illinois. While isolation is more palpable for Filipinxs in the Midwest, this observation indicates the experiential heterogeneity of the region for diasporic Filipinxs. Santos's depiction of Remedios resembles Cruz's interpretation of another Remedios in his short story "So Many Things"; both transpacific Filipinas are juxtaposed against the heartless coed (Cruz, *Transpacific Femininities*, 193).
36. Ben appears in most of the stories published in *You Lovely People*.
37. The last four stories of *Scent* appeared in *The Day the Dancers Came*.
38. Tuan, *Space and Place*, 11.
39. For more on Alumit's novel, see Sarmiento, "Diasporic Filipinx Queerness"; Ponce, *Beyond the Nation*, chap. 5; and Sohn, chap. 4.
40. E., Kim, 269, 267.
41. Ty offers a specifically Filipinx critique of U.S. empire that aligns with analyses of Santos by A. Espiritu; Campomanes, "Filipinos in the United States"; San Juan, "From Genealogy to Inventory"; and San Juan, *Racial Formations/Critical Transformations*.
42. Ty, 269.
43. Ibid., 268.
44. Tuan, *Space and Place*, 7.
45. Ibid., 6–7.
46. The unnamed narrator is plausibly the narrator of the other short stories in *Scent*, Ben, who is loosely modeled on Santos. Casper, introduction to *Scent*, ix.
47. Rodaway, 5.
48. Ibid.
49. Ibid., 61.
50. Ibid., 68.
51. Santos, *Scent*, 26, 77–79, 77.
52. Cruz's concept of "byways," which refer to "untraveled routes" and "primarily unstudied texts by Filipinas and Filipinos" (*Transpacific Femininities*, 8), and Tongson's concept of "elsewheres" as spatial imaginaries that exceed the metronormative (*Relocations*) inform my thinking here.
53. The quote in the subheading is from Santos, "The Day the Dancers Came," in *Scent*, 113.
54. Sutherland, 35.
55. Diary entry, dated Christmas Day, 1941, Santos Papers, box 2, folder 10.
56. Diary entry, dated January 5, 1942, Santos Papers, box 2, folder 10.
57. Diary entry, dated January 7, 1942, Santos Papers, box 2, folder 10.
58. Incidentally, I first wrote this paragraph during the unusually extreme subzero weather that Minnesota and much of the upper part of the United States experienced in early January 2014, during my last year in graduate school.
59. Sentence edited from Thomas Xavier Sarmiento, "Literary Perspectives on Asian Americans in the Midwest," © Oxford University Press USA, 2019; reproduced with permission of the Licensor through PLSclear. Fil counters his roommate Tony's doubt

that this will be the first time the Philippine dancers will be experiencing snow, since they have already visited New York, where snow also can fall, by rhetorically asking, "Snow in New York in early November?" "Are you crazy?" (113). Here, snow in autumn seems to be a uniquely Midwestern phenomenon.

60. Sentence edited from Thomas Xavier Sarmiento, "Literary Perspectives on Asian Americans in the Midwest," © Oxford University Press USA, 2019; reproduced with permission of the Licensor through PLSclear.

61. Santos, *Robert Taylor*, 106.

62. See Herring, chap. 1, in which he reads Willa Cather and James Weldon Johnson as pre-Stonewall anti-urbanist writers.

63. Santos, *Robert Taylor*, 107.

64. Maxine Hong Kingston's *New York Times* review of *Scent of Apples* similarly argues that Santos's "hurt men" experience both sadness and joy as exiles, thereby rendering such subjects and their ties to the United States as ambivalent and complex. Maxine Hong Kingston, "Precarious Lives," *New York Times*, May 4, 1980.

65. *Pinoy* (*Pinay* in the feminine form, *Pinxy* in the genderless form) is slang for *Filipino*, which was historically used by Filipinxs from the Philippines to refer to Filipinos in the United States, especially those of a certain socioeconomic class as denoted by Santos, but which has since traveled back to the Philippines to refer to Filipinxs in general.

66. A. Espiritu, 140–141.

67. This sentence and the preceding one edited and revised from Thomas Xavier Sarmiento, "Literary Perspectives on Asian Americans in the Midwest," © Oxford University Press USA, 2019; reproduced with permission of the Licensor through PLSclear.

68. Casper, introduction to *Scent*, ix.

69. Filemon Acayan is named after a Filipino Pullman porter whom Santos met in 1941 en route to Champaign–Urbana and refers to as "my first Filipino exile in the flesh" (*Memory's Fictions*, 79).

70. Santos, *Scent*, 116.

71. For brief histories of Filipinx Chicago, see Posadas and Guyotte; Remoquillo; Sales; and Zarsadiaz, "Raising Hell."

72. Love influences my thinking here about queerness and backward glances.

73. The quote in the subheading is from a letter from Santos to P. C. Morantte, dated July 9, 1973, Santos Papers, box 1, folder 3.

74. Santos, *Memory's Fictions*, 200.

75. Letter to P. C. Morantte, dated July 9, 1973. The bonds between the Santoses and the Filipinx Wichita community strengthen over time. He later wrote, "Without them, our stay in Wichita would have been less than what it turned out to be, memorable" (*Memory's Fictions*, 206).

76. During his interview with Roger Bresnahan in June 1980, Santos mentions his love for the "very brilliant" Filipinxs in Wichita who affectionately and respectfully called him "Uncle Ben" (*Conversations*, 90).

77. In the same interview with Bresnahan, Santos mentions not making many friends in San Francisco in 1972. He also speculates that the critical mass of Filipinxs in San Francisco may have posed a threat to White Americans and explained the hostility toward Filipinxs there (*Conversations*, 113).

78. Letter to P. C. Morantte, dated July 9, 1973.

79. Santos, *Memory's Fictions*, 199. Personal correspondences with P. C. Morantte I.

80. Santos, *Memory's Fictions*, 216.

81. Bresnahan, *Conversations*, 113.
82. Medina, 49.
83. Gordon, 5.
84. Muñoz, *Cruising Utopia*, 1.
85. Gopinath, *Impossible Desires*, 165.
86. Ibid., 186.
87. Senator Dirksen was a longtime Republican politician from Illinois.
88. Vito Russo, quoted in Carter, 261.
89. Desai, 136.
90. Ibid., 140.
91. Ibid., 142.
92. Belkin offers a similar analysis of homesickness as the literalization of nonbelonging, focusing on U.S. soldiers in the Philippines diagnosed with depressive symptoms during the Philippine–American War (171).
93. See, *Decolonized Eye*, 150–151n4.
94. Freud, "Mourning and Melancholia," 170.
95. See, *Decolonized Eye*, 7.
96. Ibid., 6.
97. For more on melancholia and the homosexual taboo, see Elliot, 152–153.
98. Bascara, "Up from Benevolent Assimilation"; Bascara, "'Within Each Crack'"; and de Jesús, "Rereading History."
99. A. Espiritu writes, "America was a space of sexual freedom, if not, transgression, as can be seen in the interracial relationships of [Carlos P.] Romulo, [Carlos] Bulosan, [José García] Villa, and [Bienvenido] Santos" (191). Likewise, in "Quicker with Arrows," Santos describes the character Val, who is living in New York City, as follows: "But Val was free and did not seem to feel the burdens and inconveniences that the war was imposing on everyone in America" (*Scent*, 142). For Val, living in the United States allows him to momentarily escape his obligation to the family company and his alleged betrothal to a Filipina and to have a relationship with Fay, a White woman he meets while attending Columbia University.
100. Casper, introduction to *Scent*, ix.
101. Sedgwick, *Between Men*.
102. Gopinath's call for queer diasporic critique to be feminist in orientation in *Impossible Desires* is apropos here. See also Sarmiento, "Diasporic Filipinx Queerness."
103. Chuh also engages Santos's work to critique Asian America studies' unwitting heterosexism (*Imagine Otherwise*, 35, 41–44). Reading the short story "Immigration Blues," the first story in *Scent* and also a chapter in *Robert Taylor*, she illustrates how U.S. imperialism has used heteronormativity as a technology of racialization and how Filipinx immigrants have disidentified with such an imperative to make do in diaspora. She writes, "Santos's story speaks of the microlevel inventions of identity that proliferate to sustain life and create community" (*Imagine Otherwise*, 43). Such attention to the particular propels the heterogeneity of racial-colonial formations.
104. Muñoz, *Cruising*, 9.
105. Celia Bocobo Olivar, "The First Pensionados," master's thesis, 1950, quoted in Sutherland, 36.
106. Ponce foregrounds liminality as a Filipinx condition that opens itself to queer diasporic reading (*Beyond the Nation*, 10–12, 26, 157, 196).
107. Casper, introduction to *Scent*, xv.

CHAPTER 4

1. *Filipinas* is an anglicized form of the Filipino/Tagalog term for the Philippines, *Pilipinas*, which also refers to girls and women of Philippine descent.
2. Turner.
3. *Edith* ran in Louisville, KY (Actors Theatre of Louisville); Atlanta, GA (Actor's Express Theatre); Coral Gables, FL (New Theatre); and Minneapolis, MN (Mu Performing Arts / Mixed Blood Theatre) as a 2011–2012 rolling world premiere (Pamatmat, 4). "Edith Can Shoot Things and Hit Them," Theater Mu, 2019, accessed October 26, 2025, https://www.theatermu.org/edith.
4. Taught by Linda España-Maram in Winter Quarter 2003 at UC San Diego.
5. Suarez, 2.
6. My thinking on alternative being is inspired by Ferguson's chapter on *Sula* in *Aberrations*.
7. For the trope of isolation in Asian Midwestern narratives, see E. Lee; J. Lee et al., introduction; Sarmiento, "Literary Perspectives"; and Trieu.
8. Galang, *HWAS*, 183.
9. Pamatmat, 6. For more on *bundok*, see De Leon.
10. Viego, 107. Manalansan and Espiritu.
11. For more on peminism, see de Jesús, *Pinay Power*; Tintiangco-Cubales; and Sarmiento, "Peminist and Queer Affiliation."
12. Aguilar-San Juan; Ku; Lewis; Logan; and Sulit. Kafka; and Ponce, *Beyond the Nation*, recognize the Midwest in their analyses of Galang's *HWAS*.
13. Ahmed, *Living a Feminist Life*, 6.
14. Cruz, *Transpacific Femininities*; and Gopinath, *Impossible Desires*.
15. McClintock.
16. Balce, 17.
17. See, *Filipino Primitive*.
18. Ponce also discusses Galang's use of second-person narration (*Beyond the Nation*, 195–196).
19. Shortridge, 8, 27, 31, 135.
20. I thank Kimball Smith for encouraging me to consider Filipinxs' relation to savagery.
21. See, for example, B. Nguyen, *Stealing Buddha's Dinner*.
22. Ninh, 6.
23. For more on hegemonic Filipinx American nationalisms, see D. Rodríguez; and Vergara, *Pinoy Capital*.
24. Noah Flora, "Jessica Hagedorn Looks Back on the Legacy of 'Dogeaters,'" *The Nation*, March 11, 2020, https://www.thenation.com/article/culture/jessica-hagedorn-dogeaters-anniversary-interview/.
25. Hagedorn, *Dogeaters*, 83, 85, 249.
26. Ahmed, *Living a Feminist Life*, 65–66.
27. Ibid., 74.
28. Ibid., 78.
29. Ibid., 82.
30. Lorrie Moore's collection of short stories, *Self-Help* (1985), "which was written entirely in the second person," inspired Galang, who "started talking to everyone in second person, all the time. When I think of that time now, I realize that the stories I was writ-

ing were mirroring my own issues of assimilation" (Carbó and Galang, 287). Here, Galang articulates how the use of second-person narration is both a distancing from oneself and an opportunity to gain insight, a kind of "working through" the psychic violences of imperial culture.

31. Coincidentally, Tongson's entry for *queer* in *Keywords for Media Studies* names Peoria to signify geographic normativity (157), further reinforcing the Midwest's normative status in the popular imaginary.

32. See, *Decolonized Eye*, xxx.

33. See, for example, Moraga and Anzaldúa. In an interview with Michel Martin for the PBS program *Amanpour and Company*, Vietnamese American writer Ocean Vuong explains how his biography influenced his debut novel, *On Earth We're Briefly Gorgeous* (2019), drawing inspiration from African American writer James Baldwin: "To use a life that was recognizable to me—Asian American life, working out of poverty within poverty in Hartford [Connecticut]—was a powerful moment for me to say this life that many people just pass on the freeway, this life gave me my imagination, in the same way Harlem gave Baldwin his." "Ocean Vuong on Race, Sexuality, and His New Novel," *Amanpour and Company*, aired October 31, 2019, https://www.pbs.org/video/ocean-vuong-race-sexuality-and-his-new-novel-xavpgo/. Bulosan's *America Is in the Heart* similarly fictionalizes the author's biography alongside the biographies of other Filipino American migrants of the early twentieth century; the novel's subtitle, *A Personal History*, encourages readers to recognize autobiographical traces in the narrative, thus blurring the line between fiction and nonfiction. The fixation on such a distinction in creative writing reveals the politics of universality, wherein an author's biographical influences often recede when they embody dominant culture.

34. Galang, "Deflowering," 209.

35. Ibid., 208.

36. Carbó and Galang, 283.

37. Bhabha, 127; emphases removed.

38. Carbó and Galang, 289.

39. See, *Decolonized Eye*; and See, *Filipino Primitive*.

40. Carbó and Galang, 283. Her brothers, however, did experience overt anti-Asian racism.

41. Carbó and Galang, 283.

42. See, for example, Ng; and B. Nguyen, *Stealing Buddha's Dinner*.

43. Lowe, *Immigrant Acts*, 71–72.

44. Ibid., 66.

45. Carbó and Galang, 292.

46. R. Lee.

47. Cruz, *Transpacific Femininities*, introduction.

48. Galang's artist statement, posted on her website, affirms this notion: "When I scan the pages of my books, my stories, and my hand-written journals, I hear the voices of the girls and women who have been traditionally silenced. I didn't mean to choose these girls, these dalagas, these women and lolas to inhabit my stories, but when I look, there they are. / Perhaps I've been looking for them in other books, but never finding them, have invited them to come forward in my fiction. Or perhaps it has to do with being born into a community that is constantly speaking and never listening. Who's going to hear you in all that chaos?" "About," M. Evelina Galang, 2023, accessed September 24, 2025, https://www.mevelinagalang.com/about.

49. See hooks, 61, on the uneven power relations between parents and children.
50. Hagedorn, *Charlie Chan*; and Ninh.
51. The hyphen between *Philippine* and *born* similarly disrupts a coherent, homogenous Filipinx subject.
52. In "Out Here and Over There," Eng considers the hyphen in *Asian-American* as discursively generative in resisting assimilationist imperatives of ethno-racial cultural nationalism and bolstering transnationality and queerness, the latter of which often runs counter to respectability politics that desire incorporation into the (U.S.) nation (36–39). Alternatively, Henry Fuhrmann points out that the hyphen "can connote an otherness, a sense that people of color are somehow not full citizens or fully American," which can have damaging effects in mainstream discourses. Henry Fuhrmann, "Drop the Hyphen in *Asian American*: On the Historical Divisiveness of an Unnecessary Punctuation Mark," *Conscious Style Guide*, January 23, 2018, https://consciousstyleguide.com/drop-hyphen-asian-american/.
53. Email communication with A. Rey Pamatmat, March 31, 2014.
54. The playscript specifies that Edith and Kenny are "Filipino-American," whereas Benji can be of "any race" (6).
55. See Edelman for a critique of queerness as un-reproductive.
56. Kazyak.
57. The playscript author's notes specify "NO GROWN UPS!" for the Mother character whom Ed mistakes for Benji's mom, while the three main characters may be "performed by young-looking adult actors, not actual teenagers," which emphasizes that the play's antagonism lies less with adults per se and more with parents and the power they wield over children.
58. T. Nguyen.
59. Ponce, "Pinoy Posteriority," 269.
60. Although Herring's and C. Johnson's works on queer rurality help to disrupt the incommensurability of queerness and rurality, they do not necessarily unseat Whiteness's entrenchment in imagining the rural.
61. Chambers-Letson offers a different sense of incommensurability that nevertheless aligns with my broader investment to suture ontoepistemes that appear incongruent.
62. While the Samuel French script does not include a reference to preparing spaghetti with ketchup, the Mu Performing Arts stage production that I saw does. Filipinx-style spaghetti features banana ketchup as an ingredient.
63. Edelman, 31.
64. Muñoz, *Cruising Utopia*, 94.
65. Ibid., 95.
66. Ibid., 22.
67. Fajardo, *Filipino Crosscurrents*; Francisco-Menchavez; Guevarra, *Marketing Dreams*; Parreñas; and R. Rodriguez, *Migrants for Export*.
68. Halberstam, *In a Queer Time and Place*; Herring; C. Johnson; and Tongson, *Relocations*.
69. Ahmed, *Living a Feminist Life*, 112.
70. Carbó and Galang, 292–293.
71. I thank Michele Janette for pointing out the cultural work Galang's text performs.
72. Sulit, 369–370.
73. Halberstam's *Wild Things* entwines *wild* and *queer*.
74. Dolan.

CHAPTER 5

1. A part of this chapter has been revised from Thomas Xavier Sarmiento, "The Empire Sings Back: *Glee*'s Queer Materialization of Filipina/o America," *MELUS: Multi-Ethnic Literature of the United States* 39, no. 2 (2014): 211–234, by permission of Oxford University Press and the Society for the Study of the Multi-Ethnic Literature of the United States. Finn's death, which the show addressed in "The Quarterback" (season 5, episode 3), was precipitated by Monteith's death in July 2013.

2. Balance; Balce; Suarez; See, *Decolonized Eye*; See, *Filipino Primitive*; Tongson, "Queer"; and Tongson, "Vocal Recognition," inform my sense of queer decolonial Filipinx aesthetics.

3. Orlando Pinatubo (played by Orlando Pabatoy) on *Strangers with Candy* (1999–2000), Suzuki St. Pierre / Byron Wu (played by Alec Mapa) on *Ugly Betty* (2007–2010), Emily Fields (played by Shay Mitchell) on *Pretty Little Liars* (2010–2017), Josh Chan (played by Vincent Rodriguez III) on *My Crazy Ex-Girlfriend* (2015–2019), Nini Salazar-Roberts (played by Olivia Rodrigo) on *High School Musical: The Musical: The Series* (2019–2022), and Mel Bayani (played by Liza Lapira) on *The Equalizer* (2021–2025) are notable examples.

4. My thinking here is inspired by Benjamin, who writes, "The past can be seized only as an image which flashes up at the instant when it can be recognized and is never seen again" ("Theses," 255).

5. Balce, 30–31.

6. "Sites of subjection" is a play on Hartman's "scenes of subjection."

7. V. Johnson.

8. *Family Matters* (1989–1998), which aired on ABC and CBS, was set in Chicago, and centered on the Winslows, a Black middle-class family, is a notable exception.

9. *Glee* cocreator Ryan Murphy, who identifies as gay and grew up in Indianapolis, Indiana, chose Lima, Ohio, as the show's setting because he was fascinated with the town as a kid after a tornado touched down there (John M. Urbancich, "Settled into a 'Glee'-ful State," cleveland.com, August 19, 2010, updated March 27, 2019, https://www.cleveland.com/sun/intermission/2010/08/post_24.html). *Superstore* showrunner Justin Spitzer chose St. Louis as the show's setting because he "wanted an area of the country with as much representation as possible" (Anna Menta, "NBC's 'Superstore' Understands Middle America Better Than Trump," *Newsweek*, November 2, 2017, https://www.newsweek.com/nbcs-superstore-understands-middle-america-better-trump-700340).

10. *Superstore* actor America Ferrera notes "the narrative that Middle America is filled with conservative white people 'only benefits those in power'" (Menta, "NBC's 'Superstore'").

11. Montalbano briefly discusses *Glee*'s setting in the Midwest and its relationship to sexual conservatism (59).

12. V. Johnson, 2–5, 33.

13. Ibid., 5. *Roseanne* (1988–1997) is one of the shows that Johnson discusses. Interestingly, it was rebooted in March 2018, giving insight into working-class America in the era of President Trump, and canceled in May 2018, after actor Roseanne Barr posted a racist tweet about Valerie Jarrett, former senior advisor to President Obama.

14. See Cantrell for more on the juxtaposition between Main Street and Wall Street.

15. Certainly, the Great Recession affected the globe; however, U.S. media representations tended to nationalize its effects.

16. For more on Midwestern populism, see Shortridge.

17. That Iowa and Ohio, along with an increasing number of adjacent states, including Michigan and Wisconsin, are key states in electoral politics further illustrates the Midwest's symbolic status as representative of the nation.

18. Tyler Clementi's suicide in September 2010 brought national attention to LGBTQ+ (cyber)bullying, and *Entertainment Weekly's* January 28, 2011, issue recognized *Glee* for leading the charge against LGBTQ+ bullying. For more on anti-bullying and queerness, see Levitt.

19. The episode aired on February 20, 2015. Iowa was the first Midwestern state to legalize same-gender marriage in April 2009; prior to this, only urban, coastal states had legalized it (Massachusetts in November 2003, California in May 2008, and Connecticut in October 2009). Although Ohio never legalized same-gender marriage, *Obergefell v. Hodges* made same-gender marriage legal across the entire United States in June 2015.

20. Duggan; Ferguson, *One-Dimensional Queer*; Muñoz, *Cruising Utopia*; and Reddy, *Freedom*.

21. Alicia Garza, Patrisse Cullors, and Opal Tometi started the Black Lives Matter movement in 2013 "in response to the acquittal of Trayvon Martin's murderer, George Zimmerman" ("Herstory," *Black Lives Matter*, accessed July 8, 2020, https://blacklivesmatter.com/herstory/).

22. The Mid-America American Studies Association's 2016 conference held at the University of Kansas was aptly themed "Battleground Midwest" to address these contradictions of the region. For the politics of race in the Twin Cities and Greater Minnesota, see Jacobs, Thompson Taiwo, and August. See also the *American Studies* double special issue on "Unsettling Global Midwests" (Perreira et al. and Sarmiento et al.). *Glee* generally ignores the structural inequities that plague its characters of color. Notably, Mr. Schuester repeatedly overlooks Mercedes, who is Black, Santana, who is Latina, and Tina, who is Asian American, for lead female roles, favoring Rachel, who is White but Jewish. Samantha Ware, who played Jane Hayward during season 6 and is Black, brought attention to the toxic work environment, alleged to have been perpetrated by Lea Michele, who played Rachel, amid the resurgence of the Black Lives Matter movement in the wake of George Floyd's murder (Elizabeth Wagmeister, "'Glee' Actor Samantha Ware on Why She Called Out Lea Michele (EXCLUSIVE)," *Variety*, June 11, 2020, https://variety.com/2020/tv/news/samantha-ware-glee-lea-michele-interview-black-actress-hollywood-1234631015/).

23. Shortridge's comment that St. Louis often is excluded from the discursive Midwest and Gonzalez's conceptualization of St. Louis as a Southern city are fitting here.

24. "Methamphetamine Seizures Continue to Climb in the Midwest," *United States Drug Enforcement Administration*, July 10, 2019, https://www.dea.gov/stories/2019/2019-07/2019-07-10/methamphetamine-seizures-continue-climb-midwest; Pine; and Alex Smith, "While Opioids Grab the Spotlight, the Meth Epidemic Grows Worse than Ever," *KCUR*, September 5, 2018, https://www.kcur.org/health/2018-09-05/while-opioids-grab-the-spotlight-the-meth-epidemic-grows-worse-than-ever.

25. Gray and Lotz; Hall; and Tongson, "Vocal Recognition," 142.

26. Squires et al.

27. Mukherjee, Banet-Weiser, and Gray, 19.

28. Joseph, 239. See also Gray, 28.

29. Joseph, 240.

30. Ferguson, "On the Postracial Question," 82.

31. Squires et al., 212.

32. Mukherjee, Banet-Weiser, and Gray, 132.

33. Joseph, 240–241.
34. Squires et al., 231.
35. Ibid., 232.
36. Although *Superstore* features a Native Hawaiian character (Sandra) and *Glee* does not, neither show (unsurprisingly) critically engages with Indigeneity and settler colonialism.
37. Balce; J. Kim; and Stoler, *Haunted*.
38. Gopinath, *Unruly Visions*, 7.
39. Balce; and Desai.
40. Balce, 4.
41. Ibid., 10.
42. Ibid., 3.
43. Ibid., 8.
44. See, *Filipino Primitive*, 49.
45. Balce, 1.
46. Criss is the first Filipinx American to win a Golden Globe. He won for his portrayal of Andrew Cunanan in the FX limited series *The Assassination of Gianni Versace: American Crime Story* (2018). Criss acknowledged his mother during his acceptance speech and his heritage during the backstage press follow-up (Dino-Ray Ramos and Nancy Tartaglione, "Darren Criss Says 'It's a Great Privilege' to Be First First [sic] Filipino American to Win Golden Globe," *Deadline*, January 6, 2019, https://deadline.com/2019/01/golden-globes-darren-criss-the-assassination-of-gianni-versace-ryan-murphy-filipino-american-1202530126/). See also E. Alex Jung, "Darren Criss on Playing Serial Killer Andrew Cunanan in ACS: Versace and Passing As White," *Vulture*, March 14, 2018, http://www.vulture.com/2018/03/darren-criss-american-crime-story-versace-and-race.html?utm_campaign=vulture&utm_source=tw&utm_medium=s1. He also used his experience as a White-passing biracial Filipino to inform his character, half-Filipinx Raymond Ainsley, in Netflix's *Hollywood* (2020) (Kristen Lopez, "'Hollywood': Janet Mock and Darren Criss Get a Chance to Rewrite History," *IndieWire*, May 5, 2020, https://www.indiewire.com/2020/05/hollywood-darren-criss-praises-ryan-murphy-1202226475/). For those who have been following Criss online, his acknowledgment of his Filipinx heritage is not new. See Darren Criss (@DarrenCriss), "@apresledeluge dude I'm half pinoy [sic] through and through. Guess they didn't want any happas [sic]. but [sic] I'm sorta glad I wasn't part of that film;)," Twitter/X, July 1, 2010, 4:47 A.M., https://x.com/DarrenCriss/status/17482021261; and Darren Criss (@DarrenCriss), "Just to clarify-1 of my favorite things about myself is that I'm half Filipino. PERIOD. I happen to not look like it, but THAT fact is not what I like. I like the fact that most people don't know it's an ace up my sleeve, an ace I'm very proud of, regardless of what I look like," Twitter/X, March 15, 2018, 12:50 A.M., https://x.com/DarrenCriss/status/974161008553013250.
47. Burns, introduction.
48. Muñoz, *Disidentifications*.
49. Burns, introduction.
50. See, *Filipino Primitive*, 142.
51. Ibid., 143. Certainly, all glee club members are "consummate mimics" as they perform covers; however, the preponderance of Filipinx singers whose voices arrest listeners in their capacity to outdo the original singer is worth considering. I thank Joe Ponce for prompting me to elaborate on this point.
52. See Sedgwick, "Paranoid Reading," for more on reparative reading.

53. Proposition 8 was an anti-same-gender marriage constitutional amendment that passed in California in 2008. "Don't Ask, Don't Tell" was the U.S. military's official policy on lesbian, gay, and bisexual servicemembers from 1994 to 2011, permitting those in the closet to serve and banning those who were open about their sexual orientation.

54. Although Kurt and Blaine identify as gay, I use *queer* to describe their nonnormative status among their peers.

55. Coach Sylvester gives Kurt the racially suggestive nickname Porcelain in lieu of calling him Lady (season 2, episode 8, "Furt"). I wish to thank Kevin Murphy for alerting me to this connection between Kurt and Hummel figurines. See also Rebecca Milzoff, "Chris Colfer Hits the High Notes on *Glee*," *Vulture*, November 16, 2009, https://www.vulture.com/2009/11/chris_colfer_on_playing_kurt_i.html. In "The End of Twerk" (season 5, episode 5), Kurt laments his "unblemished alabaster skin" after getting a grammatically incorrect tattoo.

56. Nishime, "Guilty Pleasures," 277.

57. The episode's focus on gender and sexual nonconformity also eclipses able-bodiedness elicited by Puck's decision to "help" Artie, who uses a wheelchair, as his "community service" to avoid a longer stay in juvenile detention.

58. Rachel is ethnically Jewish and appears as White. Although her biological mother, Shelby Corcoran (played by Jewish American actor and singer Idina Menzel), also appears as White, her two dads, Hiram and LeRoy Berry (played by Jewish American actor Jeff Goldblum and multiracial Black American actor and singer Brian Stokes Mitchell, respectively), could pass as White, multiracial, or non-White. The ambiguity of her biological father curiously is excised from Rachel's reception on and off the show—she is White, even if she is not blond like Quinn Fabray (who ironically is played by Jewish American actor Dianna Agron), the stereotypically all-American girl whom Rachel aspires to be. See Dubrofsky for more on Rachel's Jewishness.

59. See Nishime, *Undercover Asian*, for more on multiracial Asian American visual culture.

60. J. Lee, 189–190.

61. For fan reception, see, for example, anon, "Lea Salonga has pretty much already cast herself as Blaine's mom. . . . Blaine is supposed to be Eurasian, so I'll be disappointed if they white wash him," February 2, 2012, comment on Michael Slezak, "Glee Exclusive: Matt Bomer, Darren Criss Set to Duet With [SPOILER] Mash-Up!," *TVLine*, February 1, 2012, https://www.tvline.com/news/glee-matt-bomer-darren-criss-duran-duran-mashup-294600/; and We want Lea Salonga on Glee, "A lot of Gleeks out there want Lea Salonga to be Blaine's mom on Glee. What do you guys think?," January 27, 2012 (9:38 P.M.), Facebook wall post, https://www.facebook.com/LeaSalongaOnGlee.

62. Cooper Anderson is a play on White CNN anchor Anderson Cooper, whereas Pam Anderson is a play on blonde bombshell actor Pamela Anderson of *Baywatch* fame. The show does not introduce Blaine's father, still leaving open Blaine's racial-ethnic heritage.

63. Dubrofsky also discusses the use of humor on *Glee* as a mechanism for defusing racial tension.

64. This dynamic between allegorical American and Philippine colonial subject also occurs between Rachel and Sunshine. See Sarmiento, "Empire Sings Back."

65. During the final season (season 6), the racial politics of hair returns in the second episode, "Homecoming." In the opening sequence, Blaine provides a voice-over describing his life after Kurt, them breaking off their engagement, and his return to Ohio to coach The Warblers. "To shake things up," he decides to stop wearing hair gel. The scene

cuts to a Dalton student (listed as Terrified Dalton Student on IMDB), who looks Asian and could even pass for Filipinx (played by Korean American actor Bobo Chang), pointing at the screen and yelling, "Terrorist!" It then cuts to Blaine walking down the hall with bushy, curly hair. However, unlike the look of insecurity he had during the prom scene two seasons ago, Blaine is smiling and refuses the interpellation. This is not the only time we see Blaine without his helmet hair, however. Notably, while performing Beyoncé's "Diva" alongside Tina, Unique (played by nonbinary Black American actor and singer Alex Newell), Brittany, Kitty (played by Jewish American actor Becca Tobin), and Marley (played by White American actor Melissa Benoist) (season 4, episode 13, "Diva"), Blaine wears his hair curly, though with hair product, unlike his au naturel look during "Prom-asaurus" and "Homecoming." His "Diva" hairstyle actually is more in line with Criss's off-camera aesthetic; however, his entire look during this musical number—from hair, to makeup, to costume, to performance—presents a queer-of-color aesthetic that plays with normative scripts of gender, sexuality, class, and race.

66. Brittany had to repeat the twelfth grade because she had repressed her inner genius throughout most of her life.

67. I thank Nayan Shah for coining this phrase.

68. Trump was one of the most vocal and prominent "birther" proponents.

69. Rafael, *White Love*, chap. 2. Oddly enough, Korean American actor Ken Jeong plays Brittany's father, Pierce Pierce, although her biological father allegedly is the physicist Stephen Hawking.

70. See, for example, Katie Labovitz, "Glee-cap Season 4 Episode 3—Makeover," *Two Degrees and Separation* (blog), October 8, 2012, https://katielabovitz.wordpress.com/2012/10/08/glee-cap-season-4-episode-3-makeover/.

71. "Blaine's Time Capsule," disc 6, Murphy et al., *Glee: The Complete Fourth Season*.

72. Shoshandra, a member of rival glee club Vocal Adrenaline who appears in two episodes during season 1, is played by Filipina American actor and dancer Shelby Rabara; she has a brief speaking part in "Acafellas" (episode 3). The series features other background dancers who could be of Filipinx descent.

73. Bayani San Diego Jr., "Cheer Factor: The Real First Filipino on 'Glee,'" *Philippine Daily Inquirer*, December 4, 2011, https://entertainment.inquirer.net/23183/cheer-factor-the-real-first-filipino-on-'glee'.

74. Comments on "Howard Bamboo," *Glee Wiki*, accessed July 30, 2013, https://glee.wikia.com/wiki/Howard_Bamboo.

75. Suzanne Gardner, "Interview: Kent Avenido Talks about Being Cast as Howard Bamboo, Singing Solos, and What's Next for Howard," *Gleeks United*, June 1, 2010, http://gleeksunited.com/2010/06/01/interview-kent-avenido-talks-about-being-cast-as-howard-bamboo-singing-solos-and-whats-next-for-howard/. In this interview, Avenido expresses his desire for Lea Salonga to guest star on the show, perhaps as "one of Howard's relatives," because of their "mutual Filipino ancestry."

76. Eng, *Racial Castration*; and Parreñas Shimizu.

77. Alidio; and Rafael, *White Love*.

78. For a visual representation of the Filipino houseboy character type, see Anacleto (played by Zorro David) in John Houston's *Reflections in a Golden Eye* (1967). See, *Decolonized Eye*; and T. Nguyen present excellent readings of Anacleto.

79. Terri reappears in a few more episodes after the first season than Howard.

80. Davé, 2, 3, 6, 11, 14.

81. Ibid., 6.

82. Tongson, "Vocal Recognition," 142. Suarez also directs us toward the aurality of visual representations to recognize alternative modes of being that do not serve the ends of nationalism and globalization (113, 146).

83. See, *Filipino Primitive*, chap. 3.

84. See's call for scholars to "abandon the seductions of belonging and settling" that the university promotes influences my thinking here about settlement and movement (*Filipino Primitive*, 22).

85. Freud, "'Uncanny,'" 369–370.

86. Ibid., 399.

87. Ibid., 375.

88. Ibid.

89. Ibid., 370.

90. Ibid., 399.

91. Alexander, 49.

92. Freud, "'Uncanny,'" 383.

93. Bhabha, 129.

94. Benjamin, "Art," 220–221; and Butler, 41.

95. See, *Filipino Primitive*, 54.

96. For an extended analysis of this episode, see Sarmiento, "Empire Sings Back." Although Zyrus uses male pronouns, since Sunshine presents as female on the show, I use female pronouns when referring to the character.

97. Sunshine's performance of Beyoncé's "Listen" from the 2006 musical film *Dreamgirls* at the end of the episode is pointedly directed at Rachel and reinforces Sunshine's agency.

98. In "Throwdown" (season 1, episode 7), Sue does not single out Rachel as one of the "minority" glee club members.

99. Bhabha, 129.

100. Coincidentally, Kent Avenido briefly appears in this episode as an unnamed customer whom Jonah and Amy help.

101. Store manager Glenn assumes Mateo is Mexican (season 1, episode 3, "Shots and Salsa"). On the misrecognition of Filipinxs for Latinxs, see Coráñez Bolton, *Dos X*.

102. Gordon, 4–5.

103. Menta, "NBC's 'Superstore.'"

104. Mateo first reveals his newly discovered undocumented status to his best friend and coworker, Cheyenne, in "Election" (season 2, episode 8).

105. Kondo, 38.

106. For critical readings of Vargas's exceptional success story, see Coráñez Bolton, *Dos X*, chap. 3; and Guevarra, "Legacy of Undesirability."

107. In the introduction, I note the xenophobic and racist murder of Indian immigrant Srinivas Kuchibhotla by a White Kansas City man in February 2017. In summer 2018, President Trump used University of Iowa student Mollie Tibbetts's disappearance and murder at the hands of an undocumented Mexican immigrant to bolster support for his proposal to fortify the border wall between Mexico and the United States.

108. See Reddy, *Freedom*, for further discussion of immigration and same-gender marriage.

109. See Ahmed, *Promise of Happiness*; Berlant; and Duggan for further critiques of the "good life."

110. Hoganson, xiv.

111. Ibid., xvi.
112. Ibid., 259.
113. Ibid., 259–260.
114. For more on undocumentation, see Carroll. Joshi and Desai note that the contemporary heavy surveillance of the U.S.–Mexico border is rooted in the United States' efforts to curtail "Chinese and other Asian laborers entering through Mexico" at the turn of the twentieth century (Joshi and Desai, introduction).
115. "ICE Field Offices," U.S. Immigration and Customs Enforcement, updated March 9, 2023, https://www.ice.gov/contact/field-offices.
116. Pat Parker's poem "For the white person who wants to know how to be my friend" inspires my thinking here, quoted in Spelman, 81.
117. Doussard; Hume; Sandoval and Jennings; and Sichling and Karamehic-Muratovic indicate that St. Louis's relative attractiveness for some migrants and refugees stems from its lower cost of living and availability of entry-level job opportunities in comparison to larger cities. Bosnian refugees are the city's most visible foreign-born population.
118. Mateo immigrated to the United States with his grandmother and lives with his cousins, one of whom he tries to set Amy up with and another whom he says is out of her league (season 3, episode 12, "Groundhog Day").
119. Parikh; Park; and Wu.
120. Gopinath, *Unruly Visions*, 64.
121. See Guevarra, "Legacy of Undesirability," for more on TNTs.
122. Padrón's conception of deportability is instructive here.
123. Gopinath, *Unruly Visions*, 82.
124. Ibid., 8; Kondo, 5.
125. Balce, 10.
126. Campomanes, "New Empire's"; Campomanes, "New Formations"; Isaac, *American Tropics*; San Juan, "Configuring"; and See, *Decolonized Eye*. See also Chuh, *Imagine Otherwise*.
127. See Suarez on the productivity of difference.
128. Campomanes, "New Empire's," 165; Caronan, introduction; Cruz, *Transpacific Femininities*, 134; Isaac, *American Tropics*, 7; and See, *Decolonized Eye*, xii. Here, I am less concerned with parsing out the legalities of transpacific Filipinx movement. This notion is akin to a popular Chicanx chant—"We didn't cross the border; the border crossed us"—to emphasize the arbitrariness of juridical belonging.
129. See, *Filipino Primitive*, 104.
130. Ibid.
131. Ibid., 105.
132. Ibid., 136.
133. Ibid., 119. Here, See refers to the Filipinx concepts *utang na loob* (social obligation/indebtedness) and *kapwa* (collective sense of self). See also Fajardo, *Filipino Crosscurrents*, 87–88.
134. See Paik's important work on contemporary U.S. immigration.
135. De Genova; Ngai; and Puar.
136. General James Rusling, "Interview with President William McKinley," *Christian Advocate*, January 22, 1903.
137. My sense of queer utopia is inspired by Muñoz, *Cruising Utopia*.
138. The television show *Somebody Somewhere* (2022–2024), set in Manhattan, Kansas, presents the Midwest as somewhere rather than nowhere.

CONCLUSION

1. Ahmed, *Queer Phenomenology*.
2. Quantic, 2.
3. Martin Joseph Ponce, "Looking at Atrocity Photographs in Wing Tek Lum's *The Nanjing Massacre: Poems*," online paper presentation, Association for Asian American Studies, April 16, 2022; J. Kim; and Yoneyama. Given the map's chronological focus on mid-twentieth-century decolonization, Spanish empire seemingly would be absent, since it lost most of its colonies at the end of the nineteenth century, though it still held African territories well into the twentieth century.
4. Bascara, *Model-Minority*, 10–13; Campomanes, "New Formations"; and See, *Decolonized Eye*, xxviii.
5. I appreciate Eve Zimmerman, Weihong Bao, and audience members at my March 2023 talk at the Wellesley College Suzy Newhouse Center for the Humanities for prompting me to wrestle with these scenes of enclosure.
6. A new exhibit simply titled *The 1904 World's Fair* opened in April 2024, replacing *The 1904 World's Fair: Looking Back at Looking Forward* exhibit; it attempts to overtly reckon with the fair's imperial foundations. Ria Unson's painting *Young Spartan* (2021) is featured in the exhibit and provides a counterpoint to the dominant narrative of the fair. Unson's great-grandfather Ramon Ochoa was a pensionado who served as a waiter and guide at the Philippine Village. "Exhibit Explores Experiences of Humans Put on Display at 1904 World's Fair in St. Louis," *PBS News Hour*, PBS, May 30, 2024, https://www.pbs.org/newshour/classroom/daily-news-lessons/2024/05/exhibit-explores-experiences-of-humans-put-on-display-at-1904-worlds-fair-in-st-louis. Ria Unson, *Young Spartan*, accessed December 19, 2024, https://www.riaunson.com/young-spartan.
7. "Army Years," "The Eisenhowers," Dwight D. Eisenhower Presidential Library, Museum, and Boyhood Home, last updated April 15, 2020, https://www.eisenhowerlibrary.gov/eisenhowers/army-years; and "Chronologies," "The Eisenhowers," Dwight D. Eisenhower Presidential Library, Museum, and Boyhood Home, last updated May 7, 2021, https://www.eisenhowerlibrary.gov/eisenhowers/chronologies.
8. Manalansan et al.; and Manalansan, "'Stuff' of Archives."
9. Naramore Maher, 10.
10. Ibid., 10–11.
11. Ibid., 6.
12. McKittrick, xiv.
13. Ibid.
14. Ibid., xxxi.
15. Lowe, *Immigrant Acts*, 6–9; and Herring, introduction.
16. de Jesús, "Rereading History," 109.
17. Ahmed, *Living a Feminist Life*, 133, 134.
18. Muñoz, *Cruising Utopia*, 22.
19. My nod to impossibility is inspired by Gopinath, *Impossible Desires*.

Bibliography

Afable, Patricia O. "Journeys from Bontoc to the Western Fairs, 1904–1915: The 'Nikimalika' and their Interpreters." *Philippine Studies: Historical and Ethnographic Viewpoints* 52, no. 4 (2004): 445–473. https://www.jstor.org/stable/42634961.
Aguilar-San Juan, Karin. "Hyphen Generation." Review of *Her Wild American Self*, by M. Evelina Galang. *The Women's Review of Books* 13, no. 10/11 (1996): 35. https://www.jstor.org/stable/4022490.
Ahmed, Sara. *Living a Feminist Life*. Durham, NC: Duke University Press, 2017.
Ahmed, Sara. *The Promise of Happiness*. Durham, NC: Duke University Press, 2010.
Ahmed, Sara. *Queer Phenomenology: Orientations, Objects, Others*. Durham, NC: Duke University Press, 2006.
Alexander, M. Jacqui. *Pedagogies of Crossing: Meditations on Feminism, Sexual Politics, Memory, and the Sacred*. Durham, NC: Duke University Press, 2005.
Alidio, Kimberly. "'When I Get Home, I Want to Forget': Memory and Amnesia in the Occupied Philippines, 1901–1904." *Social Text* 17, no. 2 (1999): 105–122. https://www.jstor.org/stable/466699.
Allegro, Linda, and Andrew Grant Wood, eds. *Latin American Migrations to the U.S. Heartland: Changing Social Landscapes in Middle America*. Urbana: University of Illinois Press, 2013.
Alumit, Noël. *Letters to Montgomery Clift*. 2002. Reprint, Los Angeles: Alyson, 2003.
Alumit, Noël. *Talking to the Moon*. New York: Carroll and Graf, 2007.
Anderson, Benedict. *Imagined Communities: Reflections on the Origin and Spread of Nationalism*. Rev. ed. London: Verso, 2006.
Anderson, Donna Doan. "Acceptance for Admission: Administrations of Japanese American Relocation and the Midwestern University." *American Studies* 62, no. 3 (2023): 71–96.
Anderson, Donna Doan. "America Is in the Heartland: Land Policy, Immigration, and Rural Asian America, 1860–1950." Ph.D. diss., University of California, Santa Barbara, 2024. ProQuest (31487314).

Arondekar, Anjali. "Without a Trace: Sexuality and the Colonial Archive." *Journal of the History of Sexuality* 14, nos. 1–2 (2005): 10–27. https://www.jstor.org/stable/3704707.
Ayers, Edward L., Patricia Nelson Limerick, Stephen Nissenbaum, and Peter S. Onuf. *All Over the Map: Rethinking American Regions*. Baltimore, MD: Johns Hopkins University Press, 1996.
Balance, Christine Bacareza. *Tropical Renditions: Making Musical Scenes in Filipino America*. Durham, NC: Duke University Press, 2016.
Balance, Christine Bacareza, and Lucy Mae San Pablo Burns, eds. *California Dreaming: Movement and Place in the Asian American Imaginary*. Honolulu: University of Hawai'i Press, 2020.
Balce, Nerissa S. *Body Parts of Empire: Visual Abjection, Filipino Images, and the American Archive*. Ann Arbor: University of Michigan Press, 2016.
Baldoz, Rick. *The Third Asiatic Invasion: Empire and Migration in Filipino America, 1898–1946*. New York: New York University Press, 2011.
Baptist, Edward E. "Hidden in Plain View: Evasions, Invasions and Invisible Nations." In *Echoes of the Haitian Revolution, 1804–2004*, edited by Munro Martin and Elizabeth Walcott-Hackshaw, 1–27. Kingston, Jamaica: University of the West Indies Press, 2008.
Barillas, William. *The Midwestern Pastoral: Place and Landscape in Literature of the American Heartland*. Athens, OH: Ohio University Press, 2006.
Barritt, Majorie. "Introduction." "American-Philippine Relations" Subject Guide, University of Michigan Bentley Historical Library, 2–4. 1982. https://bentley.umich.edu/wp-content/uploads/2014/09/American_Philippine_Relations_Subject_Guide.pdf.
Bascara, Victor. *Model-Minority Imperialism*. Minneapolis: University of Minnesota Press, 2006.
Bascara, Victor. "Up from Benevolent Assimilation: At Home with the Manongs of Bienvenido Santos." *MELUS: Multi-Ethnic Literature of the United States* 29, no. 1 (2004): 61–78. https://doi.org/10.2307/4141795.
Bascara, Victor. "'Within Each Crack/A Story': The Political Economy of Queering Filipino American Pasts." In Davé, Nishime, and Oren, *East Main Street*, 117–136.
Baum, L. Frank. *The Wonderful Wizard of Oz*. 1900. Reprint, Mineola, NY: Dover, 2015.
Bauman, Robert. "Jim Crow in the Tri-Cities, 1943–1950." *Pacific Northwest Quarterly* 96, no. 3 (2005): 124–131. https://www.jstor.org/stable/40491852.
Behner, Frederick G. Papers. Bentley Historical Library, University of Michigan.
Belkin, Aaron. *Bring Me Men: Military Masculinity and the Benign Façade of American Empire, 1898–2001*. New York: Columbia University Press, 2012.
Benjamin, Walter. "Art in the Age of Mechanical Reproduction." In Benjamin, *Illuminations*, 217–251.
Benjamin, Walter. *Illuminations: Essays and Reflections*. Edited by Hannah Arendt. Translated by Harry Zohn. New York: Schocken, 1968.
Benjamin, Walter. "Theses on the Philosophy of History." In Benjamin, *Illuminations*, 253–264.
Berlant, Lauren. *Cruel Optimism*. Durham, NC: Duke University Press, 2011.
Bernabe, Jan Christian. "Queer Reconfigurations: *Bontoc Eulogy* and Marlon Fuentes's Archive Imperative." *positions: east asia cultures critique* 24, no. 4 (2016): 727–759. https://muse.jhu.edu/article/633687.
Bhabha, Homi. "Of Mimicry and Man: The Ambivalence of Colonial Discourse." *October* 28 (Spring 1984): 125–133. https://www.jstor.org/stable/778467.

Blanco, Jody. "Patterns of Reform, Repetition, and Return in the First Centennial of the Filipino Revolution, 1896-1996." In Tiongson et al., *Positively No Filipinos*, 17-25.

Blumentritt, Mia. "*Bontoc Eulogy*, History, and the Craft of Memory: An Extended Conversation with Marlon E. Fuentes." *Amerasia Journal* 24, no. 3 (1998): 75-90. https://doi.org/10.17953/amer.24.3.g21132m73h587383.

Bow, Leslie. *Partly Colored: Asian Americans and Racial Anomaly in the Segregated South*. New York: New York University Press, 2010.

Brattain, Michelle. "Miscegenation and Competing Definitions of Race in Twentieth-Century Louisiana." *Journal of Southern History* 71, no. 3 (2005): 621-658. https://www.jstor.com/stable/27648822.

Breitbart, Eric. *A World on Display: Photographs from the St. Louis World's Fair, 1904*. Albuquerque: University of New Mexico Press, 1997.

Bresnahan, Roger J. "Can These, Too, Be Midwestern? Studies of Two Filipino Writers." *MidAmerica: The Yearbook of the Society for the Study of Midwestern Literature* 8 (1986): 134-147. https://ssml.org/publications/midamerica/full-texts/.

Bresnahan, Roger J. *Conversations with Filipino Writers*. Quezon City, Philippines: New Day, 1990.

Bresnahan, Roger J. "The Midwestern Fiction of Bienvenido N. Santos." *Society for the Study of Midwestern Literature Newsletter* 13, no. 2 (1983): 28-37.

Buangan, Antonio S. "The Suyoc People Who Went to St. Louis 100 Years Ago: The Search for My Ancestors." *Philippine Studies: Historical and Ethnographic Viewpoints* 52, no. 4 (2004): 474-498. https://www.jstor.org/stable/42634962.

Bulosan, Carlos. *America Is in the Heart: A Personal History*. 1946. Reprint, Seattle: University of Washington Press, 1973.

Burns, Lucy Mae San Pablo. *Puro Arte: Filipinos on the Stages of Empire*. New York: New York University Press, 2013. Kindle.

Butler, Judith. *Gender Trouble: Feminism and the Subversion of Identity*. 1990. Reprint, New York: Routledge, 1999.

Byrd, Jodi A. *The Transit of Empire: Indigenous Critiques of Colonialism*. Minneapolis: University of Minnesota Press, 2011.

Campney, Brent M. S. *Hostile Heartland: Racism, Repression, and Resistance in the Midwest*. Urbana: University of Illinois Press, 2019.

Campney, Brent M. S. *This Is Not Dixie: Racist Violence in Kansas, 1861-1927*. Urbana: University of Illinois Press, 2015.

Campomanes, Oscar V. "Filipinos in the United States and Their Literature of Exile." In *A Companion to Asian American Studies*, edited by Kent A. Ono, 296-318. Malden, MA: Blackwell, 2005.

Campomanes, Oscar V. "The New Empire's Forgetful and Forgotten Citizens: Unrepresentability and Unassimilability in Filipino-American Postcolonialities." *Critical Mass: A Journal of Asian American Cultural Criticism* 2, no. 2 (1995): 145-200.

Campomanes, Oscar V. "New Formations of Asian American Studies and the Question of U.S. Imperialism." *positions: east asia cultures critique* 5, no. 2 (1997): 523-550.

Cantrell, Owen. "'Ya Got Trouble': River City, Main Street, U.S.A., and Nostalgia in the Imagined Midwest." In Oler, *Pieces*, 53-68.

Carbó, Nick, and M. Evelina Galang. "The Struggle for Form: A Conversation between Nick Carbó and M. Evelina Galang." *MELUS: Multi-Ethnic Literatures of the United States* 29, no. 1 (2004): 281-293. https://doi.org/10.2307/4141805.

Caronan, Faye. *Legitimizing Empire: Filipino American and U.S. Puerto Rican Cultural Critique.* Urbana: University of Illinois Press, 2015. Kindle.
Carroll, Amy Sara. "[The Fiction of a Doorframe] Further Notes on Undocumentation." *Media Fields Journal* 12 (2017): 1–10. http://mediafieldsjournal.org/the-fiction-of-a-doorframe/.
Carter, David. *Stonewall: The Riots that Sparked the Gay Revolution.* 2004. Reprint, New York: St. Martin's Griffin, 2010.
Castillo, Elaine. *America Is Not the Heart.* New York: Penguin, 2018.
Cather, Willa. *My Ántonia.* 1918. Reprint, New York: Penguin, 1994.
Cayton, Andrew R. L. "The Anti-region: Place and Identity in the History of the American Midwest." In Cayton and Gray, *American Midwest,* 140–159.
Cayton, Andrew R. L., and Susan E. Gray, eds. *The American Midwest: Essays on Regional History.* Bloomington: Indiana University Press, 2001.
Cayton, Andrew R. L., and Peter S. Onuf. *The Midwest and the Nation: Rethinking the History of an American Region.* Bloomington: Indiana University Press, 1990.
Chakrabarty, Dipesh. *Provincializing Europe: Postcolonial Thought and Historical Difference.* Princeton, NJ: Princeton University Press, 2000.
Chambers-Letson, Joshua. *After the Party: A Manifesto for Queer of Color Life.* New York: New York University Press, 2018.
Chang, Juliana. *Inhuman Citizenship: Traumatic Enjoyment and Asian American Literature.* Minneapolis: University of Minnesota Press, 2012.
Chaput, Donald. "Private William W. Grayson's War in the Philippines, 1899." *Nebraska History* 61 (1980): 355–366. https://history.nebraska.gov/wp-content/uploads/2017/12/doc_publications_NH1980GraysonWar1899.pdf.
Choy, Catherine Ceniza. *Empire of Care: Nursing and Migration in Filipino American History.* Durham, NC: Duke University Press, 2003.
Chuh, Kandice. *The Difference Aesthetics Makes: On the Humanities "After Man."* Durham, NC: Duke University Press, 2019.
Chuh, Kandice. *Imagine Otherwise: On Asian Americanist Critique.* Durham, NC: Duke University Press, 2003.
Cisneros, Sandra. *The House on Mango Street.* 1984. Reprint, New York: Vintage, 1991.
Clampitt, Cynthia. *Midwest Maize: How Corn Shaped the U.S. Heartland.* Urbana: University of Illinois Press, 2015.
Clutario, Genevieve Alva. *Beauty Regimes: A History of Power and Modern Empire in the Philippines, 1898–1941.* Durham, NC: Duke University Press, 2023.
Coffman, Franklin A. Papers. Richard L. D. and Marjorie J. Morse Department of Archives and Special Collections, Kansas State University Libraries.
Coráñez Bolton, Sony. *Crip Colony: Mestizaje, US Imperialism, and the Queer Politics of Disability in the Philippines.* Durham, NC: Duke University Press, 2023.
Coráñez Bolton, Sony. *Dos X: Disability and Racial Dysphoria in Latinx and Filipinx Culture.* Austin: University of Texas Press, 2025.
Cordova, Fred. *Filipinos: Forgotten Asian Americans; A Pictorial Essay/1763-circa-1963.* Dubuque: IA: Kendall/Hunt, 1983.
Cruz, Denise. "Jose Garcia Villa's Collection of 'Others': Irreconcilabilities of a Queer Transpacific Modernism." In "Regional Modernism," edited by Scott Herring, special issue, *Modern Fiction Studies* 55, no. 1 (2009): 11–41. https://doi.org/10.1353/mfs.0.1592.
Cruz, Denise. *Transpacific Femininities: The Making of the Modern Filipina.* Durham, NC: Duke University Press, 2012.

Cullinane, Michael. "Implementing the 'New Order': The Structure and Supervision of Local Government During the Taft Era." *Michigan Papers on South and Southeast Asia* 3 (1971): 13–75.
Curtis, Edward E., IV. *Muslims of the Heartland: How Syrian Immigrants Made a Home in the American Midwest*. New York: New York University Press, 2022.
Davé, Shilpa S. *Indian Accents: Brown Voice and Racial Performance in American Television and Film*. Urbana: University of Illinois, 2013.
Davé, Shilpa, LeiLani Nishime, and Tasha G. Oren, eds. *East Main Street: Asian American Popular Culture*. New York: New York University Press, 2005.
De Genova, Nicholas. *Working the Boundaries: Race, Space, and "Illegality" in Mexican Chicago*. Durham, NC: Duke University Press, 2005.
de Jesús, Melinda L., ed. *Pinay Power: Peminist Critical Theory; Theorizing the Filipina/American Experience*. New York: Routledge, 2005.
de Jesús, Melinda L. "Rereading History, Rewriting Desire: Reclaiming Queerness in Carlos Bulosan's *America Is in the Heart* and Bienvenido Santos' *Scent of Apples*." *Journal of Asian American Studies* 5, no. 2 (2002): 91–111. https://doi.org/10.1353/jaas.2003.0005.
De Leon, Adrian. *Bundok: A Hinterland History of Filipino America*. Chapel Hill: University of North Carolina Press, 2023.
Delmendo, Sharon. *The Star-Entangled Banner: One Hundred Years of America in the Philippines*. New Brunswick, NJ: Rutgers University Press, 2004.
Deloria, Philip J. *Indians in Unexpected Places*. Lawrence: University Press of Kansas, 2004.
Derrida, Jacques. *Specters of Marx: The State of the Debt, the Work of Mourning and the New International*. Translated by Peggy Kamuf. 1994. Reprint, New York: Routledge, 2006.
Desai, Jigna. *Beyond Bollywood: The Cultural Politics of South Asian Diasporic Film*. New York: Routledge, 2004.
Dhingra, Pawan. "Introduction to *Journal of Asian American Studies*, Special Issue on the Midwest." *Journal of Asian American Studies* 12, no. 3 (2009): 239–246. https://doi.org/10.1353/jaas.0.0044.
Dhingra, Pawan. *Life Behind the Lobby: Indian American Motel Owners and the American Dream*. Stanford, CA: Stanford University Press, 2012.
Dhingra, Pawan, ed. "The Midwest." Special issue, *Journal of Asian American Studies* 12, no. 3 (2009).
Diaz, Josen Masangkay. *Postcolonial Configurations: Dictatorship, the Racial Cold War, and Filipino America*. Durham, NC: Duke University Press, 2023.
Dolan, Jill. *Utopia in Performance: Finding Hope at the Theater*. Ann Arbor: University of Michigan Press, 2005.
Doussard, Marc. "Organizing the Ordinary City: How Labor Reform Strategies Travel to the US Heartland." *International Journal of Urban and Regional Research* 40, no. 5 (2016): 918–935. https://onlinelibrary.wiley.com/doi/10.1111/1468-2427.12435.
Dubrofsky, Rachel E. "Jewishness, Whiteness, and Blackness on *Glee*: Singing to the Tune of Postracism." *Communication, Culture and Critique* 6, no. 1 (2013): 82–102. https://doi.org/10.1111/cccr.12002.
Duggan, Lisa. *The Twilight of Equality? Neoliberalism, Cultural Politics, and the Attack on Democracy*. Boston: Beacon, 2003.
Edelman, Lee. *No Future: Queer Theory and the Death Drive*. Durham, NC: Duke University Press, 2004.
Edmunds, R. David, ed. *Enduring Nations: Native Americans in the Midwest*. Urbana: University of Illinois Press, 2008.

Edwards, Jay D. "Shotgun: The Most Contested House in America." *Buildings and Landscapes: Journal of the Vernacular Architecture Forum* 16, no. 1 (2009): 62–92. https://www.jstor.com/stable/27804896.
Eittreim, Elisabeth M. *Teaching Empire: Native Americans, Filipinos, and US Imperial Education, 1879–1918.* Lawrence: University Press of Kansas, 2019.
Elliot, Anthony. *Psychoanalytic Theory: An Introduction.* 2nd ed. Durham, NC: Duke University Press, 2002.
Eng, David L. *The Feeling of Kinship: Queer Liberalism and the Racialization of Intimacy.* Durham, NC: Duke University Press, 2010.
Eng, David L. "Out Here and Over There: Queerness and Diaspora in Asian American Studies." *Social Text* 15, nos. 3–4 (1997): 31–52. https://doi.org/10.2307/466733.
Eng, David L. *Racial Castration: Managing Masculinity in Asian America.* Durham, NC: Duke University Press, 2001.
Eng, David L., and Shinhee Han. *Racial Melancholia, Racial Dissociation: On the Social and Psychic Lives of Asian Americans.* Durham, NC: Duke University Press, 2019.
España-Maram, Linda. *Creating Masculinity in Los Angeles's Little Manila: Working-Class Filipinos and Popular Culture, 1920s–1950s.* New York: Columbia University Press, 2006.
Espiritu, Augusto Fauni. *Five Faces of Exile: The Nation and Filipino American Intellectuals.* Stanford, CA: Stanford University Press, 2005.
Espiritu, Yến Lê. *Home Bound: Filipino American Lives across Cultures, Communities, and Countries.* Berkeley: University of California Press, 2003.
Evangelista, Al. "Dancing Augmented Archives: Movement and Technology as Dramaturgical Practice." In *Dramaturgy and History: Staging the Archive,* edited by Caitlin A. Kane and Erin Stoneking. New York: Routledge, 2024.
Fajardo, Kale Bantigue. "Decolonizing Manila-Men and St. Maló, Louisiana: A Queer Postcolonial Asian American Critique." In Manalansan and Espiritu, *Filipino Studies,* 227–248.
Fajardo, Kale Bantigue. *Filipino Crosscurrents: Oceanographies of Seafaring, Masculinities, and Globalization.* Minneapolis: University of Minnesota Press, 2011.
Fajardo, Kale Bantigue. "Queering and Transing the Great Lakes: Filipino/a Tomboy Masculinities and Manhoods Across Waters." *GLQ: A Journal of Lesbian and Gay Studies* 20, nos. 1–2 (2014): 115–140. https://muse.jhu.edu/article/536498.
Fanon, Franz. *Black Skin, White Masks.* Translated by Richard Philcox. 1952. Reprint, New York: Grove, 2008.
Feng, Peter X. *Identities in Motion: Asian American Film and Video.* Durham, NC: Duke University Press, 2002.
Ferguson, Roderick A. *Aberrations in Black: Toward a Queer of Color Critique.* Minneapolis: University of Minnesota Press, 2004.
Ferguson, Roderick A. *One-Dimensional Queer.* Cambridge, UK: Polity, 2019.
Ferguson, Roderick A. "On the Postracial Question." In Mukherjee, Banet-Weiser, and Gray, *Racism Postrace,* 72–85.
Fermin, Jose D. *1904 World's Fair: The Filipino Experience.* West Conshohocken, PA: Infinity, 2004.
Francisco-Menchavez, Valerie. *The Labor of Care: Filipina Migrants and Transnational Families in the Digital Age.* Urbana: University of Illinois Press, 2018.
Freud, Sigmund. "Mourning and Melancholia." 1917. In *General Psychological Theory: Papers on Metapsychology,* edited by Philip Rieff, translated by Joan Riviere, 164–179. Reprint, New York: Touchstone, 1997.

Freud, Sigmund. "The 'Uncanny.'" 1919. In *Collected Papers, Volume IV: Papers on Metapsychology, Papers on Applied Psycho-Analysis*, edited by Joan Riviere, translated by Alix Strachey, 368–407. Reprint, London: Hogarth, 1953.

Fu, May C. "On Contradiction: Theory and Transformation in Detroit's Asian Political Alliance." *Amerasia Journal* 35, no. 2 (2009): 1–22.

Fuentes, Marlon, and Bridget Yearian, dirs. *Bontoc Eulogy*. New York: Cinema Guild, 1995. https://video.alexanderstreet.com/watch/bontoc-eulogy.

Fujita-Rony, Dorothy B. *American Workers, Colonial Power: Philippine Seattle and the Transpacific West, 1919–1941*. Berkeley: University of California Press, 2003.

Fuss, Diana. *Dying Modern: A Mediation on Elegy*. Durham, NC: Duke University Press, 2013.

Galang, M. Evelina. "Deflowering the Sampaguita." In de Jesús, *Pinay Power*, 201–209.

Galang, M. Evelina. *Her Wild American Self*. Minneapolis: Coffee House, 1996.

Galura, Joseph A., and Emily P. Lawsin. *Filipino Women in Detroit: 1945–1955; Oral Histories from the Filipino American Oral History Project of Michigan*. Ann Arbor: OSCL Press at the University of Michigan, 2002.

Gilbert, James. *Whose Fair? Experience, Memory, and the History of the Great St. Louis Exposition*. Chicago: University of Chicago Press, 2009.

Gleason, Ronald P., ed. *The Log of the "Thomas," July 23 to August 21, 1901*. https://ia600305.us.archive.org/15/items/logofthomasjuly200glea/logofthomasjuly200glea.pdf.

Gonzalez, Vernadette Vicuña. "Headhunter Itineraries: The Philippines as America's Dream Jungle." *Global South* 3, no. 2 (2009): 144–172. https://www.jstor.org/stable/10.2979/gso.2009.3.2.144.

Gonzalvez, Theodore S. *The Day the Dancers Stayed: Performing in the Filipino/American Diaspora*. Philadelphia: Temple University Press, 2009.

Gopinath, Gayatri. *Impossible Desires: Queer Diasporas and South Asian Public Cultures*. Durham, NC: Duke University Press, 2005.

Gopinath, Gayatri. "Queer Regions: Locating Lesbians in *Sancharram*." In *A Companion to Lesbian, Gay, Bisexual, Transgender, and Queer Studies*, edited by George E. Haggerty and Molly McGarry, 341–354. Malden, MA: Blackwell, 2007. https://doi.org/10.1002/9780470690864.ch18.

Gopinath, Gayatri. *Unruly Visions: The Aesthetic Practices of Queer Diaspora*. Durham, NC: Duke University Press, 2018.

Gordon, Avery F. *Ghostly Matters: Haunting and the Sociological Imagination*. Minneapolis: University of Minnesota Press, 1997.

Governor's Interracial Commission. *The Oriental in Minnesota*. St. Paul: State of Minnesota, 1949.

Gray, Herman. "Race after Race." In Mukherjee, Banet-Weiser, and Gray, *Racism Postrace*, 23–36.

Gray, Jonathan, and Amanda D. Lotz. *Television Studies*. 2nd ed. Cambridge, UK: Polity, 2019.

Guevarra, Anna Romina. "The Legacy of Undesirability: Filipino TNTs, 'Irregular Migrants,' and 'Outlaws' in the US Cultural Imaginary." In Manalansan and Espiritu, *Filipino Studies*, 355–374.

Guevarra, Anna Romina. *Marketing Dreams, Manufacturing Heroes: The Transnational Labor Brokering of Filipino Workers*. New Brunswick, NJ: Rutgers University Press, 2009.

Gupta-Carlson, Himanee. *Muncie, India(na): Middletown and Asian America*. Urbana: University of Illinois Press, 2018.

Hagedorn, Jessica, ed. *Charlie Chan Is Dead 2: At Home in the World; An Anthology of Contemporary Asian American Fiction*. New York: Penguin, 2004.
Hagedorn, Jessica. *Dogeaters*. 1990. Reprint, New York: Penguin, 1991.
Hagedorn, Jessica. *The Gangster of Love*. 1996. Reprint, New York: Penguin, 1997.
Halberstam, Jack. *In a Queer Time and Place: Transgender Bodies, Subcultural Lives*. New York: New York University Press, 2005.
Halberstam, Jack. *Wild Things: The Disorder of Desire*. Durham, NC: Duke University Press, 2020.
Hall, Stuart. "Encoding and Decoding in the Television Discourse." In *Essential Essays Vol. 1: Foundations of Cultural Studies*, edited by David Morley, 257–276. Durham, NC: Duke University Press, 2019.
Halvorson, Britt E., and Joshua O. Reno. *Imagining the Heartland: White Supremacy and the American Midwest*. Oakland: University of California Press, 2022.
Hartman, Saidiya. *Scenes of Subjection: Terror, Slavery, and Self-Making in Nineteenth-Century America*. New York: Oxford University Press, 1997.
Harvey Family Papers. Kenneth Spencer Research Library Archival Collections, University of Kansas.
Herr, Cheryl Temple. *Critical Regionalism and Cultural Studies: From Ireland to the American Midwest*. Gainesville: University Press of Florida, 1996.
Herring, Scott. *Another Country: Queer Anti-Urbanism*. New York: New York University Press, 2010. Kindle.
Hey-Colón, Rebeca L. "Ocean, Sky, Sugar, and Spirit: The Power of Pooling in Firelei Báez's *A Drexcyen Chronocommons (To win the war you fought it sideways)*." *Latin American and Latinx Visual Culture* 7, no. 2 (2025): 6–26. https://doi.org/10.1525/lavc.2025.7.2.6.
Hoganson, Kristin L. *The Heartland: An American History*. New York: Penguin, 2019.
Homiak, John P. "The Body in the Archives: A Review of Bontoc Eulogy." *American Anthropologist* 102, no. 4 (2000): 887–891. https://www.jstor.org/stable/684223.
hooks, bell. *Feminism Is for Everybody: Passionate Politics*. 2000. Reprint, New York: Routledge, 2015.
Hoorn, Jeanette. "Captivity, Melancholia and Diaspora in Marlon Fuentes' *Bontoc Eulogy*: Revisiting *Meet Me In St Louis*." In *Body Trade: Captivity, Cannibalism and Colonialism in the Pacific*, edited by Barbara Creed and Jeanette Hoorn, 195–207. London: Routledge, 2001.
Houston, Velina Hasu. *Green Tea Girl in Orange Pekoe Country*. South Gate, CA: NoPassport, 2014.
Hughes, Langston. *Not Without Laughter*. 1930. Reprint, New York: Penguin, 2018.
Hume, Susan E. "Two Decades of Bosnian Place-Making in St. Louis, Missouri." *Journal of Cultural Geography* 32, no. 1 (2015): 1–22. https://doi.org/10.1080/08873631.2015.1005880.
Hu Pegues, Juliana. *Space-Time Colonialism: Alaska's Indigenous and Asian Entanglements*. Chapel Hill: University of North Carolina Press, 2021.
Ingalls Wilder, Laura. *Little House* Complete 9-Book Box Set. New York: Harper Collins, 2008.
Isaac, Allan Punzalan. *American Tropics: Articulating Filipino America*. Minneapolis: University of Minnesota Press, 2006.
Isaac, Allan Punzalan. *Filipino Time: Affective Worlds and Contracted Labor*. New York: Fordham University Press, 2022.
Jacobs, Walter R., Wendy Thompson Taiwo, and Amy August. *Sparked: George Floyd, Racism, and the Progressive Illusion*. St. Paul: Minnesota Historical Society Press, 2021.

Janette, Michele. "Teaching Vietnamese Vietnam War Stories in the Land of the 'Big Red One.'" *Canadian Review of American Studies* 48, no. 3 (2018): 438–463. https://doi.org/10.3138/cras.2018.007.
Johnson, Colin R. *Just Queer Folks: Gender and Sexuality in Rural America*. Philadelphia: Temple University Press, 2013.
Johnson, Victoria E. *Heartland TV: Prime Time Television and the Struggle for U.S. Identity*. New York: New York University Press, 2008. Kindle.
Joseph, Ralina L. "'Tyra Banks Is Fat': Reading (*Post*-)Racism and (*Post*-)Feminism in the New Millennium." *Critical Studies in Media Communication* 26, no. 3 (2009): 237–254. https://doi.org/10.1080/15295030903015096.
Joshi, Khayti Y., and Jigna Desai, eds. *Asian Americans in Dixie: Race and Migration in the South*. Urbana: University of Illinois Press, 2013.
Justice, Daniel Heath. "Notes toward a Theory of Anomaly." *GLQ: A Journal of Lesbian and Gay Studies* 16, nos. 1–2 (2010): 207–242. https://muse.jhu.edu/article/372452.
Kafka, Phillipa. "'Cheap, On Sale, American Dream': Contemporary Asian American Women Writers' Responses to American Success Mythologies." In *American Mythologies: New Essays on Contemporary Literature*, edited by William Blazek and Michael K. Glenday, 105–127. Liverpool: Liverpool University Press, 2005.
Kaplan, Amy. *The Anarchy of Empire in the Making of U.S. Culture*. Cambridge, MA: Harvard University Press, 2005.
Kaplan, Amy, and Donald E. Pease, eds. *Cultures of United States Imperialism*. Durham, NC: Duke University Press, 1993.
Kazyak, Emily. "Midwest or Lesbian? Gender, Rurality, and Sexuality." *Gender and Society* 26, no. 6 (2012): 825–848. https://doi.org/10.1177/0891243212458361.
Kercheval, Jesse Lee. *Building Fiction: How to Develop Plot and Structure*. Cincinnati, OH: Story, 1997.
Kercheval, Jesse Lee. *The Dogeater*. Columbia: University of Missouri Press, 1987.
Khubchandani, Kareem. *Ishtyle: Accenting Gay Indian Nightlife*. Ann Arbor: University of Michigan Press, 2020.
Kim, Elaine H. *Asian American Literature: An Introduction to the Writings and Their Social Context*. Philadelphia: Temple University Press, 1982.
Kim, Jinah. *Postcolonial Grief: The Afterlives of the Pacific Wars in the Americas*. Durham, NC: Duke University Press, 2019.
Kinney, Rebecca Jo. "The Cleveland Asian Festival as Scenario: Performing and Unsettling Racial Scripts." *American Studies* 62, no. 4 (2023): 147–172.
Kinney, Rebecca Jo. *Mapping AsiaTown Cleveland: Race and Redevelopment in the Rust Belt*. Philadelphia: Temple University Press, 2025.
Kirkwood, Patrick M. "'Michigan Men' in the Philippines and the Limits of Self-Determination in the Progressive Era." *Michigan Historical Review* 40, no. 2 (2014): 63–86. https://www.jstor.org/stable/10.5342/michhistrevi.40.2.0063.
Knapp, Adeline. "A Notable Educational Expedition." In Gleason, *Log of the "Thomas,"* 11–12.
Kniffen, Fred B. "Louisiana House Types." *Annals of the Association of American Geographers* 26, no. 4 (1936): 179–193. https://www.jstor.com/stable/2569532.
Kondo, Dorinne. *World-Making: Race, Performance, and the Work of Creativity*. Durham, NC: Duke University Press, 2018.
Ku, Robert Ji-Song. Review of *Her Wild American Self*, by M. Evelina Galang. *Amerasia Journal* 23, no. 1 (1997): 190–192. https://doi.org/10.17953/amer.23.1.v68141165547p826.

La Fountain-Stokes, Lawrence. *Queer Ricans: Cultures and Sexualities in the Diaspora*. Minneapolis: University of Minnesota Press, 2009.

Lawsin, Emily P. "Pensionados, Paisanos, and Pinoys: An Analysis of the *Filipino Student Bulletin*, 1922–1939." *Filipino American Historical Society Journal* 4 (1996): 33–33P.

Lee, Erika. "Asian American Studies in the Midwest: New Questions, Approaches, and Communities." *Journal of Asian American Studies* 12, no. 3 (2009): 247–273. https://doi.org/10.1353/jaas.0.0045.

Lee, Josephine. *Performing Asian America: Race and Ethnicity on the Contemporary Stage*. Philadelphia: Temple University Press, 1997.

Lee, Josephine, Don Eitel, and R. A. Shiomi, eds. *Asian American Plays for a New Generation*. Philadelphia: Temple University Press, 2011.

Lee, Rachel C. *The Exquisite Corpse of Asian America: Biopolitics, Biosociality, and Posthuman Ecologies*. New York: New York University Press, 2014.

Lee, Richard M., and Matthew J. Miller. "History and Psychology of Adoptees in Asian America." In *Asian American Psychology: Current Perspectives*, edited by Nita Tewari and Alvin N. Alvarez, 337–363. New York: Psychology, 2009.

LeRoy, James A. *The Americans in the Philippines: A History of the Conquest and First Years of Occupation with an Introductory Account of the Spanish Rule*. Vol. 2. Boston: Houghton Mifflin, 1914.

Levitt, Rachel E. "(Dis)Appearing Subjects: Managing Violence through the Discourse of Bullying." Ph.D. diss., University of New Mexico, 2018. ProQuest (10688107).

Lewis, Krishna. Review of *Her Wild American Self*, by M. Evelina Galang. *MELUS: Multi-Ethnic Literature of the United States* 24, no. 4 (1999): 199–201. https://www.jstor.org/stable/468188.

Liliʻuokalani. *Hawaii's Story by Hawaii's Queen*. 1898. Reprint, Honolulu: Mutual, 1990.

Ling, Huping. *Chinese Americans in the Heartland: Migration, Work, and Community*. New Brunswick, NJ: Rutgers University Press, 2022.

Ling, Huping. *Chinese Chicago: Race, Transnational Migration, and Community Since 1870*. Stanford, CA: Stanford University Press, 2012.

Ling, Huping. *Chinese St. Louis: From Enclave to Cultural Community*. Philadelphia: Temple University Press, 2004.

Ling, Huping. *Voices of the Heart: Asian American Women on Immigration, Work, and Family*. Kirksville, MO: Truman State University Press, 2007.

Linmark, R. Zamora. *Rolling the R's*. New York: Kaya, 1997.

Lipsitz, George. "The Racialization of Space and the Spatialization of Race: Theorizing the Hidden Architecture of Landscape." *Landscape Journal* 26, no. 1 (2007): 10–23.

Loewen, James W. *Sundown Towns: A Hidden Dimension of American Racism*. New York: Touchstone, 2005.

Logan, Lisa. Review of *Her Wild American Self*, by M. Evelina Galang. *The Review of Contemporary Fiction* 16, no. 3 (1996): 196. Gale Literature Resource Center.

Love, Heather. *Feeling Backward: Loss and the Politics of Queer History*. Cambridge, MA: Harvard University Press, 2007.

Lowe, Lisa. *Immigrant Acts: On Asian American Cultural Politics*. Durham, NC: Duke University Press, 1996.

Lowe, Lisa. "The Intimacies of Four Continents." In Stoler, *Haunted*, 191–212.

Lowe, Lisa. *The Intimacies of Four Continents*. Durham, NC: Duke University Press, 2015.

Mabalon, Dawn Bohulano. *Little Manila Is in the Heart: The Making of the Filipina/o American Community in Stockton, California*. Durham, NC: Duke University Press, 2013.

Manalansan, Martin F., IV. *Global Divas: Filipino Gay Men in the Diaspora*. Durham, NC: Duke University Press, 2003.
Manalansan, Martin F., IV. "The 'Stuff' of Archives: Mess, Migration, and Queer Lives." *Radical History Review* 120 (2014): 94–107. https://read.dukeupress.edu/radical-his tory-review/article/2014/120/94/73309/The-Stuff-of-ArchivesMess-Migration-and -Queer.
Manalansan, Martin F., IV, and Augusto F. Espiritu, eds. *Filipino Studies: Palimpsests of Nation and Diaspora*. New York: New York University Press, 2016.
Manalansan, Martin F., IV, Chantal Nadeau, Richard T. Rodríguez, and Siobhan Somerville, eds. "Queering the Middle: Race, Region, and a Queer Midwest." Special issue, *GLQ: A Journal of Lesbian and Gay Studies* 20, nos. 1–2 (2014).
Martinez-Juan, Cristina. "*The Terms of War* and *Bontoc Eulogy*: Studies in Re-Narrativizing Archival Forms." *Southeast of Now: Directions in Contemporary and Modern Art in Asia* 3, no. 2 (2019): 113–128. https://doi.org/10.1353/sen.2019.0027.
Mason, Sarah R. "The Filipinos." In *They Chose Minnesota: A Survey of the State's Ethnic Groups*, edited by June Drenning Holmquist, 546–557. St. Paul: Minnesota Historical Society Press, 1981.
McClintock, Anne. *Imperial Leather: Race, Gender and Sexuality in the Colonial Contest*. New York: Routledge, 1995.
McKee, Kimberly D. *Disrupting Kinship: Transnational Politics of Korean Adoption in the United States*. Urbana: University of Illinois Press, 2019.
McKittrick, Katherine. *Demonic Grounds: Black Women and the Cartographies of Struggle*. Minneapolis: University of Minnesota Press, 2006.
Medina, José. *Speaking from Elsewhere: A New Contextualist Perspective on Meaning, Identity, and Discursive Agency*. Albany: State University of New York Press, 2006.
Mendoza, Victor Román. *Metroimperial Intimacies: Fantasy, Racial-Sexual Governance, and the Philippines in U.S. Imperialism, 1899–1913*. Durham, NC: Duke University Press, 2015.
Mercer, Kobena. *Welcome to the Jungle: New Positions in Black Cultural Studies*. New York: Routledge, 1994.
Mitchell, John Cameron, dir. *Hedwig and the Angry Inch*. Los Angeles: New Line Cinema, 2001.
Montalbano, Lori. "To *Glee* or Not to *Glee*: Exploring the Empowering Voice of the Glee Movement." In *Queer Media Images: LGBT Perspectives*, edited by Jane Campbell and Theresa Carilli, 55–62. Lanham, MD: Lexington, 2013.
Moraga, Cherríe, and Gloria Anzaldúa, eds. *This Bridge Called My Back: Writing by Radical Women of Color*. 2nd ed. New York: Kitchen Table: Women of Color, 1983.
Morley, David. "A Life in Essays," introduction to Hall, *Essential Essays Vol. 1: Foundations of Cultural Studies*, 1–26. Edited by David Morley. Durham, NC: Duke University Press, 2019.
Mukherjee, Roopali, Sarah Banet-Weiser, and Herman Gray, eds. *Racism Postrace*. Durham, NC: Duke University Press, 2019.
Mumford, Kevin J. *Interzones: Black/White Sex Districts in Chicago and New York in the Early Twentieth Century*. New York: Columbia University Press, 1997.
Muñoz, José Esteban. *Cruising Utopia: The Then and There of Queer Futurity*. New York: New York University Press, 2009.
Muñoz, José Esteban. *Disidentifications: Queers of Color and the Performance of Politics*. Minneapolis: University of Minnesota Press, 1999.

Murphy, Ryan, Brad Falchuk, and Ian Brennan. *Glee: The Complete First Season*. Beverly Hills, CA: Twentieth Century Fox Home Entertainment, 2010. DVD.
Murphy, Ryan, Brad Falchuk, and Ian Brennan. *Glee: The Complete Second Season*. Beverly Hills, CA: Twentieth Century Fox Home Entertainment, 2011. DVD.
Murphy, Ryan, Brad Falchuk, and Ian Brennan. *Glee: The Complete Third Season*. Beverly Hills, CA: Twentieth Century Fox Home Entertainment, 2012. DVD.
Murphy, Ryan, Brad Falchuk, and Ian Brennan. *Glee: The Complete Fourth Season*. Beverly Hills, CA: Twentieth Century Fox Home Entertainment, 2013. DVD.
Murphy, Ryan, Brad Falchuk, and Ian Brennan. *Glee: The Complete Fifth Season*. Beverly Hills, CA: Twentieth Century Fox Home Entertainment, 2014. DVD.
Murphy, Ryan, Brad Falchuk, and Ian Brennan. *Glee: The Final Season*. Beverly Hills, CA: Twentieth Century Fox Home Entertainment, 2015. DVD.
Murphy, Ryan Patrick, and Alex T. Urquhart. "Sexuality in the Headlines: Intimate Upheavals as Histories of the Twin Cities." In Twin Cities GLBT Oral History Project, *Queer Twin Cities*, 40–89.
Naramore Maher, Susan. *Deep Map Country: Literary Cartography of the Great Plains*. Lincoln: University of Nebraska Press, 2014.
Ng, Celeste. *Everything I Never Told You*. 2014. Reprint, New York: Penguin, 2015.
Ngai, Mae M. *Impossible Subjects: Illegal Aliens and the Making of Modern America*. Princeton, NJ: Princeton University Press, 2004.
Nguyen, Bich Minh. *Pioneer Girl*. New York: Penguin, 2014.
Nguyen, Bich Minh. *Stealing Buddha's Dinner*. New York: Penguin, 2008.
Nguyen, Tan Hoang. *A View from the Bottom: Asian American Masculinity and Sexual Representation*. Durham, NC: Duke University Press, 2014.
Nguyen-Dien, Giang. "The Heart(land) of Empire: 'Minnesota Nice' and the Shadows of U.S. Bene/Violent Culture in Vietnamese Refugee Lives." *American Studies* 62, no. 3 (2023): 143–168.
Ninh, erin Khuê. *Ingratitude: The Debt-Bound Daughter in Asian American Literature*. New York: New York University Press, 2011.
Nishime, LeiLani. "Guilty Pleasures: Keanu Reeves, Superman, and Racial Outing." In Davé, Nishime, and Oren, *East Main Street*, 273–291.
Nishime, LeiLani. *Undercover Asian: Multiracial Asian Americans in Visual Culture*. Urbana: University of Illinois Press, 2014.
Ocampo, Anthony Christian. *The Latinos of Asia: How Filipino Americans Break the Rules of Race*. Stanford, CA: Stanford University Press, 2016.
Oler, Andy. "Introduction: Landscape, Visibility, and the Scope of the Midwest." In Oler, *Pieces*, ix–xx.
Oler, Andy, ed. *Pieces of the Heartland: Representing Midwestern Places*. Hastings, NE: Hastings College Press, 2018.
Owen, Norman G., ed. "Compadre Colonialism: Studies on the Philippines Under American Rule." Special issue, *Michigan Papers on South and Southeast Asia* 3 (1971).
Ozeki, Ruth. *My Year of Meats*. 1998. Reprint, New York: Penguin, 1999.
Padrón, Karla. "Legal Injuries: Deportation and U.S. Immigration Policy in the Lives of TransLatina Immigrants." Ph.D. diss., University of Minnesota, 2015. https://hdl.handle.net/11299/175290.
Paik, A. Naomi. *Bans, Walls, Raids, Sanctuary: Understanding U.S. Immigration for the Twenty-First Century*. Oakland: University of California Press, 2020.
Palis, Joseph. "The Ethnographic Spectacle of the 'Other' Filipinos in Early Cinema." *GeoJournal* 74, no. 3 (2009): 227–234. https://www.jstor.org/stable/41148332.

Pamatmat, A. Rey. *Edith Can Shoot Things and Hit Them*. New York: Samuel French, 2012.
Panganiban, Leah L., and Rick Bonus. "Filipino Americans (Education)." In *Asian American Society: An Encyclopedia*, edited by Mary Yu Danico, 359–362. Thousand Oaks, CA: SAGE, 2014.
Parikh, Crystal. "Minority." In *Keywords for Asian American Studies*, edited by Cathy J. Schlund-Vials, Linda Trinh Võ, and K. Scott Wong, 162–163. New York: New York University Press, 2015.
Park, Lisa Sun-Hee. "Continuing Significance of the Model Minority Myth: The Second Generation." *Social Justice* 35, no. 2 (2008): 134–144. https://www.jstor.org/stable/297 68492.
Park Nelson, Kim. *Invisible Asians: Korean American Adoptees, Asian American Experiences, and Racial Exceptionalism*. New Brunswick, NJ: Rutgers University Press, 2016.
Parreñas, Rhacel Salazar. *Servants of Globalization: Migration and Domestic Work*. 2nd ed. Stanford, CA: Stanford University Press, 2015.
Parreñas Shimizu, Celina. *Straitjacket Sexualities: Unbinding Asian American Manhoods in the Movies*. Stanford, CA: Stanford University Press, 2012.
Pascual, Michael. "Archipelagic Memory: Reading US Filipino Literature and Visual Art Beside US Imperial Archives." Ph.D. diss., University of Michigan, 2021. ProQuest (28845231).
Patajo-Legasto, Priscelina, ed. *Philippine Studies: Have We Gone Beyond St. Louis?* Diliman, Quezon City: University of the Philippines Press, 2008.
Pate, SooJin. *From Orphan to Adoptee: U.S. Empire and Genealogies of Korean Adoption*. Minneapolis: University of Minnesota Press, 2014.
Peralta, Christine Noelle. "Handmaids of Medicine: Filipino Student Nurses' Liminality in Infant Mortality Campaigns." Master's thesis, University of British Columbia, 2011. https://dx.doi.org/10.14288/1.0072328.
Perreira, Christopher, Thomas Xavier Sarmiento, and M. Bianet Castellanos, eds. "Unsettling Global Midwests." Special issue, *American Studies* 62, no. 3 (2023).
Pha, Kong Pheng. "Colorblindness as Anti-Asian Racism in the Midwest." *American Studies* 62, no. 3 (2023): 119–142.
Pha, Kong Pheng. "'Minnesota is Open to Everything': Queer Hmong and the Politics of Community Formation in the Diaspora." *Minnesota History* 66, no. 6 (2019): 255–263. https://www.jstor.org/stable/26663128.
Pine, Jason. *The Alchemy of Meth: A Decomposition*. Minneapolis: University of Minnesota Press, 2019.
Ponce, Martin Joseph. *Beyond the Nation: Diasporic Filipino Literature and Queer Reading*. New York: New York University Press, 2012.
Ponce, Martin Joseph. "Pinoy Posterity." In Manalansan and Espiritu, *Filipino Studies*, 251–273.
Posadas, Barbara M., and Roland L. Guyotte. "Unintentional Immigrants: Chicago's Filipino Foreign Students Become Settlers, 1900–1941." *Journal of American Ethnic History* 9, no. 2 (1990): 26–48. https://www.jstor.org/stable/27500756.
Powell, Douglas Reichert. *Critical Regionalism: Connecting Politics and Culture in the American Landscape*. Chapel Hill: University of North Carolina Press, 2012.
Powers, Thomas. "Balita mula Maynila (News from Manila)." "American-Philippine Relations" Subject Guide, University of Michigan Bentley Historical Library, 5–8. 1971. https://bentley.umich.edu/wp-content/uploads/2014/09/American_Philippine_Rela tions_Subject_Guide.pdf.

Puar, Jasbir K. *Terrorist Assemblages: Homonationalism in Queer Times*. Durham, NC: Duke University Press, 2007.
Quantic, Diane Dufva. *The Nature of the Place: A Study of Great Plains Fiction*. Lincoln: University of Nebraska Press, 1995.
The Quarterly Philippinesotan. University Archives, University of Minnesota.
Quiray Tagle, Thea. "Salvage Acts: Asian/American Artists and the Uncovering of Slow Violence in the San Francisco Bay Area." *ACME: An International Journal for Critical Geographies* 18, no. 5 (2019): 1112–1127. https://acme-journal.org/index.php/acme/article/view/1702.
Quizon, Cherubim A., and Patricia O. Afable, eds. "World's Fair 1904." Special issue, *Philippine Studies: Historical and Ethnographic Viewpoints* 52, no. 4 (2004).
Rafael, Vicente L., ed. *Discrepant Histories: Translocal Essays on Filipino Cultures*. Philadelphia: Temple University Press, 1995.
Rafael, Vicente L. "Regionalism, Area Studies, and the Accidents of Agency." *American Historical Review* 104, no. 4 (1999): 1208–1220. https://www.jstor.org/stable/2649568.
Rafael, Vicente L. *White Love and Other Events in Filipino History*. Durham, NC: Duke University Press, 2000.
Reddy, Chandan. *Freedom with Violence: Race, Sexuality, and the US State*. Durham, NC: Duke University Press, 2011.
Reddy, Chandan. "Home, Houses, Nonidentity: *Paris Is Burning*." In *Burning Down the House: Recycling Domesticity*, edited by Rosemary Marangoly George, 355–379. Boulder, CO: Westview, 1998.
Remoquillo, Andi. "'I Was and Still Am Not a Subordinate': Racial Ambiguities, Politicized Invisibilities, and Locating Filipina American Identity in Chicago." *Journal of Asian American Studies* 28, no. 2 (2025): 257–287. https://dx.doi.org/10.1353/jaas.2025.a967896.
Rice, Mark. *Dean Worcester's Fantasy Islands: Photography, Film, and the Colonial Philippines*. Ann Arbor: University of Michigan Press, 2014.
Rodaway, Paul. *Sensuous Geographies: Body, Sense, and Place*. London: Routledge, 1994.
Rodríguez, Dylan. *Suspended Apocalypse: White Supremacy, Genocide, and the Filipino Condition*. Minneapolis: University of Minnesota Press, 2009.
Rodriguez, Robyn Magalit. *Migrants for Export: How the Philippine State Brokers Labor to the World*. Minneapolis: University of Minnesota Press, 2010.
Rodriguez, Robyn Magalit. "Toward a Critical Filipino Studies Approach to Philippine Migration." In Manalansan and Espiritu, *Filipino Studies*, 33–55.
Roley, Brian Ascalon. *American Son*. New York: Norton, 2001.
Roma-Sianturi, Dinah. "'Pedagogic Invasion': The Thomasites in Occupied Philippines." *Kritika Kultura* 12 (2009): 5–26. https://archium.ateneo.edu/kk/vol1/iss12/2/.
Rony, Fatimah Tobing. "The Quick and the Dead: Surrealism and the Found Ethnographic Footage Films of *Bontoc Eulogy* and *Mother Dao: The Turtlelike*." *Camera Obscura* 18, no. 1 (2003): 129–155. https://muse.jhu.edu/article/42078.
Rydell, Robert W. *All the World's a Fair: Visions of Empire at American International Expositions, 1876–1916*. Chicago: University of Chicago Press, 1987.
Sales, Joy. "'Revolutionary Care' as Activism: Filipina Nurses and Care Workers in Chicago, 1965–2016." In *Our Voices, Our Histories: Asian American and Pacific Islander Women*, edited by Shirley Hune and Gail M. Nomura, 269–284. New York: New York University Press, 2020.
Sandoval, Juan Simón Onésimo, and Joel Jennings. "Latino Civic Participation: Evaluating Indicators of Immigrant Engagement in a Midwestern City." *Latino Studies* 10, no. 4 (2012): 523–545. https://doi.org/10.1057/lst.2012.38.

San Juan, E., Jr. "Configuring the Filipino Diaspora in the United States." *Diaspora: A Journal of Transnational Studies* 3, no. 2 (1994): 117–133. https://doi.org/10.3138/diaspora.3.2.117.

San Juan, E., Jr. "From Genealogy to Inventory: The Situation of Asian American Studies in the Age of the Crisis of Global Finance Capital." *International Journal of Asia-Pacific Studies* 6, no. 1 (2010): 47–75.

San Juan, E., Jr. "One Hundred Years of Producing and Reproducing the 'Filipino.'" *Amerasia Journal* 24, no. 2 (1998): 1–33. https://doi.org/10.17953/amer.24.2.w58m448844875g82.

San Juan, E., Jr. *Racial Formations/Critical Transformations: Articulations of Power in Ethnic and Racial Studies in the United States*. Atlantic Highlands, NJ: Humanities, 1992.

Santos, Bienvenido N. *The Day the Dancers Came: Selected Prose Works*. Manila: Bookmark, 1967.

Santos, Bienvenido N. *The Man Who (Thought He) Looked Like Robert Taylor*. Quezon City, Philippines: New Day, 1983.

Santos, Bienvenido N. *Memory's Fictions: A Personal History*. Quezon City, Philippines: New Day, 1993.

Santos, Bienvenido N. Papers. Special Collections and University Archives, Wichita State University.

Santos, Bienvenido N. *Scent of Apples: A Collection of Stories*. Introduction by Leonard Casper. Seattle: University of Washington Press, 1979.

Santos, Bienvenido N. *Villa Magdalena*. Manila: Erehwon, 1965.

Santos, Bienvenido N. *The Volcano*. Quezon City, Philippines: Phoenix, 1965.

Santos, Bienvenido N. *What the Hell for You Left Your Heart in San Francisco*. Quezon City, Philippines: New Day, 1987.

Santos, Bienvenido N. *You Lovely People*. Manila: Benipayo, 1955.

Santos Aquino, Rowena. "Unremembering and Re-membering the Philippine–American War through the Composite Bodies of Reenactment." *Verge: Studies in Global Asias* 5, no. 2 (2019): 132–155. https://www.jstor.org/stable/10.5749/vergstudglobasia.5.2.0132.

Sarmiento, Thomas Xavier. "Diasporic Filipinx Queerness, Female Affective Labor, and Queer Heterosocial Relationalities in *Letters to Montgomery Clift*." *Women, Gender, and Families of Color* 5, no. 2 (2017): 105–128. https://doi.org/10.5406/womgenfamcol.5.2.0105.

Sarmiento, Thomas Xavier. "Literary Perspectives on Asian Americans in the Midwest." *Oxford Research Encyclopedia of Literature*. Oxford: Oxford University Press, 2019. https://doi.org/10.1093/acrefore/9780190201098.013.896.

Sarmiento, Thomas Xavier. "Peminist and Queer Affiliation in Literature as a Blueprint for Filipinx Decolonization and Liberation." In *Asian American Feminisms and Women of Color Politics*, edited by Lynn Fujiwara and Shireen Roshanravan, 82–104. Seattle: University of Washington Press, 2018.

Sarmiento, Thomas Xavier. "PhilippinExcess: Cunanan, Criss, Queerness, Multiraciality, Midwesternness, and the Cultural Politics of Legibility." In *Q & A: Voices from Queer Asian North America*, edited by Martin F. Manalansan IV, Alice Y. Hom, and Kale B. Fajardo, 318–330. Philadelphia: Temple University Press, 2021.

Sarmiento, Thomas Xavier. "To Return to St. Louis: Reading the Intimacies of the Heartland of U.S. Empire through 'The Dogeater.'" In "Rethinking Gendered Citizenship: Intimacy, Sovereignty, and Empire," edited by Genevieve Clutario and Rana Jaleel, special issue, *Amerasia Journal* 46, no. 2 (2020): 218–235. https://doi.org/10.1080/00447471.2020.1852701.

Sarmiento, Thomas Xavier, M. Bianet Castellanos, Christopher Perreira, and Jessica Lopez Lyman, eds. "Unsettling Global Midwests: Placekeepings." Special issue, *American Studies* 62, no. 4 (2023).

Schueller, Malini Johar. "Celebrating Imperial Education: The 2001 Thomasite Centennial in the Philippines." *American Quarterly* 74, no. 4 (2022): 945–968.

Sears, Clare. "All That Glitters: Trans-ing California's Gold Rush Migrations." *GLQ: A Journal of Lesbian and Gay Studies* 14, nos. 2–3 (2008): 383–402.

Sedgwick, Eve Kosofsky. *Between Men: English Literature and Male Homosocial Desire.* New York: Columbia University Press, 1985.

Sedgwick, Eve Kosofsky. "Paranoid Reading and Reparative Reading, or, You're So Paranoid, You Probably Think This Essay Is About You." In Sedgwick, *Touching Feeling: Affect, Pedagogy, Performativity*, chap. 4. Durham, NC: Duke University Press, 2003.

See, Sarita Echavez. *The Decolonized Eye: Filipino American Art and Performance.* Minneapolis: University of Minnesota Press, 2009.

See, Sarita Echavez. *The Filipino Primitive: Accumulation and Resistance in the American Museum.* New York: New York University Press, 2017.

Shin, K. Ian. "'The Farthest West Shakes Hands with the Remotest East': Amherst College, China, and Collegiate Cosmopolitanism in the Nineteenth Century." In *Amherst in the World*, edited by Martha Saxton, 183–200. Amherst, MA: Amherst College Press, 2020. https://www.jstor.org/stable/10.3998/mpub.11873533.14.

Shortridge, James R. *The Middle West: Its Meaning in American Culture.* Lawrence: University Press of Kansas, 1989.

Sichling, Florian, and Ajlina Karamehic-Muratovic. "'Makin' It' in the Heartland: Exploring Perceptions of Success Among Second-Generation Immigrant Youth in St. Louis." *Journal of Adolescence* 82, no. 1 (2020): 11–18. https://doi.org/10.1016/j.adolescence.2020.05.005.

Slater, Robert Bruce. "The First Black Graduates of the Nation's 50 Flagship State Universities." *Journal of Blacks in Higher Education* 13 (1996): 72–85. https://www.jstor.org/stable/2963173.

Smalkoski, Kari. "Hmong Male Youth and School Choice in a Neoliberal Era." *Hmong Studies Journal* 19, no. 1 (2018): 1–27. https://www.hmongstudiesjournal.org/uploads/4/5/8/7/4587788/smalkoskihsj19.pdf.

Sohn, Stephen Hong. *Inscrutable Belongings: Queer Asian North American Fiction.* Stanford, CA: Stanford University Press, 2018.

Spelman, Elizabeth V. "Gender and Race: The Ampersand Problem in Feminist Thought." In *Feminism and "Race*," edited by Kum-Kum Bhavani, 74–88. Oxford: Oxford University Press, 2001.

Spitzer, Justin. *Superstore.* NBC, 2015–2021. https://hulu.com/superstore.

Spivak, Gayatri Chakravorty. "Can the Subaltern Speak?" In *Marxism and the Interpretation of Culture*, edited by Cary Nelson and Lawrence Grossberg, 271–313. Urbana: University of Illinois Press, 1988.

Squires, Catherine, et al. "What Is This 'Post-' in Postracial, Postfeminist . . . (Fill in the Blank)?" *Journal of Communication Inquiry* 34, no. 3 (2010): 210–253. https://doi.org/10.1177/0196859910371375.

Steinbock-Pratt, Sarah. *Educating the Empire: American Teachers and Contested Colonization in the Philippines.* Cambridge: Cambridge University Press, 2019.

Stoler, Ann Laura. "Colonial Archives and the Arts of Governance." *Archival Science* 2, nos. 1–2 (2002): 87–109. https://doi.org/10.1007/BF02435632.

Stoler, Ann Laura, ed. *Haunted by Empire: Geographies of Intimacy in North American History*. Durham, NC: Duke University Press, 2006.
Suarez, Harrod J. *The Work of Mothering: Globalization and the Filipino Diaspora*. Urbana: University of Illinois Press, 2017.
Sulit, Marie-Therese C. "Through Our Pinay Writings: Narrating Trauma, Embodying Recovery." In de Jesús, *Pinay Power*, 351–371.
Sumida, Stephen H. "East of California: Points of Origin in Asian American Studies." *Journal of Asian American Studies* 1, no. 1 (1998): 83–100. https://doi.org/10.1353/jaas.1998.0012.
Sutherland, William Alexander. *Not by Might: The Epic of the Philippines*. Las Cruces, NM: Southwest, 1953.
Suzara, Aimee. *Souvenir*. Cincinnati, OH: WordTech, 2014.
Tadiar, Neferti X. M. *Remaindered Life*. Durham, NC: Duke University Press, 2022.
Tajima-Peña, Renee, series producer. *Asian Americans*. PBS, 2020. https://www.pbs.org/show/asian-americans/.
Takaki, Ronald T. *Strangers from a Different Shore: A History of Asian Americans*. Boston: Little, Brown, 1989.
Tintiangco-Cubales, Allyson Goce. "Pinayism." In de Jesús, *Pinay Power*, 137–148.
Tiongson, Antonio T., Jr., Edgardo V. Gutierrez, and Ricardo V. Gutierrez, eds. *Positively No Filipinos Allowed: Building Communities and Discourse*. Philadelphia: Temple University Press, 2006.
Tongson, Karen. "Queer." In *Keywords for Media Studies*, edited by Laurie Ouellette and Jonathan Gray, 157–160. New York: New York University Press, 2017. https://www.jstor.org/stable/j.ctt1gk08zz.55.
Tongson, Karen. *Relocations: Queer Suburban Imaginaries*. New York: New York University Press, 2011. Kindle.
Tongson, Karen. "Vocal Recognition: Racial and Sexual Difference after (Tele)Visuality." In Mukherjee, Banet-Weiser, and Gray, *Racism Postrace*, 135–153.
Trieu, Monica Mong. *Fighting Invisibility: Asian Americans in the Midwest*. New Brunswick, NJ: Rutgers University Press, 2023.
Tuan, Yi-Fu. "Place: An Experiential Perspective." *Geographical Review* 65, no. 2 (1975): 151–165. https://doi.org/10.2307/213970.
Tuan, Yi-Fu. *Space and Place: The Perspective of Experience*. Minneapolis: University of Minnesota Press, 1977.
Turner, Frederick Jackson. *The Frontier in American History*. New York: Henry Holt, 1920.
Twin Cities GLBT Oral History Project. *Queer Twin Cities*. Minneapolis: University of Minnesota Press, 2010.
Ty, Eleanor. "A Filipino Prufrock in an Alien Land: Bienvenido Santos's *The Man Who (Thought He) Looked Like Robert Taylor*." *Lit: Literature Interpretation Theory* 12, no. 3 (2001): 267–283. https://doi.org/10.1080/10436920108580292.
Valdés, Dionicio Nodín. *Barrios Norteños: St. Paul and Midwestern Mexican Communities in the Twentieth Century*. Austin: University of Texas Press, 2000.
Valerio-Jiménez, Omar, Santiago Vaquera-Vásquez, and Claire F. Fox, eds. *The Latina/o Midwest Reader*. Urbana: University of Illinois Press, 2017.
Vallarta, MT. "Knowing, Feeling: Toward a Queer Filipinx Poetics." Ph.D. diss., University of California, Riverside, 2022. https://escholarship.org/uc/item/4pf4j97q.
Vang, Chia Youyee. *Hmong America: Reconstructing Community in Diaspora*. Urbana: University of Illinois Press, 2010.

Vega, Sujey. *Latino Heartland: Of Borders and Belonging in the Midwest.* New York: New York University Press, 2015.

Velasco, Gina K. *Queering the Global Filipina Body: Contested Nationalisms in the Filipina/o Diaspora.* Urbana: University of Illinois Press, 2020.

Vergara, Benito M., Jr. *Displaying Filipinos: Photography and Colonialism in Early 20th Century Philippines.* Quezon City: University of the Philippines Press, 1995.

Vergara, Benito M., Jr. *Pinoy Capital: The Filipino Nation in Daly City.* Philadelphia: Temple University Press, 2009.

Viego, Antonio. *Dead Subjects: Towards a Politics of Loss in Latino Studies.* Durham, NC: Duke University Press, 2007.

Vuong, Ocean. *On Earth We're Briefly Gorgeous.* New York: Penguin, 2019.

Wei, William. *The Asian American Movement.* Philadelphia: Temple University Press, 1995.

Weisman, Karen. "Introduction." In *The Oxford Handbook of the Elegy*, edited by Karen Weisman, 1–9. Oxford: Oxford University Press, 2010.

Wilkinson, Sook, and Victor Jew, eds. *Asian Americans in Michigan: Voices from the Midwest.* Detroit: Wayne State University Press, 2015.

Williamson, Terrion L., ed. *Black in the Middle: An Anthology of the Black Midwest.* Cleveland, OH: Belt, 2020.

Winkelmann, Tessa. *Dangerous Intercourse: Gender and Interracial Relations in the American Colonial Philippines, 1898–1946.* Ithaca, NY: Cornell University Press, 2023.

Woodcock, Nicolyn. "Reading Midwest Asian America in Celeste Ng's *Everything I Never Told You*." *American Studies* 62, no. 3 (2023): 169–189.

Worcester, Dean C., and Joseph Ralston Hayden. *The Philippines Past and Present.* New edition in one volume with biographical sketch and four additional chapters by Ralston Hayden. New York: Macmillan, 1930.

Wu, Frank H. *Yellow: Race in America Beyond Black and White.* New York: Basic, 2002.

Xaykaothao, Doualy. "To Be Both Midwestern and Hmong." *Atlantic*, June 3, 2016. https://www.theatlantic.com/politics/archive/2016/06/wausau-wisconsin-southeast-asia-hmong/485291/.

Yale, Elizabeth. "The History of Archives: The State of the Discipline." *Book History* 18 (2015): 332–359. https://www.jstor.org/stable/43956377.

Yin, Cheryl. "Cambodian Refugees and Michigan Sponsors: One Story of Non-Kin Relationships in Refugee Resettlement." *American Studies* 62, no. 4 (2023): 121–144.

Yoneyama, Lisa. *Cold War Ruins: Transpacific Critique of American Justice and Japanese War Crimes.* Durham, NC: Duke University Press, 2016.

Zarsadiaz, James. "Raising Hell in the Heartland: Filipino Chicago and the Anti-Martial Law Movement, 1972–1986." *American Studies* 55/56, no. 4/1 (2017): 141–162. https://doi.org/10.1353/ams.2017.0006.

Zarsadiaz, James. *Resisting Change in Suburbia: Asian Immigrants and Frontier Nostalgia in L.A.* Oakland: University of California Press, 2022.

Index

Italicized page numbers refer to figures

9/11, 190

Abeya, Mia, 32
abjection, 35, 42, 46–47, 85, 145, 147, 153, 157, 160, 210n30
absence, 5, 11, 20, 49, 118, 146–147, 171, 196, 237n3; and archives of U.S. empire, 77, 81, 91. *See also* erasure
accumulation, 15, 19, 66, 171, 183, 188, 197
administration, 32, 63–64, 67–68, 74, 79, 83, 114, 158
adoption, 9, 23, 162, 165, 215n138
aesthetics, 12–13, 17–18, 24, 26; and Filipinas, 128, 133, 138, 148, 230n2; and St. Louis World's Fair, 53; and television, 156, 158, 160–161, 167, 187, 234n65
Aeta people, 77. *See also* Negrito people
affect, 7, 13–14, 22; and archives of U.S. empire, 63–64, 70, 84; and Filipinas, 135, 143, 146, 150; and Santos's exile literature, 95–98, 117; and St. Louis World's Fair, 34, 37, 46, 57; and television, 163, 166. *See also* emotions; feelings
African Americans, 64, 85–87, 89, 91, 126, 221n126, 221n134, 222n145, 228n33. *See also* Blackness; Black people

agriculture, 16, 19, 43; and archives of U.S. empire, 69, 77–79, 83–84, 87–89; and Santos's exile literature, 108
Ahmed, Sara, 5, 12, 128, 135, 148, 193, 199, 204n43, 215n3
Alexander, M. Jacqui, 172
alienation, 12, 20, 35, 44, 55, 195; and Santos's exile literature, 106–107, 109–111, 115, 120
Allarey, H., 74
Allarey, Macaria, 69–70, 217n36
allegory, 7, 27, 149, 152, 160, 172, 233n64
Allegro, Linda, 17, 202n18
Alma, Consolacion, 68, 73
Alma, Rufina, 71
Alumit, Noël, 101
Ambalada, Dalmacio, 73
ambivalence, 5, 17, 21, 195; and archives of U.S. empire, 65, 69, 85–87, 89–90; and Filipinas, 132, 141; and Santos's exile literature, 95–96, 98, 102, 105–106, 112–113, 117, 119–121; and St. Louis World's Fair, 34–35, 40, 43–46, 50, 56, 59; and television, 157, 167–169, 172, 174–176
American dream, the, 22, 32, 181

Americans, 210n41; and archives of U.S. empire, 68–69, 71, 82, 84–85, 88–91, 218n78; and Filipinas, 125, 130, 132, 134, 137; and Santos's exile literature, 101–102, 120, 225n77; and television, 153–154, 156–157, 160, 177, 179, 182. *See also* African Americans; Asian America/Asian Americans; Filipinx America; White men; Whiteness; White women
amnesia, 21, 27, 152–153, 160, 208n112, 210n30
Anderson, Benedict, 154
anthropology, 32, 36, 41, 46–47, 54, 102, 216n19
Aquino, Beningo "Ninoy," Jr., 177
Aquino, Corazón "Cory," 177
Arapaho people, 2, 16
archives, 6–8, 13, 15, 22–25, 27, 102, 149; and St. Louis World's Fair, 34, 37, 39–43, 46–48, 50–55, 210n44, 212n76, 212n82, 212n86; and television, 152, 160, 168, 171; of U.S. empire in the Philippines, 63–68, 72–75, 78–79, 82–83, 86, 90–92, 215n1, 216n19
Ariosto, Ludovico, 73
Artiaga, Santiago, 10
Ash, Lauren, 156
Asia/Asians, 6, 9, 11–13, 15, 18, 21, 23, 194, 198; and archives of U.S. empire, 67, 76–79, 81; and Filipinas, 125, 139, 142; and St. Louis World's Fair, 31; and television, 152, 160–162, 165, 169–171, 178, 186, 188. *See also* Asian America/Asian Americans; East Asia/East Asians; South Asia/South Asians; Southeast Asia/Southeast Asians
Asian America/Asian Americans, 7, 9–13, 15–19, 22–26, 198, 203n30, 204n38, 205n53, 206n80, 208n119; and Filipinas, 126–127, 132, 138–140, 142–143, 146, 149–150, 228n33, 229n52; and Santos's exile literature, 97, 106, 119; and St. Louis World's Fair, 31–32, 35, 44; and television, 156, 159, 161, 163, 169, 178, 186–188
Asian American literature, 12, 35, 97, 128, 138, 149, 213n113, 226n103
Asian Americans (docuseries), 31–32, 138
Asian American studies, 8–9, 11, 100, 143, 194, 202n18
assimilation, 58, 71, 96; and Filipinas, 127, 130, 142, 228n30, 229n52; and Santos's exile literature, 102, 116; and television,
163, 166–167, 173, 175, 186, 191. *See also* benevolence; imperialism
audiences, 22, 73, 75, 91, 99–100, 195–196; and archives of U.S. empire, 86, 90; and Filipinas, 130, 133, 139–140, 142, 149–150; and St. Louis World's Fair, 36, 38, 41–42, 44–46, 48–49, 51, 53, 59–60; and television, 151, 154–165, 170–171, 174–179, 182–186, 189–192
authenticity, 47, 50–51, 65, 97, 106, 153, 213n96, 223n9
Avenido, Kent, 169, 171, 235n100

Balance, Christine, 9, 50–51
Balce, Nerissa, 65, 84, 87, 91, 152, 160, 187, 210n30, 210n34
Banet-Wiser, Sarah, 158
Barillas, William, 9, 18, 203n34
Barinholtz, Jon, 189
Barritt, Marjorie, 68
Bascara, Victor, 7, 117, 119
Battle of the Little Bighorn / Battle of the Greasy Grass, 2
Baum, L. Frank, 6–7, 130, 144
Baxoje (Ioway) people, 16
Behner, Frederick George, 67, 70–74, 77
belonging, 7, 17, 19–20, 23, 27, 196; and archives of U.S. empire, 65; and Filipinas, 129, 132, 134, 142–143, 149; and Santos's exile literature, 110–114, 120–121, 226n92; and St. Louis World's Fair, 35, 44, 46, 53, 212n74; and television, 171–172, 186, 192, 235n84, 236n128
benevolence, 6–7, 71, 96, 116, 120, 166, 173, 175, 215n16. *See also* assimilation; imperialism
Bernabe, Jan Christian, 51–53
Bertrane, V. F., 71–72
Beyoncé, 173, 181, 234n65, 235n97
Bhabha, Homi, 161, 167, 172, 174
Black Lives Matter movement, 155–156, 206n80
Blackness, 61, 77, 87, 215n140
Black people, 2, 8–9, 16, 190; and archives of U.S. empire, 85–88, 221n136; Black women, 61, 175, 198–199; and St. Louis World's Fair, 43, 55, 61, 209n15; and television, 153, 155–158, 162, 178, 213n22, 230n8, 233n58, 234n65. *See also* African Americans; Black Lives Matter movement; Blackness
Blumentritt, Mia, 46, 212n79

Bocobo, Jorge, 77, 219n91
Bocobo Olivar, Celia, 120
Bodewéwadmik (Potawatomi) people, 6, 16
bodies, 1, 5, 9, 13, 18, 24, 27, 194–195, 199; and archives of U.S. empire, 64, 76, 79–81, 83–85; and Filipinas, 132, 138–139, 144, 147; and Santos's exile literature, 96, 104–105, 114, 117; and St. Louis World's Fair, 32–35, 47–54, 56–59, 210n34; and television, 152, 155, 160–161, 163, 165–167, 171, 177, 182–183, 188. See also embodiment; nudity
Bomer, Matt, 166
Bontoc people, 25, 33, 45, 47–48, 50–51, 55, 195, 213n90
borders, 2, 18–19, 24, 46, 54, 182, 210n41, 235n107, 236n114, 236n128
Borneans, 77
Bow, Leslie, 18
Bowersock, Justin De Witt, 86
Boxer Rebellion, 2
Boyd, Rekia, 17
boys, Filipino, 32, 82–83, 110, 169, 234n78; and archives of U.S. empire, 71, 73, 80–81, 88, 215n138, 221n121; and Filipinas, 127, 143–145
Brown, Michael, 17, 155, 206n80
Brown people, 1, 52, 118, 132, 138, 210n34; and television, 169–171, 179, 183
Brown v. Board of Education, 87
Bryant, William Cullen, 73
Buddhists, 9
Buffalo Soldiers, 2
Bulosan, Carlos, 12, 97–100, 226n99, 228n33
Bunin, Michael, 180
Burnett, Whit, 99
Burns, Lucy, 161

Cabrera, Antero, 31–32, 60–62
California, 1, 9–15, 21, 25, 32, 54–55, 75, 80, 126, 137; Bay Area, 46; Daly City, 12; Hollywood, 113, 116, 152, 154; Los Angeles, 12, 46, 86, 107, 153; Oakland, 39, 103; San Diego, 52, 66; San Francisco, 12, 98–99, 101, 103, 107, 110; and Santos's exile literature, 97, 100, 104, 108, 117; Stockton, 12, 103
Cambodia, 194
Campney, Brent, 17, 206n80, 222n145
Cantrell, Owen, 16, 206n77

capitalism, 18, 22, 137, 158, 183, 189; global capitalism, 12; neoliberal capitalism, 185, 188; and television, 171, 180–181, 189–191
Carbó, Nick, 138, 149
Carreon, Manuel, 75
Casper, Leonard, 117, 121
Castille, Philando, 17
Cather, Willa, 130, 143, 225n62
Catholicism, 131–132, 137, 144
Cayton, Andrew, 18
Chang, Juliana, 35, 56–57, 214n123
Cheyenne people, 2, 16
Chicago World's Fair, 125
Chickasaw people, 16
children, 6, 23, 109, 113, 165, 229n49, 229n57; and archives of U.S. empire, 70, 73, 87, 89; and Filipinas, 133, 138, 141–142, 144, 147–148; and St. Louis World's Fair, 44, 50, 52, 55, 58, 60–61, 209n15, 214n120. See also boys, Filipino; girls, Filipina
Chin, Vincent, 17
China/Chinese people, 2, 23, 77, 82, 88, 142, 166, 170–171, 204n36, 236n114
Christianity, 8, 24, 47, 82, 88, 90, 185, 189, 218n73, 219n80. See also Catholicism
Cisneros, Sandra, 130
citizenship, 20, 195, 229n52; and archives of U.S. empire, 72, 76, 87, 89; and St. Louis World's Fair, 56, 58, 210n32, 214n123; and television, 152, 167, 178–180, 186–188, 190. See also undocumented people
civilization, 7, 33, 195; and archives of U.S. empire, 69–70, 76–77, 89, 217n36; and Santos's exile literature, 99, 102; and St. Louis World's Fair, 47, 51, 57
class, social, 8, 14, 23–24, 26; and archives of U.S. empire, 75, 77, 87–89; and Filipinas, 129, 134, 141, 148; and Santos's exile literature, 100–102, 106, 110, 117, 225n65; and St. Louis World's Fair, 57–58; and television, 151–154, 156, 180, 183, 188, 190, 230n8, 230n13, 234n65
climate, 39, 60, 80, 88, 125; and Santos's exile literature, 95–96, 98, 102–107, 109–111. See also tropics
Clutario, Genevieve, 41
Coffman, Franklin "Frank" A., 78–85, *83–84*, 89, 220nn94–98
Cold War, 11, 17, 44, 114, 182, 194, 196, 202n15, 212n70
Coleman, Brandie, 17

260 / INDEX

Colfer, Chris, 155
colonialism, 2, 4–7, 9, 13, 16, 19–22, 24–27, 193–196, 198; and archives of U.S. empire, 63–75, 77–78, 80, 82, 84–86, 88–92; and Filipinas, 127, 129–130, 134, 138–140; neocolonialism, 120, 145, 158; and Santos's exile literature, 96, 98, 100, 104, 108, 114, 117, 120–121; and St. Louis World's Fair, 32–38, 40–41, 44, 46–47, 50–53, 56–59, 61; and television, 151, 153, 157–158, 160–163, 166–169, 171–172, 174–176, 185–189, 191. *See also* decolonization; postcolonialism
Columbia University, 99
commemoration, 10, 32, 34, 36, 41, 45, 76
communities, 11–12, 18, 21, 26, 106, 204n36, 205n67; and archives of U.S. empire, 73, 75, 77, 85; and Filipinas, 126–128, 133, 136, 143, 149, 228n48; and Santos's exile literature, 106–108, 110, 120, 225n75, 226n103; and St. Louis World's Fair, 44, 215n139; and television, 154
corporations, 157, 177, 180–181, 183, 185, 187–191, 194. *See also Superstore* (television show)
cosmopolitanism, 75, 88, 97, 157, 218n78, 219n92
Criss, Darren, 155, 232n46
Cruz, Denise, 22, 99, 118, 129, 214n115, 214n134, 218n75, 223n7, 224n35, 224n52
Cuba, 2, 71, 85
cultural relations, 6–16, 18, 20, 22, 24–27, 198–199; and archives of U.S. empire, 63–64, 66, 69, 73–74, 76–78, 87, 89, 91; and Filipinas, 126, 128–129, 131, 133, 135, 137–141, 143, 146, 148–150; and Santos's exile literature, 96, 100, 104–105, 108, 120–121; and St. Louis World's Fair, 32–33, 46, 50, 56–57, 59, 61; and television, 152, 154, 157–161, 171, 175, 177–178, 185–187, 189, 191–192. *See also* dominant culture; multiculturalism
cultural studies, 18, 66
Cunanan, Andrew, 21, 232n46
Custer House, 1–2, 5
Custodio, Candida, 71–72

Dakhóta (Dakota) people, 16
Dalrymple, Louis, 71
dance, 12, 49, 51, 81, 83, 143, 161, 166, 173, 191; and Santos's exile literature, 101, 104, 107–108, 114–116

Davé, Shilpa, 170, 179
Decaney, Jose Q., 75
decolonization, 7–8, 27, 61, 66, 69, 91, 145, 216, 230n2, 237n3; and television, 152, 158, 194
de Jesús, Melinda, 97, 117, 119, 223n7
Delmendo, Sharon, 84
democracy, 6, 72, 74, 89
Department of Public Instruction, Philippines, 66–67
deportation, 101, 181, 184, 187, 190, 236n122
Desai, Jigna, 18, 21, 114
desire, 13, 15, 17, 20–21, 27, 203n33, 205n55; and archives of U.S. empire, 64, 82–83, 85, 89–90; and Filipinas, 126, 132, 142–145, 147–148, 229n52; and Santos's exile literature, 96, 102, 108, 112, 117, 119; and St. Louis World's Fair, 36–37, 41, 46, 48–51, 53, 58, 212n74; and television, 159–160, 165, 167, 171–175, 180, 234n75
diaspora, Filipinx, 6–15, 17–27, 193–195, 198–199, 202n7, 202n15, 204n40, 205n67, 207n111, 208n112; and archives of U.S. empire, 63–66, 75, 77, 83, 88, 92, 215n9, 219n87, 221n121; and Filipinas, 125–130, 132–137, 139–143, 145–146, 148–149; and Santos's exile literature, 95–98, 101–104, 106–121, 224n35, 226nn102–103, 226n106; and St. Louis World's Fair, 31, 33–34, 36–37, 39–48, 50–56, 58–62, 209n17, 214n118; and television, 153, 158, 166, 176, 179, 183, 187, 191. *See also* queer diasporas
difference, 35, 45, 47–48, 50, 106, 127, 132, 146, 195, 236n127; and television, 151, 158, 160, 163, 165, 172–173, 178, 185–186, 188
Dirksen, Everett, 113
discipline, 19, 71, 98, 120, 130–135, 140–141, 144–145, 166–167
discourse, 2, 6, 9, 12–25, 95, 194–196, 198–199; and archives of U.S. empire, 64–65, 75–77, 87; and Filipinas, 126, 129, 132, 139, 149–150, 229n52; and St. Louis World's Fair, 33–34, 36–37, 40, 46, 51, 54–55, 57–60; and television, 154–155, 158, 174, 182–183, 186, 188, 191–192
dislocation, 22, 97, 102, 108
disobedient listening, 40, 50–51
diversity, 24, 76, 136, 154–155, 158, 163–165, 185–186, 191
dogeaters, 33, 40, 42, 54–62

domesticity, 59–60, 96, 209n28; and archives of U.S. empire, 74, 78–80, 82–83, 85, 89; and Filipinas, 127, 133–134, 137–138, 141, 143, 145–146, 148–149; national domesticity, 8, 17, 20, 26–27, 35, 74, 127, 158, 173, 188, 193; and television, 154, 169–170

dominant culture, 8–9, 11, 74; and Filipinas, 128, 138, 140, 145; and Santos's exile literature, 97, 105, 121; and St. Louis World's Fair, 33, 40, 56–57, 59–60; and television, 158, 160, 171, 173, 186, 191. See also hegemonies

drag, 17–18, 58

Dunn, Colton, 156

Dwight D. Eisenhower Presidential Library, Museum, and Boyhood Home, 27, 195–198, *197*

East Asia/East Asians, 139, 171, 186, 194, 197, 209n14

economics, 6–8, 16–17, 24, 43; and archives of U.S. empire, 69, 71, 89; and Filipinas, 132, 144–146, 148; and Santos's exile literature, 100, 225n65; and television, 154, 161, 181–183, 185–186, 188–189

Ecuadorian people, 187

Edelman, Lee, 147

education, 11, 21, 32, 195; and archives of U.S. empire, 87, 90; and Filipinas, 132–133, 137–138, 141, 144, 148; in the Philippines, 66–74; in the U.S., 74–85, 99–100, 102–103. See also students; teachers

Education Act (1901), Philippines, 66

Eisenhower, Dwight D., 27, 195–198, *197*

elderly people, 34, 57, 101, 110, 113–116, 119, 135–136, 188, 214n130

elegies, 33–34, 39, 48, 53, 59–61

Elezler, Gregorio, 71

embodiment, 9, 24, 26, 81, 196; and Filipinas, 127, 129, 134, 138–142, 150; and Santos's exile literature, 114, 116–117; and St. Louis World's Fair, 34, 36, 44, 53, 61; and television, 160–161, 163, 166, 168, 171–173, 177, 188. See also bodies

emotions, 50, 55, 65, 103–107, 144, 177, 181, 185, 195. See also affect; feelings

Eng, David, 20–21, 40, 44

epistemologies, 6, 9–14, 17, 19–20, 24, 26, 41, 119, 161, 194; and archives of U.S. empire, 63, 65; and Filipinas, 129, 145. See also ontoepistemologies

equality, 71, 86–87, 155–158, 177, 185

equity, 155–156, 158, 185

erasure, 2, 5, 18, 25, 63, 136, 205n60. See also absence

erotics, 35, 64, 80–81, 85, 118–119

España-Maram, Linda, 12, 74, 99

Espiritu, Augusto, 92, 102, 106

ethnicities, 7–9, 12–13, 18, 20–21, 23–24; and archives of U.S. empire, 64, 75–77; and Filipinas, 126–127, 129, 132–133, 137–140, 142, 146; and Santos's exile literature, 117, 121; and St. Louis World's Fair, 31, 33, 44, 47, 53, 55, 57, 210n39; and television, 151–152, 156, 161, 163–166, 169–171, 177, 182–189, 191, 233n58, 233n62

ethnic studies, 11, 126

ethnography, 45–48, 51, 53, 56, 82, 86, 89–90

ethnology, 56, 79, 195, 210n44

Europe, 6, 19, 43, 125, 189, 193–194, 197. See also France; Great Britain; Spain

Evangelista, Antonia, 73

everyday life, 24, 52, 64, 68, 79, 146–148, 181–183, 187

exceptionalism, 6, 15–16, 18, 99, 160, 198

exclusion, 23, 35, 102, 132, 208n119

exile, 23, 25–26, 134; and Santos's literature, 95–97, 99–104, 106–108, 110–112, 115–121, 223n13, 225n64, 225n69

expansionism, 2, 6–7, 10, 16, 24, 33, 146, 160, 209n11; and archives of U.S. empire, 64, 87

Fagen, David, 89

Fajardo, Kale, 20–21, 65, 80

families, 1, 5, 16, 21; and archives of U.S. empire, 63, 73, 79, 81, 86, 88–89; and Filipinas, 130–134, 137, 140–144, 146–149; and Santos's exile literature, 99, 101, 104, 106–107, 110–111, 118–119; and St. Louis World's Fair, 32–34, 36, 44, 46, 53, 55–56, 59, 61; and television, 153, 166, 168, 186. See also grandparents; kinship; mothers; parents

Fanon, Frantz, 61

feelings, 22, 26, 56, 127, 138, 145, 195; and Santos's exile literature, 95–97, 100, 102–103, 105–107, 110, 116–118. See also affect; emotions

Feldman, Ben, 156
femininities, 22, 70, 83; and Filipinas, 125, 127, 129–134, 137, 141, 143–145; and television, 162, 169, 172
feminism, 12, 26, 64, 118, 226n102; Black feminism, 198; and Filipinas, 128–129, 135, 137, 148; queer feminism, 70, 129. *See also* peminism
Ferguson, Roderick, 158, 203n33, 227n6
Fermin, Jose, 40
Ferrera, America, 156, 230n10
Fields, James T., 73
Filipinas, 12, 23, 26, 149, 172, 201n1; and archives of U.S. empire, 70, 73–74, 77, 80–82, 88, 218n76, 219n90; and Santos's exile literature, 101, 118, 224n35, 224n52, 226n99; and St. Louis World's Fair, 32, 38, 210n34, 214n115; and television, 161, 172, 234n72; and the Wild West, 125–132, 134–137, 140–143, 227n1. *See also* diaspora, Filipinx; girls, Filipina
Filipinx America, 8–13, 15, 20–21, 24, 26, 204n40; and archives of U.S. empire, 63–64, 68; and Filipinas, 128–129, 132–143, 146, 149; and Santos's exile literature, 97, 99–103, 107, 110, 112, 117, 120–121; and St. Louis World's Fair, 31–33, 35, 37–38, 43, 45–47, 53, 59, 61, 212n74, 215n139; and television, 159, 187, 191, 194, 232n46. *See also* diaspora, Filipinx; Pinxys
Filipinx American studies, 6, 216n24
films, 6, 8, 14, 105–106, 152, 184, 235n97; and Filipinas, 125, 134, 138, 140; and St. Louis World's Fair, 27, 33–34, 45–54, 212n86, 212n88, 213n100, 213nn90–91, 213nn103–105
Florida, 2; Orlando, 153
Florida State University, 54
Floyd, George, 17, 155, 206n80, 231n22
Fonbuena, Eugenio, 77
food, 61, 80, 82, 84–85, 132, 140, 142, 146–148, 162
Forbes, William Cameron, 88
foreignness, 8, 11, 17, 20, 58, 209n28; and archives of U.S. empire, 69–70, 73, 88–90, 218n78, 219n92; and Filipinas, 127, 142, 236n117; and Santos's exile literature, 96, 98, 110; and television, 173, 179, 188
France, 33, 54, 194
Francisco, Mateo, 10

Frank Murphy Memorial Museum, 19
Freud, Sigmund, 34, 37, 117, 172, 209n15, 213n106
Fuentes, Marlon, 25, 33–34, 45–54, *52*, 57, 59–60, 65, 195
Fujita-Rony, Dorothy, 12
Fuss, Diana, 60
futurities, 14, 19, 27, 215n1; and archives of U.S. empire, 65–66, 71; and Filipinas, 144–147; and Santos's exile literature, 104, 112, 119; and St. Louis World's Fair, 59–60; and television, 155, 171, 187, 191

Gacusana, Jose, 76–77
Gage, Jason, 17
Galang, M. Evelina, 23, 26, 126, 128, 130–144, 148–150, 227n12, 227n30, 228n48, 229n71
Garland, Judy, 113
gayness, 14, 17, 112–113, 119, 127, 231n19, 233n53, 233n57, 234n65; and television, 153, 156, 161–163, 165, 168–169, 177–179, 183, 186, 230n9, 233n54
gaze, the, 5, 23, 26, 33, 195, 207n81; and archives of U.S. empire, 66, 80–83; and Filipinas, 129, 131, 140; and St. Louis World's Fair, 37–38, 40–41, 44, 46, 48–49, 52–53, 59–60; and television, 158, 162
gender, 8–9, 12, 14, 26, 201n1; and archives of U.S. empire, 64, 69–71, 73–74, 77, 86; cisgender, 177, 198; and Filipinas, 125–130, 132–133, 136, 138–143, 147–149; and Santos's exile literature, 114, 119, 225n65; and St. Louis World's Fair, 35, 38, 61, 215n16, 218n73; and television, 151–152, 155–156, 163, 185. *See also* boys, Filipino; femininities; Filipinas; girls, Filipina; masculinities; men, Filipino; trans* people; White men; White women; women
genocide, 2, 16, 23
geographies, 8–16, 18–23, 25–27, 193–196, 198–199, 201n1; and archives of U.S. empire, 64–66, 68–69, 75, 86; and Filipinas, 125–126, 128–129, 131–133, 135–143, 145–146, 149, 228n31; and Santos's exile literature, 95–97, 100, 102–103, 106–107, 112–114, 116–117, 120; and St. Louis World's Fair, 31, 33, 35–37, 42–43, 45–48, 50–51, 53, 58–59, 209n18, 210n41; and television, 152, 159, 178, 182

Gershon, Gina, 166
Gilsig, Jessalyn, 154
girls, Filipina, 81, 125–131, 133, 135–145, 149, 219n90, 227n1, 228n48
Glee (television show), 26–27, 151–177, *164*, *167*, *170*, *174*, *176*, 188, 191, 230n9, 230n11, 231n18, 231n22, 232n36, 233n63
globalization, 18–20, 65, 83, 127, 182, 186, 194; and Filipinas, 129, 148; and television, 151–153, 155, 159, 235n82
Gonzalvez, Theodore, 12
Gopinath, Gayatri, 7, 12–14, 18–21, 23, 129, 187, 204n43, 205n55, 226n102; and archives of U.S. empire, 64–65, 85, 112, 220n112
Gordon, Avery, 112, 177
Gourlay, Candy, 32
governance, 2, 10, 35, 100, 111, 166, 191, 196–198; and archives of U.S. empire, 70–72, 77, 85–87, 90. *See also* Spain; U.S. occupation of the Philippines
grandparents, 5, 21, 68, 73, 78, 178; and Filipinas, 130–131, 134, 141; and St. Louis World's Fair, 48, 51, 55, 61
Gray, Herman, 158
Gray, John Henry, 73
Great Britain, 54, 194
Great Depression, 100
grief, 33–34, 60, 117, 119. *See also* mourning

Hagedorn, Jessica, 12, 54, 134
Haitian Revolution, 33, 209n11
Halvorson, Britt, 17
Hamilton, Dontre, 17
Han, Shinhee, 40, 44
Hart-Cellar Act (1965), 113. *See also* Immigration Act (1965)
Harvey, Sherman Allen, 85–91, 222n150
Haux, 190
Hawai'i, 71, 87–88, 97, 156, 204n41, 216n17, 232n36
Hawkins, William M., 85, 88, 91
Hawthorne, Nathaniel, 73
Hayden, Joseph Ralston, 67
Heat-Moon, William Least, 198
hegemonies, 9, 11, 26, 32–33, 54, 198–199; and archives of U.S. empire, 63, 72, 77; and Filipinas, 128, 132–133, 136, 143, 149; and television, 173, 191. *See also* dominant culture
Herr, Cheryl Temple, 18, 64

Herring, Scott, 13–15, 72, 90, 105, 133, 199, 205n67, 208n115, 229n60
heteronormativity, 11–14, 17, 21, 35, 82, 186–187, 205n43; cis-heteronormativity, 79, 198; and Filipinas, 129, 131, 134, 145, 147; and Santos's exile literature, 96, 109, 111, 118, 120, 226n103
heterosexuality, 8, 24, 61, 82; cis-heterosexuality, 23, 79, 81; and Filipinas, 126, 132, 135, 137, 146; and Santos's exile literature, 107, 109, 119; and television, 153, 164, 169, 171, 177, 186, 191
Ho-Chunk people, 16
Hoganson, Kristin, 17, 19, 64, 182
home, 6, 9–11, 15, 17, 19–21, 26–27, 193, 195, 206n81, 207n111; and archives of U.S. empire, 65, 74–75, 80, 83, 88, 91; and Filipinas, 130, 132–133, 137, 140–141, 144–146, 148–149; and Santos's exile literature, 101–106, 109–116, 119–120, 226n92; and St. Louis World's Fair, 34, 36, 49–50, 52–53, 59–61; and television, 154, 159, 169, 172, 182, 184. *See also* homelands
homelands, 16–17, 21, 25–26, 178, 207n111; and archives of U.S. empire, 65, 75, 88; and Filipinas, 130, 139, 141, 149; and Santos's exile literature, 102, 104, 106, 109–112, 115–118; and St. Louis World's Fair, 34, 46, 52–53. *See also* home
homonormativity, 96, 181, 186–187
homophobia, 17, 85, 119, 144, 148–149, 158, 163, 203n34
homosociality, 26, 79–81, 84–85, 91, 129; and Santos's exile literature, 96, 109, 117–119
Honduras, 156
Hubbell, Winifred W., 89, 222n161
Hughes, Langston, 86
humanism, 56, 58, 102, 117, 189, 214n123
humanity, 36, 53–57, 60, 87, 89, 117, 185, 187, 189–190, 203n34
Humperdinck, Engelbert, 133

identities, 6–9, 12, 17, 21, 27, 201n1, 204n36, 205n67; and archives of U.S. empire, 69, 77; and Filipinas, 126–127, 133, 137, 139, 143, 146; and Santos's exile literature, 96, 102, 113–114, 226n103; and St. Louis World's Fair, 44, 46, 52, 55–58; and television, 151, 153–154, 158, 161–166, 168, 170–171, 177, 179, 182–183, 186–187

Ifugao people, 79
Igorot people, 76, 79, 210n34, 211n63, 212n82, 212n90, 214n115, 214n120, 215n138; and St. Louis World's Fair, 31, 33, 39–40, 42, 47–48, 51, 54–60. *See also* Bontoc people
Illinois, 10, 16, 97, 137; Bloomington, 103; Chicago, 96–98, 101, 103–105, 107–108, 111, 113–115, 130, 134; Peoria, 136
Ilongot people, 88
imaginaries, 9, 11–14, 21–24, 26, 193, 195, 198, 205n53; and archives of U.S. empire, 64–65, 69, 82, 92; and Filipinas, 125–126, 134, 146; and Santos's exile literature, 97–98, 100, 103–105, 112, 115, 121; and St. Louis World's Fair, 35, 39, 41, 46, 51–52, 60, 214n115; and television, 151, 154–155, 158, 160–161, 168, 182, 191–192
immigration, 1, 5, 9–10, 22–23, 194, 199, 204n36; and Filipinas, 130, 132–134, 138–139, 141–143, 149, 228n31; and Santos's exile literature, 91, 101, 107, 110, 114, 224n52, 226n103; and St. Louis World's Fair, 31–32, 36; and television, 156, 158, 167, 178–189, 191, 235n107, 236n118. *See also* migration; undocumented people; U.S. Department of Homeland Security
Immigration Act (1965), 23, 159. *See also* Hart-Cellar Act (1965)
Immigration and Customs Enforcement (ICE), 182, 187, 189–190. *See also* deportation
imperialism, 2, 5–11, 13–15, 18–27, 193–196, 199, 208n112; anti-imperialism, 7, 86, 219n91; and archives of U.S. empire, 63–66, 68–69, 72, 74–77, 80, 82–92, 219nn91–92; cultural imperialism, 99–100, 160; and Filipinas, 125–126, 128–130, 137, 139, 141, 145–146, 149, 228n30; racial imperialism, 34, 40, 55, 87; and Santos's exile literature, 95–100, 102, 112, 114, 116–117, 120, 226n103; and St. Louis World's Fair, 31–36, 40–61, 209n15, 210n30, 212nn69–70, 237n6; and television, 151–153, 159–161, 166–168, 172–175, 186, 189, 191. *See also* amnesia; expansionism; postimperiality; U.S. occupation of the Philippines
inclusion, 17, 24, 155–156, 164, 185–186

Indiana, 16, 155, 201n2; Bloomington, 224n35; Indianapolis, 175, 230n9; Muncie, 103, 118; Terre Haute, 103
Indiana University, 74, 194, 201n2, 219n91
Indian Wars, 2, 5
Indigeneity, 43, 47, 77, 232n36
Indigenous Peoples, 1–2, 5, 9, 16, 21, 198; and archives of U.S. empire, 65, 78–80, 218n75, 220n94, 221n126; and Filipinas, 125–126, 129–130; Indigenous women, 190; and St. Louis World's Fair, 31–32, 38, 43, 47–48, 52, 58, 60, 210n39, 211n59; and television, 159, 182. *See also individual nations/groups*
Indonesia, 194
interracial relations, 2, 55, 87, 117, 155, 165, 226n99; and Filipinas, 127, 134, 146–147
intersectionality, 139, 158, 163, 168, 174, 177, 193
intimacies, 2, 19, 23, 26; and archives of U.S. empire, 64–65, 73–74, 79, 82, 84, 92; and Filipinas, 136–137, 139–140, 146, 149; and Santos's exile literature, 96, 98, 103, 109, 118–119; and St. Louis World's Fair, 35–38, 47, 51, 53–55, 58–60; and television, 153, 159, 182, 189
Iowa, 10, 16, 54, 210n2, 231n17, 231n19; Iowa City, 97, 99, 101, 106–107, 110, 223n22
Iowa State University (formerly Iowa State College of Agriculture and Mechanical Arts), 10, 74, 202n2
Iowa Writers' Workshop, 25, 54, 96–97, 99, 223n21
Isaac, Allan, 20–21
isolation, 23, 59, 79, 81, 158, 182, 207n94, 208n119; and Filipinas, 127, 132, 138, 143; and Santos's exile literature, 96, 102, 105, 107–110, 118, 120, 224n35

Japanese Americans, 190
Japan/Japanese people, 23, 38, 81, 88, 142, 156, 194; Japanese occupation of the Philippines, 5, 115, 141
Jenks, Albert, 32, 41, 60
Jew, Victor, 17
Jewish people, 154, 156, 165–166, 173, 189, 231n22, 233n58, 234n65
Jiwere (Otoe) people, 16
Johnson, Nireah, 17

Johnson, Victoria, 16, 154, 157, 230n13
Joseph, Ralina, 158
Joshi, Khyati Y., 18, 236n114

Kansas, 5, 8, 10, 16, 87–88, 91, 96, 144; Abilene, 27, 195; Emporia, 103; Flint Hills, 1, 6; Fort Riley, 1, 5–6, 23; Lawrence, 85–87; Manhattan, 79; Wamego, 6–7; Wichita, 97, 100–101, 107, 109–10
Kansas State University (formerly Kansas State Agricultural College), 10, 25, 74, 78–79, 84, 193, 202n2
Kanza people (Kaw Nation), 1, 16
Kaskaskia people, 16
Kauahi, Kaliko, 156
Kercheval, Jesse Lee, 25, 33–34, 54–60, 65, 101
Kickapoo people, 16, 19
Kim, Elaine, 102
kinship, 20–21, 25, 41, 52–53, 195; and Filipinas, 132, 138, 142–143, 148; and Santos's exile literature, 108, 113–114; and television, 163, 181. *See also* families
Kirshenblatt-Gimblett, Barbara, 46–47
Kondo, Dorinne, 179, 187
Korangy, Amir M., 183
Korea/Korean people, 23, 194
Korean Americans, 162, 234n65, 234n69
Korean War, 23
Kuchibhotla, Srinivas, 17, 235n107

Lacan, Jacques, 37, 44, 57
Lady Gaga, 173
Lakhóta (Lakota) people, 2
land-grant institutions, 1, 10, 74, 78
language, 61, 140; English language, 32, 50, 66, 70–73, 99, 114, 120, 136, 161, 170–173, 179; Filipino/Tagalog language, 52, 70, 92, 127, 136, 146, 161, 170–171, 177–179, 187; Spanish language, 120, 129, 161, 201n1, 203n33
Laos, 194
Lapuio, C., 72
Latin America/Latinx people, 155, 177, 182, 185, 190, 201n1, 209n11, 235n101
Lee, Josephine, 165
Lee, Rachel, 139
Lënape (Delaware) people, 16
Lewis and Clark Expedition, 43
LGBTQ+ people, 17, 21, 113, 148, 155, 191, 231n18

liberalism, 6, 20, 56, 58, 154, 177
liminality, 20, 34, 61, 101, 120, 132, 138, 209n28, 226n106; and archives of U.S. empire, 76, 83, 88
Lindley, Ernest, 87
Link, William, 40
Little Mix, 175
Livingston, Jennie, 17–18
localness, 1, 6–9, 14–15, 18, 129, 196, 203n34, 207n94; and archives of U.S. empire, 65–66, 69, 73–77, 79–80, 85–86, 89–90, 215n9, 219n92; and Santos's exile literature, 95, 107; and St. Louis World's Fair, 31, 44, 53, 56, 208n2, 212n69; and television, 152–154, 178, 182, 187, 191; and translocal relations, 8, 21, 24–26, 79, 88, 102, 146
loneliness, 79, 100–101, 104, 106–110, 113, 116, 118, 120
longing, 21–22, 109–110, 112, 116, 118, 120, 134
Lopez, Honorio, 73
loss, 34, 40, 52–53, 65, 90, 113–120, 211n56
Louisiana, 209n11; New Orleans, 54–55, 58–59; St. Maló, 31, 55
Louisiana Purchase (1803), 16, 24, 32–33, 37, 43, 159, 218n75
Lowe, Lisa, 36, 138–139, 199
Lynch, Jane, 155

Mabalon, Dawn, 12
MacArthur, Douglas, 196–197
Maher, Susan Naramore, 198
Malaysia/Malaysians, 77, 194
Manalansan, Martin F., IV, 21, 64, 83, 91–92, 203n30, 205n60
Manifest Destiny, 2, 37, 43, 72, 211n66
Manila, Philippines, 69, 79, 81, 134, 178, 196–197, 203n23; and St. Louis World's Fair, 31, 44, 52–53, 55, 67
Marcos, Ferdinand, 26, 96, 99, 107, 112–113, 177
marginalization, 13, 22, 27, 59, 64, 121, 199; and Filipinas, 128, 135, 137; and television, 168, 173, 176, 192
marriage, 55, 131, 140; and archives of U.S. empire, 82, 85–86, 91; and Santos's exile literature, 99, 101, 104, 106–109, 114, 117, 119; and television, 154–155, 178, 180–181, 186–187, 231n19, 233n53

Martinez-Juan, Cristina, 51, 66, 212n82, 212n86, 213n100
masculinities, 70, 74, 79, 84–85, 129, 143, 162, 169, 181, 201n1
McDonald, Laquan, 17
McHale, Kevin, 168
McKinley, William, 35, 67, 151–152, 166–167, 172, 176, 191
McKinney, Mark, 177
McKittrick, Katherine, 198
Medina, José, 112
melancholia, 25, 98, 116–117, 211n56, 211n61, 213n106; and St. Louis World's Fair, 33–35, 40–41, 44–46, 48, 50–56, 59–62
memoirs, 14, 78–81, 85–91, 96, 98, 100–102, 116, 223n22
men, Filipino, 12; and archives of U.S. empire, 80–81; and Santos's exile literature, 101, 107, 118; and St. Louis World's Fair, 38, 44, 55–56; and television, 161–169. *See also* boys, Filipino
Mendoza, Victor, 35, 205n63
Menominee people, 16
Mesquaki (Meskwaki; Fox) people, 16
mestizo people, 82, 161, 168
methodology of book, 8–27
metronormativity, 8, 12, 14–15, 69, 80, 202n18, 205n60, 224n52
metropoles, 20, 26, 64–65, 205n63; and archives of U.S. empire, 74–75, 77, 91; and Filipinas, 126, 149; and metroimperialism, 35, 40; and Santos's exile literature, 98, 104–105, 117, 120; and television, 153, 186
Mexico/Mexican people, 2, 126, 174, 182, 185, 235n101, 236n114
Michele, Lea, 165, 231n22
Michigan, 16, 19, 67, 92, 101, 111, 129, 182, 201n2, 207n90; Detroit, 103; Dowagiac, 112; Higgins Lake, 103; Kalamazoo, 97, 100, 103, 108, 118; Port Huron, 143. *See also* University of Michigan
Michigan State University, 74, 201n2
Middle East, the/Middle Eastern people, 182, 190
migration, 7, 9, 11, 14, 19, 21, 23, 25–26, 199; and archives of U.S. empire, 86, 91, 221n134; and Filipinas, 126, 140; and Santos's exile literature, 98, 100, 102–103, 113, 120; and St. Louis World's Fair, 31, 37, 59; and television, 152, 159, 173, 176, 182, 190. *See also* immigration; undocumented people
militarism, 1–6, 23, 99, 127, 139, 162, 180, 182, 195–198, 233n53; and archives of U.S. empire, 67, 79, 85; and St. Louis World's Fair, 44, 50, 212n69
mimicry, 161, 167, 172–174
Minnesota, 10, 16, 43, 77–80, 182, 201n1, 208n125, 218n77, 224n58; Minneapolis, 74–75, 126, 155, 206n80; St. Paul, 103; Twin Cities, 17, 23, 76, 126, 219n90, 231n22. *See also* Philippinesotans
Minnesota Academy of Natural Science, 67
minoritization, 8–9, 13, 26, 193–194, 200; and archives of U.S. empire, 76–77, 218n76; and Filipinas, 128, 132, 136–138; and St. Louis World's Fair, 41, 45, 48, 57, 211n59; and television, 158, 171, 177, 179, 185–186, 192, 235n98
Mississippi River, 18, 33, 43, 207n90
Missouri, 16, 159, 201n2, 209n16, 221n126; Ferguson, 155, 158, 206n80; Kansas City, 10. *See also* St. Louis, Missouri
Missouri History Museum, 25, 27, 36–40, 42, 45, 68, 195, 211n64, 212n76
Monteith, Cory, 151, 230n1
Morantte, P. C., 99, 109, 225n73
Moro people, 47
Morrill Act (1862), 78
Morris, Heather, 155
Morrison, Matthew, 154
mothers, 20, 73, 109, 161, 163, 166, 229n57, 232n46, 233n58; and archives of U.S. empire, 70, 74, 85; and Filipinas, 131–134, 141, 144, 148
Moua, Mee, 23, 208n125
mourning, 114, 117–118, 209n19, 212n82; and St. Louis World's Fair, 34, 37, 39, 41, 48, 50, 53, 55, 57, 60. *See also* grief
Mukherjee, Roopali, 158
multiculturalism, 151–152, 154, 157–158, 160–161
Muñoz, José Esteban, 11, 53, 100, 112, 119, 147, 161, 199
Murphy, Frank, 19, 71, 197, 216n23
Murphy, Ryan Patrick, 80
music, 26, 40, 49–52, 83; and television, 151, 153, 156, 161–163, 167–168, 172–176, 181, 190–191, 234n65. *See also Glee* (television show)

INDEX / 267

Muslims, 9
myaamiaki (Miami) people, 16
mythologies, 7, 16–17, 38, 154, 193, 195, 198–199, 207n94; and archives of U.S. empire, 73–74, 76; and television, 160, 162, 178, 182, 185, 188, 191

Nadeau, Chantal, 21, 205n60
Nakoda people, 16
Nancy, Jean-Luc, 53
national, the, 5, 8–16, 18–21, 23–27, 193, 195–196; and archives of U.S. empire, 63–65, 69–70, 75, 77, 88, 91–92; and Filipinas, 125–130, 132–133, 135, 137, 140, 143, 149; and Santos's exile literature, 96, 98, 104, 109–110, 117, 119–120; and St. Louis World's Fair, 31, 34–35, 37, 40, 43, 46, 53, 57–61; and television, 153–155, 157, 159, 166, 172, 182, 185, 189–190, 192. *See also* nationalism
National Archives, 46, 67
nationalism, 2, 5, 7–12, 14, 18, 22, 27; and archives of U.S. empire, 69–70, 76–77, 85, 89; and Filipinas, 127, 129, 132–133, 136, 229n52; and Santos's exile literature, 96, 100, 117; and television, 171, 178, 182, 235n82
NBC, 26, 152
Negrito people, 39, 47, 50, 77, 214n115
neoliberalism, 183, 185, 188
New Jersey, 44, 213n103; Leonia, 37, 43
New York State, 137, 216n17; Buffalo, 185; New York City, 75, 96–97, 99, 105, 162, 225n59, 226n99; Oneonta, 103
Ng, Celeste, 130
Nguyen, Bich Minh, 130
Ninh, erin Khuê, 132
Nishime, LeiLani, 163
normativity, 5, 8–9, 11–17, 19–24, 193–200, 205n67; and archives of U.S. empire, 69, 72–73, 79–80, 85, 90–91; and Filipinas, 127–129, 131–133, 135, 139–141, 143, 145–149, 228n31; and Santos's exile literature, 97–98, 103, 109, 112, 114, 117; and St. Louis World's Fair, 33–35, 50, 56–57, 60–61; and television, 152–155, 161–163, 165, 173, 177, 181, 186–188, 233n54, 234n65. *See also* heteronormativity; homonormativity; metronormativity
North Dakota, 10, 16, 182, 201n2

Northwest Ordinance (1787), 16, 130, 159
nostalgia, 14, 16, 25, 44, 56, 60, 154; and Santos's exile literature, 96, 98, 108–109, 112, 114–117
nowhere, 7, 21–23, 45, 65, 91, 111–112, 196, 198, 208n115; and Filipinas, 146, 169; and television, 192, 236n138
nudity, 35, 56, 58, 80–81, 84–85, 104
Nutachi (Missouria) people, 16

Obama, Barack, 8, 157, 167, 230n13
objectification, 118, 160, 194–195, 211n63; and archives of U.S. empire, 66, 81; and Filipinas, 129, 140; and St. Louis World's Fair, 33, 36, 38, 41, 43–50, 53, 56–57, 59–60
Obusan, Enrico, 49, 213n91
Ohio, 16, 66–67, 137, 201n2, 231n17, 231n19; and *Glee*, 151–152, 154–155, 157, 159, 162, 168, 171, 176, 230n9, 233n65
Ohio State University, The, 74, 201n2
Ojibwe people, 16
Oler, Andy, 7, 205n59
Omaha people, 16
O'Malley, Mike, 154
Ono, Kent, 158
ontoepistemologies, 26, 34–35, 91, 178, 193, 199; and Filipinas, 128–129, 145, 229n61; and St. Louis World's Fair, 36, 39, 45, 51, 209n28
ontologies, 10, 13, 15, 17–18, 20, 24, 26, 36, 199; and Filipinas, 134, 138, 145, 147; and Santos's exile literature, 96–97, 112, 116; and television, 152, 159, 175, 189. *See also* ontoepistemologies
Orientalism, 49, 138–141, 171
Osage people, 16
Otherness, 4, 14, 116, 194, 199; and archives of U.S. empire, 69, 82; and Filipinas, 129, 140, 229n52; and St. Louis World's Fair, 59–60; and television, 172, 191
Overstreet, Chord, 154
Ozeki, Ruth, 130
Oz Museum, 6–7

palimpsests, 36, 42, 54, 115, 127, 152–153, 170, 191–193
Pamatmat, A. Rey, 26, 126–128, 130, 133–136, 143, 147–150
Panama–California Exposition, 52

parents, 1–2, 4–6, 21, 36, 209n15, 213n106, 220n97, 223n3; and archives of U.S. empire, 69, 84, 87; and Filipinas, 131–134, 137, 141–148, 229n49, 229n57
past, the, 5, 14, 19, 27, 195, 198, 209n16, 230n3; and archives of U.S. empire, 65, 76, 91, 215n1; and Filipinas, 147–148; and Santos's exile literature, 108, 112, 115, 119, 121; and St. Louis World's Fair, 33–35, 41–42, 47–48, 50–53, 55, 58–59; and television, 153, 158–160, 171, 174
patriarchy, 89, 130, 147; heteropatriarchy, 56, 61, 102, 114, 117, 127–130, 132, 135, 144–145, 191
Pawnee people, 16
PBS, 23, 31, 228n33
Pearl Harbor attack, 98, 104
Pemberton, Johnny, 156
peminism, 12, 23, 26, 128, 132, 134–136, 140, 147–149
Pensionado Act (1903), 74
pensionadxs, 10, 25, 77, 218n74, 219n91, 223n30, 237n6; and Santos's exile literature, 95–100, 103, 105, 107, 120
Peoria people, 16
performativity, 8, 13, 15, 26–27; and archives of U.S. empire, 81, 83, 90; and St. Louis World's Fair, 32, 34, 42, 50, 53, 58–59; and television, 161, 168, 173, 179
Philippine Air Corps, 197
Philippine-American War, 2–4, 32, 66, 77, 87
Philippine Army, 196–197
Philippine Bureau of Aeronautics, 197
Philippine Bureau of Agriculture, 78–79
Philippine Commissions, 66–67, 70
Philippine Government-in-Exile, 99
Philippine Insular Government, 67
Philippine Republic, 108
Philippine Revolution, 31, 72
Philippines, the: Albay, 99, 106; Baguio, 79; Bataan Province, 82; Bicol, 25, 44, 73, 99, 102, 110; Cagayan River Valley, 85–86, 88, 90–91; Camarines Sur, 44, 99; Cordillera Mountains, 31, 51, 209n16; Daet, 44; and independence, 2, 27, 72, 76, 90, 108, 120, 196; La Carlota Experiment Station, 78–84, 83; Luzon, 31, 44, 47, 49–50, 65, 79, 212n82; Mangaldan, 44; Negros, 79–80; Taal Lake, 84, 85; Tayabas Province, 68–69, 73; Visayas region, 79, 91. *See also* diaspora, Filipinx; Filipinas; Filipinx America; Manila, Philippines
Philippinesotans, 75–78
photography, 31–32, 38, 41, 56, 59, 105, 116, 196–197, 213n91; and archives of U.S. empire, 64, 68, 75, 78–79, 81, 84–85
Piankashaw people, 16
Pinxys, 126, 145, 225n65, 232n46
politics, 8–10, 15, 17, 19–20, 22, 26–27, 195–199; and archives of U.S. empire, 66–67, 71–72, 77, 85–86, 89–90, 217n41, 219n87; and Filipinas, 127–128, 132, 135–136, 138, 145, 147, 228n33, 229n52; necropolitics, 147; and Santos's exile literature, 99, 107, 112–113, 226n87; and St. Louis World's Fair, 35–36, 51; and television, 152–158, 166–168, 172, 174–178, 181–183, 185–186, 189–192, 231n17, 231n22, 233n65. *See also* democracy; governance
Ponca people, 16
Ponce, Martin Joseph, 21–22, 145, 203n33, 226n106, 228n18, 232n51
Porter, Linda, 188
postcolonialism, 21, 26–27, 64, 117, 194, 209n17, 215n1; and Filipinas, 126, 128–129; and St. Louis World's Fair, 33–35, 37, 40–41, 51, 59; and television, 159, 161, 166, 168, 173, 175
postimperiality, 26–27, 128, 149, 152–153, 157–159, 171–177, 183–185, 188, 191
postracialism, 27, 152–155, 157–159, 165, 168, 171–178, 183–185, 191
present, the, 2, 11, 19, 24, 27, 76, 145–147, 191; and Santos's exile literature, 112, 119–121; and St. Louis World's Fair, 34, 41–42, 51–53, 60; and television, 152, 159
primitivity, 33, 36, 47, 50, 80, 129, 209n16, 210n39. *See also* savagery
progressivism, 13, 16, 19, 33, 47, 145, 148, 216n23; and archives of U.S. empire, 69–72, 77, 90; and television, 155, 158, 181, 185, 187
Proposition 8 (2008, CA), 162, 233n53
provinciality, 11, 18, 69, 73, 79–81, 84, 88, 110, 203n34
public sphere, 18, 22, 103, 138, 148, 196, 198; and archives of U.S. empire, 63, 66–67, 69–70, 76, 78, 83; and St. Louis World's Fair, 35, 55, 59; and television, 153–154, 160, 169, 171, 179
Puerto Rico, 71, 87
Purdue University, 74, 201n2

Quantic, Diana Dufva, 193
Quapaw people, 16
queer diasporas, 20, 22, 24–25, 27, 61, 195, 198–199; and archives of U.S. empire, 65–66, 88; and Filipinas, 127, 143, 149; and Santos's exile literature, 95, 112, 117, 119; and television, 158, 176, 183, 187, 191
queer Filipinxness, 8, 11–12, 14–15, 20–27, 33, 194–195, 199–200, 205n67; and archives of U.S. empire, 65, 82, 91; and Filipinas, 126, 143, 146, 150; and Santos's exile literature, 95–96, 121; and television, 152–153, 157, 161, 168, 173, 176–178, 191
queerness, 1, 6–8, 10–20, 22–26, 193, 195, 198–199; and archives of U.S. empire, 64–65, 69–70, 73–74, 78–79, 81–85, 89–92; and Filipinas, 126–129, 132–134, 140, 143–150; QTBIPOC, 22–23, 205n60; queer feminism, 70, 129; queers of color, 11, 14, 18, 24, 155, 161, 168, 195, 203n33, 234n65; queer theory, 9, 22–23, 200, 213n107; and Santos's exile literature, 96–98, 109, 112–113, 116–121; and St. Louis World's Fair, 33–34, 51, 53, 59–61; and television, 152–155, 161–163, 166–167, 171, 173, 177, 181, 183, 186–187, 190–191. *See also* queer diasporas; queer Filipinxness
Quezon, Manuel, 196–197

race, 8, 11, 13–15, 27, 204n38, 209n15; and archives of U.S. empire, 75, 77, 86–88, 90–91; biraciality, 157, 165, 232n46; and Filipinas, 125–130, 132–133, 138–139, 142, 145–147, 150, 229n54; multiraciality, 165; and racial formation, 13, 19, 139, 160, 163, 166, 181, 185, 188; and the racial inhuman, 56–58, 60; and Santos's exile literature, 96, 102–103, 117, 121; and St. Louis World's Fair, 33, 40, 43, 45, 53, 61–62; and television, 151–168, 171–175, 177–180, 183–190, 234n65; transraciality, 165. *See also* interracial relations; postracialism; racialization; racism
racialization, 4, 8–9, 12–13, 17–20, 23–24, 26–27, 204n38; and archives of U.S. empire, 64, 83, 86, 90, 215n16; and Filipinas, 126, 128, 139–140, 142, 147–148; and Santos's exile literature, 96, 98, 103, 114, 117, 226n103; and St. Louis World's Fair, 31, 34–35, 38, 40–41, 44–46, 50–51, 53, 55–61; and television, 158–160, 165, 168–169, 171, 174, 179, 182, 186, 191
racism, 5, 23, 203n34, 204n35, 209n14; anti-Asian, 138; anti-Black, 87, 206n80; anti-racism, 135, 158; and archives of U.S. empire, 71, 76–77, 86–87, 89; and Filipinas, 137–139, 146, 228n40; and Santos's exile literature, 102, 114; and St. Louis World's Fair, 34, 43, 57, 212n69, 222n145; and television, 155, 158, 160, 167, 176, 184, 230n13, 235n107
Rafael, Vicente, 84
Rañola, Andres, 69
Reddy, Chandan, 17
refugees, 9, 16, 23, 111, 182, 184–185, 189, 194, 236n117
regional, the, 5, 7–27, 193, 196, 198–200, 203n34, 204n40; and archives of U.S. empire, 64–66, 69, 73, 75, 77, 79, 82, 84–85, 88, 90–92, 215n9; and Filipinas, 125–126, 128–135, 138–139, 141–142, 145, 149–150; and Santos's exile literature, 96–97, 102, 104, 109, 114, 119; and St. Louis World's Fair, 31, 33–34, 37, 39–40, 43–48, 54, 56, 58–59, 62, 209n16; and television, 153–157, 166, 182, 185–187, 190–191; transregional relations, 44, 48, 54, 59, 79
Reno, Joshua, 17
Republicans, 85–86, 226n87
Revolutionary War (U.S.), 1
Riley, Amber, 162
Rivera, Naya, 155
Rizal, José, 10, 77, 90, 219n87
Rockoff, Hugh, 7
Rodaway, Paul, 103
Rodríguez, Dylan, 12
Rodríguez, Richard, 21
Rony, Fatimah Tobing, 51
rurality, 5, 8, 11, 13–15, 18, 43, 205n67, 206n94, 207n86; and archives of U.S. empire, 69, 79, 86–89, 91, 217n32; and Filipinas, 133–134, 143, 145–146, 148, 150, 229n60; and Santos's exile literature, 97, 101, 110; and St. Louis World's Fair, 43–44; and television, 155, 157
Ruskin, John, 73

saawanwa (Shawnee) people, 16
Sakura, Nichole, 156
Salazar, George, 187
San Agustin, Felisa, 74, 218n73
Sanchez, Jessica, 174–175
Santos, Beatriz, 99, 107, 109–110, 129
Santos, Bienvenido "Ben," 23–25, 92, 102–113, 129–130, 150, 193, 224n41, 224n46; biography of, 95–102, 219n78, 223n7, 223n22, 223n26, 223nn12–13, 225n69; and loss, 113–121, 219n87, 224n35, 225nn64–65, 225nn75–77, 226n99, 226n103
Santos, Nico, 156, 178
Sauk (Sac) people, 16
Savage, Dan, 147
savagery, 3, 33, 60, 77, 128–129, 131, 134, 195, 227n20. *See also* primitivity; wildness
Schueller, Malini Johar, 68
Sears, Clare, 80
Sedgwick, Eve, 118
See, Sarita, 5, 13–14, 19, 22–24, 34, 66, 71, 117; and Filipinas, 129, 136, 138; and television, 160, 171, 173, 188–189
Seneca people, 16
sexism, 49, 130, 137, 149, 158, 176, 203n34; heterosexism, 119, 146, 163, 226n103
sexualities, 7–19, 23, 26, 35, 207n81, 209n15, 233n53; and archives of U.S. empire, 81, 86, 91; and Filipinas, 125–126, 128–129, 131–133, 139, 141, 145–147, 149–150; and Santos's exile literature, 109, 111, 114, 117, 119, 226n99; and sexual relations, 137, 144, 147, 165, 186–187, 209n15; and television, 151–155, 162–165, 173, 181, 186–187, 191, 230n11, 233n57, 234n65. *See also* erotics; gayness; heteronormativity; heterosexuality; homonormativity; queerness
sexualization, 35, 114, 127, 139, 142
Shortridge, James, 16, 131, 231n23
short stories, 14, 25–26, 33, 54–62, 227n30; and Galang, 126–128, 130, 132, 136–144, 148–150; and Santos, 97–101, 103–105, 113, 224n35, 224n46, 226n103
Shum, Harry, Jr., 166
Singapore, 194
slavery, 7, 16, 85, 87, 109n15
Smithsonian Museum, 46, 212n82
social relations, 7–9, 11–15, 18, 20, 22, 24–26, 199; and archives of U.S. empire, 68, 71–72, 74–77, 79, 90, 217n32; and

Filipinas, 127–129, 132, 134–135, 137–140, 143, 145–147; and Santos's exile literature, 96, 98, 107–108, 117–120; and St. Louis World's Fair, 35, 37, 40, 44, 57, 59; and television, 154, 156–157, 159, 161, 178, 183, 186–188. *See also* homosociality
Somerville, Siobhan, 21, 205n60
sound, 92, 105, 133, 195; and St. Louis World's Fair, 39–40, 47–52; and television, 152, 170–171, 179, 181, 190–191
South Asia/South Asians, 170–171, 190, 196
Southeast Asia/Southeast Asians, 64, 139, 194, 196, 201n1, 209n14
sovereignty, 67, 71, 74, 76, 88, 147, 188
Spain, 54, 72, 115, 237n3; Spanish occupation of the Philippines, 2, 5, 7, 71, 77, 90, 194
Spanish–American War, 2, 6, 10, 85–86, 151
spatiality, 8–16, 19–24, 193–195, 198–200, 203n21, 204n38, 204n40, 205n67; and archives of U.S. empire, 64–65, 68, 74, 78, 80, 82, 84, 90–92; and Filipinas, 125, 127, 131–133, 143, 146–147, 149; and Santos's exile literature, 95, 102–103, 112–114, 119, 121, 226n99; and St. Louis World's Fair, 33–39, 41, 45–47, 49–54, 58–59, 61–62, 214n115, 216n19; and television, 153, 161, 169, 171, 173, 178, 188, 191
spectrality, 4, 82, 114, 117–118, 127, 132, 149; and St. Louis World's Fair, 37–38, 42, 44; and television, 159–160, 172, 182, 191
Squires, Catherine, 158
Steere, Joseph Beal, 10, 67
stereotypes, 9, 41, 55–59, 63, 136, 169, 177, 179, 209n14
St. Louis, Missouri, 27, 32, 38–53, 58–60, 68, 103, 194; and television, 152, 154, 156–157, 159, 182, 185–186, 188. *See also* St. Louis World's Fair (1904)
St. Louis World's Fair (1904), 10, 22, 24–25, 27, 129, 131, 159, 194; and archives of U.S. empire, 42, 68, 77, 81, and the Filipinx Midwest, 24, 31–41, 46–48, 51–52, 56, 59, 61, 209nn15–17, 211n64. *See also* Fuentes, Marlon; Suzara, Aimee
Stonewall Riots, 113, 225n62
students, 10, 26, 54, 86, 92, 194; in the Philippines, 66–78, 216n25, 217n32; and student presses, 75–78, 87; and television, 166, 173–174, 191, 234n65; in the U.S., 74–85, 99–100, 212n76, 218n74, 218n76, 218n78, 219n90, 235n107

Suarez, Harrod, 20, 127, 202n7, 235n82
subalternity, 8, 95, 161; and archives of U.S. empire, 63–64, 68–69, 74, 89–90, 216n19; and St. Louis World's Fair, 35, 38, 40, 51, 53–54, 56
subjecthood, 5, 17, 23–24, 26, 141, 194–195, 199; and archives of U.S. empire, 69, 75, 90; and Santos's exile literature, 95–96, 98, 100, 117; and St. Louis World's Fair, 32–33, 35–36, 40–42, 46, 48, 55; and television, 152, 160–162, 168–169, 171, 173, 175, 179, 183, 185–189, 191
subjection, 59–60, 69, 129, 153, 195
subjectivities, 4, 13, 19, 22, 26, 193, 213n112; and archives of U.S. empire, 65–66, 69–70, 72–73, 83, 88, 91; and Filipinas, 126, 129, 133, 135, 138–140, 145, 149; and Santos's exile literature, 97, 100–101, 106, 109–110, 112, 114–116, 120–121; and St. Louis World's Fair, 32, 34–38, 40–44, 46–49, 51, 53, 56–61; and television, 161, 163, 168, 171
Sulit, Marie-Therese C., 149
Sumida, Stephen, 32
Superstore (television show), 26–27, 152–154, 156–160, 176–191, *179*, 194, 230nn9–10, 232n36
Sutherland, William, 99, 103
Suzara, Aimee, 24, 33–48, 52–54, 57–61, 65, 81, 195, 211n66, 212n69, 215nn139–140
Syria/Syrians, 183–185

Taft, William Howard, 66
Taft Commission, 66, 72, 74
Tagalog people, 41, 47, 91
Taino, Leoncia, 68
Taiwan, 194
Taylor, Robert, 101, 113, 116
teachers, 66–71, 73–74, 99, 169, 215nn16–17
Teahan, Marguerite Murphy, 71
Teena, Brandon, 17
temporalities, 8, 11, 18, 22, 24, 200; and archives of U.S. empire, 64, 66, 69, 90, 92; and Filipinas, 125, 147–149; and Santos's exile literature, 95, 101, 107, 109–110, 113–114, 116–117, 119, 121; and St. Louis World's Fair, 34, 37, 39, 41, 45–47, 51–54, 56, 59; and television, 168, 187. *See also* futurities; past, the; present, the
Tennyson, Alfred, 73
Theater Mu, 126
Theba, Iqbal, 154

Tongson, Karen, 14–15, 22, 24, 171, 204n43, 205n67, 224n52, 228n31
transnational relations, 8, 10–11, 19–21, 24, 196, 203n30; and archives of U.S. empire, 77–78, 219n92; and Filipinas, 136, 149, 229n52; and Santos's exile literature, 98, 121; and St. Louis World's Fair, 31, 46, 48, 59, 61
transoceanic relations, 10, 24, 33, 53, 64, 78, 87. *See also* transpacific relations
transpacific relations, 5, 8, 10, 19–20, 22–24, 193, 196; and archives of U.S. empire, 64, 86, 91; and Santos's exile literature, 100, 224n35; and St. Louis World's Fair, 33, 35, 44–45, 47, 53, 61; and television, 159, 170, 191, 236n128
trans* people, 9, 17, 113, 154, 173, 211n59
transphobia, 17, 158
trauma, 34, 40, 56–57, 139, 149, 175
Trieu, Monica, 17
tropics, 2, 10, 38, 60, 98, 103, 107, 134, 141; and archives of U.S. empire, 79–81, 88, 90
Trump, Donald, 8, 157–158, 178, 180, 230n13, 234n68, 235n107
Tuan, Yi-Fu, 14, 101–102
Turner, Frederick Jackson, 125
Twin Cities GLBT Oral History Project, 17
Ty, Eleanor, 102

uncanny, the, 115, 151–152, 160, 166, 172, 195, 198
unconscious, the, 15, 37, 45–47, 57, 117, 156, 158, 168, 171, 173
undocumented people, 156, 177–190, 235n104, 235n107
University of Chicago, 74, 201n2
University of Illinois Urbana-Champaign, 25, 74, 96, 98, 105, 201n2
University of Iowa, 99, 201n2, 235n107
University of Kansas (KU), 25, 85–88, 202n2
University of Michigan, 10, 25, 67–68, 74, 78, 92, 201n2, 216n19, 216n23; Museum of Natural History, 19
University of Minnesota, 25, 32, 74–76, 201n2, 214n116, 218n78, 219n84
University of Nebraska-Lincoln, 74, 201n2
University of Santo Tomas, 90
University of Wisconsin-Madison, 54, 74, 201n2
urbanism, 13–15, 18, 26, 43, 59, 200, 205n60, 231n19; and archives of U.S. empire, 76,

urbanism *(continued)*
  88, 91; and Filipinas, 133, 136, 141–142, 145, 150; and Santos's exile literature, 97, 104–105, 225n62; suburbanism, 14–15, 23–24, 61–63, 130, 136–137, 141, 152–153, 157, 188, 203n32, 205n67
Urquhart, Alex, 80
U.S. Air Force, 1
U.S. Army, 1–2, 5–6, 66, 107; Cavalry and First Infantry Division Museums, 1–6, 3–4, 195
U.S. Congress, 74
U.S. Department of Agriculture (USDA), 78
U.S. Department of Homeland Security, 17, 19, 182–183, 190
Ushkowitz, Jenna, 162
U.S. occupation of the Philippines, 5–6, 35, 56, 58, 60, 194, 196; and archives of U.S. empire, 63–64, 69, 72, 75, 86, 88; and Filipinas, 129, 134, 141; and Santos's exile literature, 112, 115; and television, 151–152, 159–160, 166, 170, 172, 175–176, 188
U.S. Office of Education, 103
U.S.-Philippine relations, 65–68, 73, 89, 196–197; and television, 172, 175. *See also* Philippine–American War; U.S. occupation of the Philippines
utopianism, 11, 53, 65, 87, 112, 121, 145, 191

Vang, Cha, 17
Vargas, Jose Antonio, 180
Vergara, Benito, 12
Versace, Gianni, 21
Vietnam/Vietnamese people, 23, 194, 228n33
Vietnam War, 1, 23
Villavicenind, Vicente, 72
violence, 3, 16–17, 22–23, 204n36, 206n78; and archives of U.S. empire, 63, 65, 83, 87–88, 91, 216n25, 222n145; and Filipinas, 126, 139, 228n30; and Santos's exile literature, 104, 109; and St. Louis World's Fair, 32, 35, 50, 55–57; and television, 155, 159–160, 175, 180–181, 185, 188–190
Visayan people, 39, 47

Washington, 97, 108; Kennewick, 37, 43–44; Seattle, 12, 60, 215n139
Washington, DC, 46, 75, 78, 99–100, 105, 112, 116
Wea people, 16

Weisman, Karen, 34, 209n18
White men, 61, 193; and archives of U.S. empire, 70, 73, 78–80, 82, 84–85, 87–88; and television, 154–155, 161, 163, 166, 168, 175, 177, 180
Whiteness, 4–5, 8, 10–11, 14, 16–17, 23–24, 193, 198; and archives of U.S. empire, 64, 78, 86–90; and Filipinas, 125–127, 131–134, 136, 138, 142, 146–147; and Santos's exile literature, 95, 102–103, 107, 118; and St. Louis World's Fair, 32–33, 35–36, 38, 40–41, 43–44, 47, 49, 54–56, 58–60; and television, 153, 155–161, 165–167, 169–171, 175, 179, 182, 185, 190–191. *See also* White men; White supremacy; White women
White supremacy, 16, 56–57, 61, 89, 145, 191; and television, 156–158, 165, 173, 178, 182, 185
White women, 38, 49, 55, 193, 226n99; and archives of U.S. empire, 77, 81–82, 85; and television, 155–156, 165–166, 168–169, 173
Wichita State University, 25, 96, 99, 101, 110, 193
Wilder, Laura Ingalls, 130
wildness, 13, 23, 26, 132, 229n73; and Filipinas, 125, 127–135, 137, 141, 143, 145, 149, 172
Wilkinson, Sook, 17
Wisconsin, 16, 137, 231n17; Brookfield, 127, 136–138, 142; Milwaukee, 130, 137, 141
women, 111, 126, 128, 135, 139–140, 190; and archives of U.S. empire, 70, 74, 81–82; and television, 173–175, 177, 185; women of color, 61, 81, 128, 137, 142–143, 156, 208n125. *See also* Filipinas; White women
The Wonderful Wizard of Oz, 6–7, 130, 144
Wood, Andrew Grant, 17
Worcester, Dean Conant, 67, 76, 79, 89, 216n19
Worcester, Nanon Fay Leas, 89, 222n161
World War I, 2
World War II, 23, 26, 86, 190, 196, 209n17; and Santos's exile literature, 98, 100, 103, 107, 115–117, 120
Wounded Knee Massacre, 2
Wyandot people, 16

Zedd, 175
Zyrus, Jake, 173, 235n96

Thomas Xavier Sarmiento is an award-winning Associate Professor of English at Kansas State University.

Also in the series *Asian American History and Culture*:

Timothy K. August, *The Refugee Aesthetic: Reimagining Southeast Asian America*

L. Joyce Zapanta Mariano, *Giving Back: Filipino America and the Politics of Diaspora Giving*

Manan Desai, *The United States of India: Anticolonial Literature and Transnational Refraction*

Cathy J. Schlund-Vials, Guy Beauregard, and Hsiu-chuan Lee, eds., *The Subject(s) of Human Rights: Crises, Violations, and Asian/American Critique*

Malini Johar Schueller, *Campaigns of Knowledge: U.S. Pedagogies of Colonialism and Occupation in the Philippines and Japan*

Crystal Mun-hye Baik, *Reencounters: On the Korean War and Diasporic Memory Critique*

Michael Omi, Dana Y. Nakano, and Jeffrey T. Yamashita, eds., *Japanese American Millennials: Rethinking Generation, Community, and Diversity*

Masumi Izumi, *The Rise and Fall of America's Concentration Camp Law: Civil Liberties Debates from the Internment to McCarthyism and the Radical 1960s*

Shirley Jennifer Lim, *Anna May Wong: Performing the Modern*

Edward Tang, *From Confinement to Containment: Japanese/American Arts during the Early Cold War*

Patricia P. Chu, *Where I Have Never Been: Migration, Melancholia, and Memory in Asian American Narratives of Return*

Cynthia Wu, *Sticky Rice: A Politics of Intraracial Desire*

Marguerite Nguyen, *America's Vietnam: The Longue Durée of U.S. Literature and Empire*

Vanita Reddy, *Fashioning Diaspora: Beauty, Femininity, and South Asian American Culture*

Audrey Wu Clark, *The Asian American Avant-Garde: Universalist Aspirations in Modernist Literature and Art*

Eric Tang, *Unsettled: Cambodian Refugees in the New York City Hyperghetto*

Jeffrey Santa Ana, *Racial Feelings: Asian America in a Capitalist Culture of Emotion*

Jiemin Bao, *Creating a Buddhist Community: A Thai Temple in Silicon Valley*

Elda E. Tsou, *Unquiet Tropes: Form, Race, and Asian American Literature*

Tarry Hum, *Making a Global Immigrant Neighborhood: Brooklyn's Sunset Park*

Ruth Mayer, *Serial Fu Manchu: The Chinese Supervillain and the Spread of Yellow Peril Ideology*

Karen Kuo, *East Is West and West Is East: Gender, Culture, and Interwar Encounters between Asia and America*

Kieu-Linh Caroline Valverde, *Transnationalizing Viet Nam: Community, Culture, and Politics in the Diaspora*

Lan P. Duong, *Treacherous Subjects: Gender, Culture, and Trans-Vietnamese Feminism*

Kristi Brian, *Reframing Transracial Adoption: Adopted Koreans, White Parents, and the Politics of Kinship*

Belinda Kong, *Tiananmen Fictions outside the Square: The Chinese Literary Diaspora and the Politics of Global Culture*

Bindi V. Shah, *Laotian Daughters: Working toward Community, Belonging, and Environmental Justice*

Cherstin M. Lyon, *Prisons and Patriots: Japanese American Wartime Citizenship, Civil Disobedience, and Historical Memory*

Shelley Sang-Hee Lee, *Claiming the Oriental Gateway: Prewar Seattle and Japanese America*

Isabelle Thuy Pelaud, *This Is All I Choose to Tell: History and Hybridity in Vietnamese American Literature*

Christian Collet and Pei-te Lien, eds., *The Transnational Politics of Asian Americans*

Min Zhou, *Contemporary Chinese America: Immigration, Ethnicity, and Community Transformation*

Kathleen S. Yep, *Outside the Paint: When Basketball Ruled at the Chinese Playground*

Benito M. Vergara Jr., *Pinoy Capital: The Filipino Nation in Daly City*

Jonathan Y. Okamura, *Ethnicity and Inequality in Hawai'i*

Sucheng Chan and Madeline Y. Hsu, eds., *Chinese Americans and the Politics of Race and Culture*

K. Scott Wong, *Americans First: Chinese Americans and the Second World War*

Lisa Yun, *The Coolie Speaks: Chinese Indentured Laborers and African Slaves in Cuba*

Estella Habal, *San Francisco's International Hotel: Mobilizing the Filipino American Community in the Anti-eviction Movement*

Thomas P. Kim, *The Racial Logic of Politics: Asian Americans and Party Competition*

Sucheng Chan, ed., *The Vietnamese American 1.5 Generation: Stories of War, Revolution, Flight, and New Beginnings*

Antonio T. Tiongson Jr., Edgardo V. Gutierrez, and Ricardo V. Gutierrez, eds., *Positively No Filipinos Allowed: Building Communities and Discourse*

Sucheng Chan, ed., *Chinese American Transnationalism: The Flow of People, Resources, and Ideas between China and America during the Exclusion Era*

Rajini Srikanth, *The World Next Door: South Asian American Literature and the Idea of America*

Keith Lawrence and Floyd Cheung, eds., *Recovered Legacies: Authority and Identity in Early Asian American Literature*

Linda Trinh Võ, *Mobilizing an Asian American Community*

Franklin S. Odo, *No Sword to Bury: Japanese Americans in Hawai'i during World War II*

Josephine Lee, Imogene L. Lim, and Yuko Matsukawa, eds., *Re/collecting Early Asian America: Essays in Cultural History*

Linda Trinh Võ and Rick Bonus, eds., *Contemporary Asian American Communities: Intersections and Divergences*

Sunaina Marr Maira, *Desis in the House: Indian American Youth Culture in New York City*

Teresa Williams-León and Cynthia Nakashima, eds., *The Sum of Our Parts: Mixed-Heritage Asian Americans*

Tung Pok Chin with Winifred C. Chin, *Paper Son: One Man's Story*

Amy Ling, ed., *Yellow Light: The Flowering of Asian American Arts*

Rick Bonus, *Locating Filipino Americans: Ethnicity and the Cultural Politics of Space*

Darrell Y. Hamamoto and Sandra Liu, eds., *Countervisions: Asian American Film Criticism*

Martin F. Manalansan IV, ed., *Cultural Compass: Ethnographic Explorations of Asian America*

Ko-lin Chin, *Smuggled Chinese: Clandestine Immigration to the United States*

Evelyn Hu-DeHart, ed., *Across the Pacific: Asian Americans and Globalization*

Soo-Young Chin, *Doing What Had to Be Done: The Life Narrative of Dora Yum Kim*

Robert G. Lee, *Orientals: Asian Americans in Popular Culture*

David L. Eng and Alice Y. Hom, eds., *Q & A: Queer in Asian America*

K. Scott Wong and Sucheng Chan, eds., *Claiming America: Constructing Chinese American Identities during the Exclusion Era*

Lavina Dhingra Shankar and Rajini Srikanth, eds., *A Part, Yet Apart: South Asians in Asian America*

Jere Takahashi, *Nisei/Sansei: Shifting Japanese American Identities and Politics*

Velina Hasu Houston, ed., *But Still, Like Air, I'll Rise: New Asian American Plays*

Josephine Lee, *Performing Asian America: Race and Ethnicity on the Contemporary Stage*

Deepika Bahri and Mary Vasudeva, eds., *Between the Lines: South Asians and Postcoloniality*

E. San Juan Jr., *The Philippine Temptation: Dialectics of Philippines–U.S. Literary Relations*

Carlos Bulosan and E. San Juan Jr., eds., *The Cry and the Dedication*

Carlos Bulosan and E. San Juan Jr., eds., *On Becoming Filipino: Selected Writings of Carlos Bulosan*

Vicente L. Rafael, ed., *Discrepant Histories: Translocal Essays on Filipino Cultures*

Yen Le Espiritu, *Filipino American Lives*

Paul Ong, Edna Bonacich, and Lucie Cheng, eds., *The New Asian Immigration in Los Angeles and Global Restructuring*

Chris Friday, *Organizing Asian American Labor: The Pacific Coast Canned-Salmon Industry, 1870–1942*

Sucheng Chan, ed., *Hmong Means Free: Life in Laos and America*

Timothy P. Fong, *The First Suburban Chinatown: The Remaking of Monterey Park, California*

William Wei, *The Asian American Movement*

Yen Le Espiritu, *Asian American Panethnicity*

Velina Hasu Houston, ed., *The Politics of Life*

Renqiu Yu, *To Save China, To Save Ourselves: The Chinese Hand Laundry Alliance of New York*

Shirley Geok-lin Lim and Amy Ling, eds., *Reading the Literatures of Asian America*

Karen Isaksen Leonard, *Making Ethnic Choices: California's Punjabi Mexican Americans*

Gary Y. Okihiro, *Cane Fires: The Anti-Japanese Movement in Hawaii, 1865–1945*

Sucheng Chan, *Entry Denied: Exclusion and the Chinese Community in America, 1882–1943*

www.ingramcontent.com/pod-product-compliance
Lightning Source LLC
Chambersburg PA
CBHW032033300426
44117CB00009B/1041